Word 2007

THE MISSING MANUAL

*The book that
should have been
in the box*®

Word 2007

THE MISSING MANUAL

Chris Grover

POGUE PRESS™
O'REILLY®

Beijing • Cambridge • Farnham • Köln • Paris • Sebastopol • Taipei • Tokyo

Word 2007: The Missing Manual

by Chris Grover

Copyright © 2007 O'Reilly Media, Inc. All rights reserved.
Printed in the United States of America.

Published by O'Reilly Media, Inc., 1005 Gravenstein Highway North, Sebastopol, CA 95472.

O'Reilly books may be purchased for educational, business, or sales promotional use. Online editions are also available for most titles (*safari.oreilly.com*). For more information, contact our corporate/institutional sales department: (800) 998-9938 or *corporate@oreilly.com*.

Printing History:

December 2006:   First Edition.

 This book uses RepKover™, a durable and flexible lay-flat binding.

ISBN-10: 0-596-52739-X
ISBN-13: 978-0-596-52739-6
[C]

Table of Contents

Part Three: Sharing Documents and Collaborating with Other People

Part Four: Customizing Word with Macros and Other Tools

The Missing Credits

About the Author

 Chris Grover got his first computer in 1982 when he realized it was easier to write on a computer than an IBM Selectric. He never looked back. Chris has worked as a technical writer, advertising copywriter, and product publicist for more than 25 years. He is the coauthor of *Digital Photography: The Missing Manual*. In addition to computer topics, he's written book reviews, software reviews, and articles on subjects ranging from home remodeling to video recorder repairs. His latest project is the launching of Bolinas Road Creative (*www.bolinasroad. com*), an agency that helps small businesses promote their products and services. Chris lives in Fairfax, California with his wife and two daughters, who have learned to tolerate his computer and gadget obsessions.

About the Creative Team

Nan Barber (editor) has worked with the Missing Manual series since its inception—long enough to remember installing Word from floppy disks. Email: *nanbarber@oreilly.com*.

Peter Meyers (editor) works as an editor at O'Reilly Media on the Missing Manual series. He lives with his wife and cats in New York City. Email: *peter.meyers@gmail. com*.

Michele Filshie (editor) is O'Reilly's assistant editor for Missing Manuals and editor of *Dont Get Burned on eBay*. Before turning to the world of computer-related books, Michele spent many happy years at Black Sparrow Press. She lives in Sebastopol. Email: *mfilshie@oreilly.com*.

Dawn Mann (technical reviewer) has been with O'Reilly for over three years and is currently an editorial assistant. When not working, she likes rock climbing, playing soccer, and generally getting into trouble. Email: *dawn@oreilly.com*.

Greg Guntle (technical reviewer) is a Windows veteran covering Office, Programming, Networks and Operating Systems. He's been providing technical editing services for the past 20 years.

Rick Jewell (technical reviewer) has been in the technical industry since 1995. He's now a Beta Support Engineer for Microsoft. Since Microsoft acquired Groove in April of 2005, he's been a technical support engineer supporting the Groove product suite, which will be incorporated into the Premium edition of Microsoft Office 2007 when it's released.

Jill Steinberg (copy editor) is a freelance writer and editor based in Seattle and has produced content for O'Reilly, Intel, Microsoft, and the University of Washington. Jill was educated at Brandeis University, Williams College, and Stanford University. Email: *saysjill@mac.com*

Acknowledgements

Many thanks to the whole Missing Manuals creative team, especially to Nan Barber, who had her work cut out for her making my prose readable. Peter Meyers helped shape the book and gently kept us all on track. Dawn Mann, Greg Guntle, and Rick Jewell checked and double-checked the technical details. Thanks to Michele Filshie for editing, indexing, and working weekends.

As always, thanks to my beautiful wife Joyce, my collaborator in that other project—life. And hugs for Mary and Amy who help me approach everything I do with fresh enthusiasm and a bundle of questions.

—*Chris Grover*

The Missing Manual Series

Missing Manuals are witty, superbly written guides to computer products that don't come with printed manuals (which is just about all of them). Each book features a handcrafted index and RepKover, a detached-spine binding that lets the book lie perfectly flat without the assistance of weights or cinder blocks.

Recent and upcoming titles include:

Access 2003 for Starters: The Missing Manual by Kate Chase and Scott Palmer

Access 2007 for Starters: The Missing Manual by Matthew MacDonald

Access 2007: The Missing Manual by Matthew MacDonald

AppleScript: The Missing Manual by Adam Goldstein

AppleWorks 6: The Missing Manual by Jim Elferdink and David Reynolds

CSS: The Missing Manual by David Sawyer McFarland

Creating Web Sites: The Missing Manual by Matthew MacDonald

Digital Photography: The Missing Manual by Chris Grover and Barbara Brundage

Dreamweaver 8: The Missing Manual by David Sawyer McFarland

eBay: The Missing Manual by Nancy Conner

Excel 2003 for Starters: The Missing Manual by Matthew MacDonald

Excel 2003: The Missing Manual by Matthew MacDonald

Excel 2007 for Starters: The Missing Manual by Matthew MacDonald

Introduction

Word. Microsoft Word has been the world's most popular word processor for so long, it needs only one name—like Oprah or Madonna. Unlike certain celebrities, though, Word has undergone a makeover that goes well beyond cosmetic. Microsoft has redesigned the way you interact with the program and has redefined the underlying document format (don't worry; your old Word documents will still work).

Some things haven't changed: Word 2007 still makes it easy to create professional-looking letters, business reports, and novels. But Microsoft has loaded the program with new features to make designing and formatting attractive documents easier than ever. So even if you're well acquainted with its predecessors, Word 2007 needs an introduction and a new book too. Some of the commands that are old favorites—like Cut and Paste—are in new places. And some high tech features that you may have found counterintuitive or inaccessible—like mail merge and indexing—are now out in the open and easier to use.

The New Word

In the past, when Microsoft introduced new versions of Word, it seemed as if the developers simply tacked new features on top of the old program wherever they'd fit. Sometimes the result was sort of like putting fins on a Volkswagen Beetle. With Word 2007, however, Microsoft listened to the critics who complained about Word's maze of menus and dialog boxes. There were also legitimate complaints about illogically placed commands and important tools that were buried. With Word 2007, all commands have been reorganized according to task and function. Is the new system going to put a smile on everyone's face? No, probably not. Is it an improvement that makes Word easier to use for most people? Yes.

Another concern was security. Microsoft has made major changes in Word's file formats to minimize the chance that you'll open a document containing a virus. It would be naive to think these steps will eliminate virus threats, but they'll certainly help.

So c'mon, pop the hood, kick the tires, and take a look at Word's new chassis.

- **Meet the ribbon.** The first thing you notice when you fire up Word 2007 is that it looks different from other Windows programs you've used. The old menus are gone and so are the toolbars. In their place you have the ribbon, which is sort of a hybrid of the two, as shown in Figure I-1. Where you used to see menu names, you see the names on tabs. Click a tab, and you see a ribbon full of buttons, tools, and commands. Unlike Word's previous toolbars, these buttons and tools are big, visual, and often include labels. Buttons clearly state what they do with both words and pictures, and if you see a down arrow, you can be assured it opens a menu of closely related commands.

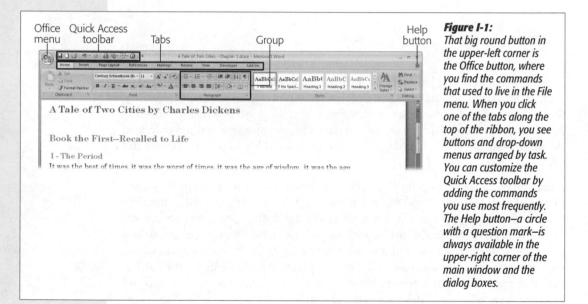

Figure I-1:
That big round button in the upper-left corner is the Office button, where you find the commands that used to live in the File menu. When you click one of the tabs along the top of the ribbon, you see buttons and drop-down menus arranged by task. You can customize the Quick Access toolbar by adding the commands you use most frequently. The Help button—a circle with a question mark—is always available in the upper-right corner of the main window and the dialog boxes.

Tip: Word's new ribbon is one of those features that's easier to understand when you see it in action. You can see a *screencast* (onscreen demonstration) of the ribbon over on the Missing Manuals Web site. Head over to the "Missing CD" page at *www.missingmanuals.com*. Look for other screencasts throughout this book.

- **Building Blocks for better docs.** Word 2007's Building Blocks save time and stress if you consider yourself a writer (or a doctor, or a manager), not a designer. Building Blocks are predesigned, preformatted elements that you can easily drop into your document. Microsoft has thrown in dozens of headers, footers, tables of contents, fax cover pages, and more. Choose a Building Block with the look you want, and then pop it into your document, knowing it will look good and include any pertinent details, like page number, document title, even your name.

- **Instant gratification with Live Preview.** Have you ever paused with your mouse over a command or a formatting option and wondered what it would do to your document? Those days are over. Live Preview is a new feature in Word 2007. Now when you hold your mouse over a formatting style, Building Block, or color, you see a preview right within your document. If you like the look, click your mouse button. If you don't, move your mouse away from the button or menu option, and your document snaps back to its previous appearance. And, of course, you can preview some more options.

- **More art for the masses.** Each version of Word includes more of everything, and Word 2007 is no different in that respect: more clip art; more charts and graphs; and more lines, shapes, and arrows. There's even a new type of artwork called SmartArt. Developed for business presentations, SmartArt makes it a breeze to create flow charts, organizational charts, and other graphics that combine words and pictures. You provide the words, and SmartArt takes care of all the sizing and formatting.

- **Help! Get me security.** That was the cry of many Word users when they opened a document only to let loose a virus on their poor, unsuspecting computer. Microsoft has tackled security problems from several different directions. For example, Word 2007 has a new file format that makes it easier to ferret out documents that may contain virus-infected programs. (When it comes to Word viruses, the main culprits are Visual Basic for Applications and the tools it creates, called ActiveX controls.) In Word 2007, it's also easier than ever to add digital signatures to documents to make sure files come from a trusted source and haven't been tampered with.

- **File this way, please.** The groans are audible any time an industry standard like Microsoft Word makes major changes to its file format. The *file format* is the way a program writes information to a computer disc. As mentioned earlier, Microsoft is switching to a new file format for the best of reasons—to make all our computers safer from viruses. The downside of a new file format is that you can't open the new documents with older versions of Word unless you install a compatibility pack for the older programs. (You can read all the gory details on page 355.)

About This Book

Microsoft expects you to get all the information you need about Word from the Help button in the upper-left corner of the window. Word's help system contains a wealth of information, and it's great in a pinch. But the helps screens are a little long on computer geek-speak and short on useful tips and explanations that make sense to the rest of us. In fact, some of the help screens are on Microsoft's Web site, so you can't even read them without an Internet connection. If you're on the road and can't afford a hotel with a wireless connection, you're out of luck.

This book is the manual you need but Microsoft didn't give you. You'll even find some things in here that Microsoft would never say. If a feature isn't up to snuff, you'll read about it in these pages. What's more, *Word 2007: The Missing Manual* is designed to accommodate readers at every technical level. You won't be lost even if you've never used any version of Microsoft Word. Look for the sidebars called Up To Speed if you feel like you need to catch up on a topic. For the advanced beginner and intermediate readers, there are plenty of details. Word's a humongous program, and this book pokes into all the nooks and crannies. You'll find examples and step-by-step instructions for many of Word's more complicated features and functions. For even more detail on the advanced topics, look for the Power Users' Clinic sidebars.

About the Outline

Word 2007: The Missing Manual is divided into four parts, each containing several chapters:

- Part 1, *Word Basics for Simple Documents*, starts at the very beginning and gets you up and running fast, whether you're a Word veteran or a newcomer. This part covers creating, opening, and saving documents—complete with a description of Word's new file formats. You'll learn how to view your Word documents as outlines, Web pages, and in special print preview and reading modes.

  You'll find chapters devoted to editing text and setting up new documents with custom margins, headers, and footers. You'll learn how to use Word's templates and themes—special tools that make it easy for you to create professional-looking documents. You probably know that Word includes reference tools that check your spelling and help you find the right word, but have you ever used Word's language translation tools or created a custom dictionary of your own technical terms? Now's your chance to learn how it's done. Part 1 wraps up with a complete discussion about printing Word documents.

- Part 2, *Creating Longer and More Complex Documents*, helps yougraduate to the next level of Word creations. When you work with long documents, it's more important than ever to plan ahead, so outlines are covered first. Word can automatically create a table of contents, an index, and a bibliography for your long document, but you'll want to learn some of the tips and tricks for using these tools. This section also explains the pros and cons of using a master document to manage the parts of a very long document. These chapters cover all the elements you're likely to add to longer and more complex documents, like tables, pictures, and even video and sound clips. Last but not least, this part includes a chapter that reveals the mysteries of mail merge and takes you through step-by-step examples.

- Part 3, *Sharing Documents and Collaborating with Other People*, covers ways you can share your Word documents and collaborate with colleagues on projects. Whether you're creating a Web page or creating a form, you'll find the details here. If you're ready for a little tech talk and a glimpse of the future, read the chapter on the way Word makes use of XML (Extensible Markup Language). These days, documents often pass through many hands before they're ready for publication, so you'll learn about Word's tools to make that process go smoothly.

- Part 4, *Customizing Word with Macros and Other Tools*, moves into intermediate and advanced territory, but you'll be ready for it when you get there. The first chapter in this part covers how you can set up Word to work the way you like to work. If security is an important issue for you, be sure to read the chapter that covers Word's Trust Center and other features for safe computing. You'll learn how to automate tasks in Word using macros, and you'll find an introduction to Visual Basic. If you're planning on creating documents for other people to use, you'll be interested in the final chapter on creating themes and templates.

About These Arrows

Throughout this book, and throughout the Missing Manual series, you'll find sentences like this one: "Click Start → All Programs → Microsoft Office → Microsoft Office Word 2007." That's shorthand for a much longer instruction that directs you to click the Start button to open the Start menu, and then choose All Programs. From there, click the Microsoft Office folder, and then click Word's icon to launch it.

Similarly, this kind of arrow shorthand helps to simply the business of choosing commands and menus, as shown in Figure I-2.

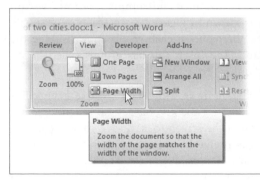

Figure I-2:
In this book, arrow notations help to simplify Word's ribbon structure and commands. For example, "Choose View → Zoom → Page Width" is a more compact way of saying: "Click the View tab, and then go to the Zoom group and click Page Width," as shown here.

The Very Basics

If your fingers have ever graced a computer keyboard, you're probably familiar with the following: Press the keys on your keyboard, and text appears in your document. Hold the Shift key down to type capitals or to enter the various punctuation marks you see above the numbers keys (!@#$*&^). Press Caps Lock, and your keyboard types only capital letters, but the numbers and other symbols continue to work as usual. To correct an error you've just made, you can use the Backspace key. Press it down once, and the cursor moves backward one space, erasing the last character you typed. If you continue to hold it down, it will keep on going, eating up your work like a starving man at a smorgasbord. The Delete (or Del) key, usually on or near the numerical keypad, does the same thing but for the character in *front* of the insertion point.

If you've got that under your belt, then you're ready for the rest of *Word 2007: The Missing Manual*. This book assumes you're familiar with just a few other terms and concepts:

- **Clicking.** This book gives you three kinds of instructions that require you to use your computer's mouse or trackpad. To *click* means to point the arrow cursor at something on the screen, and then—without moving the cursor at all—to press and release the clicker button on the mouse (or laptop trackpad). To *right-click* means to do the same thing, but with the right mouse button. To *double-click*, of course, means to click twice in rapid succession, again without moving the cursor at all. And to *drag* means to move the cursor while pressing the button.

- **Shift-clicking.** Here's another bit of shorthand. *Shift-click* means to hold down the Shift key, and then to click before releasing the key. If you understand that much, then instructions like Ctrl-click and Alt-click should be clear.

- **The ribbon.** Like the older menu system, Word's ribbon shows names across the top of the window—Home, Insert, Page Layout, and so on. In this book, these names are referred to as *tabs*. The buttons and commands on the ribbon change when you click each tab, as shown in Figure I-3. The ribbon organizes buttons and commands in *groups*; the name of each group appears along the bottom of the ribbon. For example, the Insert tab has groups called Pages, Tables, Illustrations, Links, and so on.

- **Keyboard shortcuts.** If you're typing along in a burst of creative energy, it's sometimes disruptive to take your hand off the keyboard, grab the mouse, and then travel all the way up to the top of the screen to, say, save your document. That's why many computer mavens prefer to trigger commands by pressing certain combinations on the keyboard. For example, in most programs you can press Ctrl+S to save the file you're currently working on. When you read an instruction like "press Ctrl+S," start by pressing the Ctrl key; while it's down, type the letter S, and then release both keys.

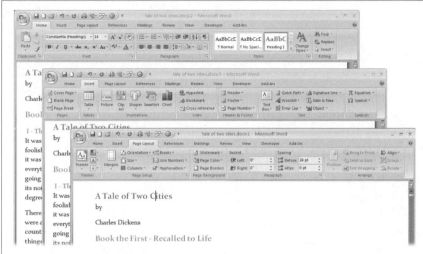

Figure I-3:
The tools on the ribbon change when you click different tabs. From top to bottom, these examples show the Home tab, the Insert tab, and the Page Layout tab.

About MissingManuals.com

At the *www.missingmauals.com* Web site, click the "Missing CD" link to reveal a neat, organized, chapter-by-chapter list of the downloadable practice files mentioned in this book. The Web site also offers corrections and updates to the book (to see them, click the book's title, and then click Errata). In fact, you're invited and encouraged to submit such corrections and updates yourself. In an effort to keep the book as up to date and accurate as possible, each time we print more copies of this book, we incorporate any confirmed corrections you've suggested. We also note such changes on the Web site, so you can mark corrections in your own copy of the book, if you like.

Safari® Enabled

When you see a Safari® Enabled icon on the cover of your favorite technology book, that means the book is available online through the O'Reilly Network Safari Bookshelf.

Safari offers a solution that's better than e-books. It's a virtual library that lets you easily search thousands of top tech books, cut and paste code samples, download chapters, and find quick answers when you need the most accurate, current information. Try it for free at *http://safari.oreilly.com*.

Part One: Word Basics for Simple Documents

1

Creating, Opening, and Saving Documents

Every Word project you create—whether it's a personal letter, a TV sitcom script, or a thesis in microbiology—begins and ends the same way. You start by creating a document, and you end by saving your work. Sounds simple, but to manage your Word documents effectively, you need to know these basics and beyond. This chapter shows you all the different ways to create a new Word document—like starting from an existing document or adding text to a predesigned template—and how to choose the best one for your particular project.

You'll also learn how to work faster and smarter by changing your view of your document. If you want, you can use Word's Outline view when you're brainstorming, and then switch to Print view when you're ready for hard copy. This chapter gets you up and running with these fundamental tools so you can focus on the important stuff—your words.

Tip: If you've used Word before, then you're probably familiar with opening and saving documents. Still, you may want to skim this chapter to catch up on the differences between this version of Word and the ghosts of Word past. You'll grasp some of the big changes just by examining the figures. For more detail, check out the gray boxes and the notes and tips—like this one!

Launching Word

The first time you launch Word after installation, the program asks you to confirm your name and initials. This isn't Microsoft's nefarious plan to pin you down: Word uses this information to identify documents that you create and modify.

Word uses your initials to mark your edits when you review and add comments to Word documents that other people send to you (page 376).

You have three primary ways to fire up Word, so use whichever method you find quickest:

- **Start menu.** The Start button in the lower-left corner of your screen gives you access to all programs on your PC—Word included. To start Word, choose Start → All Programs → Microsoft Office → Microsoft Office Word.

- **Quick Launch toolbar.** The Quick Launch toolbar at the bottom of your screen (just to the right of the Start menu) is a great place to start programs you use frequently. Microsoft modestly assumes that you'll be using Word a lot, so it usually installs the Word icon in the Quick Launch toolbar. To start using Word, just click the W icon, and voilá!

Tip: When you don't see the Quick Launch toolbar, here's how to display it: On the bar at the bottom of your screen, right-click an empty spot. From the menu that pops up, choose Toolbars → Quick Launch. When you're done, icons for some of your programs appear in the bottom bar. A single click fires up the program.

- **Opening a Word document.** Once you've created some Word documents, this method is fastest of all, since you don't have to start Word as a separate step. Just open an existing Word document, and Word starts itself. Try going to Start → My Recent Documents, and then, from the list of files, choose a Word document. You can also double-click the document's icon on the desktop or wherever it lives on your PC.

Tip: If you need to get familiar with the Start menu, Quick Launch toolbar, and other Windows features, then pick up a copy of *Windows XP: The Missing Manual*, Second Edition or *Windows Vista: The Missing Manual.*

So, what happens once you've got Word's motor running? If you're a newcomer, you're probably just staring with curiosity. If you're familiar with previous versions of Word, though, you may be doing a double take (Figure 1-1). In Word 2007, Microsoft combined all the old menus and toolbars into a new feature called the ribbon. Click one of the tabs above the ribbon, and you see the command buttons change below. The ribbon commands are organized into groups, with the name of each group listed at the bottom. (See Figure 1-1 for more detail on the ribbon.)

Creating a New Document

When you start Word without opening an existing document, the program gives you an empty one to work in. If you're eager to put words to page, then type away.

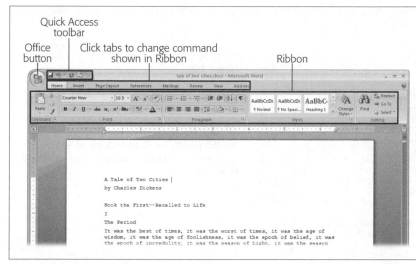

Quick Access toolbar

Office button

Click tabs to change command shown in Ribbon

Ribbon

Figure 1-1:
When you start Word 2007 for the first time, it may look a little top-heavy. The ribbon takes up more real estate than the old menus and toolbars. This change may not matter if you have a nice big monitor. But if you want to reclaim some of that space, you can hide the ribbon by double-clicking the active tab. Later, when you need to see the ribbon commands, just click a tab.

Sooner or later, though, you'll want to start *another* new document. Word gives you three ways to do so:

- **Creating a new blank document.** When you're preparing a simple document—like a two-page essay, a note for the babysitter, or a press release—a plain, unadorned page is fine. Or, when you're just brainstorming and you're not sure what you want the final document to look like, you probably want to start with a blank slate or use one of Word's templates (more on that in a moment) to provide structure for your text.

- **Creating a document from an existing document.** For letters, resumes, and other documents that require more formatting, why reinvent the wheel? You can save time by using an existing document as a starting point (page 15). When you have a letter format that you like, you can use it over and over by editing the contents.

- **Creating a document from a template** (page 17). Use a template when you need a professional design for a complex document, like a newsletter, a contract, or meeting minutes. Templates are a lot like forms—the margins, formatting, and graphics are already in place. All you do is fill in your text.

Tip: Microsoft provides a mind-boggling number of templates with Word, but they're not the only source. You can find loads more on the Internet, as described on page 136. Your employer may even provide official templates for company documents.

To start your document in any of the above ways, click the Windows logo in the upper-left corner of the screen. That's Office 2007's new *Office button*. Click it, and a drop-down menu opens, revealing commands for creating, opening, and saving documents. Next to these commands, you see a list of your Word documents. This list includes documents that are open, as well as those that you've recently opened.

The Office button is also where you go to print and email your documents (Figure 1-2).

Figure 1-2:
The phrase most frequently uttered by experienced Word fans the first time they start Word 2007 is, "Okay, where's my File menu?" Never fear, the equivalent of the File menu is still there—it's just camouflaged a bit. Clicking the Office button (the one that looks like a Windows logo) reveals the commands you use to create, open, and save Word documents.

Creating a New Blank Document

Say you want a new blank document, just like the one Word shows you when you start the program. No problem—here are the steps:

1. **Choose Office button → New.**

   The New Document dialog box appears.

2. **In the upper-left corner of the large "Create a new Word document" panel, click "Blank document" (Figure 1-3).**

   The New Document box presents a seemingly endless number of options, but don't panic. The "Blank document" option you want is on the left side of the first line.

3. **At the bottom of the New Document dialog box, click Create.**

   The dialog box disappears, and you're gazing at the blank page of a new Word document.

Better get to work.

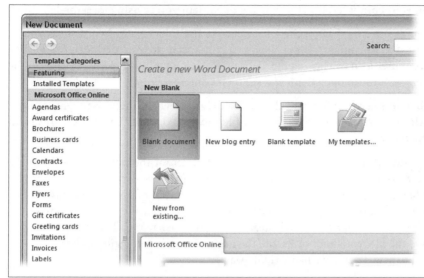

Figure 1-3:
Open the New Document box (Office button → New, or Alt+F, N), and Word gives you several ways to create a new document. Click "Blank document" to open an empty document, similar to the one Word shows when you first start the program. Or you can click "New from existing" to open a document that you previously created under a new name.

Creating a New Document from an Existing Document

A blank Word document is sort of like a shapeless lump of clay. With some work, you can mold it to become just about anything. Often, however, you can save time by opening an existing document that's similar to the one you want to create. Imagine that you write the minutes for the monthly meetings of the Chief Executive Officer's Surfing Association (CEOSA). When it's time to write up the June minutes, it's a lot faster to open the minutes from May. You keep the boilerplate text and all the formatting, but you delete the text that's specific to the previous month. Now all you have to do is enter the text for June and save the document with a new name: *JuneMinutes.docx*.

Note: The .docx extension on the end of the filename is Word 2007's new version of .doc. The switch from three-letter to four-letter filename extensions indicates a change in the way Word stores documents. (If you need to share documents with folks using earlier versions of Word, choose Office button → Save As → Word 97-2003 document when you save the file. See the box on page 17 for details.)

Word gives you a "New from existing" document-creation option to satisfy your desire to spend more time surfing and less time writing meeting minutes. Here's how to create a new document from an existing document:

1. **Choose Office button → New (Alt+F, N) to open the New Document window. Then click "New from existing…" (it sits directly below the "Blank document" button).**

   The three dots at the end of the button's title tell you that there's another dialog box to come. And sure enough, when you click "New from existing…", it opens another box, appropriately titled New from Existing Document (Figure 1-4). This box looks—and works—like a standard Windows Open File box. It lets you navigate to a specific folder and open a file.

---

2. **On your computer, find the existing document you're using for a model.**

   You can use the bar on the left to change the folder view. Word starts you in your My Documents folder, but you can switch to your desktop or your My Computer icon by clicking the icons on the left. Double-click folder icons in the large window to open them and see their contents.

3. **Click to select the file, and then click Create New (in the lower-right corner). (Alternatively, just double-click the file's icon to open it. This trick works in all Open File boxes.)**

   Instead of the usual Open button at the bottom of the box, the button in the New from Existing Document box reads Create New—your clue that this box behaves differently in one important respect: Instead of opening an existing file, you're making a *copy* of an existing file. Once open, the file's name is something like *Document2.docx* instead of the original name. This way, when you save the file, you don't overwrite the original document. (Still, it's best to save it with a new descriptive name right away.)

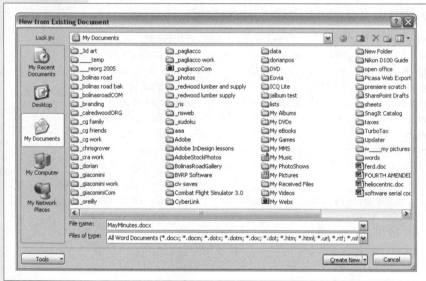

Figure 1-4:
Use the New from Existing Document box to find an existing Word document that you'd like to open as a model for your new document. When you click Create New at bottom-right, Word opens a new copy of the document, leaving the original untouched. You can modify the copy to your heart's content and save it under a different file name.

Tip: Windows' Open File boxes, like New from Existing Document, let you do a lot more than just find files. In fact, they let you do just about anything you can do in Windows Explorer. Using keyboard shortcuts, you can cut (Ctrl+X), copy (Ctrl+C), and paste (Ctrl+V) files. A right-click displays a shortcut menu with even more commands, letting you rename files, view Properties dialog boxes, and much more. You can even drag and drop to move files and folders.

Word's New File Formats: .docx and .docm

With Office 2007, Microsoft took the drastic step of changing its file formats in hopes of improving your computer's security. Malicious programmers were using Office's macros to do nasty things to unsuspecting computers. The *.docx* format, the new standard for Word files, doesn't permit macros, making it safe from those threats. The *.docm* format indicates that a document contains macros or other bits of programming code. When opening one of these files, play it safe: If you don't know who created the .docm file, then don't open it.

The downside of the new file formats is that older versions of Word don't know how to open these .docx and .docm documents. To open Word 2007 files with an older version (even Word 2003), you need to install the Microsoft Office Compatibility Pack.

This software fix gives pre-2007 versions of Word the power to open documents in the new formats. Even then, you may not be able to use or edit parts of the file that use new Word features (like themes, equations, and content controls). To download the free compatibility pack, go to *www.office. microsoft.com* and type *office 2007 compatibility* into the search box at the top of the page.

Also, if you're preparing a Word document for someone who's using an older Word version, then you have to save it in a compatible format, as described in the tip on page 15. (Fortunately, the compatibility issue doesn't go both ways: Word 2007 can open old .doc docs just fine.)

Creating a New Document from a Template

Say you're creating meeting minutes for the first time. You don't have an existing document to give you a leg up, but you do want to end up with handsome, properly formatted minutes. Word is at your service—with *templates*. Microsoft provides dozens upon dozens of prebuilt templates for everything from newsletters to postcards. Remember all the busy stuff in the New Document box in Figure 1-3? About 90 percent of the items in there are templates.

In the previous example, where you use an existing document to create the meeting minutes for the Chief Executive Officer's Surfing Association (CEOSA), each month you open the minutes from the previous month. You delete the information that pertains to the previous month and enter the current month's minutes. A template works pretty much the same way, except it's a generic document, designed to be adaptable to lots of different situations. You just open it and add your text. The structure, formatting, graphics, colors, and other doodads are already in place.

Note: The subject of Word templates is a lengthy one, especially when it comes to creating your own, so there's a whole chapter devoted to that topic—Chapter 20.

Here's how to get some help from one of Microsoft's templates for meeting minutes:

1. **Choose Office button → New (Alt+F, N) to open the New Document window.**

    On the left of the New Document box is a Template Categories list. The top entry on this list is Installed Templates—the ones Word has installed on your computer.

You could use any of these, but you also have a world of choice waiting for you online. On its Web site, Microsoft offers hundreds of templates for all sorts of documents, and you can access them right from the New Document box. If you have a fast Internet connection, then it's just as quick and easy to use an online template as it is using the ones stored on your computer. In fact, you'll use an online template for this example.

Note: If you can't connect to the Internet right now, then simply choose one of the installed templates instead. Click Create, and then skip to step 4.

2. **Scroll down the Template Categories list to the Microsoft Office Online heading. Under this heading, select Minutes.**

   In the center pane, you'll see all different types of minutes templates, from PTA minutes to Annual shareholder's meeting minutes (Figure 1-5). When you click a template's icon, a preview appears in the pane on the right.

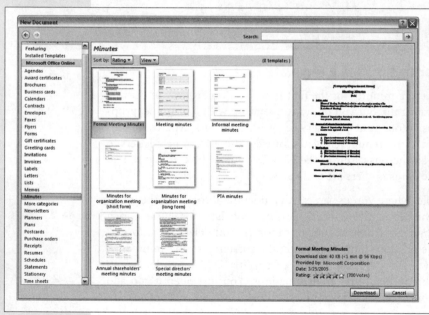

Figure 1-5:
The New Document box lists prebuilt templates that live at Microsoft Office Online in categories like Agendas, Brochures, Calendars, and Minutes. Below the thumbnail you see an estimate of how long it takes to download the template from the Microsoft Office Online Web site. A rating, from 0 to 5 stars, tells you what other people think of the template (the rating system is kind of like the one at Amazon.com).

3. **When you're done perusing the various styles, click the Formal Meeting Minutes icon. (After all, CEOSA is a very formal organization.) Then click Download.**

   Word downloads and opens the document.

4. **Start writing up the minutes for the CEO Surfers.**

   To follow the template's structure, replace all the words in square brackets ([ ]) with text relevant to CEOSA.

Tip: If you'd rather not download the Formal Meeting Minutes template every time you use it, then you can save the file on your computer as a Word template. The steps for saving files are just around the corner on page 29.

Opening an Existing Document

If you've mastered creating a document from an existing document and creating a document from a template, you'll find that opening an existing document is a snap. The steps are nearly identical.

1. **Choose Office button → Open (Alt+F, O). In the Open window (Figure 1-6), navigate to the folder and file you want to open.**

   The Open window starts out showing your My Documents folder, since that's where Word suggests you save your files. When your document's in a more exotic location, click the My Computer icon, and then navigate to the proper folder from there.

Tip: When you open a document you've used recently, you may see its name right on the Office button → Recent Documents menu. If so, simply click to open it without a trip to the Open dialog box.

2. **With the file selected, click Open in the lower-right corner.**

   The Open box goes away and your document opens in Word. You're all set to get to work. Just remember, when you save this document (Alt+F, S or Ctrl+S), you write over the previous file. Essentially, you create a new, improved, and only copy of the file you just opened. If you don't want to write over the existing document, use the Save As command (Alt+F, A), and then type a new name in the File Name text box.

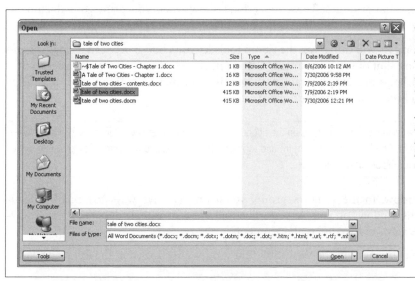

Figure 1-6:
This Open dialog box shows the contents of the tale of two cities *folder, according to the "Look in" box at the top. The file* tale of two cities. docx *is selected, as you can see in the "File name box" at the bottom of the window. By clicking Open, Mr. Dickens is ready to go to work.*

Tip: Opening a file in Word doesn't mean you're limited to documents *created* in Word. You can choose documents created in other programs from the Files of Type drop-down menu at the bottom of the Open dialog box. Word then shows you that type of document in the main part of the window. You can open Outlook messages (.msg), Web pages (.htm or .html), or files from other word processors (.rtf, .mcw, .wps).

Your Different Document Views

Now that you know a handful of ways to create and open Word documents, it's time to take a look around the establishment. You may think a document's a document—just look at it straight on and get your work done. It's surprising, though, how changing your view of the page can help you work faster and smarter. When you're working with a very long document, you can change to Outline view and peruse just your document's headlines without the paragraph text. In Outline view, you get a better feeling for the manuscript as a whole. Likewise, when you're working on a document that's headed for the Web, it makes sense to view the page as it will appear in a browser. Other times, you may want to have two documents open on your screen at once (or on each of your two monitors, you lucky dog), to make it easy to cut and paste text from one to the other.

The key to working with Word's different view options is to match the view to the job at hand. Once you get used to switching views, you'll find lots of reasons to change your point of view. Find the tools you need on the View tab (Figure 1-7). To get there, click the View tab (Alt+W) on the ribbon (near the top of Word's window). The tab divides the view commands into four groups:

- **Document Views.** These commands change the big picture. For the most part, use these when you want to view a document in a dramatically different way: two pages side by side, Outline view, Web layout view, and so on.

- **Show/Hide.** The Show/Hide commands display and conceal Word tools like rulers and gridlines. These tools don't show when you print your document; they're just visual aids that help you when you're working in Word.

- **Zoom.** As you can guess, the Zoom tools let you choose between a close-up and a long shot of your document. Getting in close makes your words easier to read and helps prevent eyestrain. But zooming out makes scrolling faster and helps you keep your eye on the big picture.

Tip: In addition to the Zoom tools on the ribbon, handy Zoom tools are available in the window's lower-right corner. Check out the + (Zoom In) and – (Zoom Out) buttons and the slider in between them. See page 23 for the details on using them.

- **Window.** In the Window group, you'll find creative ways to organize document windows on your screen—like split views of a single document or side-by-side views of two different documents.

All the commands in the View tab's four groups are covered in the following pages.

Note: This section provides the short course on viewing your Word documents. For even more details and options for customizing your Word environment, see Chapter 17.

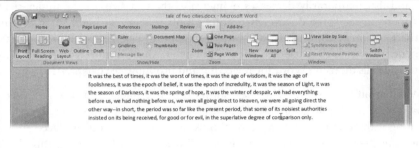

Figure 1-7:
The View tab is your document-viewing control center. Look closely, and you see it's divided into four groups with names at the bottom of the ribbon: Document Views, Show/Hide, Zoom, and Window. To apply a view command, just click the button or label.

Document Views: Five Ways to Look at Your Manuscript

Word gives you five basic document views. To select a view, go to the View tab (Alt+W) and choose one of the Document Views on the left side of the ribbon (Figure 1-8). You have another great option for switching from one view to another that's always available in the lower-right corner of Word's window. Click one of the five small buttons to the left of the slider to jump between Print Layout, Full Screen Reading, Web Layout, Outline, and Draft views. Each view has a special purpose, and you can modify them even more using the other commands on the View tab.

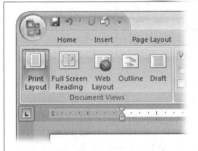

Figure 1-8:
On the left side of the View tab, you find the five basic document views: Print Layout, Full Screen Reading, Web Layout, Outline, and Draft. You can edit your document in any of the views, although they come with different tools for different purposes. For example, Outline view provides a menu that lets you show or hide headings at different outline levels.

Note: Changing your view in no way affects the document itself—you're just looking at the same document from a different perspective.

- **Print Layout (Alt+W, P).** The most frequently used view in Word, Print Layout, is the one you see when you first start the program or create a new blank document. In this view, the page you see on your computer screen looks much as it does when you print it. This view's handy for letters, reports, and most documents headed for the printer.

- **Full Screen Reading (Alt+W, F).** If you'd like to get rid of the clutter of menus, ribbons, and all the rest of the word-processing gadgetry, then use Full Screen Reading view. As the name implies, this view's designed primarily for reading documents. It includes options you don't find in the other views, like a command that temporarily decreases or increases the text size. In the upper-right corner you see some document-proofing tools (like a text highlighter and an insert comment command), but when you want to change or edit your document, you must first use the View Options → Allow Typing command. For more details on using Word for reviewing and proofing, see Chapter 16.

- **Web Layout (Alt+W, L).** This view shows your document as if it were a single Web page loaded in a browser. You don't see any page breaks in this view. Along with your text, you see any photos or videos that you've placed in the document—just like a Web page. Page 317 has more details on creating Web pages with Word.

- **Outline (Alt+W, U).** For lots of writers, an outline is the first step in creating a manuscript. Once they've created a framework of chapters and headings, they dive in and fill out the document with text. If you like to work this way, then you'll love Outline view. It's easy to jump back and forth between Outline view and Print Layout view or Draft view, so you can bounce back and forth between a macro and a micro view of your epic. (For more details on using Word's Outline view, see page 185.)

- **Draft (Alt+W, V).** Here's the no-nonsense, roll-up-your-sleeves view of your work (Figure 1-9). You see most formatting as it appears on the printed page, except for headers and footers. Page breaks are indicated by a thin dotted line. In this view, it's as if your document is on one single roll of paper that scrolls through your computer screen. This view's a good choice for longer documents and those moments when you want to focus on the words without being distracted by page breaks and other formatting niceties.

Show and Hide Window Tools

Word gives you some visual aids that make it easier to work with your documents. Tools like rulers and gridlines don't show up when you print your document, but they help you line up the elements on the page. Use the ruler to set page margins and to create tabs for your documents. Checkboxes on the View tab let you show or hide tools, but some tools aren't available in all the views, so they're grayed out. You can't, for example, display page rulers in Outline or Full Screen Reading views.

Use the checkboxes in the Show/Hide group of the View tab (Figure 1-10) to turn these tools on and off:

- **Ruler.** Use the ruler to adjust margins, set tabs, and position items on your page. For more detail on formatting text and paragraphs, see Chapter 4.

- **Gridlines.** When you click the Gridlines box, it looks like you created your document on a piece of graph paper. This effect isn't too helpful for an all-text document, but it sure comes in handy if you're trying to line up photos on a page.

Figure 1-9:
In Draft view, you see most text and paragraph formatting, but headers, footers, and other distracting page formatting features are hidden. Your text appears as a continuous scroll, with the margins hidden. Page breaks appear as dotted lines.

- **Message Bar.** The Message Bar resides directly under the ribbon, and it's where you see alerts about a document's behavior. For example, when a document is trying to run a macro and your Word settings prohibit macros, an alert appears in the Message Bar. Click the checkbox to show or hide the Message Bar.

- **Document Map.** If you work with long documents, you'll like the Document Map. This useful tool appears to the left of your text (you can see it in Figure 1-10), showing the document's headings at various levels. Click the little + and − buttons next to a heading to expand or collapse the outline. Click a heading, and you jump to that location in your document.

- **Thumbnails.** Select the Thumbnails option, and you see little icons of your document's pages in the bar on the left. Click a thumbnail to go to that page. In general, thumbnails are more useful for shorter documents and for pages that are visually distinctive. For longer documents, you'll find the Document Map easier to use for navigation.

Zooming Your View In and Out

When you're working, do you ever find that you sometimes hold pages at arm's length to get a complete view, and then, at other times, you stick your nose close to the page to examine the details? Word's Zoom options (Figure 1-11) let you do the same thing with your screen—but without looking nearly as silly.

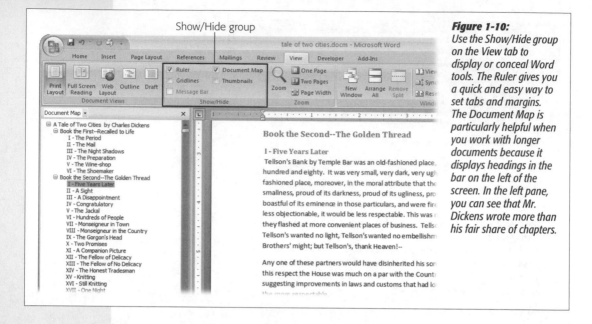

Figure 1-10:
Use the Show/Hide group on the View tab to display or conceal Word tools. The Ruler gives you a quick and easy way to set tabs and margins. The Document Map is particularly helpful when you work with longer documents because it displays headings in the bar on the left of the screen. In the left pane, you can see that Mr. Dickens wrote more than his fair share of chapters.

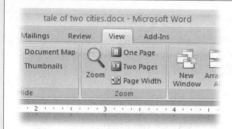

Figure 1-11:
The Zoom group of options lets you view your document close up or at a distance. The big magnifying glass opens the Zoom dialog box with more controls for fine-tuning your zoom level. For quick changes, click one of the three buttons on the right: One Page, Two Pages, or Page Width.

Note: Even though the text appears to get bigger and smaller when you zoom, you're not actually changing the document in any way. Zoom is similar to bringing a page closer so you can read the fine print. If you want to actually change the font size, then use the formatting options on the Home tab (Alt+H, FS).

On the View tab, click the big magnifying glass to open the Zoom dialog box (Figure 1-12). Depending on your current Document View (see page 20), you can adjust your view by percentage or relative to the page and text (more on that in a moment). The options change slightly depending on which Document View you're using. The Page options don't really apply to Web layouts, so they're grayed out and inactive if you're in the Web Layout view.

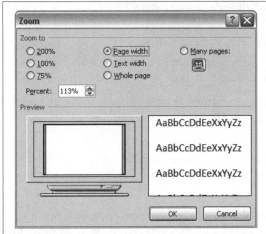

Figure 1-12:
The Zoom dialog box lets you choose from a variety of views. Just click one of the option buttons, and then click OK. The monitor and text sample at the bottom of the Zoom box provide visual clues as you change the settings.

Zooming by percentage

In the box's upper-left corner, you find controls to zoom in and out of your document by percentage. The view varies depending on your computer screen and settings, but in general, 100% is a respectable, middle-of-the-road view of your document. The higher the percentage, the more zoomed in you are, and the bigger everything looks—vice versa with a lower percentage.

The three radio buttons (200%, 100%, and 75%) give you quick access to some standard settings. For in-between percentages (like 145%), type a number in the box below the buttons, or use the up-down arrows to change the value. For a quick way to zoom in and out without opening a dialog box, use the Zoom slider (Figure 1-13) in the lower-right corner of your window. Drag the slider to the right to zoom in on your document, and drag it to the left to zoom out. The percentage changes as you drag.

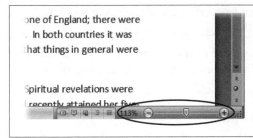

Figure 1-13:
The Zoom slider at the bottom of the document window gives you a quick and easy way to change your perspective. Drag the slider to the right to zoom in on your document, and drag it to the left to zoom out. To the left of the slider are five View buttons: Print Layout, Full Screen Reading, Web Layout, Outline, and Draft (page 22). Since the first button is selected, this document is in Print Layout view.

Zooming relative to page or text

Not everyone's a number person. (That's especially true of writers.) So you may prefer to zoom without worrying about percentage figures. The Zoom dialog box (on the View tab, click the magnifying-glass icon) gives you four radio buttons with plain-English zoom settings:

Page width. Click this button, and the page resizes to fill the screen from one side to the other. It's the fastest way to zoom to a text size that most people find comfortable to read. (You may have to scroll, though, to read the page from top to bottom.)

Text width. This button zooms in even farther, because it ignores the margins of your page. Use this one if you have a high-resolution monitor (or you've misplaced your reading glasses).

Whole page. When you want to see an entire page from top to bottom and left to right, click this button. It's great for getting an overview of how your headings and paragraphs look on the page.

Many pages. This view is the equivalent of spreading your document out on the floor, and then viewing it from the top of a ladder. You can use it to see how close you are to finishing that five-page paper, or to inspect the layout of a multi-page newsletter.

Warning: When you're zoomed out to Whole or "Many pages" view, watch those fingers on the keyboard. You can still make changes to your text in these views, even though you can't see what you're doing.

Changing page view from the ribbon

The ribbon offers radio buttons for three popular page views. (You can see them back in Figure 1-11, to the Zoom tool's right.) They're a quick and dirty way to change the number of pages you see onscreen without fiddling with zoom controls.

- **One Page.** This view shows the entire page in Word's document window. If your screen is large enough, you can read and edit text in this view.

- **Two Pages.** In this view, you see two pages side by side. This view's handy when you're working with documents that have two-page spreads, like booklets.

- **Page Width.** This button does the exact same thing as the Page Width button in the Zoom dialog box (page 23). It's more readable than the One Page and Two Page options, because the page fills the screen from edge to edge, making the text appear larger.

The Window Group: Doing the Splits

Back when dinosaurs roamed the earth and people used typewriters (or very early word processors), you could work on only one document at a time—the one right in front of you. Although Word 2007 has more options for viewing multiple documents and multiple windows than ever, some folks forget to use them. Big mistake. If you ever find yourself comparing two documents or borrowing extensively from some other text, then having two or more documents visible on your screen can double or triple your work speed.

The commands for managing multiple documents, views, and windows are in the View tab's Window group (Figure 1-14).

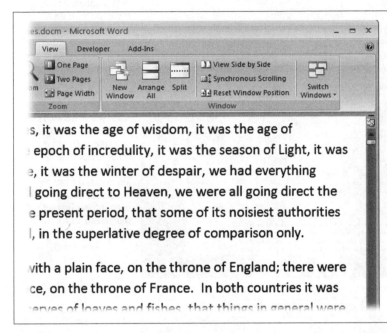

Figure 1-14:
In the Window group, the three commands on the left—New Window, Arrange All, and Split—let you open and view your work from multiple vantage points. The commands in the middle—View Side by Side, Synchronous Scrolling, and Reset Window Position—are helpful when reviewing and comparing documents. The big Switch Windows button lets you hop from one document to another.

- **New Window (Alt+W, N).** When you're working on a long document, sometimes you want to see two different parts of the document at the same time, as if they were two separate documents. You may want to keep referring to what you said in the Introduction while you're working on Chapter 5. Or perhaps you want to keep an Outline view open while editing in Draft view. That's where the New Window command comes in. When you click this button (or hit this keystroke), you've got your document open in two windows that you can scroll independently. Make a change to one window, and it immediately appears in the other.

- **Arrange All (Alt+W, A).** Great—now you've got documents open in two or more windows, but it takes a heck of a lot of mousing around and window resizing to get them lined up on your screen at the same time. Click Arrange All and, like magic, your open Word document windows are sharing the screen, making it easy to work on one and then the other. Word takes an egalitarian approach to screen real estate, giving all windows an equal amount of property (Figure 1-15).

- **Split (Alt+W, S).** The Split button divides a single window so you can see two different parts of the same document—particularly handy if you're copying text from one part of a document to another. The other advantage of the Split command is that it gives you more room to work than using Arrange All for multiple windows because it doesn't duplicate the ribbon, ruler, and other Word tools (Figure 1-16).

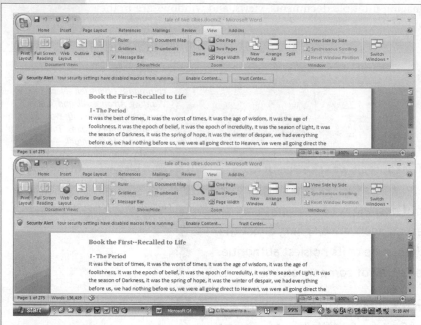

Figure 1-15:
One downside of Office 2007's ribbon: It takes up more space on your computer's screen than menus or even the older button bars. When you open a couple of windows, you're not left with much space to do your work, especially when you're working on an ultra-portable laptop or a computer with a small screen. You can double-click the active tab to hide the ribbon, but in most cases, you're better off working with a split screen, as shown in Figure 1-16.

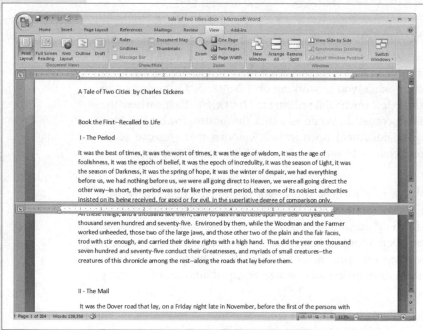

Figure 1-16:
When you're viewing two different parts of a single document, use the Split command; it leaves you more room to work than two separate windows, as shown in Figure 1-15. Each section of the split window has a scroll bar, so you can independently control different parts of your document. If you want to fine-tune your split, just drag the middle bar exactly where you want it. When you're done, click Remove Split to return to a single screen view.

Viewing multiple windows

One common reason for wanting to see two documents or more on your screen at once is so you can make line-by-line comparisons. Imagine you have two Word documents that are almost identical, but you have to find the spots where there are differences. A great way to make those differences jump out is to put both versions on your screen side by side and scroll through them. As you scroll, you can see differences in the paragraph lengths and the line lengths. Here are the commands to help you with the process:

- **View Side by Side (Alt+W, B).** Click the View Side by Side command and Word arranges two windows vertically side by side. As you work with side-by-side documents, you can rearrange windows on your screen by dragging the very top of the Window frame. You can resize the windows by pointing to any edge of the frame. When you see a double arrow, just drag to resize the window. Synchronous Scrolling (described next) is automatically turned on.

- **Synchronous Scrolling (Alt+W, Y).** The Synchronous Scrolling feature keeps multiple document windows in lock step. When you scroll one window, the other windows automatically scroll too. Using the same button or keystroke, you can toggle Synchronous Scrolling on and off as you work with your documents.

- **Reset Windows Position (Alt+W, T).** If you've moved or resized your document windows as described earlier under View Side by Side, then you can click this button to reset your view so the windows share the screen equally.

Saving and Closing Documents

From the earliest days of personal computing, the watchword has been "save early, save often." There's nothing more frustrating than working half the day and then having the Great American Novel evaporate into the digital ether because your power goes out. So, here are some tips to protect your work from disasters human-made and natural:

- Name and save your document shortly after you first create it. You'll see the steps to do so later in this section.

- Get in the habit of doing a quick save with Alt+F, S (think *File Save*) when you pause to think or get up to go to the kitchen for a snack. (Note for old-timers: Ctrl+S still works for a quick save too.)

- If you're leaving your computer for an extended period of time, save and close your document with Alt+F, C (think *File Close*).

Where Are My Keyboard Shortcuts?

Ribbons, buttons, and menus are all well and good when you're doing something new or complicated. But when you know where you're going, a good keyboard shortcut can save time. Word 2007 has dozens of keyboard shortcuts. If you don't have your favorites memorized, use the Alt key to reveal them.

Press the Alt key, and you see small badges with letters and numbers pop up next to menus and buttons. These are your shortcuts. If you're looking for the keyboard shortcut to close your document, follow these steps:

1. Press and release the Alt key to show the keyboard shortcut badges.

   When you do this, the badges appear over menu items and ribbon buttons. (The Alt key acts as a toggle. If you change your mind and don't want to use a shortcut, then press the Alt key again and you're back in normal typing mode.)

2. Press F to open the Office menu.

   Pressing F (which used to stand for File menu) does the same thing as clicking the button with your mouse, except that now it sports little keyboard shortcut badges.

3. Press C to close your document.

   Looking at the bottom of the Office menu, you see the Close command. A small C badge indicates that pressing C closes your document.

As you can guess, most keyboard shortcuts are based on the initial letter of the actual command words. This doesn't always work out for popular letters. As a result, you have cases like the References tab, which has the keyboard shortcut S.

Even if you don't deliberately work to memorize the keyboard shortcuts, you'll find that you begin to learn your favorites as you use them. Before long, your fingers will tap them out automatically.

If a substantial portion of your brain is occupied by keyboard shortcuts from previous versions of Word, never fear. Most of those old commands still work—including Ctrl+B for Bold, Ctrl+N for new document, and F7 for spell checking.

The Many Ways to Save Documents

It's the Microsoft Way to give you multiple ways to do most everything. Whether that's because the company's programmers believe in giving you lots of choices, or because they can't make up their minds about the best way to do something is a question best left to the philosophers. But the point is, you do have a choice. You don't have to memorize every keystroke, button, and command. Especially with saving, the important thing is to find a way you like and stick with it. Here's a list of some ways you can save the document you're working on:

Saving by keyboard shortcut

- **Ctrl+S.** If you're an old hand at Word, this keyboard shortcut may already be burned in your brain. It still works with Word and other Office programs. This command quickly saves the document and lets you get back to work.

- **Alt+F, S.** This keyboard shortcut does the exact same thing as Ctrl+S. Unlike Ctrl+S, though, you get visual reminders of which keys to press when you press the Alt key. See the box above.

Saving by menu command

- **Office button → Save.** If you don't want to use keyboard shortcuts, you can mouse your way to the same place using menus. Like the options above, this command saves your file with its current name.

- **Office button → Save As.** The Save As option lets you save your file with a new name (Figure 1-17). When you use this command, you create a new document with a new name that includes any changes you've made. (The individual steps are described in the next section.)

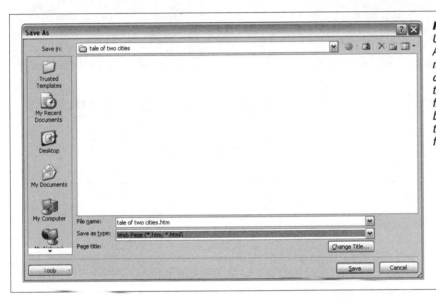

Figure 1-17:
Use Office button → Save As to save your file with a new name or in a different file format. In this example, the Word file tale of two cities *is being saved as an HTML type file—a format used for Web pages.*

- **Office button → Close.** When you close a document, Word checks to see if you've made any changes to the file. When you've made changes, Word always asks whether you'd like to save the document (Figure 1-18).

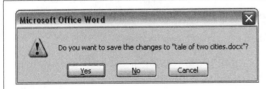

Figure 1-18:
When you see this message box, you have three choices: Yes saves your document before closing it; No closes your document without saving it; Cancel leaves your document open without saving it.

Saving with a new name

When you save a new document or save a document with a new name (Save As), you've got three things to consider: a filename, a file location, and a file format.

Preventing and Recovering from Disaster

Lightning strikes. Children trip over power cords. Computers crash. Saving your work frequently and keeping backup copies of your documents are important safeguards. You can have Word save backup copies every time you save a document, so you always have the last two versions of your work stored on your computer. Word doesn't automatically save backup copies of your files, but it's easy enough to change this setting. Click the Office button, and then click Word Options at the bottom of the box.

After the Word Options dialog box opens, scroll down to the Save group, and turn on the "Always create backup copy" checkbox. Choose Office button → Open to find and open your backup file (Figure 1-19).

When disaster strikes in spite of your meticulous preventive measures, Word can help too. Word's new file formats have been designed to be easier to recover and repair. In many cases, if a picture or a table is corrupted in the file, you can still retrieve everything else (Figure 1-20).

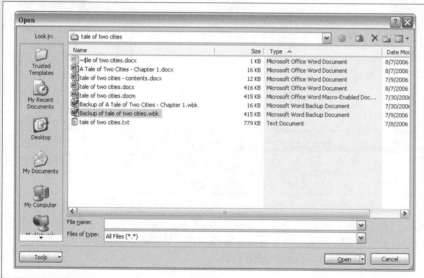

Figure 1-19:
To open a backup file, choose All Files (.*) in the "Files of type" drop-down menu at the bottom of the Open dialog box. Look for a file that begins with the words "Backup of." Double-click to open the file.*

Here are the steps for saving a file, complete with a new name:

1. **Choose Office button → Save As to open the Save As box.**

   You use the Save As command when you're saving a file with a new name. Word also displays the Save As box the first time you save a new document.

2. **Use the "Save in" drop-down list or double-click to open folders in the window to find a location to store your file.**

   The buttons in the upper-right corner can also help you navigate. See the details in Figure 1-21. Word doesn't care where you save your files, so you can choose your desktop or any folder on your computer.

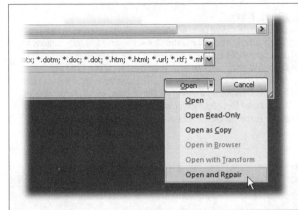

Figure 1-20:
When you can't open a file with a normal Open command, click the arrow to the right of the Open button, and choose Open and Repair from the drop-down menu. Some parts of your file may still be damaged, but you can usually recover most of your work.

Tip: The more files you save on your computer, the more helpful it is to have a logical folder and file system. If you keep hundreds of Word documents, you may want to have different folders named: letters, memos, reports, and newsletters.

---

3. **At the bottom of the Save As dialog box, type a name in the File name box.**

   Word accepts long names, so you don't need to skimp. Use a descriptive name that will help you identify the file two weeks or two years from now. A good name saves you time in the long run.

4. **Use the "Save as type" box to choose a file type.**

   In most cases you don't need to change the file type. Word automatically selects either *.docx* or *.docm* depending on the contents of your file, but Word can save files in over a dozen different formats. If you're sharing the file with someone who's using an older version of Word, then choose Word 97-2003 Document to save the document in .doc format. If you're sharing with someone who uses a Mac or Linux computer, then you may want to use the more universal Rich Text Format (.rtf).

Tip: If you want to use your document as a template in the future, then choose Word Template (.dotx). Use the Word Macro-Enabled format (.dotm) if you've created any macros (page 434).

   Unless you're sharing your file with someone using an older version of Word or a different operating system or making a template, stick with the new standard Word file types .docx (for normal Word files) and .docm (for files that run macros). See the box on page 17 for a complete rundown.

5. **Click Save.**

   Word does the rest. All you need to do is remember where you saved your work.

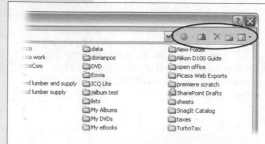

Figure 1-21:
*The Save As dialog box has all the controls you need to navigate
to any location on your computer—including five nifty buttons in
the upper-right corner. From left to right: The left arrow button
steps you backward through your past locations (just like the
back button in a Web browser). The up arrow takes you out to
the folder enclosing the one you're in now. The X button deletes
folders and files—be careful with it. Click the folder with the star
in the corner to create a new folder.*

UP TO SPEED

Understanding Word File Types

When you save your first file in Word 2007, you'll find a
bewildering array of file types. Don't sweat it—you'll use
some new file types on the list frequently, but you'll probably ignore a lot of types. The two you'll use most often are
.docx and **.docm**.

- **.docx.** New format for most Word documents. Pre-
  2007 versions of Word can't open these documents
  without the help of the Office Compatibility Pack, as
  described in the box on page 17.

- **.docm.** New format for Word documents containing macros. (Microsoft is making an effort to
  increase computer security by reining in Office macros.)

- **.dotx.** New format for templates.

- **.dotm.** New format for templates containing
  macros.

- **.doc.** Format for all the previous versions of Word
  including: Word 6.0, Word 95, and Word 97-2003.

- **.dot.** The template format for previous versions of
  Word.

- **.pdf.** Adobe Reader (also known as Acrobat) files.
  PDF stands for Portable Document Format.

- **.xps.** XML Paper specification. As explained on page
  405, this format is Microsoft's answer to PDF for
  creating documents that anyone can open on any
  computer.

- **.mhtm, .mhtml.** Single file Web page. In other
  words, all the files that make up a Web page (including images) are contained in one single file. (There's
  no difference between .mhtm and .mhtml files;
  they're just four-letter and five-letter versions of the
  same filename extension.)

- **.htm, .html.** Standard Web page format. This format is for the Web pages you see on the Internet.
  When the page includes photos or other files, links
  on the page point to those external files. (There's no
  difference between .htm and .html; both mean the
  same thing.)

- **.rtf.** Rich Text Format, a file format used to exchange
  files with other word processors and other types of
  computers like Macs and Linux computers.

- **.txt.** This plain text format doesn't have a lot of the
  formatting you can do in Word. It makes for a nice,
  small file size, and you can open it on any computer, but it's not pretty.

- **.xml.** eXtensible Markup Language is a standard language for describing many different types of data.

- **.wps.** This format indicates a document created in
  Office's little sibling, Microsoft Works.

Entering and Editing Text

Despite advanced features like grammar checking, indexing, and image editing, Word is still, at heart, a word processor. You probably spend most of your time entering text and massaging it into shape. Amidst all the slick graphics and gee-whiz automation, Word 2007 makes it faster and easier than ever for you to enter and edit your text. A quick read through this chapter will reveal timesaving techniques that'll help you spend less time hunting, pecking, and clicking, so you can move on to the important stuff—polishing your prose and sharing it with the world.

This chapter starts with a quick review of the basics—putting words on the page and moving around your document. You'll also learn how to cut, copy, paste, and generally put text exactly where you want it. To top it off, you'll explore the Find and Replace features and learn how to save keystrokes using Word's Quick Parts.

Typing in Word

Whenever you're entering text into Word, the *insertion point* is where all the action takes place (Figure 2-1). It's that vertical, blinking bar that's a little taller than a capital letter. When you press a key, a letter appears at the insertion point, and the blinking bar moves a space to the right. To type in a different spot, just click somewhere in your text, and the insertion point moves to that location.

Press Shift to type capitals or to enter the various punctuation marks you see above the numbers keys (!@#$*&^). When you want to type several words in uppercase letters, press the Caps Lock key. You don't have to keep holding it down. It works like a toggle. Press it once and you're in caps mode. Press it again and you're back to lowercase.

The Backspace key and the Delete key both erase characters, but there's a difference: The Backspace erases the characters behind the insertion point, while the Delete key eliminates characters in front.

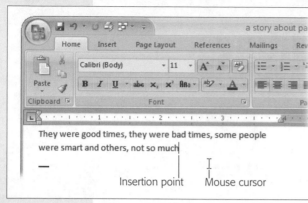

Figure 2-1:
As you type, the characters appear at the insertion point. Sometimes people call the insertion point the "cursor," but the insertion point and the mouse cursor are actually two different things. You use the mouse cursor to choose commands from the ribbon, select text, and place the insertion point in your document. The cursor can roam all over the Word window, but the insertion point remains hard at work, blinking patiently, waiting for you to enter the next character.

Note: Word's cursor changes its appearance like a chameleon, hinting at what will happen when you click the mouse button. When you move the cursor over the ribbon, it turns into an arrow, indicating that you can point and click a command. Hold it over your text, and it looks like an I-beam, giving you a precise tool for placing the insertion point between characters.

But if all you do with Word is type, you're missing out on 95 percent of its potential. What makes Word a 21st-century tool is the ease with which you can edit text, as described next.

Click and Type for Quick Formatting

Word's *Click and Type* feature makes it easy to position and align text on a blank spot on the page. It's great for those jobs where you want to position a block of text in an unusual place. Imagine you're putting together a title page for a report and you want the title about a third of the way down on the right side of the page with text aligned to the right. All you have to do is position your mouse cursor where you want the text. Notice, as you move the cursor around the page, sometimes four small lines appear near the I-beam. When the cursor's on the right side of the page, the lines trail off to the left (Figure 2-2). When the cursor's in the center of the page, the lines are centered at the bottom of the I-beam. As usual, the cursor is giving a hint about what will happen next.

If you double-click when the cursor's on the right side of the page (with the lines trailing off to the left), then several things happen. Most noticeable, your insertion point is exactly where you clicked. Behind the scenes, Word makes several other adjustments. If necessary, Word positions the insertion point vertically and horizontally on the page by adding paragraph marks and tabs as needed. Word changes the paragraph alignment setting to Align Right—it's just as if you clicked the button on the ribbon. Fortunately, you don't need to worry about these details; all you have to do is type the text (Figure 2-3).

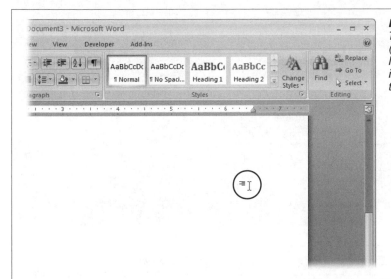

Figure 2-2:
The Click and Type cursor changes (circled) depending on where it's located on the page. Here the cursor indicates that text will be aligned to the right.

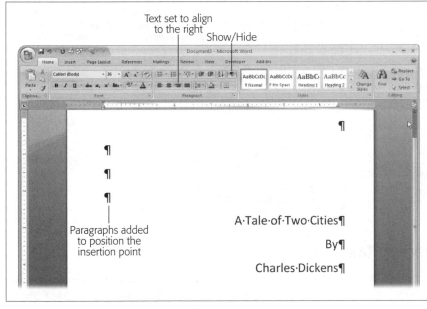

Figure 2-3:
When you double-click with the Click and Type cursor shown in Figure 2-2, Word adds several paragraph marks to position the insertion point down the page. When you type some text, it's right-aligned—just as the cursor indicated. (To see these usually hidden paragraph marks, click the Show/Hide button on the Home tab.)

POWER USERS' CLINIC

Entering Special Characters

Letters, numbers, and punctuation are the common currency of most documents. Still, you may want to use a bunch of other fairly common characters, like © and ®, that don't show up on your keyboard. And where are all those foreign characters, math symbols, and fractions?

They're waiting for you on the Insert tab. Choose Insert → Symbols → Symbol. If the character you need is on the menu, then click to insert it into your text. When you don't see it, click "More symbols" to see a much more comprehensive list of characters (Figure 2-4). The first group—Symbols—gives you access to every character Word can put on the page.

Use the Font box on the left to select your typeface. If you want to use the typeface you're currently using in your document, as is often the case, then leave this set to "(normal text)." Use the Subset drop-down menu to choose a language (like Greek, Cyrillic, or Latin), or choose from other groupings (accented letters, math symbols, and so on). You can also use the scroll bar on the right to visually search for a symbol. Symbols that you've used recently are lined up near the bottom of the dialog box, so you can grab them quickly.

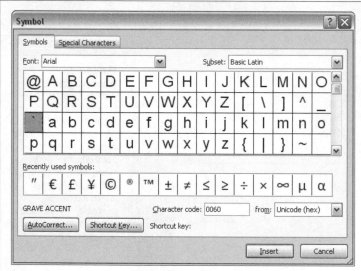

Figure 2-4:
To insert a character in your text, either double-click the character or single-click it, and then click Insert. The right-hand tab—Special Characters—contains a list of specialized punctuation marks like dashes and nonbreaking hyphens.

Selecting Text

Even among the best writers, the first draft needs a lot of editing before it's ready for public viewing. You'll need to change words, delete boring parts, and move sentences (or even whole paragraphs) to reorganize your text.

In Word, as in most programs, you have to *select* something before you can do anything to it. Say you want to change the word "good" to "awesome": Select "good," and then type your new, improved adjective in its place. To delete or move a block of text, first select it, and then use the mouse, keyboard, or ribbon

UP TO SPEED

Choosing Between Insert and Overtype Mode

Most of the time, you type in *insert mode*. Put your cursor in the middle of a sentence, start typing, and Word inserts the letters you type at that point. Existing text scoots along to the right to make room.

In the other mode—*overtype mode*—every time you type a character, it *writes over* and erases the next one. Before Word 2007, most people stumbled upon overtype mode by accident. They'd click in the middle of a sentence and start typing—and the letters to the right of the cursor started to disappear! In those earlier versions of Word, pressing the Insert key threw you right into overtype mode. It was an easy mistake to make, since Insert is just above the much-used Delete key (on most keyboards).

Microsoft made overtype mode harder to get to, so people would not accidentally type over all their hard work.

Now the Insert key doesn't do anything unless you make a few tweaks to Word's settings.

If you miss that old overtype mode and want to toggle back and forth with the Insert key, follow these steps.

1. Go to Office button → Word Options to open the Word Options dialog box.

2. In the left bar, select Advanced.

3. In the first group of options, called Editing Options, turn on the "Use the Insert Key to control overtype mode" checkbox.

If you want to use overtype mode as your regular text entry mode, turn on the "Use overtype mode" checkbox.

commands to do the deed. Since selection is such a fundamental editing skill, Word gives you many different and new (see Figure 2-5) ways to do it. If you've been dragging your mouse around for the past 20 years, you're lagging behind. This section shows you some timesaving selection techniques—with and without the mouse.

Figure 2-5:
As you make selections, you'll notice the Mini Toolbar pops up occasionally. It's faint at first, but when you move the mouse toward the toolbar, it comes into focus, giving you easy access to the most often used formatting commands, including the format painter.

Selecting with the Mouse

The mouse is an easy, visual, intuitive way to make selections. It's the first way most people learn, and besides, it's right there on your desktop. Here's how to select various document parts using your mouse:

- **Select individual characters.** Click to place the insertion point at the beginning of the text you want to select. Press and hold the left mouse button and drag over the characters. As you drag, the characters you select are highlighted to indicate they're part of the selection (Figure 2-6).

Tip: Word doesn't care if you move forward or backward as you select text. It simply uses the point where you click as either the beginning or the ending point of the selection. These examples describe how to select text moving forward, but most of the techniques, including the keyboard techniques, work going backward too. Don't be afraid to experiment. Before you know it, you'll be proficient selecting text with both the mouse and the keyboard.

- **Select a word.** Double-click the word. The entire word's highlighted.

- **Select a sentence.** Ctrl-click the sentence. The entire sentence is highlighted.

- **Select a line of text.** Move the cursor into the left margin. The cursor changes to an arrow. Click right next to the line you want to select. The line's highlighted, showing that it's selected.

- **Select a whole paragraph.** Move the cursor into the left margin. When it changes into an arrow, double-click next to the paragraph. The entire paragraph is highlighted. To add more paragraphs, keep your finger on the mouse button and drag until the cursor points at another paragraph, and another....

- **Select a block of text.** Click to place the insertion point at the beginning of the block you want to select. (No need to keep pressing the mouse button.) Hold the Shift key down, and then click at the other end of the selection. The block of text is highlighted, and your wrist is happy. Everybody wins.

- **Select an entire document.** Move the cursor into the left margin, so that it changes into an arrow. Click the left mouse button three times. Your entire document's highlighted. (In other words, do the same thing as for selecting a paragraph, except you triple-click instead of double-click.)

Tip: This section focuses on selecting text, but the same techniques apply to tables, pictures, charts, and other objects that Word handles as parts of your text. You'll learn all the details when you encounter these features in later chapters.

Selecting with the Keyboard

When it comes to selecting fine details, like a single letter, the mouse can make you feel like you're trying to thread a needle with mittens on. And if you're a fast typist, taking your hands away from the keyboard to grasp the mouse causes a

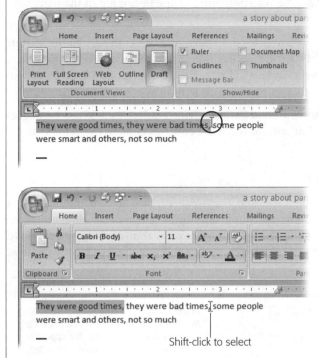

Figure 2-6:
Top: To select text with your mouse, drag your cursor (circled) over the text. The selected text is highlighted to show you what's included in the selection.

Bottom: Or use the Shift-click trick. Shift-clicking at the end of "bad times" extends the selection to include both phrases: "They were good times, they were bad times," As you can see, Dickens still has some wordsmithing to do.

Shift-click to select

needless loss of time. Word nerds, in fact, do as much as possible from the keyboard, even selecting. If you've never selected text using the keyboard before, prepare to be amazed:

- **Select individual characters.** Tap the arrow keys to place the insertion point on one end of the selection. Press the Shift key as you use the left or right arrow keys to highlight the characters you want to select.

- **Select a word.** Start with the insertion point at the beginning or end of the word. Press Ctrl+Shift+right arrow to select the word to the right or Ctrl+Shift+left arrow to select the word to the left. To select more words, just keep hitting the arrow key.

- **Select a sentence.** Put the insertion point at the beginning of the sentence. Press Shift+right arrow repeatedly until you reach the end of the sentence. (OK, so this method is a workaround. Word doesn't have a single keyboard command to select an entire sentence.)

- **Select to end of line.** Press Shift+End. Word highlights all the text from the insertion point to the end of line.

- **Select to beginning of line.** Press Shift+Home to select text from the insertion point to the beginning of the line.

- **Select a paragraph.** Place the insertion point at the beginning of the paragraph and press Ctrl+Shift+down arrow.

- **Select a block of text.** Click to place the insertion point at the beginning of your selection. Hold the Shift key down and use any of the arrow keys (up, down, left, and right) or navigation keys (Home, End, Page Up, and Page Down) to mark your selection.

- **Select an entire document.** Press Ctrl+A. (Think select All.) Word highlights the entire document. You can also select the entire document by pressing the F8 key repeatedly.

Extending a Selection

What if you've selected some text and then realize you'd like to add a little bit more to your selection? You have a couple of options. The most common method: Extend your selection by Shift-clicking in your text, as shown in Figure 2-7. Word highlights the text between the previous selection and your Shift-click and includes it in the new selection.

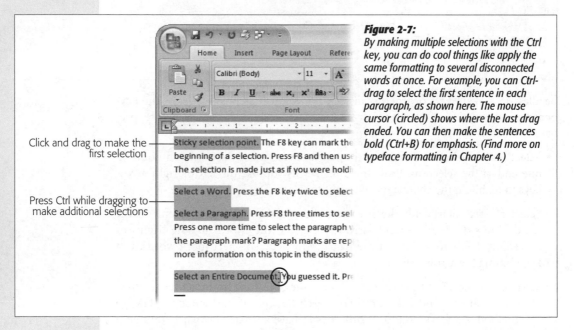

Click and drag to make the first selection

Press Ctrl while dragging to make additional selections

Figure 2-7:
By making multiple selections with the Ctrl key, you can do cool things like apply the same formatting to several disconnected words at once. For example, you can Ctrl-drag to select the first sentence in each paragraph, as shown here. The mouse cursor (circled) shows where the last drag ended. You can then make the sentences bold (Ctrl+B) for emphasis. (Find more on typeface formatting in Chapter 4.)

A similar, but even more elegant way to extend a selection is with the F8 key. Pressing F8 sets one end of your selection at the insertion point. Click either forward or backward in your document, and everything in between the insertion point and your click is instantly highlighted and selected. F8 has several other surprising selection powers. See the box on page 43 for all the details.

F8—The Selection Superhero

For an unassuming function key sitting there almost unused at the top of your keyboard, the F8 key has surprisingly powerful text selection skills. Pressing it helps you select much more than you can with any other single keystroke or mouse click.

- **Sticky selection end point.** Pressing F8 at the beginning of your intended selection makes any selection method you use stay "on" without your having to press any keys. Here's how it works: Put your insertion point at the beginning of where you want to start a selection. Press F8 once (don't hold it down), and then use the mouse or arrow keys to complete the selection. Look ma, no hands! Word makes the selection just as if you were pressing the Shift key while navigating to a new point.

- **Select a word.** Press F8 twice to select a whole word. Used this way, F8 works just like double-clicking the word.

- **Select a sentence.** Press F8 three times to select a sentence.

- **Select a paragraph.** Press F8 four times to select all the text in a paragraph.

- **Select an entire document.** Press F8 five times. Voila! The whole document is selected.

The F8 key with its sticky behavior keeps selecting text left and right until you turn it off. Press the Esc key to deactivate the F8 key's selection proclivities. Then you can once again move the insertion point without selecting text.

Selecting Multiple Chunks of Text in Different Places

If you're into efficiency and multitasking, Word's multiple selection feature was made for you. Multiple selections save you time by applying formatting to similar, but disconnected elements. Say you have several paragraphs of text and you decide you'd like to make the first sentence in each paragraph bold (Figure 2-8) for emphasis. After you select the sentences, you can format them all at once. You can also collect items from several locations and then copy and paste them into a new spot. See page 49 for more on cutting and pasting.

To make a multiple selection, simply make your first selection and then press the Ctrl key while you make another. The areas you select don't need to be connected.

Tip: You can also use just about any of the selection techniques mentioned earlier in this section to add to the multiple selection. For example, when you want to add an entire paragraph to your selection, press Ctrl while you double-click in the left margin next to the paragraph.

So, here are the steps to follow for the example in Figure 2-7:

1. **Drag to select the first sentence in the first paragraph.**

   Word highlights the sentence to indicate it's selected.

2. **Press Ctrl, and keep holding it as you drag to select the first sentence in the** *next* **paragraph.**

   Word highlights each sentence you select but nothing in between. Repeat this step for each sentence you want to select.

3. **Press Ctrl+B.**

   Word makes the selected sentences bold and leaves them highlighted. You can enter another command if you want—bold italics, anyone?

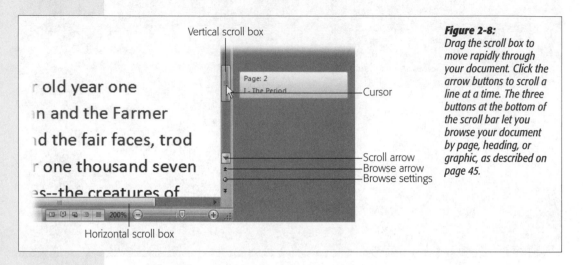

Vertical scroll box

Cursor

Scroll arrow
Browse arrow
Browse settings

Horizontal scroll box

Figure 2-8:
Drag the scroll box to move rapidly through your document. Click the arrow buttons to scroll a line at a time. The three buttons at the bottom of the scroll bar let you browse your document by page, heading, or graphic, as described on page 45.

Moving Around Your Document

Using that nice blue scrollbar on the right side of your document is the most obvious way to navigate your document. And if your mouse has a wheel on it, then using it to scroll is pretty speedy too. But when your document's more than a few pages long, trying to scroll to the exact point you're looking for is just plain inefficient.

Word's most powerful ways of boogieing around your document don't involve scrolling at all. You can use the keyboard to hop from place to place. For really long documents, as with long journeys, the best way to get around is by using landmarks. For example, you can check all the graphics in a document by jumping directly from one to the next. Or you can go directly to a specific heading in a 400-page business report by telling Word to find it for you. You can even create your own landmarks using Word's bookmarking feature. Word's got the tools, and this section tells you how to use 'em.

Tip: If you're working with a large document, then Word has some other great ways to find your way around. You can use Outline view (View → Documents View → Outline) to easily navigate between chapter and section headings (page 21). The Document Map (View → Documents View → Document Map) shows a similar view in the bar along the left side of your document (page 24). If your pages include distinctive graphics, then the Thumbnail View (View → Show/Hide → Thumbnails) can help you find the spot you want by eye (page 196).

Keyboarding Around Your Document

You've heard it before: You lose time every time you take your hands off the keyboard to fumble for the mouse. For short jaunts especially, get in the habit of using these keyboard commands to move the insertion point:

- **Move left or right.** Left/right arrow keys.

- **Move to the beginning or the end of a line.** Home/End. (On most keyboards, these keys are just above the arrow keys. On most laptops, the Home and End keys are either along the right side or in the top-right corner.)

- **Move up or down a line.** Up/down arrow keys.

- **Move up or down a paragraph.** Ctrl+up/down arrow.

- **Move up or down one screenful of text.** Page up/down.

- **Move to the beginning or the end of a document.** Ctrl+Home/End.

Using the Scroll Bars

If you've used Word or any of the other Microsoft Office programs in the past, that skinny bar down the right side of your document should look familiar. In the center of the bar is a box that you drag to move up or down your document. The bar also has some arrow buttons at top and bottom for finer control (shown in Figure 2-8). Click the buttons to scroll just a line or two at a time. To cover big distances, click in the bar above or below the box, and the document scrolls one screen at a time.

Easier still, you can scroll without using the scroll bar at all; see Figure 2-9 and Figure 2-10 for instructions.

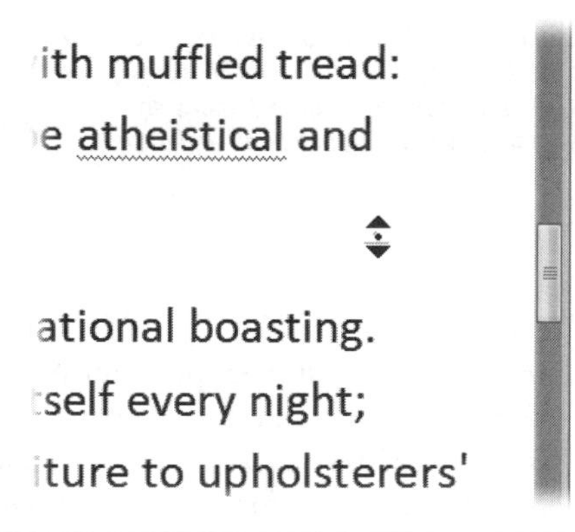

ith muffled tread:

e atheistical and

ational boasting.

self every night;

ture to upholsterers'

Figure 2-9:
Click the mouse wheel, and you see the scroll symbol shown here. When this symbol is present, you can scroll your document by moving the mouse cursor away from the symbol. Move your cursor down to start to scroll down. The further you move the cursor down the screen, the faster the document scrolls. Click the wheel button to stop the auto-scrolling.

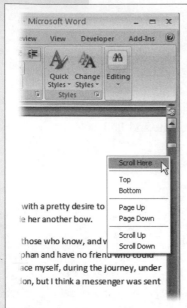

Figure 2-10:
Right-click the scroll bar, and you see a pop-up menu with navigation shortcuts. At the top of the list is Scroll Here, which is the equivalent of dragging the scroll box to the location you clicked on the scroll bar. (In previous versions of Word, you could Shift-click for the same result.) Other shortcuts take you to the beginning or the end of your document and scroll a line or a screenful at a time.

Browsing by Headings and Other Objects

For longer documents, the most interesting controls are at the bottom of the scroll bar: two double arrows separated by a round button. What makes these *Browse buttons* so handy is the fact that you can customize their behavior to match your needs. The round button puts you in control. Click it, and you see the Browse Settings menu (Figure 2-11).

Figure 2-11:
The Browse Settings menu lets you set the behavior of the Browse buttons and perform other useful navigation tasks. For example, you can set the buttons to browse by headings, pages, or even graphics within your document. These settings make the Browse buttons an extremely powerful navigation feature. It's a shame they're overlooked and underused.

At first, the icons in the "Browse by" toolbar may seem a little cryptic, but never fear, you can get help. Hold the cursor over the icons, and their function is explained in the text box at the top. The "Open the Go To box" and "Open the Find box" options open the dialog box where you can search for specific text and jump to a certain location in your document, as described later in this chapter (page 56). The rest of the options determine what happens when you click the double-arrow Browse buttons. For example, when you click Browse by Headings, clicking the Browse arrows then takes you forward (or back) through your document, jumping from one heading to the next and skipping everything in between.

As you learn to use more advanced features like end notes and comments, described later in this book, you'll find it very convenient to use them as your landmarks, as well.

Browsing by Bookmark

The bookmarks that slip between the pages of books are elegant in their simplicity, even decorative, but they're kind of primitive. They only do one thing—mark a point between two adjacent pages—and if they fall out, well then they don't do anything at all. Word's electronic bookmarks let you get much more specific. You can use them to mark the exact *word* where you left off. And since there's no limit on how many you can put in a document, you can use them to help organize a long document as you work your way through it. Bookmarks don't show up when you print the document; they're just reference points that let you jump instantly to places you want to return to most often.

Creating bookmarks

You can create as many bookmarks as you want in a document with just a few mouse clicks. Bookmarks are invisible in your documents, but that's just Word's factory setting. You can change your Word Options to show bookmarks in your text. (Maybe Microsoft turns them off because the bookmarks are sort of unattractive—they appear as brackets around the bookmarked text.)

To see bookmarks in your text, choose Office button → Word Options → Advanced. (The Word Options button is at the bottom of the Office menu, near the Exit button.) Scroll down to the options under "Show document content," and then turn on the "Show bookmarks" checkbox.

Here's how to insert a bookmark in your Word document:

1. **Select the text you want to bookmark.**

   The selected text is the location of the bookmark. If the text moves as you edit, the bookmark stays with the text.

   You can also create a bookmark without selecting text: Word simply places the bookmark at the insertion point. However, it's a little easier to keep track of your bookmarks if you select text.

2. **Go to Insert → Links → Bookmark.**

   The Bookmark dialog box opens (Figure 2-12).

3. **In the "Bookmark name" box, type a name for the bookmark.**

   Use a descriptive name, one that describes the location in the text, or perhaps the work you need to do at that spot. For example, if you're marking a place to come back and add something about guillotines, name it LaGuillotine.

Note: For its own computerish reasons, Word doesn't let you use spaces in your bookmark name. To separate words, you can use dashes or underscores instead.

---

4. **Click Add.**

When you click Add, the dialog box disappears, and your bookmark is set and ready for use.

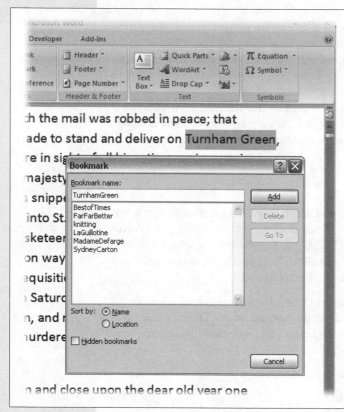

Jumping to bookmarks

Using bookmarks is even easier than creating them. The quickest way to use a bookmark is to hit F5 key to bring up the Go To dialog box (Figure 2-13). From the "Go to what" list, select Bookmark. When you've done that, the drop-down list at right shows all the bookmarks in your document. Select one, and then click the Go To button. Your document scrolls to put the highlighted, bookmarked text at the top of your screen. Click Close to hide the dialog box. After you've searched for a bookmark, you can use the Browse buttons below the scroll bar to jump to other bookmarks (page 47).

Tip: The Find, Replace, and Go To dialog boxes have memory. While you're working in a document, it remembers the tab and list items you last used. So, if earlier you found a particular bookmark, then the next time you click Go To (or press F5), Word finds that same bookmark.

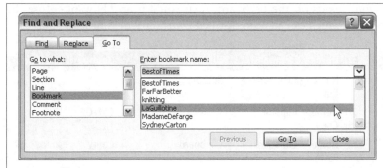

Figure 2-13:
Bookmarks are useful if you need to jump back and forth between different locations. To move to a bookmark, open the Go To dialog box (F5), and then select Bookmark from the list at left. The drop-down list at right lists all the bookmarks in your document. Simply choose one from the list.

Deleting bookmarks

About the only reason you'd want to delete a bookmark is if your list's getting cluttered and it's hard to find the bookmark you want. In any case, it's easy to delete a bookmark using the same dialog box you use to create them (Figure 2-12). Just pick the soon-to-be-terminated bookmark from the list and click Delete. It's a goner.

UP TO SPEED

The Many Paths to Go To

The Go To, Find, and Replace dialog boxes are actually three different tabs in the same window. You either open the dialog box directly to one of the tabs, or, if it's already open, then just click a tab at the top of the box. As usual, Microsoft provides many ways to open this particular box:

- **Home → Editing → Find.** Opens the Find tab.

- **Home → Editing → Replace.** Opens the Replace tab.

- **Home → Editing → Go To.** Opens the Go To tab.

- **Browse Settings button.** Click Browse Settings (the tiny circle in the window's lower-right corner, as shown in Figure 2-8), and then click the Go To (arrow) or Find (binoculars).

- **Ctrl+F.** Opens the Find tab.

- **Ctrl+H.** Opens the Replace tab.

- **Ctrl+G or F5.** Opens the Go To tab.

- **Double-click Status bar.** Double-clicking the status bar in the lower-left corner also opens the Go To tab.

Cutting, Copying, and Pasting

When it comes time to edit your text and shape it into a masterpiece of communication, the job is all about cutting, copying, and pasting. Compared to actually using scissors and paste (which is what writers and editors did in the pre-PC era), Word makes manipulating text almost effortless. You're free to experiment, moving words, sentences, and paragraphs around until you've got everything just right.

By now, you've probably figured that most Word functions can be done in at least two ways—by keyboard and by mouse. That's certainly the case when it comes to the basic editing functions, as shown in the table. If you're typing away and don't

---

want to take your hands off the keyboard, then you'll probably want to use the keyboard shortcuts, which can all be performed with a flick of your left hand.

Command	Ribbon Command	Ribbon Icon	Keyboard Shortcut
Cut	Home → Clipboard → Cut	Scissors	Ctrl+X
Copy	Home → Clipboard → Copy	2 pages	Ctrl+C
Paste	Home → Clipboard → Paste	Clipboard	Ctrl+V

Editing with the Ribbon

- Word's new ribbon is where all the commands live, and it's hardly a surprise that cut, copy, and paste are the first commands on the first tab (Home) in the first group (Clipboard). As you can see in Figure 2-14, these commands are conveniently located right near another place you frequently mouse over to, the Office button.

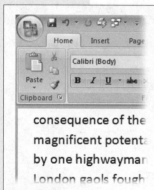

Figure 2-14:
The basic editing commands Cut, Copy, and Paste are easy to find. Go to Home → Clipboard, and there they are. As always, the first step is to select the text that you want to cut (scissors) or copy (two pages). Then, position the insertion point at the location where you want to paste (clipboard) the text.

Once you've found the commands, here's how to use 'em:

- **Cut (Home → Clipboard → Cut).** Again, you need to select text (or an object, like a picture or a table) before you can cut it from your document. When you invoke the Cut command, your selected item disappears, but Cut is very different from a Delete or a Clear command. The Cut command actually stores the cut item on the Office Clipboard, where you can bring it back later using the Paste command. You can actually open this Clipboard and see recently cut and copied items. The Office Clipboard works across all Microsoft Office programs, so you can cut a paragraph from your novel and paste it into an Outlook email or PowerPoint slide.

- **Copy (Home → Clipboard → Copy).** As you may expect, Copy makes a duplicate of the selected text or object and stores it on the Clipboard. It leaves the selection in place in its original location.

- **Paste (Home → Clipboard → Paste).** Before you use the Paste command, you must first cut or copy some text (or a picture or other object). Then, put the insertion point exactly where you want to place the item, and then paste away.

Note: See page 53 for more about working with Word's Clipboard.

Editing with Keyboard Shortcuts

The keyboard shortcuts are the quickest and easiest editing commands to use as you're typing along, because you don't need to take your hands off the keyboard. You can use the Cut, Copy, and Paste commands with only a couple fingers of the left hand. These shortcuts use the Ctrl key in combination with nearby keys on the bottom row—X, C, and V. As an added bonus, the adjacent Z key is used for the Undo command—another oft-used editor's tool. These keys perform the exact same functions as the ones run when you use the ribbon commands using Word's ribbon:

- **Cut.** Ctrl+X.

- **Copy.** Ctrl+C.

- **Paste.** Ctrl+V.

- **Undo.** Ctrl+Z.

Editing with the Mouse

After Cut, Copy, and Paste, the next great leap forward for writers and editors was the *graphical user interface* (GUI) and the ability to use a mouse to drag and drop text. After all, most of editing is deleting unneeded words and pushing the others around into the most effective positions. With a mouse, you can really see what you're doing: Take *this* and drag it over *there*.

But some people are never satisfied. And lo and behold, Microsoft added a right mouse button. When you right-click, you get a pop-up menu that includes Cut, Copy, Paste, and other commands, right where you need them (Figure 2-15). The pop-up menu contains only the most common commands, to save you a trip all the way up to that ribbon. To get to more advanced commands (like line spacing or alphabetic sorting), you do have to use the ribbon.

It's easy to drag and drop text to a new location using just your mouse. Take your hands off the keyboard, lean back in your chair, grab the mouse, and follow these steps:

1. **Click (the left mouse button) and drag to select the text that you want to relocate.**

    Word highlights the text to show you what you've selected. Let go of the mouse button when you're done.

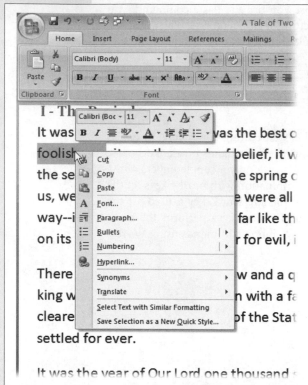

Figure 2-15:
Right-click in your text to display the Edit shortcut menu. If you've selected text, you can use the Cut and Copy commands. Word 2007 adds a slew of additional commands, including language translation, hyperlink creation, and formatting options. As an added bonus, you see the Mini Toolbar with formatting commands above the edit commands.

2. **Click the selected text and, holding down the mouse button, drag the mouse to the new location for the text.**

   As shown in Figure 2-16 (top), a little rectangle below the cursor means you're dragging something. As you move the mouse, the insertion point follows, marking where the moved text will appear.

3. **Release the mouse button.**

   Releasing the mouse button finishes the job, placing the moved text at the insertion point, as shown in Figure 2-16 (bottom).

Moving Text Between Two Documents

Moving text from one document to another isn't much different from moving it from place to place within a document. You can use keyboard or ribbon commands to cut and paste, or you can drag and drop between documents (Figure 2-17). In fact, it's just as easy to move text between documents created by different programs. For example, you can cut or copy text in Word and paste it into documents created in Outlook, PowerPoint, Access, Excel, and many non-Microsoft programs, too. Even the same keyboard shortcuts do the trick: Ctrl+X (Cut), Ctrl+C (Copy), and Ctrl+V (Paste). Of course, you can also use menu commands if you insist.

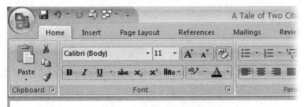

Figure 2-16:
Gutenberg would be amazed at how easy it is to reset type with Word. Top: Select the text you want to move, and then point to it and click. Continue to hold the left mouse button while you drag the text to a new location.

Bottom: When you release the mouse button, Word plops the text into the new location.

Viewing and Pasting Clippings

More often than not, when you cut or copy text, a picture, or an object, you want to paste it into a new location right away. But what if you wanted to copy several items and paste them into the same location? Or, what if you want to again paste an item that you copied several edits ago? Enter the Office Clipboard. The Clipboard's nothing new to Microsoft Office programs, but the 2007 version gives this familiar tool a new look (Figure 2-18). As you cut and copy text, graphics, and other objects, Word (or whatever Office program you're in) stashes them here for reuse. The Clipboard lets you view the stored items and lets you paste them into other documents with just a click or two.

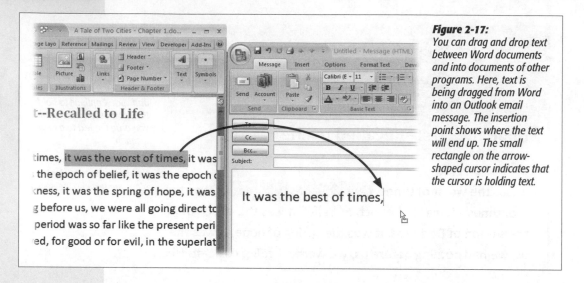

Figure 2-17:
You can drag and drop text between Word documents and into documents of other programs. Here, text is being dragged from Word into an Outlook email message. The insertion point shows where the text will end up. The small rectangle on the arrow-shaped cursor indicates that the cursor is holding text.

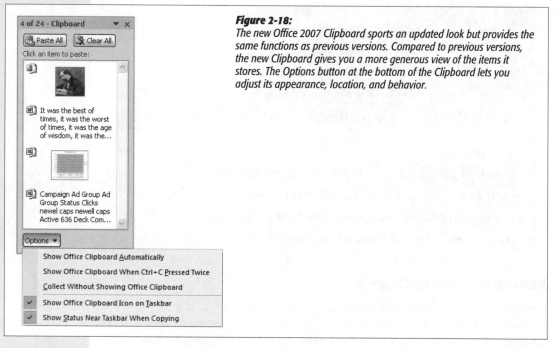

Figure 2-18:
The new Office 2007 Clipboard sports an updated look but provides the same functions as previous versions. Compared to previous versions, the new Clipboard gives you a more generous view of the items it stores. The Options button at the bottom of the Clipboard lets you adjust its appearance, location, and behavior.

Your most recent cut items or copied items appear at the top of the Clipboard and move down as you add more. When you use the Paste command (Ctrl+V), Word is simply pasting the item at the top of the Clipboard at the insertion point. That's what happens whether the Clipboard is open or closed. To paste a different item instead of the most recent, just place the insertion point where you want it, and then click that item on the Clipboard, as shown in Figure 2-19.

Working with the Clipboard Task Pane

Open the Clipboard task pane by clicking the launcher in the lower-right corner of the Clipboard group (Home → Clipboard). (You find it in exactly the same spot in Access, Excel, and PowerPoint.) With the Clipboard task pane open, you see all the items you recently cut or copied. Click an item to paste it into your Word document at the insertion point. Or, if you want, you can switch to another program (Alt+Tab) and paste it there. Point to an item on the Clipboard, and you see a drop-down menu with two options: Paste and Delete. It's easier to simply click to paste an item, but Delete gives you a handy way to clean up the Clipboard contents before you use the Paste All command. The Paste All and Clear All buttons are at the top of the Clipboard task pane.

The Options menu (at bottom) is where you fine-tune the Clipboard's behavior:

- **Show Office Clipboard Automatically.** Turn on this option to have the Clipboard appear whenever you copy an item.

- **Show Office Clipboard when Ctrl+C Pressed Twice.** This option works easily as you're typing. Press Ctrl+C once to copy selected text; press Ctrl+C a second time, and you see the Clipboard.

- **Show Office Clipboard Icon on Taskbar.** With this option selected, the Office Clipboard appears in the Taskbar in the lower-right corner of your screen.

- **Show Status Near Taskbar when Copying.** Each time you cut or copy an item, a screen tip appears near the Taskbar detailing how many items are on the Clipboard.

But wait—the Clipboard's coolness is just getting warmed up. Not only can you see multiple pasteable items, you can paste them in bunches too. The Clipboard acts as a collection palette. For example, suppose you've created a dinner menu for your restaurant in Word, and you want to create a new lunch menu that includes just a few of the items from the dinner menu. Follow these steps to collect and paste those tasty morsels into a new document:

1. **With the source document open in front of you (in this case, the dinner menu), go to Home → Clipboard, and then click the small square next to the Clipboard group label.**

   This square, with an arrow in the lower-right corner, is called the Clipboard *launcher*, and its job is to open and close the Clipboard. Initially, the Clipboard opens in a panel on the left side of the window, but you can drag it from that location and use it like a freestanding palette.

2. **At the top of the Clipboard, click Clear All to remove any previously copied items.**

   If you've been working on other projects, there may be items already on your Clipboard, including those from other Office programs. Since you probably don't want all that stuff on your lunch menu, clear the decks with the Clear All button.

Note: Clippings stay on the Office Clipboard until you clear them—or until you exit all Microsoft Office programs (Word, Outlook, Excel, and PowerPoint).

---

3. **Copy (Ctrl+C) the entrees, side dishes, and beverages you want to put on the lunch menu.**

   Use any of the methods described in this chapter to find, select, and copy the items. As you copy each item, Word adds it to the clipboard.

4. **Open a new document (Office button → New → Blank) to use as your lunch menu.**

   A new Word window opens, but notice that you still have access to the Clipboard with all your copied menu entries.

5. **Click Paste All.**

   When you click Paste All, the Clipboard's entire contents appear in your new document. (Now all you need to do is figure out the lunch prices.)

Figure 2-19:
Use the Office Clipboard to paste text, graphics, and other objects into your documents. Unlike the Cut and Paste commands, the Clipboard isn't limited to the last item you cut or copied. You can choose from an appetizing menu of words and images that you recently edited. Deleting removes the item from the Clipboard.

Finding and Replacing Text

Scanning every word of your 400-page novel to find the exact spot where you first mentioned Madame DeFarge is drudgery with a capital D. Fortunately, Word performs this task quickly and without whining or demanding overtime pay. What's more, it's just as easy to find and then replace text. Suppose you decide to change the name of the character from Madame DeFarge to Madame de Stael. Simple—here's how to do a Find and Replace:

1. **Open the Replace dialog box (Figure 2-20). For example, press Ctrl+H.**

   You have many ways to open the Replace dialog box, as explained in the box on page 59. If your hands are on the keyboard, then Ctrl+H is the fastest.

When the dialog box opens, you see tabs at the top for each of the panels: Find, Replace, and Go To. The controls and options under the Find and Replace tabs are nearly identical. The main difference is that the Replace tab includes *two* text boxes—"Replace with" as well as "Find what."

2. **In the "Find what" box, type the text you want to find, and, in the "Replace with" box, type the replacement text.**

For example, type *Madame DeFarge* in "Find what" and *Madame de Stael* in "Replace with."

Note: The "Find what" is a drop-down box that remembers your past searches. So the next time you go to this box, Madame DeFarge will be there waiting for you.

---

3. **If you wish, click More to reveal additional Find options.**

When you click More, the box expands, and you see a number of additional controls that can fine-tune your search. For example, if you're searching for "Madame DeFarge" but you don't know how it's capitalized, then make sure the Match Case checkbox is turned off. That way, Word finds every occurrence even if you didn't capitalize it the same way throughout. For an explanation of all the Search options, see the box on page 59.

The Format button at the bottom of the screen lets you refine your search by including formatting details. For instance, you can limit your search to a specific paragraph style such as Heading 1.

The Special button at the bottom of the box helps you find characters that aren't easy to enter with your keyboard, like paragraph marks, column breaks, and em dashes. These sound like odd things to search for, but they're enormously helpful when you're reformatting a document. For example, imagine someone sends you a document and they followed the odious practice of using two carriage returns at the end of each paragraph. You can search for all the double paragraph marks and replace them with a single paragraph mark. Problem solved.

Tip: A better way to leave extra space between paragraphs is to include it in the paragraph formatting itself. See page 103 for details.

---

4. **Click Find Next to begin your search and replace mission.**

The search begins at the insertion point, so if you want to find all the instances of Madame DeFarge, start at the beginning of your document. A quick Ctrl+Home takes you there. Word finds the text and highlights it in the document. If you need a better look at your text, you can click the top edge of the Replace box and drag it to another position.

5. **Examine the text and make sure you want to replace this instance of Madame DeFarge with Madame de Stael. Click Replace, and the text is swapped.**

   Word automatically finds the next instance of your search text.

6. **If you're certain that you want to replace every instance of Madame DeFarge, click Replace All.**

   Word makes all the changes and reports back with the number of replacements it made.

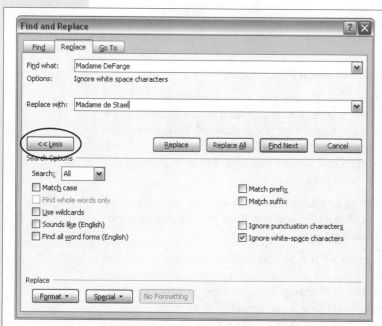

Figure 2-20:
Initially, the Replace box is pretty simple, but when you click More, you see a number of options for fine-tuning your search. (And the More button turns into a Less button, as shown here.) The box on page 59 explains all the Search options in detail.

Saving Keystrokes with Quick Parts

Suppose your company has an extremely long name and an even longer address (complete with 9-digit Zip code). Now say you type in the name and address about three times an hour. Wouldn't it be great to just type *address* and have Word fill in the whole shebang? That's exactly the kind of magic you can do with Word 2007's Quick Parts feature. You can have Word memorize whole chunks of text, and then spit them back out when you type an abbreviation word followed by the F3 key.

Quick Parts evolved from the AutoText feature found in earlier versions of Word. AutoText was one of the program's most overlooked and underused features. Quick Parts work like this: You store text, graphics, or anything else you've created in Word in a Quick Part and give it a name, preferably something short and memorable. When you want to retrieve the Quick Part, simply type that name, and then press F3. Word replaces the name with the entire contents of the Quick Part. Few keystrokes, mucho text.

Search Options Explained

Computers are dumb. They don't know that, if you type *bird* in the Find dialog box, you're looking for flying things, not some Mr. Birdley. So Microsoft gives you the Find and Replace dialog boxes with some options to help you make them smarter.

Here's what the options do when you turn on their checkboxes:

- **Match case.** Find shows you only words that exactly match the uppercase and lowercase letters of your search entry. So, *DeFarge* finds "DeFarge" but not "defarge."

- **Find whole words only.** Find only shows you complete words that match your entry. For example, if you enter *some*, the search shows you the word "some" but not the word "somewhere."

- **Use wildcards.** Wild cards let you expand your search. For example, ^? is the wildcard that matches any character. A search for ^*?ill* returns the words "will," "bill," "kill," "dill," and so forth.

- **Sounds like.** Finds words that sound like your entry. (Consider this help for the spelling-impaired.) If, say, you enter *inglund*, then Word finds "England."

- **Find all word forms.** Type *is,* and Word finds "was," "were," and "being."

- **Match prefix.** Finds characters at the beginning of a word, so *re* finds "reason" but not "are." (In this option and the next, Word doesn't consider prefix and suffix in a grammatical sense; it's just looking for the beginning and the ending of words.)

- **Match suffix.** Use this option to find characters at the end of a word. For example, *ed* finds "mashed" but not "eddy."

- **Ignore punctuation characters.** Word doesn't include periods, commas, hyphens, apostrophes, and other punctuation marks when it makes a match. For example, *coachlamps* finds coach-lamps.

- **Ignore white-space characters.** Word leaves paragraph marks, spaces, tabs, and other non-printing, "space" characters out of the search. In this case, *coachlamps* finds "coach lamps."

Here are step-by-step instructions for creating a new Quick Part:

1. **Select the text you want to save as a Quick Part.**

   Your selection can include text, pictures, and other objects that Office recognizes. There's virtually no size limit. You can even use an entire document as a Quick Part (like a rejection letter that you send out every day).

2. **Use Alt+F3 to open the Create New Building Block dialog box (Figure 2-21).**

   The Alt+F3 keyboard shortcut's the quickest route to creating a new Quick Part Building Block. (And, after all, speed's the name of the Quick Part game.) You see six boxes in the Create New Building Block dialog box, but the first one, Name, is the most important.

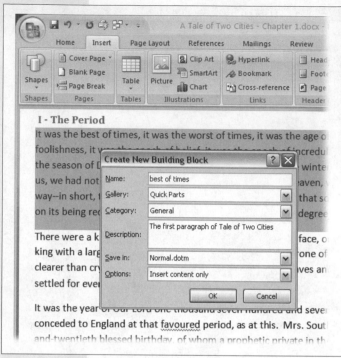

Figure 2-21:
When you want to create a Quick Part entry quickly, press Alt+F3 to display the Create New Building Block dialog box. At a minimum, you need to give your Quick Part a name, which is also what you type to retrieve your Quick Part and place it in your document. In this example, the entire first paragraph of A Tale of Two Cities is named "best of times." In the future, to insert the paragraph into a document, you type best of times, and then press F3. Word replaces the name with the entire paragraph.

3. **Give your Quick Part a Name.**

   Think carefully when you type a name for your Quick Part, because the name is the key you use to retrieve the Quick Part. The name can be as short or as long as you want. For speed's sake, shorter is better, but you don't want to make it so cryptic you can't remember it.

4. **Type a Description and, if you wish, choose a Category for your Quick Part.**

   A description is optional, but it's helpful for other people who use Word, or even for you, a couple of years down the road. And if you create a lot of Quick Parts, then you may find it helpful to store them in different categories as a way to organize them. For example, you can create a Help Desk category with answers to frequently asked questions and a Contracts category with a legal boilerplate.

Tip: You can use the Gallery drop-down menu to store your entry as something other than a Quick Part. For example, you could store it as a Cover Page or as a Bibliography.

---

5. **Leave the "Save in" drop-down menu set to Building Blocks.dotx.**

   The Quick Part is saved in Building Blocks.dotx, a Word template that's available to any document. You can find more information about using templates on page 134.

NOSTALGIA CORNER

Easy Access to AutoText

If you're a fan of the way AutoText worked in earlier versions of Word, you may be dismayed to see it buried as one of the Galleries in the Building Blocks Organizer. Fortunately, it's as easy as ever to create and retrieve an AutoText entry using the F3 key. The steps are nearly identical to creating a Quick Part:

1. Select the text you want to save as an AutoText entry.

2. Press Alt+F3 to open the Create New Building Block box, as shown in Figure 2-21.

3. Enter a name for the AutoText entry.

4. From the Gallery drop-down menu, choose AutoText.

5. Enter a Category and Description (optional).

6. Click OK to save the entry.

To insert an AutoText entry in your text, just type the name (entered in step 2 above), and then press F3. Word replaces the name with the entire AutoText entry. Now the only thing that's missing is a menu that provides quick and easy access to your AutoText entries.

You can resolve this issue too, by adding AutoText to your Quick Access toolbar. Follow these steps:

1. In Word's upper-left corner, right-click anywhere on the Quick Access toolbar.

2. From the shortcut menu, choose "Customize Quick Access Toolbar" to open the Word Options box.

3. In the "Choose commands from" drop-down menu, choose All Commands (it's at the very bottom of the list).

4. Scroll down to AutoText (the options are alphabetized). Double-click to add the command to the box on the right.

5. Click OK to close the box.

The AutoText drop-down menu is now part of the Quick Access toolbar. When you click the icon that looks like a keyboard with a hand pointing to it, you see visual representations of your AutoText entries (Figure 2-22). As an added bonus, a button at the bottom of the menu lets you save any selection as an AutoText entry.

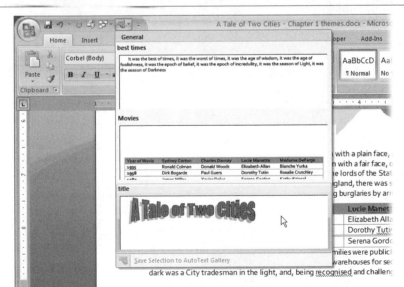

Figure 2-22:
Add the AutoText drop-down menu to your Quick Access toolbar for easy, visual access to all your AutoText entries. See the box above for instructions.

6. **From the Options menu, choose how you want the text to appear every time you press F3.**

The first option, **Insert content only**, is a good one to use if you plan to use the Quick Part within paragraphs. The second option, **Insert content in its own paragraph**, works well for address blocks or entire paragraphs, such as the answers to frequently asked questions. The last option, **Insert content in its own page**, is a logical choice for a memo or other text that rightfully belongs on its own.

Setting Up the Document: Margins, Page Breaks, and More

Your document makes a first impression before anyone reads a word. The paper size, color, and borders give the reader an overall sense of the document's theme and quality. Margins, the text layout, and perhaps a watermark send further visual clues. Making the right choices about your document setup helps you send the right message to your readers. Say you're working on an invitation; using a smaller, elegant paper size and adding a subtle border lets your recipients know right away that they're in for a sophisticated event.

In this chapter, you'll learn how to set and change all the page layout features that people notice first, starting with paper size, orientation, and margins. You'll also learn how to adjust margins and make changes to the headers and footers. Finally, you'll learn how to work with multiple columns and how to control Word's hyphenation inclinations.

Choosing Paper Size and Layout

When you edit a document in Word, what you see on your computer screen looks almost exactly like the final printed page. To get that correct preview, Word needs to know some details about the paper you're using, like the page size and orientation. You have two different ways to change the page settings: using the Page Layout tab (Figure 3-1) or the Page Setup dialog box (Figure 3-2). When you click the Page Layout tab, the ribbon's buttons and icons change to show you options related to designing your page as a whole. Your options are organized in five groups: Themes, Page Setup, Page Background, Paragraph, and Arrange.

Of Menus and Boxes

Word gives you two ways to set options: through ribbon menus and dialog boxes. In general, the ribbon's drop-down menus give you access to quick, predesigned solutions, while dialog boxes give you greater control over more details. Menu options usually focus on one or two settings, while dialog boxes are much more complex affairs, letting you change several settings at once.

The Page Layout → Page Setup → Size menu, shown in Figure 3-1, lets you choose a standard paper size with one click. But what if you're not using one of the standard paper sizes on the Size menu? In that case, click More Paper Sizes (at the bottom of the Size menu).

The Page Setup dialog box opens to the Paper tab (Figure 3-2). Here, you can customize the page size—by entering numbers in the Width and Height text boxes—and tweak other paper-related settings. These other settings, such as the Paper Source settings (which let you tell your printer which tray to take the paper from), are typical of the fine-tuning controls you find in dialog boxes.

On the Margins and Layout tabs, you can control your document's margins, orientation, headers, and footers. You'll learn more about all of these settings later in this chapter.

Changing Paper Size

If you want to quickly change the page size to a standard paper size like letter, legal, or tabloid, the Page Layout → Page Setup → Size menu is the way to go (Figure 3-1). With one quick click, you change your document's size. If there's text in your document, Word reshapes it to fit the page. Say you change a 10-page document from letter size to the longer legal-size page. Word spreads out your text over the extra space, and you'll have fewer pages overall.

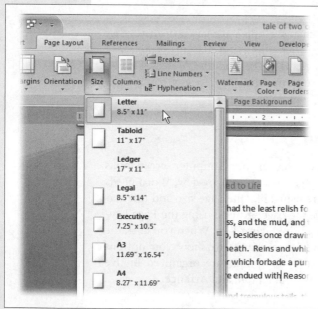

Figure 3-1:
The Size menu, like many Word 2007 menus, uses icons as well as text to give you quick visual cues. Your choices include Letter (8.5"x 11"), Tabloid (11" x 17"), and more. If you're using standard-size paper (including standard international sizes like A3 and A4), you can click one of these choices, and you're done. If you're using an oddball size paper, see the steps on the following pages.

Customizing paper size and source

If you can't find the paper size you need on the Size menu, then you need to customize your paper size, which you do in the Page Setup dialog box's Paper tab. Here are the steps:

1. **Choose Page Layout → Page Setup → Size. At the bottom of the Size menu, click More Paper Sizes.**

   The Page Setup dialog box appears, with the Paper tab showing (Figure 3-2). Why the Paper tab? Because you opened the box using the More Paper Sizes button.

2. **In the Width and Height boxes, enter the size of your custom paper.**

   The quickest way to change the Width and Height settings is to select the numbers in the boxes and type your new page dimensions. Your new numbers replace the previous settings. You can also click the up and down arrows to the right of the text boxes, but it's slow going as the sizes change in tenths of an inch. Notice that as you change the dimensions, the Preview image at the bottom of the Page Setup box changes to match.

3. **Click OK at the bottom, to close the dialog box and make the changes.**

   The Page Setup box closes, and your custom-sized document shows in Word.

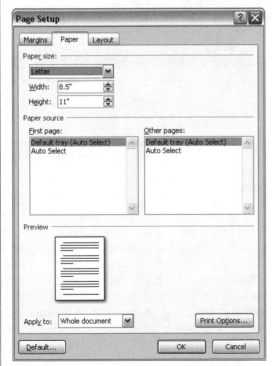

Figure 3-2:
Using the Paper tab of the Page Setup box, you can choose from standard paper sizes or set your own custom paper size. Dialog boxes are great for making several changes at once. On this tab you can also choose a paper source (if you're lucky enough to have a printer with more than one paper tray). You can read more about printing in Chapter 7.

Note: At the bottom of the Page Setup dialog box is an "Apply to" option with two choices: "Whole document" and "This point forward." If you choose "Whole document," Word applies these paper size and other page layout settings to your entire document. If you choose "This point forward," Word creates a page break at the insertion point, and starts using the new settings only after the break. As page 385 explains, Word lets you break a document into sections, each with its own unique formatting. Using sections, you can create a cover page, table of contents, chapter breaks, and more.

Setting Paper Orientation

Most business documents, school papers, and letters use a *portrait* page orientation, meaning the page is taller than it is wide. But sometimes you want a short, wide page—*landscape* page orientation—to accommodate a table, chart, or photo, or just for artistic effect. Whatever the reason, using the Orientation menu (Page Layout → Page Setup → Orientation) is the easiest way to make the change (Figure 3-3). Just click one of the two options: Portrait or Landscape.

If you've already got the Page Setup box open, you'll find the Orientation options on the Margins tab (Page Layout → Page Setup → Margins → Custom Margins).

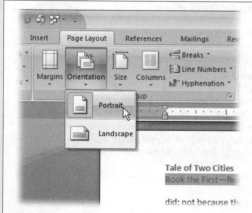

Figure 3-3:
Click Portrait or Landscape to choose a page orientation for your document.

Setting Document Margins

Page margins are more than just empty space. The right page margins make your document more readable. Generous page margins make text look inviting and give reviewers room for notes and comments. With narrower margins, you can squeeze more words on the page; however, having too many words per line makes your document difficult to read. With really long lines it's a challenge for readers to track from the end of one line back to the beginning of the next. Margins become even more important for complex documents, such as books or magazines with facing pages. With Word's margins and page setup tools, you can tackle a whole range of projects.

Selecting Preset Margins

Word's Margins menu (Page Layout → Page Setup → Margins) gives you a way to quickly apply standard margins to your pages. The preset margins are a mixed bag of settings from a half inch to one and a quarter inches. For most documents, you can choose one of these preset margins and never look back (Figure 3-4).

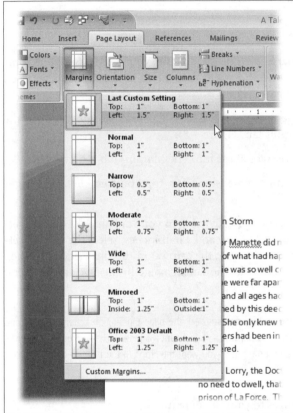

Figure 3-4:
The Margins menu provides some standard settings such as the ever popular one inch all the way around. Word calls this favorite of businesses and schools the Normal margin. If you've customized your margins, your most recent settings appear at the top of the menu.

For each of the preset margin options you see dimensions and an icon that hints at the look of the page.

- **Normal** gives you one inch on all sides of the page.

- **Narrow** margins work well with multicolumn documents, giving you a little more room for each column.

- **Moderate** margins with three-quarter inches left and right let you squeeze a few more words in each line.

- The **Wide** preset gives you more room for marginal notes when you're proofing a manuscript.

To select one of the preset margins, go to Page Layout → Page Setup → Margins, and then click one of the options. You can also use the shortcut key *Alt+P, M*, and then use your up and down arrow keys to highlight one of the margins. Press Enter to use the highlighted margin.

> **Note:** Word measures margins from the edge of the page to the edge of the body text. Any headers and footers that you add (page 76) appear *in* the margin areas.

Setting Custom Margins

What if none of the preset margins on the menu suits your needs? Say your company's style guide insists on one-and-a-half-inch margins for all press releases. Here's how to customize your margins:

1. **Go to Page Layout → Page Setup → Margins → Custom Margins to open the Page Setup box to the Margins tab (Figure 3-5).**

   The Page Setup box has three tabs at the top. The Margins tab is on the left.

2. **At the top of the box, enter dimensions for top, bottom, left, and right margins.**

   The boxes in the Margins section already contain your document's current settings. To change the Top margin to one and a half inches, select the current setting, and then type *1.5*, or you can click the arrows on the right side of the box to change the margin number. Make the same change in the Bottom, Left, and Right margin text boxes.

> **Tip:** While you're here in the Page Setup box, double-check the page Orientation setting. Margins and page orientation have a combined effect. In other words, if you want a quarter-inch top margin, make sure the orientation is set correctly depending on whether you want the "top" of the page to be on the long side or the short side of the paper.

3. **Click OK to apply the changes to your document.**

   The Page Setup box closes and your document takes shape with the new margins. If the changes are substantially different from the previous settings, you may find that you have a different number of pages in your document.

Setting Margins for Booklets

The vast majority of the documents spewing forth from our collective printers are printed on a single side of the page. If they're bound at all, it's likely to be with a staple or a paper clip in the upper-left corner. Documents like this don't need fancy margins or page setups. But, if you're putting together a booklet, corporate report, or newsletter, you need more sophisticated tools.

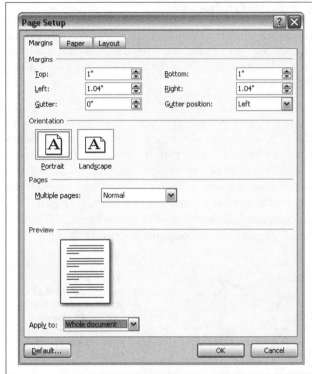

Figure 3-5:
*The Margins tab is divided into four groups of
controls: Margins, Orientation, Pages, and Preview.
Use the text boxes at the top to set your top, bottom,
and side margins. Use the gutter settings to specify
the part of the page that's hidden by a binding.*

Open the Page Setup box to the Margins tab (Page Layout → Page Setup → Margins → Custom Margins or Alt+P, MA). In the Pages group, click the "Multiple pages" drop-down menu to see the options.

• **Normal** is the setting you use for most single-sided documents.

• **Mirror margins** are great for documents with facing pages, like bound reports or newsletters. This setting makes outside and inside margins identical. Outside margins are the left margin on the left page and the right margin on the right page. Inside margins are in between the two facing pages. Documents with facing pages may also have a gutter, which is a part of the page that is hidden when the document is bound.

• **2 pages per sheet** prints two pages on a single side of the paper. If you've defined headers and footers, they'll show up on both pages. Usually you cut these pages after printing to create separate pages.

• **Book fold** is similar to the option above and prints two pages on one side of the paper. The difference is that the book fold layout is designed so you can fold the paper down the middle to create a booklet with facing pages.

When you make a selection from the "Multiple pages" menu, some of the other options in the Margins box change too. For example, if you choose "Mirror margins," the labels above for the Right and Left margins change to Inside and Outside.

Adding Page Background Features

While every document has a paper size, orientation, and margins, Word has some specialized formatting features that you'll use less frequently. You'll find the options for watermarks, page color, and borders in the middle of the Page Layout tab. These tools let you get a little fancy.

Adding Watermarks

A true watermark is created in a process where a water-coated metal stamp imprints a design into the paper's surface during manufacture. The design is usually a paper company's logo. The presence of a watermark can also indicate a document's authenticity. Word can't create a real watermark, but it can replicate the effect by printing one faintly on the page, seemingly beneath the text (Figure 3-6). A watermark could be your company logo, or it could be words like CONFIDENTIAL, DRAFT, or DO NOT COPY, emblazoned diagonally across the page.

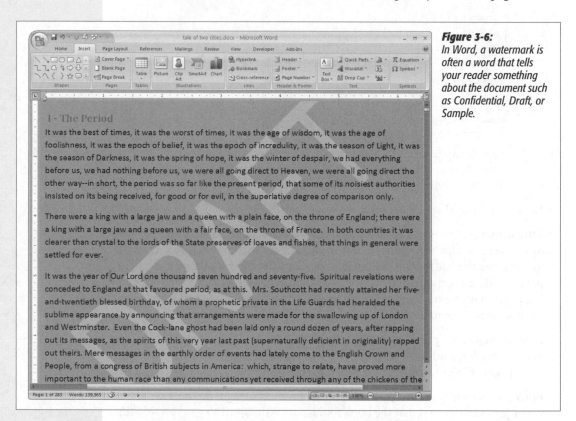

Figure 3-6:
In Word, a watermark is often a word that tells your reader something about the document such as Confidential, Draft, or Sample.

Suppose you'd like to have your company logo appear as a classy watermark on your document. Using your logo picture file as a watermark takes just a few steps:

1. **Go to Page Layout → Page Background → Watermark.**

   When the Watermark menu drops down, you see a dozen predesigned water-mark options. You can choose one of these options, or you can take a few more steps to customize your watermark.

2. **At the bottom of the menu, click Custom Watermarks to open the Printed Watermark dialog box (Figure 3-7).**

   The Printed Watermark box has three radio button options arranged vertically: No watermark, Picture watermark, and Text watermark.

Figure 3-7:
Using the Printed Watermark box, you can brand your document with a word of your choice. Simply type it in the Text box. Use the Font, Size, Color, and Layout options to change the text's appearance.

3. **Select the "Picture watermark" radio button.**

   When you click one of these buttons, the appropriate fine-tuning options become available and the others fade to gray. For example, when you choose "Picture watermark," the Text watermark options are grayed out.

4. **Click the Select Picture button to open the Insert Picture box.**

   The Insert Picture box is a standard Windows file box. Use the buttons on the left and the "Look in" drop-down menu at the top to navigate to the folder with your logo's picture file.

5. **Double-click the picture file to use it for your watermark, or, as an alternative, select your picture, and then click Insert.**

   The Insert Picture box closes, and you see the More Watermarks box again. Next to the Select Picture button, you see the name of your picture file.

6. **Set the Scale and Washout options.**

   Now that you've chosen your picture file, you can use two more settings to make your watermark look spiffy. Use the Scale drop-down menu to adjust the size of your image so that it looks good on the page. You can choose from preset sizes of 50%, 100%, 150%, 200%, or 500%. Or you can choose the Auto setting, which scales your image to fit comfortably on the page. The Washout checkbox fades your image, making it easier to read text over the watermark.

7. **Click Apply to see your watermark in action, and then click Close to finish up.**

   Use the Apply button to see how your watermark will look on the printed page. If you need a better view, click the top bar of the Printed Watermark box, and then drag it out of the way. When you're happy with the results, click Close to close the Printed Watermark dialog box. Your new watermark appears on every page of your document. To back out of the deal, select "No watermark" at the top of the box.

Tip: To get rid of an existing watermark, open the Watermark drop-down menu and, at the bottom, click Remove Watermark.

Choosing a Page Color

The Page Color option applies more to Web pages than to printed pages. When you're working with paper, you'll usually print on a different colored paper rather than printing a colored background on white paper. However, with heavy stock, you can use this feature on occasion to create postcards, colored covers, and so on.

When you're creating a Web page in Word (Chapter 4), you can use this feature to add background colors, textures, patterns, and even background pictures—not that it's always a good idea. Nothing screams "Amateur designer!" more than background colors and images that fight with the text on the page. Homespun Web pages are the most flagrant violators of good taste. But whether you're working for screen or paper, if you use a dark text color, make sure you use a light page color and vice versa. Avoid extremely busy background patterns, textures, and images that make it hard to read your text.

Go to Page Layout → Page Background → Page Color drop-down menu to see a palette of options (Figure 3-8). If you move your mouse over a color (without clicking), then you see the page change color, immediately giving you a preview. In fact, if you're previewing a very dark page color, Word's smart enough to change the text from black to white. That doesn't mean it's impossible to come up with some garish page color options. Click a color to set your page color.

If you don't like the colors on the menu, you can open the Colors box that's used in all the Office programs (Figure 3-9). The Standard tab shows colors arranged as hexagons within a hexagon. Click a color or a gray shade (at the bottom) to make a selection. The Custom tab gives you more control over your color selection. To use it, click the rainbow-colored box on the left, and you get a crosshair cursor to choose a color with. Position the crosshairs on the color in the spectrum you want, and then click the slider on the right to adjust your chosen color's lightness or darkness. Using these two controls, you can select any color your computer can create. As you work with the Colors spectrum and the slider, the New and Current

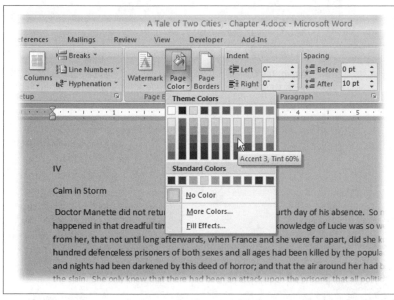

Figure 3-8:
*The Page Color menu is divided
into two sections. Theme Colors
shows you a palette of colors
that are part of the document's
current theme format. (For more
on themes, see page 126.) The
Standard Colors palette gives
you access to several basic,
bright colors.*

boxes show you a preview of how you're changing the color. This system is easy to use but makes it hard to recreate the same color twice in a row. To do that, you need to color by numbers—see the box on page 75.

Applying Page Borders

A tasteful, properly applied border can add a certain flare to your document. However, an inappropriate border can make your document look cheesy (Figure 3-10). Enough said.

Okay, now that you've been warned, here's how to add page borders:

1. **Choose Page Layout → Page Background → Page Borders to open the Borders and Shading box (Figure 3-11).**

   The Borders and Shading box has three tabs. Make sure you're using the *Page* Border tab. (The first Borders tab puts borders around paragraphs, pictures, and other objects on the page.)

2. **On the left, choose a setting to define the border.**

   Start with the five settings on the left, to define the border in broad strokes ranging from no border to drop shadows. You can select only one of these settings.

3. **Choose a line style, color, and width, or choose an art border.**

   Decide whether your border will be a line or an art border—trees, hearts, pieces of cake, and so on. If you're going with a line border, choose a style of line from the drop-down menu. You can choose from more than two dozen lines, including solid, dotted, double, and wavy. Then use the drop-down menus to choose a line color and width.

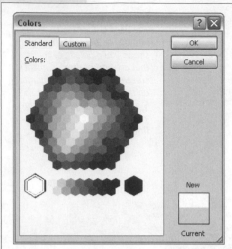

Figure 3-9:
The Office 2007 Colors box lets you pick colors in two ways.

Top: The Standard tab is the easiest to use—just click a color swatch.

Bottom: The Custom tab gives you great color control, but requires a couple extra clicks or knowledge of one of two standard color models, RGB or HSL, as the box on page 75 explains.

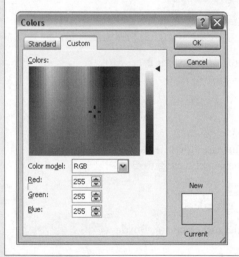

If you want an art border, select your design from the menu. Note that some of the art styles use different patterns for different sides of the page and for the corner design.

Note: Whether you choose lines or art for your border, you can adjust the width. You can increase line widths to a thick 6 points and art widths to 31 points.

4. **Preview the border, and then select the sides of the page that will have borders.**

The Preview on the right side of the Borders and Shading box shows what sides of your page will have borders. Click the borders to toggle them on or off. Using this technique, you can choose to show a border on a single side of the page or on any combination of sides.

Specifying Colors by Numbers

When Web designers talk about color, they use a numerical system from 0 to 255, where any color imaginable can be described as a combination of red, green, and blue. A value of 0 means that the color contains none of that hue, with 255 being the maximum amount. These numbers let you describe color with great precision. For example, R197, G216, B255 specifies a particular shade of blue. To create this color in Word's Colors box, type 197 in the Red box, 216 in the Green box, and 255 in the Blue box. This numerical system minimizes the chances for misunderstandings. If you're collaborating on a Web site, the Web designer can give you an RGB color to use for the Web page background and be absolutely certain that you're both talking about the same color.

(When you click a color and move the lightness/darkness slider in the Colors box, you're still using the RGB system, but Word fills in the numbers for you.)

The other color model used in the Colors box is HSL, which stands for hue, saturation (intensity), and luminosity (brightness). Saturation refers to the amount of the actual color (hue) in the mix, and luminosity determines the amount of white or black mixed in to create degrees of lightness and darkness. Here, too, you can type numbers if you know them, or just use the color spectrum and slider until you've got the color you want.

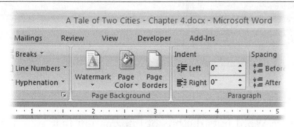

h the Doctor tried hard, and never ceased trying, to get Charles Damay
t him brought to trial, the public current of the time set too strong and
the king was tried, doomed, and beheaded; the Republic of Liberty, E
lared for victory or death against the world in arms; the black flag wave
owers of Notre Dame; three hundred thousand men, summoned to rise
rose from all the varying soils of France, as if the dragon's teeth had bee

Figure 3-10:
You can find the Page Borders button in the Page Background group on the Page Layouts tab. Don't get carried away with borders, or you can make bad decisions. This cake border is a bad choice for Marie Antoinette and most other adults.

5. **In the lower-right corner of the box, use the "Apply to" control to set the pages that will have borders.**

   Maybe you want your first page to have a different border from the rest of the document. If the first page of your document uses letterhead, you may want a first page with no border at all, so select "This section – all except first page." Or, to put a border around the cover page but no other pages, choose the "This section – first page only" setting. As with paper size and other page layout settings, Word lets you apply borders differently in different sections of your document.

6. Click OK to accept the settings and to close the Borders and Shading box.

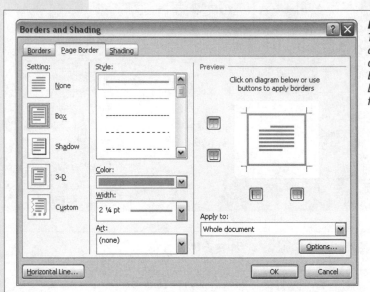

Figure 3-11:
The Borders and Shading box lets you apply borders to paragraphs, pictures, or pages. Make sure you're on the Page Border tab if you're applying page borders. You can use lines or artwork to form your borders.

Adding Headers and Footers

Headers and footers are where Word puts the bits of information that appear at the top or bottom of every page of most multipage documents (Figure 3-12). They remind you of the page number, chapter title, and so on, as you read along. For business memos and reports, headers are a great place to repeat the document's subject and publication date. (If you're the author of the report and want your boss to know, consider adding your name under the title.)

Note: Word's *fields* are bits of text automated with the help of some behind-the-scenes computer code. You can insert fields into your document to show information that's likely to change, like today's date or a page number. Because it's a field, this text updates itself automatically.

Introducing the Header and Footer Tools

Unlike some of the other features in this chapter, the header and footer tools are on the Insert tab (not the Page Layout tab). As you can see in Figure 3-13, three menus appear in the Header & Footer group—Header, Footer, and Page Number. Each of the menus provides predesigned page elements, known in Word-speak as Building Blocks. So, for example, if you select a header Building Block, it may add text and several graphic elements to the top of your page.

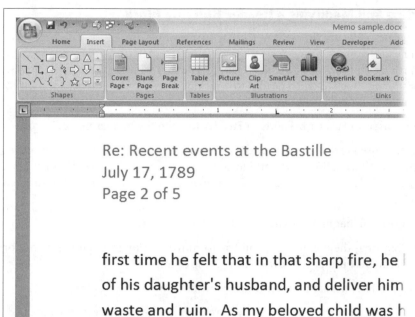

Figure 3-12:
Document headers give the reader additional information that's not found in the text. For example, the header for a business memo can include the subject, date, and page number. Word lets you enter this information manually or with the help of fields that automatically update the information.

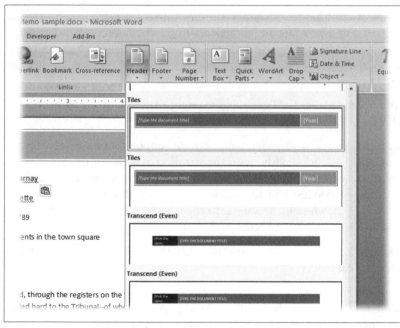

Figure 3-13:
The Header, Footer, and Page Number menus help you insert predesigned page elements, known as Building Blocks, into your document. You can see what each one looks like right on the menu. At the bottom of the menu, you find options to create (or remove) custom headers, footers, and page numbers.

Inserting and Modifying a Header Building Block

Go to Insert → Header & Footer → Header, and you see more than a dozen prede-signed header options. You can keep these canned headers as they are, or use them as a starting point for your own imagination. The following steps show you how to use a Building Block to add a header to your document and then tweak it a bit by inserting an additional field.

1. **Go to Insert → Header & Footer → Header to open the Header menu.**

   If you've used earlier versions of the program, you'll notice that the drop-down menus in Word 2007 are larger and much more visual. The Header menu is a good example, as it gives you a clear representation of the available predesigned headers.

2. **Use the scroll bar on the right to find the Tiles header.**

   You can drag the box in the scroll bar to move quickly through the menu, or use the arrow buttons to browse through the examples.

3. **Click the Tiles header to insert it into your document.**

   When you select the Tiles header, you're adding more than text to your docu-ment: A Building Block comes with all its own accessories. The Tiles header includes a box with a rule around it and two tiles of color. Inside the tiles are bracketed words.

   When you insert a header, a couple of other things happen too. The Header menu closes and a new Design tab appears on your ribbon, with a Header & Footer Tools tab above. Along with that, a whole slew of new buttons and tools appear on the ribbon (left to right): Header & Footer, Insert, Navigation, Options, Position, and the Close Header and Footer button.

4. **Click the bracketed words "Type the document title," and then type a title of your choice.**

   The bracketed words are a prompt that you're supposed to enter new text in that spot. A single click anywhere on the words selects the entire group. Type your title, say, *A Tale of Two Cities*. When you type, the other words and the brackets disappear. When you add a title to the header, Word uses this text to update the title shown in the Document Properties (Office button → Prepare → Properties). For details, see the box on page 80.

5. **Click the bracketed word "Year," and then use the calendar control to update the header's Year field.**

   This standard Word tool lets you enter a date by selecting it. At the top, you see the month and year. Click the buttons on either side to move backward or for-ward through the months. Click a date on the calendar below to select a spe-cific date. Word uses the year from the date you selected to update the Year text in the header. Or you can enter a year simply by typing it.

You can modify Building Blocks after you add them to your document by typing your own text, which you'll do next.

6. **Click the header to the right of your title. If the title is highlighted, use the right arrow key to deselect the title, and then type a hyphen (-) followed by a space.**

   You can also add automatically updating text by inserting a field, which is how Word creates those ever-changing dates and page numbers. Word has fields for lots of other stuff too. You can't create (or edit) a field by typing directly in your document, though. You must use the Field dialog box.

7. **Choose Insert → Quick Parts → Field.**

   The Field dialog box opens showing an alphabetical list of field names on the left side, as shown in Figure 3-14. Fields store information about your document and keep track of other information that you can use in your documents.

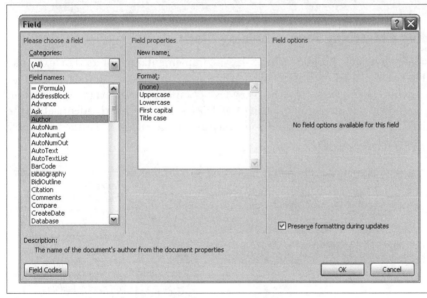

Figure 3-14:
Using fields, you can add automatically updating page numbers, dates, and names. The Field dialog box shows a whole list of fields (left) and provides ways to format them (right) so that they work just right.

8. **Double-click the Author field name to insert it into the header.**

   The author's name appears next to the title in the header. (If you're working on your own computer, it's probably your name.) This text is grayed out to show that it's a field and that you can't edit it directly.

9. **Double-click anywhere on the document's body text to close the Header & Footer Tools contextual tab.**

   You have two options for closing the header and going back to editing your document. You can double-click anywhere outside the header, or, on the right side of the ribbon, you can click the Close Header and Footer button. Either way, the header fades out and the text of your document sharpens up. Your insertion point appears back in the body text, and you're ready to work.

Inspecting Your Document's Properties and Fields

When you type to replace placeholder text in a Quick Part (like the header title in step 3 on page 78), something else happens behind the scenes. Every Word document has *properties*—defining information like author, title, and subject. You can check them out in the Document Information Panel: Choose Office button → Prepare → Properties. (When you're done, click the X button at the upper right to close the box.) When you give the header a new title, Word takes those words and inserts them in the Title field of the Document Information Panel.

Word keeps track of the title and other document properties and uses them to fill in the fields you insert into your documents. You can insert a field in a header, a footer, or indeed anywhere in your document by choosing Insert → Quick Parts → Field. For example, the number of pages in a document is stored in the NumPages field. So if you'd like to put "Page X of XX pages" in your header or footer, just replace X with the Page field and XX with the NumPages field.

Adding a Matching Footer Building Block

Most of the header Building Blocks have complementary footers. For example, the Tiles header used in the step-by-step example provides title and date information, while the Tiles footer provides company and page information (Figure 3-15). The steps for inserting the Tiles footer are nearly identical to the header steps. Just start with the Footer menu: Choose Insert → Header & Footer → Footer or press Alt+N, O.

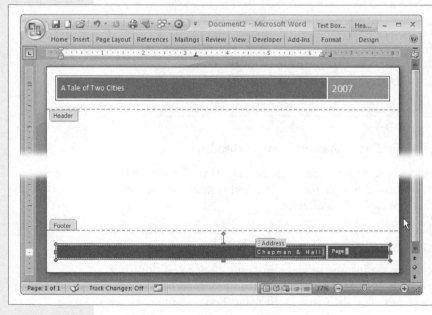

Figure 3-15:
Most of the header and footer Building Blocks come in pairs. By using a header and footer with the same name, you can be sure of having a consistent design. You can modify Building Blocks—like this predesigned header and footer—after you insert them in your text. Just edit as you would any text. It's best to leave the page numbers as they are, though. This page number is grayed out to indicate that it's a field that automatically changes for each page.

Creating Custom Headers and Footers

Microsoft provides a lot of competently designed headers and footers with Word, but you're free to create your own. After all, Microsoft's Building Blocks may not be to your taste, or maybe you have to follow company guidelines for your documents. It's not difficult to create your own headers in Word. Here's how to create a custom footer with a company name on the left and page numbers on the right:

1. **Go to Insert → Header & Footer → Footer → Edit Footer.**

   The insertion point moves from the body of your document to the footer space at the bottom.

2. **Type your company name, press Enter, and then type your city and country.**

   Pressing Enter puts the city and country on a new line below the company name. Text that you type directly into the footer appears on every page unless you make changes to the header and footer options.

3. **Press Tab twice to move the insertion point to the right side of the footer.**

   The first time you press Tab, the insertion point moves to the center of the page. If you enter text at that point, Word centers the text in the footer. The second time you press Tab, the insertion point moves to the right margin. Text that you enter there is aligned on the right margin.

4. **Type *Page*, and then press the Space bar.**

   As you type, the insertion point remains on the right margin and your text flows to the left.

5. **Choose Header & Footer Tools | Design → Insert → Quick Parts → Field (or press Alt+JH, Q, F) to open the Field dialog box.**

   The Quick Parts menu shows several different options: Document Property, Field, and Building Blocks Organizer.

6. **In the list of Field Names, double-click Page to insert the Page field in the footer.**

   Remember, if you simply type a number into the footer, you'll end up with the same number on every page. Instead, you place the Page field in your footer to tell Word to insert the correct number on each page. The page number appears in the footer next to the word "Page." The number is grayed out, indicating that it's a field and you can't edit the number.

7. **Type *of* and then a space. Press Alt+JH, Q, F to open the Field box again, and then double-click the NumPages field to insert it in your footer after the space.**

   The NumPages field keeps track of the number of pages in your document. When you're done, your footer looks like the one in Figure 3-16.

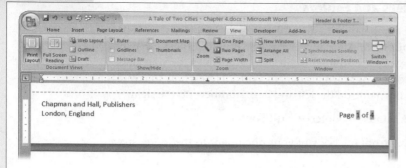

Figure 3-16:
This custom footer may not be as flashy as Microsoft's Building Blocks, but what Chapman and Hall wants, Chapman and Hall gets. The company name and city are plain typed-in text, while the page number and number of pages are fields that update automatically.

Removing Headers, Footers, and Page Numbers

It's easy to remove any headers, footers, or page numbers that you've added to your document. You'll find a command at the bottom of each of the respective menus to do just that. If you want to remove a header, follow these steps:

1. **Go to Insert → Header & Footer → Header to open the Header menu.**

   You see the same menu that you used to insert the header Building Block into your document. At the bottom of the menu, below all the Header examples, you see the Remove Header command.

2. **Click Remove Header.**

   The Header menu closes, and the entire header disappears from your document—text, graphics, and all.

The steps for removing a footer or a page number Building Block are nearly identical. Just start with the Footer menu (Insert → Header & Footer → Footer) or the Page Number menu (Insert → Header & Footer → Page Number).

Working with Multiple Columns

Word makes it easy to work with multiple newspaper-style columns. Instead of your having to use tabs or spaces to separate the column one line at a time, Word lets you set up the column guidelines and then type away. When you type text in a multicolumn layout, your words appear in the left column first. After you reach the end or bottom of the column, the insertion point jumps to the top of the next column and you begin to fill it, from top to bottom.

To use multiple columns, go to Page Layout → Page Setup → Columns, and then click one of the following options:

- **One.** Whether you know it or not, every page in Word has a column layout. The standard layout is one big column stretching from margin to margin.

- **Two.** With two columns, your document begins to look like a pamphlet or a school textbook.

- **Three.** Three columns are about as much as a standard 8.5 × 11-inch page can handle, unless you switch to Landscape orientation. In fact, you may want to reduce the body text size to about 9 or 10 points and turn on hyphenation. Otherwise, you can't fit very many words on a line.

- **Left.** This layout has two columns, with the narrower column on the left. The narrow column is a great place to introduce the text with a long heading and subheading or a quote pulled from the larger body text.

- **Right.** The mirror image of the Left layout, this option uses two columns with a narrow column at right.

- **More Columns.** Use the More Columns option to open the Columns dialog box (Figure 3-17) where you can create a customized column layout.

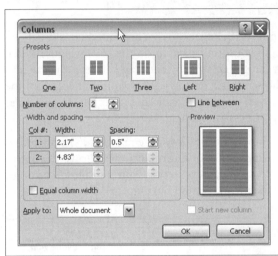

Figure 3-17:
At the top of the Columns dialog box, you see the same presets as on the Columns menu. Below them, controls let you create your own multicolumn layouts. The preview icon on the right changes as you adjust the settings.

Tip: If you want to use keyboard shortcuts to select column options, press Alt+P, J and then use the up and down arrow keys to highlight one of the options. With your choice highlighted, hit Enter.

When you get to the bottom of a column, Word automatically flows your text to the top of the next one, but you can also force Word to end the column and jump to the next one. There are two ways to create a *column break*. The quickest way while you're typing is to use the keyboard shortcut Ctrl+Shift+Enter (or Alt+P, BC). Or, if you forget the shortcut, you can use the ribbon: Page Layout → Page Setup → Breaks → Column.

Customizing Columns

Go to Page Layout → Page Setup → Columns → More Columns to open the Columns box (Figure 3-17) where you can create custom page layouts with multiple columns. By entering a number in the "Number of columns" text box, you can create more than three columns per page.

Choosing Between Columns and Tables

Word gives you two tools to divide your text into strips—Columns and Tables. Even though they may look the same on paper, they work and act differently. If you're writing a newsletter or a pamphlet, you probably want newspaper-style columns, so you can just type (or paste in) your text and let Word distribute it smoothly from one column to the next. But if you're listing the names of volunteers who joined the PTA each semester, you're better off using a table to create the columns, so you can keep each name on its own line.

As a rule of thumb, use newspaper-style columns (Page Layout → Page Setup → Columns) when you need a consistent number of evenly spaced columns on each page and when you expect the reader to read from the top to the bottom of a column before moving to the next column. Use tables to organize information in rows and columns, like a spreadsheet. Readers are just as likely to read tables left to right as they are from top to bottom. There's more information on tables on page 235.

If you turn on the "Equal column width" checkbox, Word automatically sets all the columns to the same width, so you don't have to do the math (Figure 3-18). Turn off this checkbox, and you can get creative by entering a different width and spacing for each column. Use the scroll bar on the right if you can't see all of the columns. Turn on the "Line between" box to place a line (also known as a *rule*) between your columns for a crisp professional look.

Near the bottom of the Columns box is a drop-down menu labeled "Apply to." If you want to use your column settings for your entire document, leave this set to "Whole document." If you want to create a new section with the column settings, select "This point forward" from the menu (see the Tip on page 66).

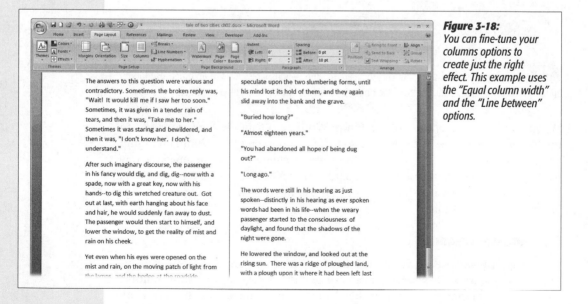

Figure 3-18:
You can fine-tune your columns options to create just the right effect. This example uses the "Equal column width" and the "Line between" options.

Line Numbers

Line numbers are a favorite feature of lawyers and screenwriters. Just as page numbers keep count of a document's pages, line numbers help you keep track of your line count (Figure 3-19). Suppose you mail a printed copy of your short story, with line numbering, to an editor on the other side of the country. The editor can call you on the phone with comments and refer to specific lines and words. Line numbering is also helpful for students and journalists who have to write pieces of a certain length.

To turn on basic line numbering, choose Page Layout → Page Setup → Line Numbers → Continuous.

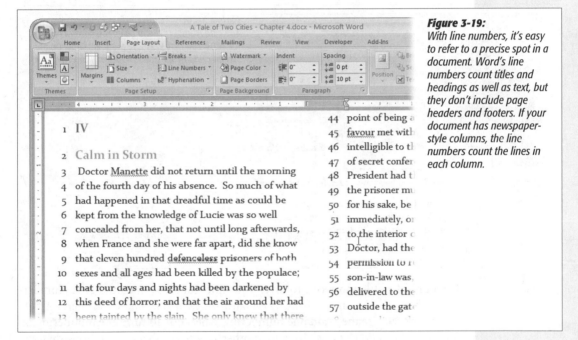

Figure 3-19:
With line numbers, it's easy to refer to a precise spot in a document. Word's line numbers count titles and headings as well as text, but they don't include page headers and footers. If your document has newspaper-style columns, the line numbers count the lines in each column.

Word also gives you some tools to set up your line numbers just the way you want them. Go to Page Layout → Page Setup → Line Numbers to see the Line Numbers menu (Figure 3-20).

Note: Line numbers appear only in Print Layout view and Full Screen Reading view. If you're expecting line numbers but don't see them, make sure you're in one of these two views.

- **None (Alt+P, LN, N).** Don't show any line numbers.

- **Continuous (Alt+P, LN, C).** Show line numbers throughout the document.

- **Restart Each Page (Alt+P, LN, R).** The first line on every page is line 1.

- **Restart Each Section (Alt+P, LN, E).** The first line of each section resets the line count to 1.

- **Suppress for Current Section (Alt+P, LN, S).** Line numbers in the current section don't show and the lines aren't included in the overall count. (The current section is the section with the insertion point.)

- **Line Numbering (Alt+P, LN, L).** Click this button to fine-tune the way line numbers appear in your document. It takes two steps to reach the Line Numbers box (Figure 3-21). Your first click opens the Page Setup box to the Layout tab. Click the Line Number button in the bottom right of the box to open the Line Numbers box.

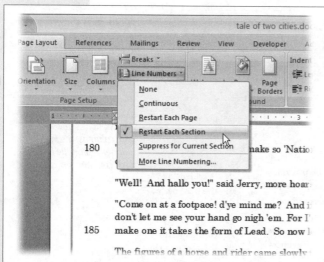

Figure 3-20:
The Line Numbers menu gives you several options for controlling the way line numbers show on the screen and in your printed document.

If you need a little more control over your line numbers, open the Line Numbers dialog box. Here's a not-so-short keyboard shortcut that takes you there: Alt+P, LN, L, Alt+N. Use the "Add line numbering" checkbox to turn line numbering on and off. The radio buttons give you another way to set the same options that you find on the Line Numbers menu. It's the three text boxes that offer something different:

- **Start at.** Use the "Start at" box to set the starting number for the count. Say you want to start at number 1001 instead of 1—just type *1001* in this box.

- **From text.** This box lets you position the line numbers on your page. Enter a larger number to move the line numbers farther away from your text.

- **Count by.** Sometimes you don't need a line number at every line; it makes your page needlessly cluttered. Set the count by number to, say, 5 and you'll see numbers only at line 5, 10, 15, and so forth.

Figure 3-21:
The radio buttons in the Line Numbers dialog box repeat commands from the Line Numbers menu. However, the text boxes give you some handy tools for fine-tuning the appearance and behavior of line numbers.

Hyphenation

Without hyphenation, if a word is too long to fit on the line, Word moves it down to the beginning of the next line. If a word is particularly long, it can leave some pretty big gaps at the end of the line. Justified text is aligned on both the left and right margins, like most of the text in this book. If you have justified text and no hyphenation, you often get large, distracting gaps between words, where Word is trying to spread out the text along the line. When used properly, hyphenation helps make text more attractive on the page and easier to read. In most cases, you can relax and let Word handle the hyphenating.

You just have to choose one of three basic hyphenation styles from the Page Layout → Page Setup → Hyphenation menu (Alt+P, H), as shown in Figure 3-22:

- **None.** No hyphenation at all. For informal letters, first drafts, and many reports, you may choose not to use hyphenation. It's a good-looking choice for documents that have fairly long lines (60 to 80 characters) and left-aligned text.

- **Automatic.** Word makes hyphenation decisions based on some simple rules that you provide. Consider using automatic hyphenation for documents that have line lengths of about 50 characters or less, including documents that use newspaper-style columns.

- **Manual.** In this scheme, Word asks you about each word it wants to hyphenate, giving you the final decision. Use manual hyphenation when you need to be particularly scrupulous about your grammar and when you need to be certain that you don't hyphenate a company name, a person's name, or some other equally important word.

Automatic Hyphenation

It's easy to turn on automatic hyphenation. Just choose Page Layout → Page Setup → Hyphenation (or press Alt+P, H). Still, you may want to assert some control over how and when Word uses hyphenation. To do that, open the Hyphenation box (Figure 3-23) by choosing Page Layout → Page Setup → Hyphenation → Hyphenation Options (Alt+P, HH). This box has two important options that let you control hyphenation:

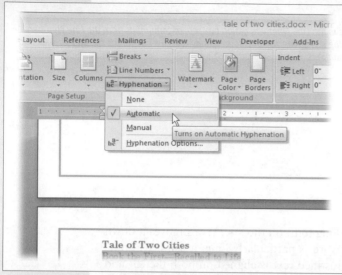

Figure 3-22:
Choose Automatic from the hyphenation menu, and Word takes care of all hyphenation decisions. Word's hyphenation feature works quite well and usually needs no help from you.

Hyphenation Rules of Thumb

Hyphenation rules are notoriously complicated, and, to make matters worse, they change by language and country. For example, Americans and British hyphenate differently. Still, you should follow these basic rules of thumb:

- **Use hyphenation with documents that have shorter lines.** A document that uses two or three columns on the page needs hyphenation to avoid large gaps in the text.

- **Use hyphenation with justified text.** Justified text, which is aligned on both the left and right margins, makes documents look formal and tidy—but not if big gaps appear between letters and words. Avoid those gaps by letting Word hyphenate your justified text.

- **Avoid hyphenating company names and proper names.** Most people don't like to have their name messed with, and your boss feels the same way about the company name. Use manual hyphenation (covered on the following page) to prevent Word from dividing certain words.

- **Avoid hyphenating more than two lines in a row.** According to many standard style guides, it's wrong to use hyphenation on more than two consecutive lines. Use manual hyphenation to remove a hyphen if you see too many in a row.

- **Avoid overusing hyphens.** Excessive hyphenation, even if not on consecutive lines, distracts the eye and makes a document more difficult to read.

- **Hyphenation zone.** This zone is the maximum space that Word allows between the end of a word and the right margin. If the space is larger than this, Word hyphenates a word to close the gap. For most documents, .25" (a quarter of an inch) is a reasonable choice. A larger distance may give you fewer hyphens but a more ragged look to your right margin.

- **Limit consecutive hyphens to.** A "ladder" of three or more hyphens makes text difficult to read. Enter 2 in this box, and Word won't hyphenate more than two lines in a row.

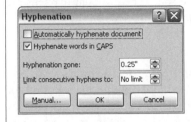

Figure 3-23:
Use the Hyphenation box to set the ground rules for hyphenation. Turn on the "Automatically hyphenate document" checkbox at top to have Word automatically hyphenate words according to the rules you set.

Manual Hyphenation

The term *manual hyphenation* sounds like more work than it actually is. *Computer-assisted hyphenation* would be a better term. When you turn on manual hyphenation (Alt+P, HM), Word automatically finds and shows you words that fall within the hyphenation zone, using the hyphenation rules you set in the Hyphenation box (Figure 3-23). As shown in Figure 3-24, Word gives you the word in a box and suggests where to place the hyphen. If you agree, click Yes. If you'd rather hyphenate the word in a different spot, click to put the insertion point where you want the hyphen, and then click Yes.

Figure 3-24:
You may not always agree with Word when it comes to hyphen placement. In this case, the hyphen is in the wrong spot in the word "mischance." To manually set the hyphen, click to put the insertion point between the "s" and the "c," and then click Yes.

Tip: It's best to run the Manual Hyphenation command (Page Layout → Page Setup → Hyphenation → Manual or Alt+P, HM) immediately before you print or save the final draft of your document. If last-minute edits change the line lengths and line breaks, you need to run manual hyphenation again.

Optional hyphens

Optional hyphens are like saying to Word, "If you're going to hyphenate this word, do it here." You can place an optional hyphen in any word by placing the insertion point where you want the hyphen and then pressing Ctrl+- (hyphen). Optional hyphens appear on the printed page only when the word is split between lines. Otherwise, the optional hyphen is a hidden, non-printing character.

Tip: You can change your Word Options to show all optional hyphens. Go to Office button → Word Options → Display. Under the heading "Always show these formatting marks on the screen," turn on the "Optional hyphens" checkbox that's labeled. In your text, optional hyphens look like this: ¬.

When you use manual hyphenation, you're actually inserting optional hyphens in your text. Each time you click Yes, Word inserts an optional hyphen in your document. If you change your text, words that you hyphenated may no longer fall within the hyphenation zones and they won't be split. The optional hyphens are still there, as you see if you use the tip to show optional hyphens on the screen.

Hyphenating selected text

You don't have to hyphenate an entire document. If you select a chunk of text and then start manual hyphenation (Alt+P, HM), Word looks within the selection for words that should be hyphenated. You can choose to hyphenate the words by clicking Yes, or you can move the hyphen by clicking elsewhere in the word. If you don't want to hyphenate the word at all, then click No. After Word is finished hyphenating the selection, a box appears asking if you want to hyphenate the remainder of the document.

Nonbreaking hyphens

Some words always have hyphens, and some of those are words that you don't want to split between two lines. Suppose the CEO of Coca-Cola decreed that under no circumstances should the company name or product ever straddle two lines of text. That could be a problem because whenever Word sees a typed hyphen, it feels free to break the word at the point. What you need is a *nonbreaking* hyphen, which, despite the oxymoronic name, is easy to use. To make a hyphen nonbreaking, press down the Ctrl and Shift keys when you press the hyphen key (Ctrl+Shift+-). A hyphen appears at the insertion point, but it's a nonbreaking hyphen and has enough glue to hold Coca and Cola together no matter what.

Removing Hyphenation from Your Document

It's easier to remove hyphenation from your document if you've used automatic rather than manual hyphenation. In the case of automatic hyphenation, you simply turn it off: Choose Page Layout → Page Setup → Hyphenation → None, or use the keyboard shortcut Alt+P, HN. All the automatic hyphens in your document disappear and the words rearrange themselves accordingly.

But when you use manual hyphenation, Word inserts optional hyphens in your document that don't go away even if you turn hyphenation off. If you set Hyphenation to None (Alt+P, HN), then Word continues to split words at the end of lines using the optional hyphens. The only way to find and delete the optional hyphens is with Word's Find and Replace dialog box (Figure 3-25).

Here are the steps to remove optional hyphens from your document:

1. **Choose Home → Replace (or press Ctrl+H) to open the Find and Replace dialog box to the Replace tab.**

   If you don't see a Special button at the bottom, click the More button on the left to expand the box. (If the box is expanded, the More button is labeled "Less" and clicking it shrinks the box.)

2. **Click in the "Find what" box to put the insertion point in the box.**

   Normally, you'd just type in the text that you're searching for, but the optional hyphen is a special character that you won't find on your keyboard. Searching for optional hyphens requires a couple of extra steps.

3. **Click the Special button to reveal the list of special characters.**

   The Find and Replace tool can search for a number of special characters. Some of them, like the optional hyphen and the paragraph mark, are nonprinting characters. Others, like the em dash need more than a single keystroke to produce.

4. **From the menu of special characters, choose Optional Hyphen.**

   The Special menu closes when you make a choice from the list. In the "Find what" box, you see ^-, the code Word uses to indicate an optional hyphen. Leave the "Replace with" box empty, because you want to replace the optional hyphens with nothing, which effectively removes them.

5. **Click Replace All to remove all optional hyphens from your text.**

   Word quickly removes the optional hyphens and displays a message telling you how many changes were made. Click Close to dismiss the alert box, and then, in the Find and Replace box, click Close. Mission accomplished.

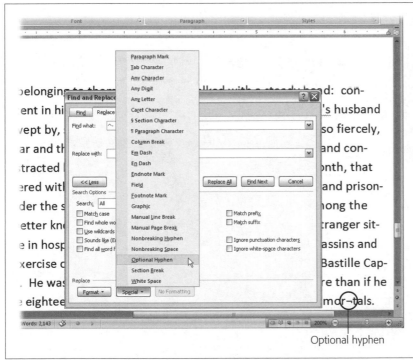

Figure 3-25:
Click the Special button on the Replace tab (Ctrl+H) to enter nonprinting characters like optional hyphens in the "Find what" or "Replace with" field. You can change your display settings to always show optional hyphens. When they aren't at the end of a line, optional hyphens look like the character between the "r" and "t" in the word "mortals" (circled).

Optional hyphen

Formatting Text, Paragraphs, and Headings

Formatting is the fine art of making your documents effective and attractive. Good formatting distinguishes different parts of your text and helps your readers take in your message. You can apply formatting to just about every element of your document, from a single character to entire paragraphs. Body text needs to be readable and easy on the eyes. Headings should be big and bold, and they should also be consistent throughout your document. Important words need to resonate with emphasis. Quotes and references should be set off from the other text.

This chapter starts with the basics: how to format individual characters and words—selecting fonts and making characters bold, italicized, underlined, or capitalized. You learn how to format paragraphs with indents and spacing, and how to control the way Word breaks up the words in a line and the lines in a paragraph. Finally, you find out how to copy and reuse formatting with tools like the Format Painter and style sets.

Formatting Basics

Word deals with formatting on three levels encompassing small and specific on up to big and broad—through characters, paragraphs, and sections. You apply different types of formatting to each of these parts. Character formatting includes selecting a font, a font size, bold or italics, and so on. At the paragraph level, you apply indents, bullets, and line spacing. For each section of your document (even if there's only one), you set the page size, orientation, and margins, as described in the previous chapter. Sometimes it helps to think of the parts of a document as Russian nesting dolls: Characters go inside paragraphs, which go inside sections, which fit inside your document.

Each type of formatting has its own dialog box, giving you access to all possible settings. You can also apply most types of formatting via the ribbon, the mini-toolbar, or the keyboard shortcut.

- **Characters.** Use the Font dialog box (Alt+H, FN) to format characters. Letters, numbers, and punctuation marks are all printable characters and, as such, you can format them. Once you select a character or a group of characters, you can apply any of the formatting commands on the Home tab's Font group (Alt+H). You can choose a font and a size for any character in your document. You can make characters bold, underlined, superscript, or change them to just about any color of the rainbow.

Note: Prior to the use of computers, groups of letters, numbers, and punctuation of a certain style, such as Helvetica or Bodoni, were called *typefaces*. The term *font* was more specific, referring to variations within a typeface such as bold, narrow, or italic. Today, the terms are interchangeable. Word uses the term *font*, probably because it's shorter and therefore easier to fit into a dialog box.

- **Paragraphs.** Use the Paragraph dialog box (Alt+H, PG) to format paragraphs. You can set formatting for text alignment, indents, line spacing, line breaks, and paragraph breaks. You don't have to select a paragraph to format it; just click to place the insertion point within a paragraph. Because characters are part of paragraphs (remember those Russian nesting dolls), every paragraph includes a basic font description. When you select characters within a paragraph and change the font settings, you override the basic font description in the paragraph's style.

- **Sections.** Use the Page Setup dialog box (Alt+P, SP) to format sections. When you change margins, page orientation, page size, and the number of columns per page (all described in Chapter 3), you're formatting the section. Many documents have only one section, so when you make formatting changes to a section, you're actually formatting the entire document.

Note: This chapter explains how to format characters and paragraphs. Section formatting is covered in Chapter 9, beginning on page 197.

Formatting Characters

Every character in your document is formatted. The formatting describes the typeface, the size of the character, the color, and whether or not the character is underlined, bold, or capitalized. It's easy to change the formatting, and Word gives you quite a few different ways to do it. The easiest and most visual way is with the ribbon (Home → Font). You can further fine-tune the font formatting using the Font dialog box (Alt+H, FN).

For quick formatting, you may not need to go any further than the mini-toolbar that pops up when you select text for formatting. And when you get really good, you can do most of your formatting with keyboard shortcuts, never even slowing down long enough to reach for the mouse.

Whichever method you use, formatting is a two-step process. First, tell Word which text you want to format by selecting it. Then format away. Or, you can set up your formatting options first, and then begin to type. Your letters and words will be beautifully formatted from the get-go.

Formatting with the Ribbon or the Font Dialog Box

Since character formatting is one of the most often used Word features, Microsoft put the most popular settings right on the Home tab. If you don't see what you're looking for there, then you must open the Font dialog box. The good thing about the dialog box is that it puts all your character formatting options in one place so you can quickly make multiple changes. It's one-stop shopping if you want to change the typeface and the size, and add that pink double-underline.

Here are the steps:

1. **Select a group of characters, as shown in Figure 4-1.**

   You can use any of the selection methods described in Chapter 2. You can drag to select a single character. You can double-click to select a word. Or you can move the mouse cursor to the left side of a paragraph, and then double-click to select the whole paragraph.

   Of course, if you haven't typed anything yet, you can always go right to the ribbon and make your formatting choices first. Then type away.

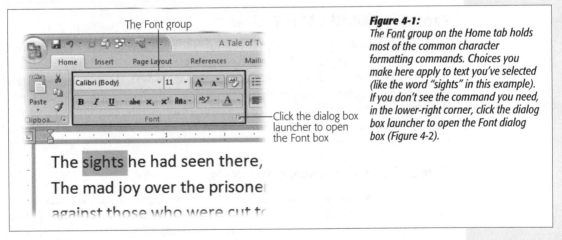

The Font group

Click the dialog box launcher to open the Font box

Figure 4-1:
The Font group on the Home tab holds most of the common character formatting commands. Choices you make here apply to text you've selected (like the word "sights" in this example). If you don't see the command you need, in the lower-right corner, click the dialog box launcher to open the Font dialog box (Figure 4-2).

2. **Go to Home → Font or the Font dialog box (click the little launcher button shown in Figure 4-1 or press Alt+H, FN) and make your formatting choices.**

   Many of the buttons in the Font group act like toggles. So, when you select text and click the underline button, Word underlines all the characters in the selection. When you click the underline button again, the underline goes away.

If you can't find the command you want on the ribbon, or if you want to make several character formatting changes at once, then open the Font box (Figure 4-2).

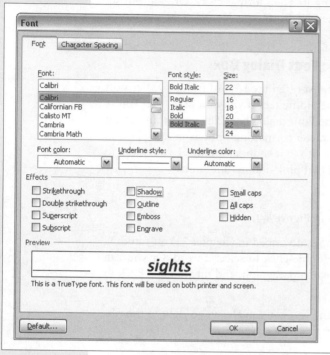

Figure 4-2:
Open the Font box (Alt+H+FN) to change the typeface, style, size, color, and other effects. Like many dialog boxes, the Font box gives you access to more commands than you find on the ribbon.

Formatting with the Mini Toolbar

Word's Mini Toolbar isn't quite as much fun as your hotel room's mini-bar, but there are times when you'll be glad it's there. A new feature in Word 2007, the Mini Toolbar pops up after you've selected text (Figure 4-3). It's faint at first, but if you move your mouse toward it, the Mini Toolbar comes into focus showing commands, most of which are character formatting commands. Just click one of the buttons to format your selection (or move your mouse away from the toolbar if you want it to go away).

Formatting with Keyboard Shortcuts

When you're typing away and the muses are moving you, it's a lot easier to hit Ctrl+I to italicize a word than it is to take your hands off the keyboard and grab a mouse. Because most formatting commands work like toggles, formatting options like bold, underline, and italics become second nature. For example, to italicize a word, just press Ctrl+I at the beginning, type the word, and then press Ctrl+I at the end. Table 4-1 is your cheat sheet to every character formatting shortcut known to Word.

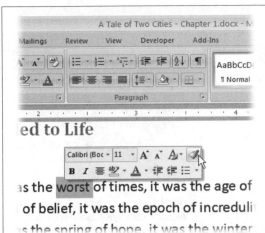

Figure 4-3:
The mini-toolbar gives you access to the most commonly used commands. It just so happens that most of these commands are character formatting commands.

Table 4-1. *As a result of Word's evolution, most formatting commands have more than one keyboard shortcut. A new set of keyboard shortcuts is part of the reorganization that came up with Word 2007's new ribbon feature. But if commands like Ctrl+B for bold and Ctrl+U for underline are permanently burned into your brain, don't worry: Those commands from previous versions still work just fine.*

Command	Keyboard Shortcut	Old Keyboard Shortcut	Description
Font	Alt+H, FF; arrow keys; Enter	Ctrl+D; arrow keys; Enter	Alt+H, FF selects the font drop-down menu; use the arrow keys to highlight the font; press Enter to finish the selection.
Font Size	Alt+H, FS; arrow keys; Enter	Ctrl+Shift+P; arrow keys; Enter	Alt+H, FS selects the font size drop-down menu; use the arrow keys to highlight the size; press Enter to finish the selection.
Increase Font Size	Alt+H, FG	Ctrl+>	Increases font size.
Decrease Font Size	Alt+H, FK	Ctrl+<	Decreases font size.
Bold	Alt+H,1	Ctrl+B	Toggles bold on and off.
Italic	Alt+H,2	Ctrl+I	Toggles italics on and off.
Underline	Alt+H, 3; Enter	Ctrl+U	Toggles underline on and off.
Double underline	Alt+H, 3; down arrow; Enter	Ctrl+Shift+D	Toggles double underline on and off.
Underline style	Alt+H, 3; arrow keys		Alt+H, 3 selects the underline style drop-down menu; use the arrow keys to highlight the style; press Enter to finish the selection.
Strikethrough	Alt+H, 4		Toggles strikethrough on and off.

Command	Keyboard Shortcut	Old Keyboard Shortcut	Description
Subscript	Alt+H, 5	Ctrl+=	Toggles subscript on and off.
Superscript	Alt+H, 6	Ctrl++	Toggles superscript on and off.
Change Case	Alt+H, 7; arrow keys	Shift+F3	Toggles through five case options: sentence case, lowercase, uppercase, capitalize each word, toggle case.
Color	Alt+H, FC; arrow keys; Enter		Alt+H, FS FC selects the font color drop-down menu; use the arrow keys to highlight the color; press Enter to finish the selection.
Highlight Text	Alt+H, I; Enter		Alt+H, I selects the highlight drop-down menu; Enter highlights the selection.
Clear formatting	Alt+H, E	Ctrl+Spacebar	Removes text formatting from the selection.

NOSTALGIA CORNER

Where's the Animated Type?

In what may be an unprecedented move, Microsoft actually *reduced* the number of text formatting options in Word 2007. Fortunately, the defunct feature is something most folks won't miss—animated type. In Word 2003, Alt+O, FX opened the Effects panel on the Font dialog box. There you found such animated effects as Blinking Background, Las Vegas Lights, Marching Black Ants, Marching Red Ants, Shimmer, and Sparkle. (Microsoft intended these effects for use on Web sites, of course, not on printed documents.)

Presumably, the general public had good enough taste to shun these annoying type effects, and Microsoft dropped them due to disuse.

In any case, if you absolutely must have red marching ants dancing around the perimeter of your letters, the only way to enlist them is to cut and paste preformatted text from an older version of Word.

Changing Capitalization

Any letter can be uppercase or lowercase, but when you get to words and sentences, you find some variations on the theme. It's not unusual to have a heading or a company name where all the letters are capitalized. Sentences start with an initial cap on the first word only, and titles usually have the major words capped. In an effort to automate anything that can possibly be automated, Microsoft provides the Change Case menu (Alt+H, 7) on the ribbon (Figure 4-4).

The Change Case command defies the usual rules about selecting before you apply character formatting. If you don't select anything, Word assumes you want to apply the Change Case command to an entire word, so the program selects the word at the insertion point. If you've selected text, the command works, as you'd expect, only on the selection.

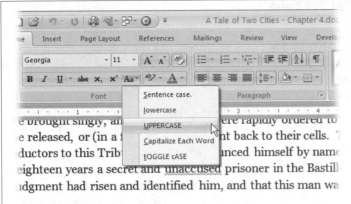

Figure 4-4:
The Change Case menu gives you five ways to change the case of a selection. To open it, click the button that looks like two letter As.

Small caps for headers

Small caps (Figure 4-5) are another variation on the capitalization theme. You won't find this option on the Change Case button; for small caps you have to use the Font dialog box, which you find on the right side under Effects (where underline or strikethrough are). Small caps are great for headings and letterhead (especially if you're a lawyer or an accountant), but you wouldn't want to use them for body text. It's difficult to read all capitalized text for an entire paragraph.

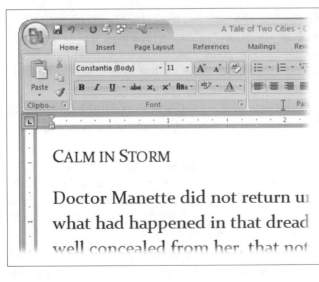

Figure 4-5:
Small caps are a great way to distinguish a heading or subheading from body text, like the words "Calm in Storm." Initial letters get full-sized capitals while the letters that would normally be lowercase get small capitals.

Formatting Paragraphs

Formatting a paragraph usually entails changing its shape. You may be squeezing it in with indents or stretching it out with additional line spacing. Other kinds of formatting change a paragraph's very nature, like adding a border or making it part of a numbered or bulleted list. The Paragraph formatting group (Home → Paragraph) is right next door to the Font group (Figure 4-6). You don't need to *select* text to format a paragraph; just make sure the insertion point is in the paragraph you want to format. However, if you want to format several paragraphs at once, select them all before you apply a command.

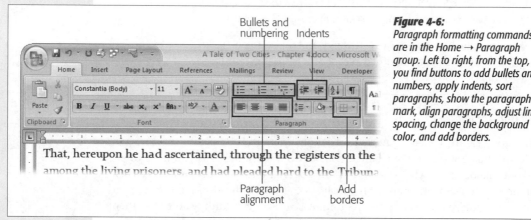

Figure 4-6:
Paragraph formatting commands are in the Home → Paragraph group. Left to right, from the top, you find buttons to add bullets and numbers, apply indents, sort paragraphs, show the paragraph mark, align paragraphs, adjust line spacing, change the background color, and add borders.

Aligning Text

It's easy to apply alignment to text. With your insertion point in the paragraph you want to change, click one of the alignment buttons in the Paragraph group on the Home Tab. For example, Home → Paragraph → Left sets the current paragraph's alignment. As shown in Figure 4-7, you have four choices when it comes to aligning your paragraphs:

- **Left (Alt+H, AL).** Aligns the lines in the paragraph flush on the left side and ragged on the right. Left alignment is standard for letters, reports, and many business documents.

- **Centered (Alt+H, AC).** Centers each line in the paragraph, leaving both left and right margins ragged. This setting is appropriate for headings and short chunks of text, as in invitations and advertisements. Avoid using centered text for long paragraphs, since it's hard for readers' eyes to track from the end of one line to the beginning of the next when the left margin is uneven.

- **Right (Alt+H, AR).** Aligns the lines in the paragraph flush on the right side and ragged on the left. This unusual alignment is most often used for setting captions or quotations apart from the main text.

- **Justified (Alt+H, AJ).** Adds space between letters and words so that both the left and right sides of the paragraph are straight and flush with the margins. Justified margins give text a more formal look suitable for textbooks or scholarly documents. If your justified text looks odd because big gaps appear between the letters or words, try using a long line—that is, putting more characters per line. You can do this by extending the margins (Alt+P, M) or by changing the size of your font (Alt+H, FS).

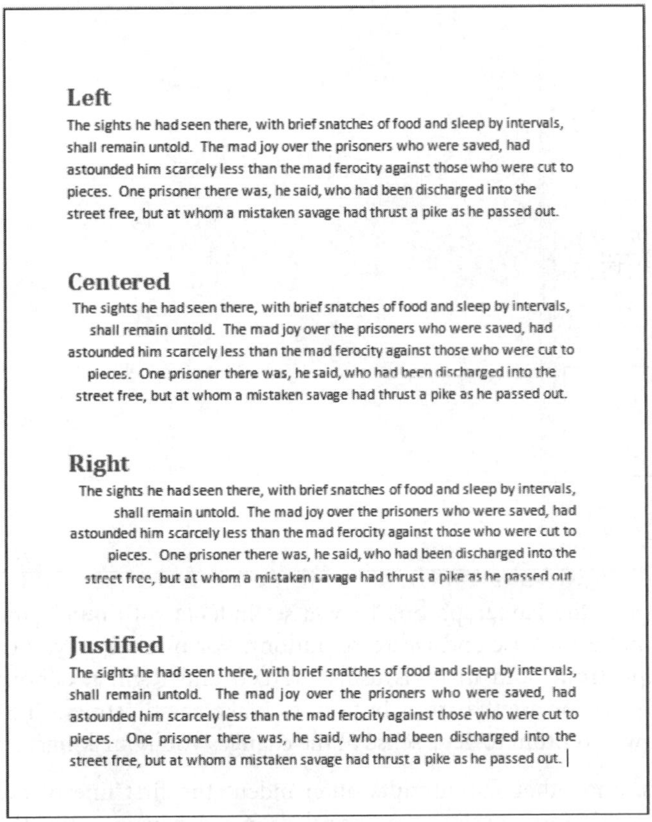

Figure 4-7:
Set the alignment of your paragraphs using the buttons on the ribbon. Four settings are available: Left, Centered, Right, and Justified.

Left

The sights he had seen there, with brief snatches of food and sleep by intervals, shall remain untold. The mad joy over the prisoners who were saved, had astounded him scarcely less than the mad ferocity against those who were cut to pieces. One prisoner there was, he said, who had been discharged into the street free, but at whom a mistaken savage had thrust a pike as he passed out.

Centered

The sights he had seen there, with brief snatches of food and sleep by intervals, shall remain untold. The mad joy over the prisoners who were saved, had astounded him scarcely less than the mad ferocity against those who were cut to pieces. One prisoner there was, he said, who had been discharged into the street free, but at whom a mistaken savage had thrust a pike as he passed out.

Right

The sights he had seen there, with brief snatches of food and sleep by intervals, shall remain untold. The mad joy over the prisoners who were saved, had astounded him scarcely less than the mad ferocity against those who were cut to pieces. One prisoner there was, he said, who had been discharged into the street free, but at whom a mistaken savage had thrust a pike as he passed out

Justified

The sights he had seen there, with brief snatches of food and sleep by intervals, shall remain untold. The mad joy over the prisoners who were saved, had astounded him scarcely less than the mad ferocity against those who were cut to pieces. One prisoner there was, he said, who had been discharged into the street free, but at whom a mistaken savage had thrust a pike as he passed out. |

Indenting Paragraphs

One of the most common reasons for indenting a paragraph is to set off quoted text from the rest of the document. Usually, you move the paragraph's left edge in about a half inch from the left margin. Word makes it easy to indent text in this way. Just use the Increase Indent button on the ribbon (shown back in Figure 4-6) or the shortcut Alt+H, AI. If you change your mind and want to remove the indent, use the companion command Decrease Indent (Alt+H, AO).

The ribbon buttons handle most everyday indentation chores, but what if you need to customize your indents? To do that, open the Paragraph dialog box to the

Indents and Spacing tab (Alt+H, PG), and you see the Indentation tools in the middle of the tab (Figure 4-8).

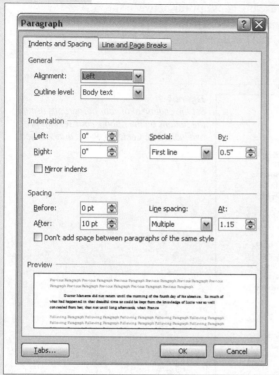

Figure 4-8:
The Paragraph box is divided into four sections. From the top you see: General, Indentation, Spacing, and Preview. As you adjust your paragraph formatting using tools from the first three groups, you see the changes take place in an example paragraph in the Preview window.

The indentation tools in the Paragraph box let you set indents with much more precision than the simple Increase and Decrease buttons. For one thing, you can indent your paragraph from both margins using the Left and Right text boxes. Type a number in the box or use the arrow buttons to make an adjustment. Look in the Preview window at bottom to get a sense of the changes you're making.

Novels, short stories, and other manuscripts often indent the first line of each paragraph. To set up this format, click the Special drop-down menu, and then choose "First line." Type a number, in inches, in the By box on the right. A quarter inch (.25") is usually an attractive first-line indent.

Tip: By the way, don't hit Tab to create a first-line indent. For one thing, it creates an amateurish, type-writer-like half-inch indent. And you lose all the benefits of paragraph formatting. For example, when you press Enter to start a new paragraph, Word automatically carries your settings forward, with a perfect first-line indent just like the paragraph above. If you use the Tab key, you have to remember to hit it at the beginning of every paragraph, and there's the danger of messing up your indents if you change the tab settings (page 109).

For the reverse of the "First line" indent, choose the hanging indent where the first line extends to the left margin, while the rest of the paragraph is indented the amount shown in the By box. This kind of indentation makes great looking glossaries, bibliographies, and such.

Spacing Between Paragraphs

For documents like business letters or reports that use block-style paragraphs, there's usually a little space between each. You can adjust this spacing between paragraphs to set off some blocks of text from the rest.

Use the Paragraph dialog box (Figure 4-8) to adjust the distance between paragraphs. On the left, you can enter numbers to set the space before the paragraph and the space after. With body text paragraphs, it's good to set the same, relatively small distance before and after—say, three points. For headers, you may want to put a little extra space before the header to distance it from the preceding text. That space makes it clear that the header is related to the text beneath it. Generally speaking, the more significant the header, the larger the type and the greater the spacing around it.

Spacing Between Lines

In the Paragraph box, to the right of the paragraph spacing controls, you find the "Line spacing" tools. Use these controls to set the distance between lines *within* paragraphs. You have three presets and three custom settings:

- **Single** keeps the lines close together, with a minimum amount of space between. Single spacing is usually easy to read, and it sure saves paper.

- **1.5 lines** gives your text a little more breathing room, and still offers a nice professional look.

- **Double** is the option preferred by teachers and editors, so there's plenty of room for their helpful comments.

- **At least** is a good option if you have a mix of font sizes or include inline graphics with your text. This option ensures that everything fits, as Figure 4-9 illustrates.

- **Exactly** puts you in control. Type a number in the At box, and Word won't mess with that setting.

- **Multiple** is the oddball of the bunch. Think of Multiple as a percentage of a single line space: 1=100 percent; .8=80 percent; 1.2=120 percent; and so on.

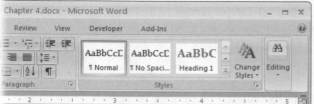

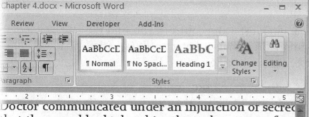

Figure 4-9:
Line spacing controls the space between lines within a paragraph. These examples show the same paragraph, with two different settings. All the type is set to 11 points except for the word "by," which is 24-point type.

Top: Using the "At least" option with 12 points entered in the At box, this setting adjusts so that the oversized word fits.

Bottom: Using the Exactly option with 12 points in the At box, the b and y get clipped off.

Inserting Page Breaks and Line Breaks

Some things just look wrong, such as a heading at the bottom of a page with no text beneath it. That heading should be at the top of the next page. Sure, you could force it over there with a page break (Ctrl+Enter), but that can cause trouble if you edit your text and things move around. You could end up with a page break in some weird spot. The solution is to adjust your Line and Page Break settings so that headings and paragraphs behave the way you want them to.

On the Paragraph box's Line and Page Breaks tab (Figure 4-10), you can adjust how paragraphs handle these breaks. The behavior becomes part of the paragraph's formatting and travels with the text no matter where you move the text or breaks. The keyboard shortcut to get there is Alt+H, PG, Alt+P. You can use four settings:

- **Widow/Orphan control.** Single lines abandoned at the top (widows) or bottom (orphans) of the page look out of place. Turn on this checkbox, and Word keeps the whole family, er, *paragraph* together.

- **Keep with next.** Certain paragraphs, like headings, need to stay attached to the paragraph that comes immediately after them. Choose the "Keep with next" option for your headings, and they always appear above following paragraph.

- **Keep lines together.** Sometimes you have a paragraph that shouldn't be split between two pages, like a one-paragraph quote or disclaimer. Use this option to keep the paragraph as one unit.

- **Page break before.** Use this command with major headings to make sure new sections of your document start on a new page.

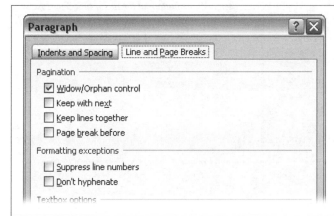

Figure 4-10:
Use the Line and Page Break settings to control the appearance of your text and to avoid awkward transitions between pages.

Creating Bulleted and Numbered Lists

Bullets and numbers add impact and help organize information. The bullets in the previous section call attention to the Line and Page Breaks commands and show that the commands are related to each other. Numbered paragraphs send a different signal, implying that the items listed are sequential or have a hierarchy. This book uses numbered paragraphs for step-by-step instructions. Meeting minutes are usually numbered, both as a point of reference and to indicate the order of the meeting's events.

Like the other paragraph formatting options, you don't have to select a paragraph to format it. It's enough just to have the insertion point in the paragraph. When using bullets or numbers, you usually want to format more than one paragraph. To do that, make a selection, and then click the bullet or number button.

Bulleted paragraphs

It's easy to turn an ordinary paragraph into a bulleted paragraph—Word does all the heavy lifting for you. You may spend more time choosing a bullet style than applying it.

Here's how to create a bulleted list:

1. **Go to Home → Paragraph, and then click the triangle next to the Bullet button to open the Bullets menu (or press Alt+H, U).**

   At the top of the menu (Figure 4-11), you see bullet styles that you used recently. In the middle, you see your Bullet Library. The bottom section shows bullet styles that have already been used in the document. At the very bottom are two commands for customizing bullets.

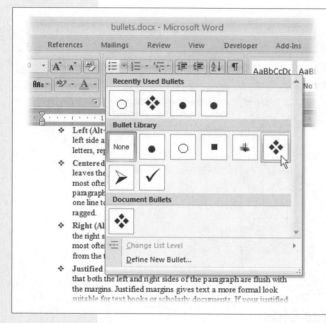

Figure 4-11:
The Bullet menu provides choices from the traditional filled circle to more contemporary options. If you have your own ideas for bullet design, at the bottom of the menu click Define New Bullet.

2. **On the Bullets menu, click to choose a bullet style.**

   When you click a bullet to apply that style to the paragraph, a couple of things happen. Word adds the bullet and automatically formats the paragraph with a hanging indent (page 101), so that the first line of the paragraph extends farther to the left than the other lines. The bullet appears in this overhang, calling attention to the bullet and setting off the paragraph from the other body text.

3. **Type some text, and then press Enter to start a new paragraph.**

   When you hit Enter to create a new paragraph, Word assumes that you're continuing with your bulleted list, so it adds the same bullet and indent automatically. You don't have to do anything; just keep on writing.

4. **When you're through with your bulleted list, press Enter, and then click the Home → Paragraph → Bullet button again to turn off bullet formatting.**

   The paragraph with the insertion point changes from a bulleted paragraph to a normal paragraph.

If you have a few paragraphs that you've already written, and you want to change them to bulleted paragraphs, just select all the paragraphs, and then click the Bullet button.

Customizing bullets

You don't have to settle for the bullets shown on the menu—Word has more choices tucked away. You can even use your own graphics for bullets, like a miniaturized version of your company logo. To explore the Bullet options available to you, open the Bullet menu (Alt+H, U), and then, at the bottom of the menu, click Define New Bullet. The Define New Bullet Box opens, showing you three buttons at the top: Symbol, Picture, and Font. Use the Symbol to browse through additional bullet options that are built into Word's type libraries. Use the Font button to apply character styles to your choice such as font size, shadow, or bold formatting.

The middle button is the most interesting—it opens the Picture Bullet box (Figure 4-12) where you see a whole slew of bullets based on picture files. These files are the same sort used for drawings and photographs, with filename extensions like .jpg, .gif, .pct, and .emf. In addition to these dozens of bullet options, you can use your own picture or graphic files as bullets. Just click the Import button at the bottom-left corner to open the Add Clips to Organizer box. Use this Windows file box to select any picture on your computer and add it to your bullet library.

Numbered paragraphs

In most cases, numbered paragraphs work just like bulleted paragraphs. You can follow the step-by-step instructions in the previous section for making bulleted paragraphs to make numbered paragraphs. Just click the Numbering button, and then choose a number style (Figure 4-13).

The main distinction between the numbered paragraphs and the bulleted paragraphs is in the options. For numbered paragraphs, you can choose from Arabic numbers, Roman numerals, numbers set off by parentheses, and alphabetic sequences. You can even use words such as One, Two, Three, or First, Second, Third.

Multilevel lists

Multilevel lists are a more advanced numbering format. They help you create project and document outlines, as well as legal documents divided into articles and sections. In a multilevel list, each new level is indented (nudged to the right), and usually each new level has a new number format (Figure 4-14). In addition to

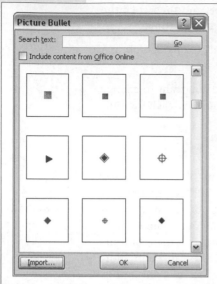

Figure 4-12:
Open the Picture Bullet box to see bullets based on picture files like JPEG and GIF. If you have pictures or drawings on your computer that you want to use as bullets, then click the Import button in the lower-left corner.

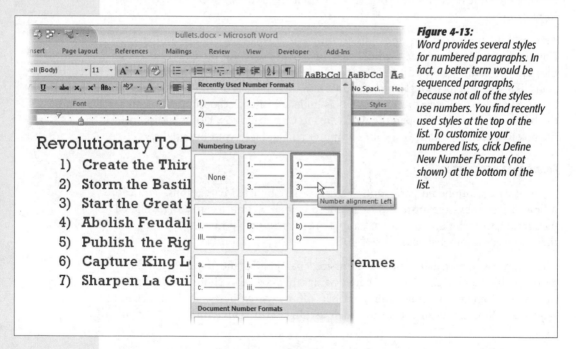

Figure 4-13:
Word provides several styles for numbered paragraphs. In fact, a better term would be sequenced paragraphs, because not all of the styles use numbers. You find recently used styles at the top of the list. To customize your numbered lists, click Define New Number Format (not shown) at the bottom of the list.

outline and legal numbering, multilevel lists can use bullets instead of numbers. So for example, you can create a bulleted list that uses squares for level one, triangles for level two, and circles for level three. If you choose a bulleted multilevel list, the lines within the levels aren't sequenced; they're just bulleted.

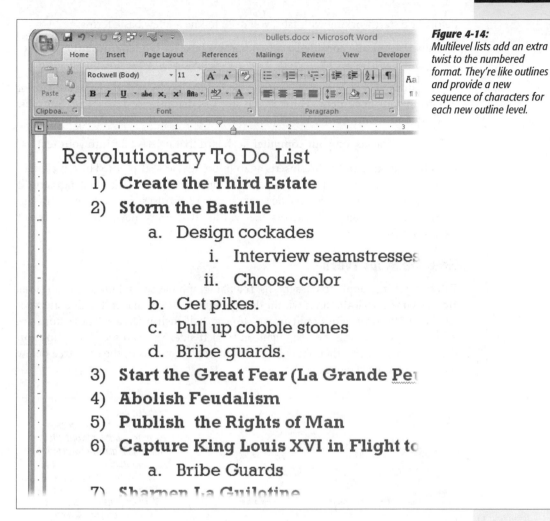

Figure 4-14:
Multilevel lists add an extra twist to the numbered format. They're like outlines and provide a new sequence of characters for each new outline level.

Setting Tabs

The lowly Tab key contains more power than you may think. Sure, you can use the Tab key to scoot the insertion point across the page in half-inch increments. But Word's tab tool is capable of much loftier feats: You can use it to design a dinner menu, create a playbill, or develop a series of consistently formatted reports.

Tab stops are all about precision alignment, giving you control over the way you present text and numbers to your readers. For example, on your dinner menu you can use *tab leaders* (dotted lines like the ones in this book's table of contents) so that your reader's eye tracks from Wild Salmon to the exceptionally reasonable price you're asking. Once you have settings you like, you can save and reuse them. (How's that for efficiency?)

Before you start working with tabs, you need to know a few basic terms:

- **Tabs.** Technically considered *tab characters*, tabs are hidden formatting characters, similar to space characters. Tabs are embedded in your document's text.

- **Tab stops.** These paragraph settings define the position and characteristics of tabs in your document. Think of tab stops as definitions, describing your tabs. To define them, you use Word tools, like the Ruler or the Tabs dialog box.

- **Tab key.** The key on your computer keyboard that inserts tabs into your text.

Press the Tab key, and Word inserts a tab in the text at that point. The tab character makes the insertion point jump left to right and stop at the first tab stop it reaches. If you haven't set any new tab stops, Word uses the built-in set of tab stops—one every half inch across the width—that every new, blank document starts out with.

How Tab Stops Work

Tab stop settings apply to paragraphs. If a paragraph has several lines, the tab stops are the same for all the lines within that paragraph. If you haven't deliberately set tab stops, Word provides built-in tab stops at half-inch intervals. These stops are left tab stops, meaning the text aligns on the left side. You can see all tab stops on the horizontal ruler—they show as small vertical tick marks in the gray area below the number scale (Figure 4-15).

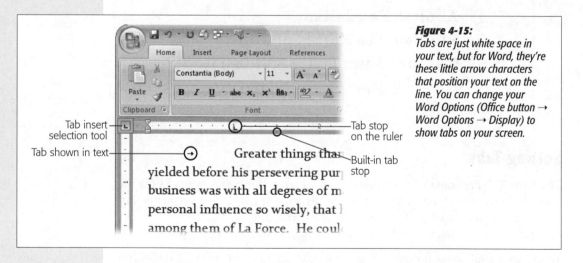

Figure 4-15:
Tabs are just white space in your text, but for Word, they're these little arrow characters that position your text on the line. You can change your Word Options (Office button → Word Options → Display) to show tabs on your screen.

Tab insert selection tool

Tab shown in text

Tab stop on the ruler

Built-in tab stop

Greater things that yielded before his persevering pur business was with all degrees of m personal influence so wisely, that l among them of La Force. He coul

---

Tip: If you don't see tab stops in the ruler, click within a paragraph. Remember, tab stops are paragraph settings, so your insertion point must be in a paragraph to see them.

Viewing Tab Marks in Your Text

Tabs are invisible on the printed page, like spaces or paragraph marks. Sometimes, when your document behaves unexpectedly, it helps to reveal the hidden characters so you can see if tabs are the culprit. After all, when they're hidden, all you see is white space on the page, however, spaces, tabs, and indents each behave quite differently.

To view tabs within your text:

1. **Choose Office button → Word Options to open the Word Options dialog box (Figure 4-16).**

   The Word Options button is at the bottom of the Office menu.

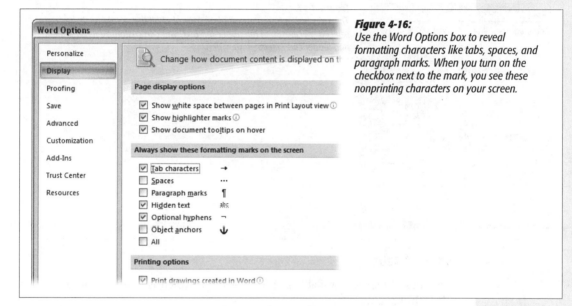

Figure 4-16:
Use the Word Options box to reveal formatting characters like tabs, spaces, and paragraph marks. When you turn on the checkbox next to the mark, you see these nonprinting characters on your screen.

2. **On the left side of the Word Options box, choose the Display option.**

   The panel on the right is divided into three parts. The top section shows page display options, the middle section shows formatting marks, and the bottom section holds printing options.

3. **In the middle group, turn on the "Tab characters" checkbox to make your tabs visible.**

   An icon next to this checkbox shows you the symbol for tab characters. This mark shows up on your computer screen but not in printed text.

4. **Click OK to save the settings and close the dialog box.**

   The box closes and you see the tabs as small arrows in your text.

Deleting and Editing Tabs

Because tabs are characters within your document, you can delete, copy, and paste them, just as you would any other character or text fragment. Maybe you want to delete a tab just click immediately after a tab character, and then press the Backspace key. You can also use the Tabs box (Figure 4-17) for to control tabs.

With tabs, you can use almost any editing trick that you'd use on other characters. You can select and drag a tab to a different place in your text. You can use shortcut keys, such as Ctrl+X to cut a tab and Ctrl+V to paste it someplace else. (All of these activities are much, much easier when you've set your Word Options to view tab marks as described previously.)

Figure 4-17:
The Tabs box puts you in complete control of all things tabular. When you select a specific tab in the upper-left box, you can customize its alignment and leader characters.

Types of Tabs

Five types of tabs are available in Word—one of which isn't a true tab but works well with the others:

- **Left tab.** The most common type of tab, it aligns text at the left side; text flows from the tab stop to the right. When you start a new, blank document, Word provides left tabs every half inch.

- **Center tab.** Keeps text centered at the tab stop. Text extends evenly left and right with the tab stop in the middle.

- **Right tab.** Aligns text to the right. Text flows backwards from the tab stop, from right to left.

- **Decimal tab.** Used to align numbers, whether or not they have decimals. Numbers align with the decimal point centered on the tab stop. Numbers without decimal points align similar to a right tab.

- **Bar tab.** The Bar tab is the oddball of the group and, no, it has nothing to do with your local watering hole. It also has nothing to do with aligning text. It inserts a vertical bar in your text as a divider. The bar appears in every line in the paragraph. This tab stop ignores tabs inserted in your text and behaves in the same manner whether or not tab characters are present.

Note: There may be a certain Microsoftian logic in grouping the bar tab with the tab feature, but Word provides other ways to place vertical lines on your pages that you may find more intuitive. You can use Insert → Insert Shapes → More and choose the line for free-form lines. Or you can use borders for paragraphs or tables.

Tab Leaders

Tab leaders help readers connect the dots by providing a trail from one tabbed item to the next. They're ideal for creating professional-looking menus, playbills, and more.

Here are some examples:

```
Hamlet, Prince of Denmark..........Sir Laurence Olivier
Ophelia, daughter to Polonius.......Roseanne Barr
```

Four Leader options can be used with each type of tab stop except the bar tab:

```
None                          No leader here
Dotted..........................You've seen this before
Dashed_ _ _ _ _ _ _ _ _ _ _ _ _ _  For a different, intermittent look
Underline_____  When only a solid line will do
```

As visual aids, leaders are quite helpful, and they work equally well for text and numbers.

Using Word's Rulers

If you're visually oriented, you may prefer the ruler for futzing with tab stops, page margins, and indents. Two rulers are available—horizontal and vertical. The horizontal ruler appears at the top of the page, giving you quick access to your tab, indent, and margin settings. To make the rulers visible, press Alt+W, R, or click the View Ruler button at the top of the righthand scroll bar (Figure 4-18).

Tip: The ruler marks off your page in the measuring units of your choice. The factory setting uses inches, but if you want to make changes, you can do that in Word Options. Go to Office button → Word Options → Advanced. Scroll down to the group under Display, and then change the drop-down menu labeled "Show measurements in units of" to your preferred units of measurement.

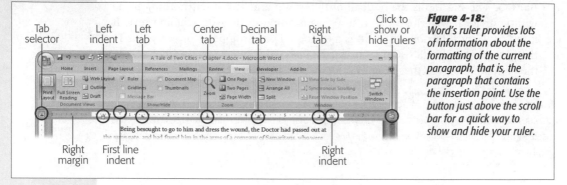

Figure 4-18:
Word's ruler provides lots of information about the formatting of the current paragraph, that is, the paragraph that contains the insertion point. Use the button just above the scroll bar for a quick way to show and hide your ruler.

Managing Tab Settings with the Ruler

In Figure 4-18, the ruler measures the page in inches. The grayed areas at both ends of the ruler indicate the page margins. The numbers on the ruler mark the distance from the left margin in both directions, left and right. Note the number 1, at the left edge of the ruler in Figure 4-18.

Setting tab stops

Word's every-half-inch tab stops can work for many of your documents, but sooner or later, you may need to put a tab stop in a different place or change its style. No problem—it's easy enough to do with the ruler.

Setting a new tab stop is a two-step process:

1. **Using the selection box to the left of the ruler, choose the type of tab you want.**

   The icon in this box shows what kind of tab you're about to apply—Left, Center, Right, Decimal, or Bar. When you hold your cursor over the box for a second or two, a little screen tip appears describing the formatting option. Click the box to cycle through the tab stop and indent options.

2. **Once you've selected the tab type you want, click the ruler to position the tab.**

   Click the point on the ruler where you want to place the tab stop. An icon appears on the ruler showing the position and the type of tab stop.

Tip: If you find the tab icons a little confusing, here's some help: Think of the vertical line as the tab stop and the horizontal line at the bottom as the direction your text flows. For example, the Left tab icon is L shaped, indicating that text flows to the right, away from the tab stop. The Center tab icon has the vertical line in the middle.

You can add an almost limitless number of tab stops—one for every tick mark on the ruler. If you need greater precision, use the Tab dialog box described on page 109. Setting a tab stop removes all the built-in tab stops to its left, but the ones to the right remain.

Adjusting and removing tab stops with the ruler

If a tab stop isn't exactly where you want it, you don't have to delete it—just drag it to a new position on the ruler. If you wish to remove a tab stop, drag it up or down off the ruler, and it disappears. When you make these changes, your document shows the consequences. Any tabs in your text shift over to the next readily available tab stop, which can be a built-in tab stop or one that you've set.

Setting Margins with the Ruler

You can always use the Page Layout tools (Page Layout → Page Setup → Margins or Alt+P, M) to set your margins with a click of the mouse, but for visual control, nothing beats the ruler (Figure 4-19). The lighter part of the ruler shows the text area, and the darker part shows your margins. Making adjustments is simply a matter of clicking and dragging the margin to a new location. Keep in mind that changing your margin affects the entire document section; more often than not, that means it affects the entire document because many documents are a single section. (For more details on working with sections, see page 197.)

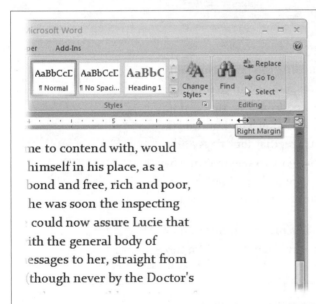

Figure 4-19:
Hold your cursor over the margin boundary on the ruler, and it changes to a double arrow, as shown here. The screen tip shows what you're pointing to— the right margin, in this case. Drag the boundary to a new location to change your document margins.

Tip: To avoid confusion, remember that indents are used to change the width of a single paragraph, while margins are used to change the paragraph width for an entire section or document.

Adjusting Paragraph Indents with the Ruler

Using the ruler to adjust indentation is similar to changing margins. It's just a matter of clicking and dragging. Indents are bit more complicated because you have a few more options, and that means more tools and widgets (Figure 4-20).

It can take awhile to get used to adjusting paragraph indents with the ruler. For one thing, you need a steady hand and accurate clicking to zero in on those little triangle buttons. The top triangle sets the first line indent and moves independently. The bottom triangle creates a hanging indent, and you can move it independently too, as long as you grab only that triangle. That little box below the triangle is your left indent, and if you drag it, both it and the top (first line) indent marker move together.

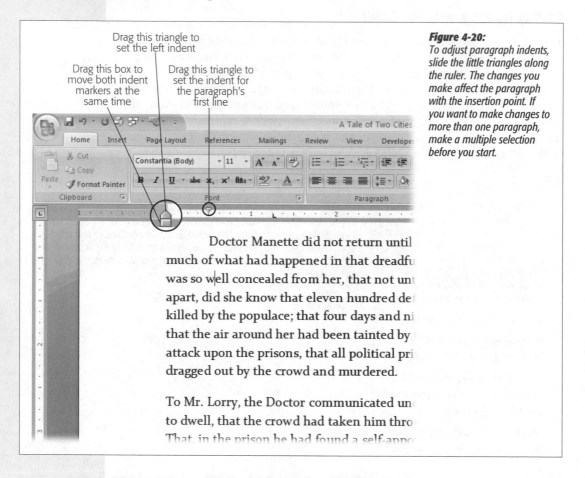

Figure 4-20:
To adjust paragraph indents, slide the little triangles along the ruler. The changes you make affect the paragraph with the insertion point. If you want to make changes to more than one paragraph, make a multiple selection before you start.

Fast Formatting with Format Painter

Whether it's a special heading or a paragraph of text, formatting a paragraph just the way you want it is a lot of work. Once you have the margins, indents, and tabs in place, and you've got the font style and size set, you've invested a chunk of time in the project. Fortunately, you can capitalize on that investment. The Format Painter works like magic. You can use it to copy the formatting of a word, heading, or paragraph onto something else. You don't have to worry about any of the formatting details. You don't even need to *know* how something is formatted, so long as you like the way it looks.

Here's how it works:

1. **Select the character or paragraph with the formatting that you want to copy.**

   You can copy and paint either the character or the paragraph formatting. If you want to copy just text formatting (font, size, text color, and so on), select a few letters or a word with that formatting, not the whole paragraph. Selecting an entire paragraph, complete with the paragraph mark at the end, copies both the character formatting and the paragraph formatting. If you don't select anything, the Format Painter uses the formatting from the current paragraph, so to copy paragraph formatting alone (for example, tabs and indents), just click anywhere in the paragraph.

2. **Go to Home → Clipboard and click the Format Painter button, or just press Alt+H, FP.**

   Your cursor acquires a tiny paintbrush icon. If you have only one quick change to make, just click the Format Painter once. However, if you want to copy the same formatting to several different locations, double-click the Format Painter. When you double-click, the button stays locked down, indicating that it will stay on and let you paint multiple times until you're ready to stop.

3. **Drag the Format Painter over the text or paragraph that you want to change.**

   Here's the fun part. Like magic, your selection takes on all the formatting that you copied. If you double-clicked for multiple format painting, you can keep on dragging over text or clicking paragraphs. When you're through, hit Esc. The Format Painter button pops back up, and your cursor changes back to its normal I-beam appearance.

Formatting with Styles

Like the Format Painter, Word's styles are great time-savers because they let you apply a whole bunch of formatting commands in one fell swoop. Unlike Format Painter, Word's styles are permanent repositories of formatting information that you can always apply with one click. So, if you've discovered or created the perfect style (formatting) for a heading, you can apply that same style to headings today, tomorrow, or a week from tomorrow.

Microsoft provides sets of predesigned Quick Styles. These sets include a Normal style for body text and a number of Heading styles. You can also find a variety of styles for lists, quotes, references, and for paragraphs or text that deserve special emphasis. With a click of your mouse, you can apply any one of these styles and make dramatic changes to your document (Figure 4-21).

Some styles define character formatting, such as font, font size, font style, and special effects such as underlining or strikethrough. Other styles define both character formatting and paragraph formatting. Paragraph formatting includes things like paragraph alignment, line spacing, bullets, numbering, indents, and tab settings.

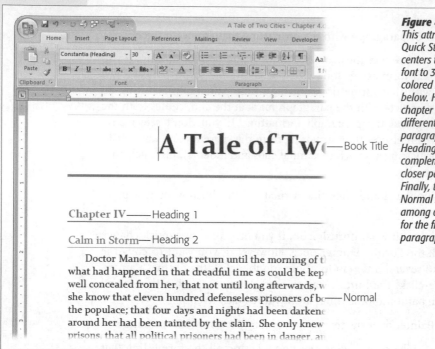

Figure 4-21:
This attractive page uses four Quick Styles: Book Title style centers the text and sets the font to 30-point Constantia with colored borders above and below. Heading 1 for the chapter heading uses a different color and generous paragraph spacing. The Heading 2 spec uses a complementary color and closer paragraph spacing. Finally, the body text uses the Normal style, which provides, among other things, an indent for the first line of each paragraph.

Applying Quick Styles

It's easy to preview and apply a style to your text. The action takes place in the Styles group on the Home tab. Follow these steps:

1. **Select the text or paragraph that you want to format.**

   When you want to apply a style to an entire paragraph, just click to put the insertion point in that paragraph. When you want to apply a style to text, you need to select the text first.

2. **Go to Home → Styles and hold your cursor over a style to see a live preview in your document.**

   The Styles group shows a few styles right on the ribbon. To see more styles, use the arrows on the right to scroll through the list, or click the button at bottom to open the entire menu (Figure 4-22).

   When you hold the mouse cursor over a style, the text in your document changes, showing you the effect of applying that style.

3. **Click to apply the style.**

   When you click a style on the ribbon or in the menu, Word applies that style to your paragraph or text selection.

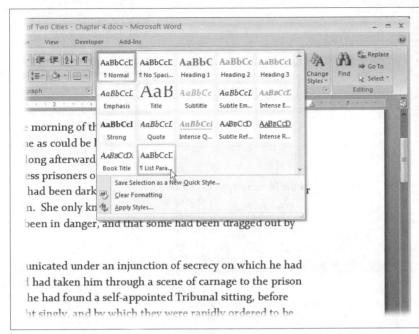

Figure 4-22:
Each style is a collection of formatting commands that you can apply with a mouse click. To browse the available styles, go to Home → Styles. When you hold your mouse over a style, the text in your document changes, giving you a live preview of the style. Word offers dozens of predesigned Quick Styles, or you can create your own.

Modifying Styles

When you apply a style to a paragraph of text, you do more than just change its formatting. In essence, you've attached that style to the paragraph. If you make changes to that style later, the paragraph reflects those changes. Imagine that you have a style called Heading 1 that centers the headings on the page. You've used this style repeatedly throughout your 400-page novel about the French Revolution. Say, you decide your novel would look better with that heading aligned on the left margin rather than centered. Instead of making the change to each individual heading, you edit the Heading 1 style. When you change the style definition, all your headings that are based on the Heading 1 style change to match.

Here are the steps to modifying a style. In this example, you give the Heading 1 style left alignment:

1. **Go to Home → Styles and click the Styles dialog box launcher (Figure 4-23).**

   In the Styles box, you can click to apply any one of the styles to your current selection or paragraph. Even when the Styles box is open, you can click within your text to move the insertion point to a different paragraph. And you can use the scroll bar, the PageUP and PageDN keys, or any other method to navigate through your document.

   When you hold your cursor over a style, a screen tip pops up showing you details. Turn on the Show Preview checkbox at bottom to see a more visual representation of each of the styles.

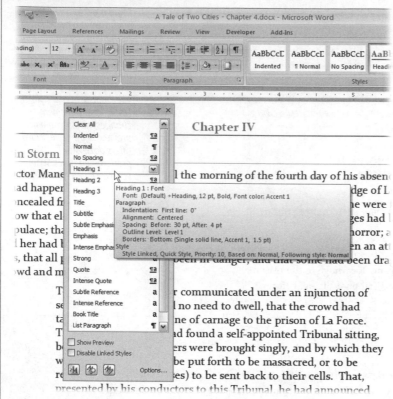

Figure 4-23:
Open the Style dialog box to see a complete list of all available styles. On the right side, a paragraph mark shows that a style includes paragraph formatting. The lowercase "a" shows that the style includes character formatting. Click the down arrow button to open a menu where you can modify the style definition.

2. **Right-click Heading 1 (or whatever style you want to change), and then choose Modify from the shortcut menu.**

   The Modify Style dialog box opens (Figure 4-24). Here you can get under the hood and tinker with all the formatting options.

   Tip: When you right-click anywhere on the style name, or click the V button in the Styles dialog box, a context menu shows you several choices for changing and working with the selected style. At the top of the list is "Update Heading 1 to Match Selection." This option changes all the formatting in the selected style so that it's identical to the current paragraph or selection.

3. **In the lower-left corner of the Modify Style box, click the Format button, and then choose Paragraph.**

   The Paragraph dialog box opens. Yep, it's exactly the same box you open when you click the Paragraph dialog box launcher on the ribbon or press Alt+H, PG (see Figure 4-8). In fact, the Format button leads you to many familiar dialog boxes, from Fonts to Borders to Tabs. The difference, of course, is that you're now changing a style format, not just a few paragraphs.

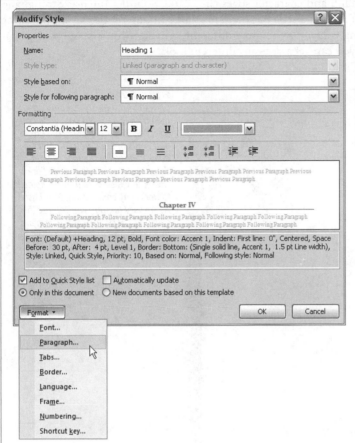

Figure 4-24:
The Modify Style box is command central for tinkering with your style definitions. The properties at the top determine the behavior of the styles when you're working with text. The preview window in the center shows an example of the style in action. Use the format button in the lower-left corner to open dialog boxes to make changes in the character and paragraph formatting.

4. **At the top of the Paragraph box, in the General group, click the Alignment drop-down menu, and then choose Left.**

   In this example, you're just making a single change, but you can also make changes to any of the other formatting options in this box.

5. **Close the Paragraph box, the Modify Style box, and the Styles box.**

   Everything's done except the cleanup. Close each of the boxes you've opened to go back to your text and continue editing.

Managing Style Sets

A *style set* is a collection of styles. Microsoft includes several predesigned style sets with Word, with names like Classic, Distinctive, Elegant, Formal, and Modern. Go to Home → Styles → Change Styles (or press Alt+H, FQ) to see them listed under the Change Styles button (Figure 4-25). Each of Word's predesigned style sets includes a Normal style, several heading styles (Heading 1, Heading 2, and so on), and other paragraph and character styles (like Title, Subtitle, Intense, Strong, and Reference). Even though a style has the same name in different sets—like Heading 1—the formatting is likely to be quite different. So when you change your document's style set, you can get a radically different look.

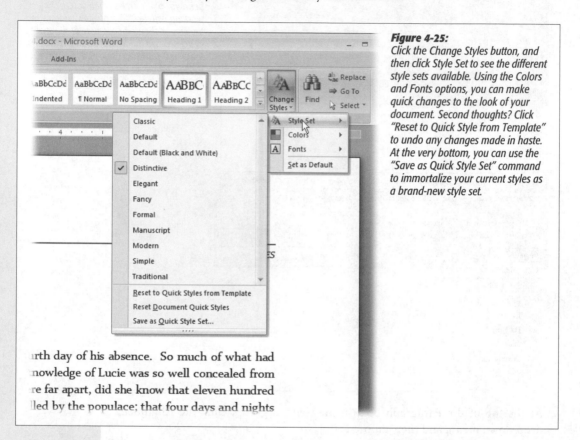

Figure 4-25:
Click the Change Styles button, and then click Style Set to see the different style sets available. Using the Colors and Fonts options, you can make quick changes to the look of your document. Second thoughts? Click "Reset to Quick Style from Template" to undo any changes made in haste. At the very bottom, you can use the "Save as Quick Style Set" command to immortalize your current styles as a brand-new style set.

The style set that's in use has a checkmark next to the name. If you move your cursor over the name of a different style set, Live Preview shows you your text formatted with that new style set. To make the change permanent, just click the name. The menu closes, and your text has a whole new look.

Creating Your Own Style Set

The best way to create your own style set is to start with one of Microsoft's predesigned sets, and then modify it. Here's a basic procedure for customize an existing style set to meet your needs.

1. **Use live preview to browse the existing style sets and choose one that's a reasonably close match to what you have in mind.**

   For example, open a document to a place where you can see a few different types of styles, like body text, some headings, and maybe a numbered or bulleted list.

2. **Go to Home → Styles → Change Styles → Style Set (Alt+H, GY). Work your way down the list of style sets, and click one that has a look that's similar to the one you want.**

The Style Sets submenu lists the style sets available. Hold your mouse cursor over the name of a style set, and live preview shows you how that style set changes your document. In the next steps, you'll modify the style set to be exactly what you want.

3. **If necessary, modify the colors and fonts using the options on the Change Styles menu.**

The first and most obvious changes you can make are to the colors and fonts. The commands to make those changes are right there on the Change Styles menu (Home → Styles → Change Styles). The previewing procedure is the same: Just hold your mouse cursor over a Font or Color style, and you see your document change. Click to choose a color or font style.

Start with the Normal paragraph style. Consider the font, font size, color, and any other character formatting that you may want to change. (But don't get crazy; after all, this is the *Normal* paragraph style.) After the Normal paragraph style, move on to the Heading styles. The font size and color you choose for your headings set the tone for your entire document.

4. **Examine the existing paragraph styles, and if necessary, make changes.**

Consider the line spacing and indents for normal paragraph. Do you want more or less space around them on the page? Choose the paragraph spacing for each heading style. Think about borders—perhaps you'd like a nice line above or below a heading.

Work your way through any of the existing paragraph or character styles that you know you'll use.

5. **Consider the paragraph styles you need, and add new ones if they're missing.**

After you've modified the existing styles, think about styles that you'd like to have but aren't part of the set. Maybe you need a numbered list, or a special sidebar paragraph with a border running all the way around it. Create whatever styles you need, and then add them to your style set.

Don't worry if you can't think of everything just now. You can always add new styles later when you're using the style set.

6. **When you're done customizing your style set, go to Home → Styles → More → Save Selection as Quick Style Set (or Atl+H, L), and then save it with a new name.**

The Save command is at the very bottom of the submenu. As a last step, save your style with a name, and it becomes one of the available style sets (Figure 4-26).

A standard Windows Save dialog box opens. Type a name for your style set in the "File name" text box, and then click Save. After you've saved it, your customized style shows on the Change Styles menu with all the rest.

Figure 4-26:
You can create a custom style set that's fine-tuned to your own specs. Once saved, your style set shows up on the Change Styles menu.

Themes and Templates

Formatting your text, headings, lists, and other page elements individually—as described in the previous couple of chapters—takes time that you may not have. And with so many choices in fonts, colors, and graphic ornaments, putting together a good-looking document can be overwhelming. No wonder so many people stuck with Times New Roman body text and Arial headings! Fortunately, graphic designers at Microsoft have created *themes*, a new Word 2007 feature that lets you apply a complete, coordinated package of fonts, colors, heading styles, and more with a single click.

While themes are all about style and appearance, *templates* are about content. Part of Word for more than a decade, templates provide boilerplate text and blank spaces for you to fill with your own information. Templates also set you up with snappy graphics and consistent margins, indents, and paragraph formatting. A good template even provides cues to tell you what information you need to fill in the blanks.

Word's themes and templates help you make your documents look like they came from a Fortune 500 company's publications division. Even if you don't know a font from a fondue, you can crank out professional looking business proposals, resumés, and more.

Note: This chapter shows you how to choose and apply Word's themes and templates. If you're interested in creating your own themes and templates, see Chapter 20.

Choosing a Theme

When you're on deadline putting together, say, a business proposal, you don't want to waste precious minutes worrying about fonts, heading colors, and the design of tables, charts, and graphs. Instead, simply choose a theme with a click of your mouse, and you've got a professional looking document (Figure 5-1).

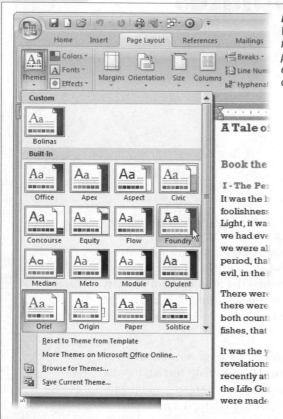

Figure 5-1:
Word 2007's themes are prepackaged collections of colors, fonts, and effects that work together to create attractive pages. Hold your mouse cursor over a theme to preview its effect on your document. Applying a theme is as simple as clicking the design you like best.

Themes are made up of three parts:

- **Colors.** Each theme contains twelve colors, each of which is assigned to a specific document part. One color (usually black) is used for body text. Another color (dark blue, say) is used for Heading 1 paragraphs. Lesser headings—like Heading 2 and Heading 3—may use a lighter shade of the same color. Other complementary colors are used for accent and hyperlinks (links to the Internet).

- **Fonts.** Each theme specifies one or two fonts—one for the body text and one for headings. Also known as typefaces, fonts define the actual shape of the letters on the screen and on the page. They have a subtle but significant effect on the appearance and feeling of a document. Some typefaces don't always play well with others, but fortunately, you don't have to worry about that when you choose themes, since their typeface combinations are always compatible.

- **Effects.** Each theme uses one of Word's 20 built-in graphic effects. These effects include design touches like shadows, line styles, 3-D, and so on. Most of these effects have more of an impact in PowerPoint presentations than in Word documents, but they come with the theme's package.

When you choose a theme, you're applying color, font, and effect formatting to the elements in your document (Figure 5-2).

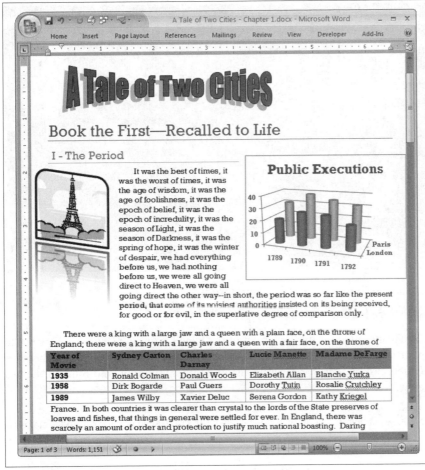

Figure 5-2:
This document shows the Foundry theme in all its glory. The theme defines the fonts and the colors used for headings, chart objects, picture borders, and tables. As you can see, even with professionally designed themes, amateurish excess can still produce an ugly page.

Here are examples of the parts of your document that take their formatting cues from the selected theme:

- **Body text.** Font, size, style, and color.

- **Headings.** Font, size, style, and color.

- **Tables.** Font specs (same as above), border and line styles, and colors.

- **Charts.** Font specs, borders, lines, chart graphic styles, and colors.

- **Picture.** Border colors.

- **Smart-Art.** Font specs, graphic colors.

- **Clip art.** Major outline and border colors.

- **Drop caps.** Font specs and color.

- **WordArt.** Font colors change, but the actual typestyle remains the same.

NOSTALGIA CORNER

PowerPoint Themes Come to Word

Microsoft first introduced *themes* in PowerPoint, the ubiquitous tool of boardroom and classroom presentations. PowerPoint themes help corporate types create attractive slides with coordinated background, highlight, and font colors, and text formatting. Themes also provide consistent formatting and colors for tables, charts, graphs, and photos. (After all, most MBA programs don't include a course in graphic design.)

With Office 2007, themes bring this same easy-to-use formatting power to Word and Excel. By using a consistent theme, you give your documents, spreadsheets, and presentations a unified, professional look.

When you're making a presentation to the board, your handouts will coordinate impressively with the onscreen presentation. Themes also make it easier to copy and paste between programs. When your Word document and spreadsheet use the same theme, you won't have to worry about changing fonts and colors after the fact. Say you use the Metro theme in Word and PowerPoint. You can do your writing in Word, and then paste excerpts of your text into your PowerPoint presentation—no reformatting necessary. As you can see in Figure 5-3, everything has a consistent look.

Here's how to choose a theme for your document:

1. **Go to Page Layout → Themes (or press Alt+P, TH).**

   The Themes menu is on the far left of the Page Layout tab (Figure 5-1). It's like an artist's palette where you see sample colors and typefaces. Themes are divided into two categories with Custom themes at the top and Built-In themes below.

Note: You see Custom Themes only if you've created your own custom document themes. For tips on how to roll your own themes, see page 449.

---

2. **If the themes aren't all visible, drag the scroll bar on the right to get a better view.**

   In the lower-right corner, the three dots indicate that you can click that spot to drag the corner and resize the menu. If you'd rather have the menu stretch across the top of your window so you can see your document beneath, then just drag the corner.

3. **With your mouse, point to a theme (but don't click) to see a Live Preview.**

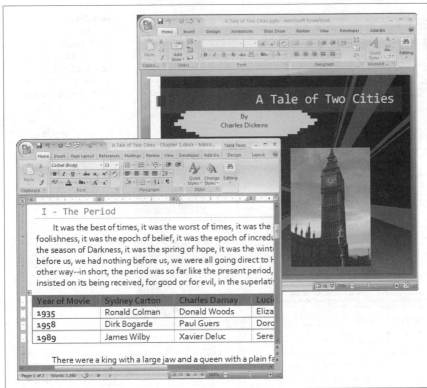

Figure 5-3:
Word, PowerPoint, and Excel share the same themes. This Word document (front) and PowerPoint presentation (rear) both use the Metro theme, giving them consistent typestyles and graphic specifications.

The Themes menu uses Microsoft's new Live Preview feature—all you have to do is point to a theme, and your document changes to show you how it will look using that theme. You can quickly view and compare the available choices. (See, computer games aren't the only programs that use all of your computer's graphics power.)

4. **Once you decide on a theme, click to select it.**

   One click chooses a theme and applies formatting changes throughout your document. Headings, borders, and lines change color. Body text, headings, and title fonts also change (Figure 5-4).

Finding More Themes

Word comes with 20 built-in themes, but you may still find yourself looking for more. Perhaps you work in an office on a computer that was set up by your employer, and someone has created official company themes that you need to use. If that's the case, then you need to know where to look for those themes on your computer, especially if you (or someone you love) have inadvertently moved them. You can also look beyond your computer: Creative types are constantly coming up with new, exciting themes and sharing them on the Web.

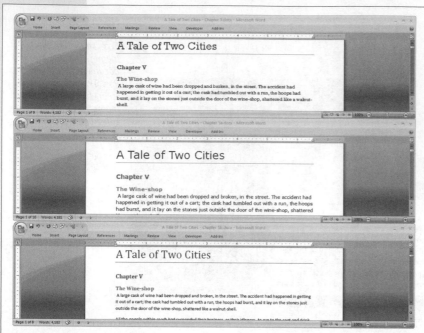

Figure 5-4:
Here's the same document with three different themes. On top is the Foundry theme with a font that looks a little like something that would come out of a typewriter. In the middle is the Aspect theme featuring Verdana—a modern looking sans-serif type. On the bottom is the Office theme, ensconced in hues of Microsoft.

Tip: It's not hard to create your own custom themes, especially if you start with an existing theme and make modifications. You'll find the details on customizing and creating your own themes on page 449.

Browsing for themes on your computer

Open the Themes menu (Page Layout → Themes → Themes or Alt+P, TH), and you find custom themes at the top of the list (Figure 5-5). Custom themes are ones that you or someone else created, and they're stored in the Document Themes folder inside your Template folder (*C:\Documents and Settings\[Your Name]\Templates\Document Themes*).

If themes are stored (or moved) somewhere else on your computer, then they won't show up on the Themes menu, but Word can help you look for them. To search for themes, click the Browse for Themes button near the bottom of the Themes menu. The Choose Theme or Themed Document box opens. As shown in Figure 5-6, this standard Windows file box is set up to show you *.thmx, *.docx, *xlsx*, and other file types that contain Office themes. The "Files of type" menu is set to Office Themes and Themed Documents, which acts as a filter, so the main window shows you only files that match these types (and folders that contain them).

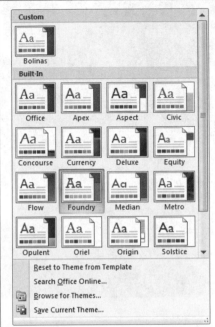

Figure 5-5:
The Themes menu shows two types of themes—Built-In and Custom. Built-In themes are predesigned themes that come with Word. Themes that you or someone else created appear at the top of the list.

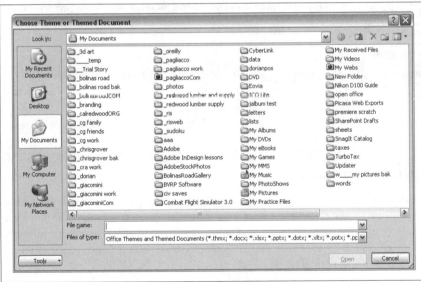

Figure 5-6:
If you click Browse for Themes, then you get a standard Windows file box. You can use this box to navigate through your system to seek out files that end in ".thmx." And if you can't find themes this way, see the box on page 133 for another way to search.

Moving Themes to Your Themes Folder

If you frequently browse to use a custom theme, then you'll save time copying the theme to your Document Themes folder. That way, the theme always shows up in the Custom group on the Themes menu, and you'll never have to search for it again. Here's how to move a theme from your My Documents folder to your Document Themes folder:

1. Choose Page Layout → Themes → Themes → Browse for Themes to open the Choose Theme or Themed Document box (Figure 5-6).

2. Use the buttons on the left and the drop-down menu at the top to hunt down a folder with Office themes. (Theme files end in .thmx.)

3. When you find the file you want to copy, right-click it, and then choose Copy from the File shortcut menu.

4. Navigate to your Document Themes folder. If you sign on to your computer with the name *Christopher*, then start in your My Computer window, and go to *C:\Documents and Settings\Christopher\Templates\Document Themes* (Figure 5-7).

5. Right-click an empty spot in the Document Themes folder, and then choose Paste.

You see your Themes document added to the Document Themes folder. Open your Themes menu, and it's there at the top of the list.

Figure 5-7:
Word stores themes in a folder inside your Templates folder. Microsoft likes to hide this folder so you won't find it with your other files in your My Documents folder. Instead, you must look in the Documents and Settings folder on your hard drive. On most computers that's Local Disk (C:).

Searching for themes online

You can look for themes on the Internet, too. A good place to start is Microsoft Office Online (*www.microsoft.com/office*), shown in Figure 5-8. As time goes on, it's likely that more themes, fonts, and colors will be available. And don't forget to do a Google search. Type *Office 2007 themes* in Google's search box, and you'll see at least a half million entries.

Searching for Themes on Your Computer

If you think themes may be hiding on your computer that aren't in your My Documents folder, then you can search them out using Windows Explorer.

1. Go to Start → My Documents.

   Windows Explorer opens and you see the contents of a folder in the large box on the right. The panel on the left changes as you click buttons and menu commands.

2. Near the top of the window, click Search (or press Ctrl+F) to open the Search task pane.

   At the pane's left, click the "All files and folders" button (since you want to search your entire computer).

3. In the "All or part of the file name" box, type *.thmx. (The asterisk (*) character is a wild card that matches any file name with any number of characters.)

So when you enter *.thmx you're telling your computer to look for all files that end with ".thmx.")

4. In the "Look in" drop-down menu at the bottom, choose My Computer to tell Windows Explorer to search *all* the files and folders on your computer. (Those theme files can't hide from you!)

5. Click Search. Before long, you'll see some files ending in .thmx start to pop up in the window on the right.

Ignore the themes that show up in expected places, such as *Program Files\Microsoft Office\Document Themes 12* and *Templates\Document Themes*, because all these themes already show up in Word's Theme menu. You're looking for themes in other locations. When you find likely candidates, copy and paste them into your *C:\Documents and Settings\Christopher\Templates\Document Themes* folder.

Figure 5-8:
Microsoft's Office Web site is a good source for information and add-ons. Currently you'll find help files, predesigned templates, and an active Office community. More themes, colors, and font sets should be available soon.

Choosing a Template

When you use a template, you're taking advantage of the work and wisdom of those who have gone before you. As the saying goes, "Why reinvent the wheel?" Microsoft must adhere to this philosophy because, in Word 2007, they've made templates an even more integral part of the program. Just look at the New Document dialog box (Alt+F, N). Your computer screen fills up with templates (Figure 5-9). You'll find templates for resumés, newsletters, calendars, and greeting cards. The business category alone contains hundreds of templates. When you're working on deadline or you need a professionally designed document, finding the right template to do the job will save time in the long run.

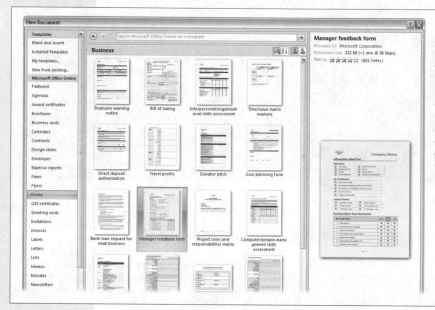

Figure 5-9:
Open the New Document box and suddenly you see more than a dozen template options. The list on the left shows installed templates at the top. In the lower part of the list are hordes of templates that you can access from the Microsoft Office Online site.

Here's a partial sampling of the types of templates you'll find. In the New Document dialog box, they appear alphabetically in the left panel:

- **Planning.** Agendas, calendars, lists, planners, schedules.

- **Stationery and mailing.** Business cards, greeting cards, envelopes, faxes, invitations, labels, letters, postcards.

- **General business.** Contracts, forms, invoices, memos, minutes, purchase orders, receipts, reports, resumés, statements, time sheets.

- **Marketing.** Award certificates, brochures, gift certificates, flyers, newsletters.

If that's not enough, in typical Microsoftian overkill there's even a category called More Categories, where, believe it or not, you find 50 more categories, which run the gamut from Address Books, Games, and Paper Folding projects to Quizzes and Scorecards.

When you use a template, you're not opening a template file, you're opening a copy of it, sort of like pulling the top sheet off a pad of forms. The original template file remains untouched. Here are some of the goodies you'll find in a new document you've opened from a template:

• **Graphics.** Templates for brochures, business cards, greeting cards, and newsletters almost always include drawing, clip art, lines, and borders. Frequently you'll find templates that include photos (Figure 5-10).

Figure 5-10:
When you use a template, you get a professionally designed, preformatted document. Many templates include impressive graphics and high quality photos. All you need to do is fill in your message.

• **Formatting.** Setting up the page formats, indents, and line spacing, and positioning every single bit of text on the page can be a big job. For projects like forms, purchase orders, and invoices, you may end up tearing your hair out. Fortunately, using a template is a lot easier on your scalp.

• **Boilerplate text.** Often in templates the text is just there for position. You replace the text with your own words. However, some templates include boilerplate text that you want to leave in place. Contracts, fax cover pages, forms, and even resumés may include body text or headings that you want to keep.

- **AutoText entries.** Sophisticated templates sometimes add automated features like AutoText entries (page 470). A template designed to handle a common complaint may include a lengthy AutoText entry that begins, "We are so very sorry that the widget didn't live up to your expectations." To insert the diatribe, all you have to do is type *sorry*, and then press the F3 key.

- **Content controls.** Some templates include widgets, like text boxes and dropdown menus, that let you create electronic forms in Word, just like the forms you fill out on Web sites. You can learn how to use these *content controls* on page 341.

- **Macros.** Templates that include a lot of automatic features probably use macros—mini-programs that run inside Word documents—to create their magic. Macros let you run several commands with the click of a button or a keyboard shortcut, as explained beginning on page 433.

Templates Behind the Scenes

Every Word document has at least one template attached to it, whether you know it or not. Even when you start a blank document, the Normal template is what provides a basic page layout and serves up your preferred font and AutoText entries. The tools and formats in the Normal template are always available to all your documents, so it's called a *global template*.

Document templates are different from global ones. They often provide extensive formatting, boilerplate text, and in some cases macros and other tools to help you get the job done. The settings and tools in document templates are available only to documents that are based on that template. So you won't find AutoText from your invoice template in a document you created using a greeting card template.

Starting a Document from a Template

The New Document dialog box lets you access the hundreds of Office templates that are available online—many more than Word installs on your computer. If you have a computer with a cable or DSL Internet connection, then using an online template is almost as fast as using an installed one.

Here's how to download a business card template and use it to create your own cards:

1. **Go to Office button → New (or press Alt+F, N).**

   The New Document box opens, offering several ways to create a new document (Figure 5-9). To find a business card template, look to the Templates categories list on the left.

2. **In the left panel, under the Microsoft Office Online heading, click "Business cards."**

   Each category contains dozens of templates. When you select "Business cards," you see cards for just about every industry on earth—except English Novelist (Figure 5-11).

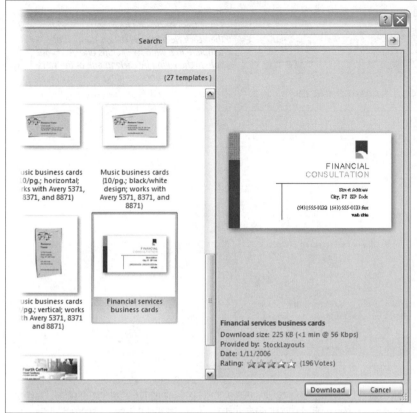

Figure 5-11:
*Use the New Document box
to see previews of
templates before you
download them for use. If
you click one of the
categories at left, then you
see thumbnails and
descriptions. Click a
thumbnail to see a larger
version in the preview
window at right. Like what
you see? Click the
Download button.*

3. **Scroll down the middle panel, and then click the "Financial services business cards" template to preview it in the rightmost panel.**

   The preview shows how your document will look. It creates 10 cards per page when you print on a full-sized sheet. You'll find some additional details about the card below the preview panel. Note the file size is 225 KB. Even a 56 Kpbs (slow dial-up Internet access) takes less than a minute to download this template.

   At bottom is a rating showing that this particular design has received four out of five stars, according to votes from 196 people like you. The rating system is a way for you to learn if a certain template has been helpful to others. You can vote on this template, too, as described in Figure 5-12.

4. **In the middle panel, double-click the template to start the download.**

   If all goes well, then you see an alert box telling you that the download is taking place (Figure 5-13). When the download is complete, Word opens a new document based on the template.

Figure 5-12:
In the New Document box, select a template, and then click Help to view details about that template in a window like this one. Add your vote to the rating by clicking one of the stars under the Feedback heading.

Note: The Microsoft Genuine Advantage box may rear its head during the download process. When you see this message box, Microsoft is checking whether you have legal and licensed versions of their programs. If you don't, then you won't be able to download the template.

Figure 5-13:
The download alert box appears when the download begins. If you change your mind, click Stop. Otherwise, the box automatically goes away when the download is complete.

5. **Replace the boilerplate text with your own text.**

As with any template, you need to replace the boilerplate text with your own information. Figure 5-14 compares the newly inserted text next to the original template. In the case of the business cards, you need to copy (Ctrl+C) and paste (Ctrl+V) your text in each of the cards on the page.

6. **Save the file with a new name.**

When you're happy with the changes, save your document in a folder where you can find it later.

7. **Print the document.**

When you're ready, run the presses. You probably don't want to print business cards on regular flimsy paper. Instead, you can find sturdier card stock at an office supply store. Avery, one company that makes labels and other forms, has several products for business cards including some with micro-perforated edges that give you a clean, professional result.

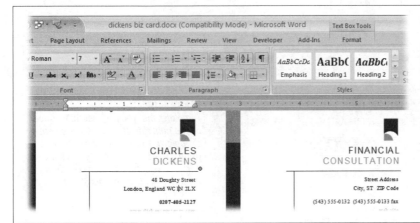

Figure 5-14:
The card on the right shows the boilerplate text for the Financial Services business card. The card on the left shows the text changed to accommodate a more creative and noble profession.

Using Installed Templates

Using a template that's already on your computer isn't much different than using one of the templates from Microsoft Office Online (Figure 5-15). After you open the New Document box (Alt+F, N), click Installed Templates at the top of the left panel. The middle panel shows you thumbnails of all templates on your computer. (You won't find as much variety here as you get online.)

You can preview the installed templates just like you did the online counterparts. Click a template thumbnail to preview it in the right panel. Using an installed template works exactly the same as using one from Microsoft Office Online, as described in the previous section, except that you skip the download process. Just double-click the template to open a new document from it, and then get to work as you normally would.

After you've used a template, the next time you start a new document, you'll see the template's name in the Recently Used Templates list Figure 5-16). The templates that you use most frequently end up as permanent members of this list—how's that for handy?

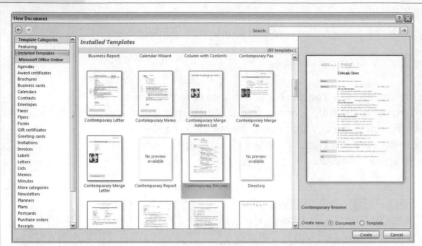

Figure 5-15:
If you're lucky enough to have a fast Internet connection, then you'll hardly notice whether your templates are online or installed on your computer. The process of selecting, previewing, and using a template is almost exactly the same.

Figure 5-16:
Templates that you used recently appear on the right side of the New Document dialog box. To create a new document using a template, just double-click the name, or select it, and then click Create in the lower-right corner (not shown).

Spelling, Grammar, and Reference Tools

When you've worked for hours on a resumé or a report, the last thing you want to do is send it out with goofs. Word's spelling and grammar tools help you avoid that kind of embarrassment. In this chapter, you'll learn how to use these tools. You'll also get a clear understanding of when and how Word makes automatic changes to your text. Even more important, you'll learn how to set up these tools to work the way you like to work.

If you really want to sound smart, Word can help you with some extra research, giving you access to a comprehensive Web based reference library, including dictionary, encyclopedia, thesaurus, Web search, and language translation tools (Figure 6-1).

Turning on Spelling and Grammar Checking

Spelling errors make any document look unprofessional, so ignoring Word's spell checker is just plain silly. And while grammar and style are largely subjective, the grammar-checking tool can help you spot glaring errors (like mixing up "it's" and "its"). When Microsoft first added these tools to Word, some people resented the intrusion, as discussed in the box on page 144. The fact is, you're in control. You can choose whether you want Word to check your work as you type, flagging misspelled words and questionable grammar (Figure 6-2), or whether you prefer to get the words on the page first, and then review the spelling and grammar at the end.

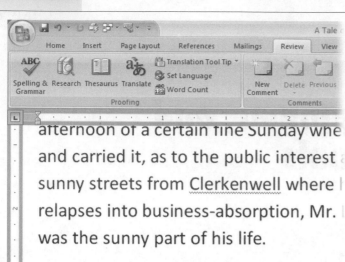

Figure 6-1:
Access to Word's Spelling and Grammar checker is on the Review → Proofing group, along with the thesaurus, the translation tool, and a slew of Web-based research tools.

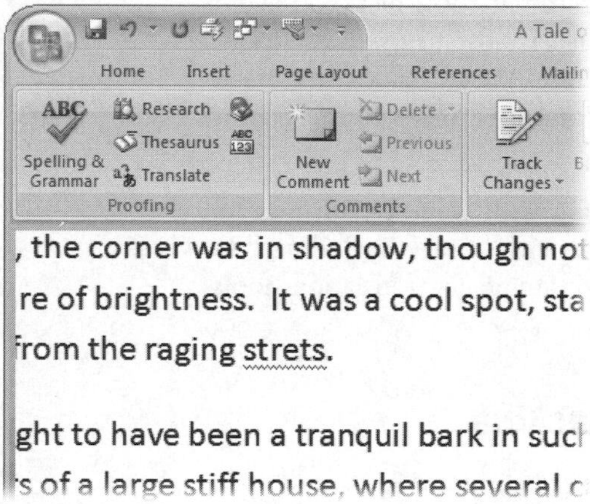

Figure 6-2:
When you use the "Check spelling as you type" option, Word places wavy red lines under possibly misspelled words. Some people consider this a distraction from their writing and choose to do a manual spell check when they've finished writing.

Follow these steps to set up Word's spelling and grammar-checking tools to work the way you like to work:

1. **Click the Office button (Alt+F) and in the lower-right corner of the menu, click Word Options.**

   The list on the left gives you several buttons that divide the Options into different groups. The options for the spelling and grammar tools are in Proofing.

2. **Click the Proofing category (Figure 6-3).**

The panel on the right changes to show checkboxes and buttons grouped into four categories: "AutoCorrect options," "When correcting spelling in Office programs," "When correcting spelling in Word," "When correcting grammar in Word," and "Exceptions for."

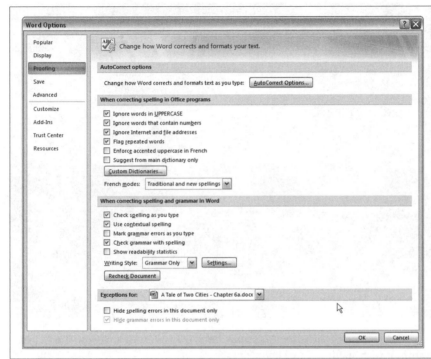

Figure 6-3:
Not only can you choose whether Word checks your spelling and grammar as you type, but Word also gives you a bunch of ways to fine-tune the program's level of persnicketyness. (By the way, this chapter was originally written in Word, and that last word was flagged with a red underline.)

3. Turn on the options in "When correcting spelling for Office programs" for the types of errors you want Word *not* to worry about.

   For example, Internet addresses and filenames often set off the spell checker, resulting in a distracting sea of red waves. You can also tell Word to ignore words in uppercase and words that include numbers, which are often company names or special terms that Word doesn't know how to spell. Use the checkboxes to have the spell checker ignore these types of words.

   Tip: You can "teach" Word how to spell these unfamiliar words and include them in spell checks by adding them to Word's spelling dictionary (page 148).

   ---

4. Word starts out with background spell checking turned on; if it annoys you, turn off the "Check spelling as you type" checkbox.

   This unassuming checkbox is the most important option. Turning it on turns on the wavy red lines under misspelled words.

Sometimes the word you type is spelled correctly, but it's the wrong word in the context. For example, "I'll see you in too weeks" is a contextual error. Word checks for this type of mistake if you turn on the "Use contextual spelling" checkbox.

The Wavy Line Debate

When Microsoft first introduced background spell checking and the wavy red line, it was roundly pooh-poohed by a large portion of the Word-using population. Some people didn't like the distraction of the red snakes popping up all over. These lines interfered with their concentration on their work. Other people noticed that background spell checking slowed down already slow computers. And, of course there were the folks who considered it unnecessary. "I always check my spelling when I'm *finished* writing." Microsoft continued to ship Word with background spell checking turned on. After all, people who didn't like it had the option to turn it off.

Over the years, the wavy lines have won some converts. Folks who once found background spell checking distracting began to leave it on as they upgraded Word.

Those people who were new to Word probably didn't know they could turn it off. Computers continued to increase in horsepower, so speed was no longer a big issue. If your computer can edit video, it probably won't be stressed by handling spell checking in the background, even for a very long document. The Automatic spell checking isn't going away and the solution is the same as always. Pick your path to pristine prose and set up Word accordingly.

By the way, if you *don't* want Word to check spelling in the background, you can make it stop. Open Word Options (Alt+F, I), and then click the Proofing option on the left. The third group of options is named "When correcting spelling and grammar in Word." Turn off the "Check spelling as you type" checkbox, and you've turned off background spell checking.

5. **If you're interested in some grammar help from Word, turn on the "Check grammar with spelling" checkbox.**

   This setting makes Word flag questionable construction as you work, with a wavy *green* underline. Or you can leave it turned off and check grammar when you're through writing, as described on page 150.

   If you don't want Word checking your grammar at all, turn off the "Check grammar with spelling" checkbox.

Tip: To fine-tune your grammar options, click the Settings button to open the Grammar Settings box (Figure 6-4). In this box, you can control whether the grammar checker flags capitalization, run on sentences, and so on.

---

6. **Click OK to close the Word Options box.**

   Your new spelling and grammar settings go into effect.

Figure 6-4:
You encounter even more debate and personal opinion when it comes to setting rules about grammar and style. Word gives you more options for controlling the program's tendency to flag your immortal prose.

Checking Spelling

Word's spell checker reads every word in your document and looks it up in its behind-the-scenes dictionary file. If the word isn't in the dictionary, the spell checker flags it as a possibly misspelled word. Spell checker handles misspelled words in three ways:

- **AutoCorrect.** The spell checker looks to see if the word is in its list of words to correct automatically. Words like "hte" for "the" or "shwo" for "show," for example, are in the AutoCorrect list. (You can add and remove words from the AutoCorrect list, and if you prefer, you can turn off AutoCorrect entirely. To see how, flip ahead to page 153.)

- **Check spelling as you type.** If you've set up Word to check spelling errors as you type, the spell checker puts a wavy red line under the word in question (Figure 6-2).

- **Check spelling manually.** Check spelling in one pass. The spell checker asks you about each questionable word when you run a manual spell check.

Checking Spelling As You Type

Unless you've turned this option off, as described in the previous steps, Word checks the spelling of each word you type, comparing it to its spelling dictionary. When a word is not in the dictionary, the spell checker brings it to your attention—not with a whack across the knuckles with a ruler, but with a wavy red underline (Figure 6-2).

To correct a word flagged with a wavy red line, right-click it. A shortcut menu shows suggested spellings for the word you flubbed (Figure 6-5). To choose a word from the list, just click it, and the correctly spelled word replaces the misspelled word.

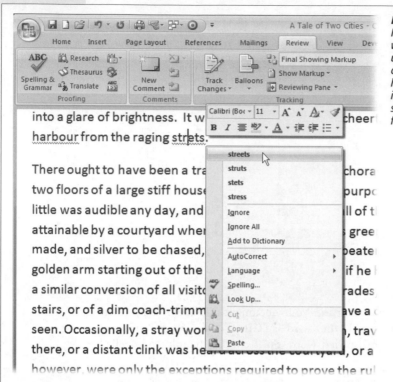

Figure 6-5:
Right-click words flagged with the wavy red line, and you see a pop-up menu suggesting a few correctly spelled possibilities. You have some other options, including adding the word to your spelling dictionary so it won't be flagged again.

Sometimes the spell checker flags a word, but you want to keep it in your document just the way it is (and make Word stop underlining it, for heaven's sake). For these words, the shortcut menu gives you three courses of action (Figure 6-6):

- **Ignore.** Click Ignore, and the spell checker ignores this instance of the word (in this document only) and removes the underline.

- **Ignore All.** When you choose this option, the spell checker doesn't flag any occurrence of the word in this document. No more wavy red lines for that baby.

- **Add to Dictionary.** When you add a word to the dictionary, you'll never see a wavy line under the word again, in this document or any other. Word adds the word to a file named CUSTOM.DIC. Over time, your custom dictionary collects all the special words that you don't want flagged in a spell check.

Checking Spelling Manually

When you opt for manual spelling and grammar checking, you can do these tasks in one pass, at your leisure, like after you've finished writing. To start a spelling and grammar check, choose Review → Proofing → Spelling and Grammar or press Alt+R, S. (F7, that old favorite spelling key, still works too.) You see a dialog box like the one in Figure 6-7.

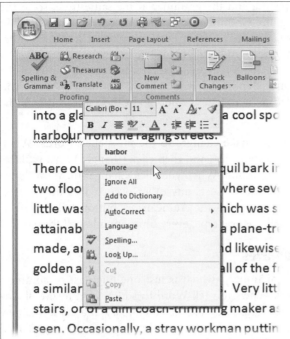

Figure 6-6:
In addition to a spelling suggestion, Word gives you three other options. You can ignore the word just this once, you can ignore all occurrences of the word in the document, or you can add the word to your dictionary, so that Word won't flag it as misspelled in any document.

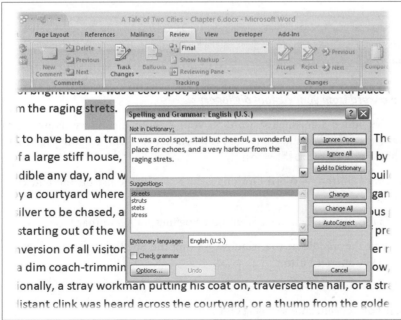

Figure 6-7:
When you use the manual spell checker, you work in this dialog box. The top text box shows you your word in context. The bottom text box offers suggested spellings.

Often, you're checking the spelling and the grammar at the same time, so in the upper-left corner, the Spelling and Grammar box tells you about the problem. In the case of a misspelled word, you see "Not in Dictionary" over a text box that shows the entire sentence with the word highlighted. The box below offers suggestions. On the right side of the dialog box, you see several buttons. Use one of the top three buttons—Ignore Once, Ignore All, and Add to Dictionary—when you want to keep the word spelled as it is. These options do the same thing as the shortcut menu options.

The bottom three buttons let you make changes to the misspelled words. When you select a word from the Suggestions list, and then click Change, Word replaces the highlighted word with the suggestion. When you click Change All, Word looks through your whole document, and corrects any other occurrences of the misspelled words at the same time. Clicking the AutoCorrect button tells Word to make the correction automatically, as you type, every time you misspell the word.

Managing Custom Dictionaries

Word has a standard spelling dictionary, which is just one huge list of common words in their correct spellings. When you tell Word to add a word to the dictionary, it doesn't actually add the word to its standard dictionary. It adds it to a new file that's all yours. This file, CUSTOM.DIC, contains your personal preferred spellings. Over time, your CUSTOM.DIC file collects the oddly spelled names of your friends and family, slang terms you frequently use, and a host of other words.

Tip: You can transfer your custom dictionary to another computer by simply copying your CUSTOM.DIC file to the new machine. (Your CUSTOM.DIC file lives in a folder named *C:\Documents and Settings\User Name\Microsoft\Application Data\Proof*.)

Removing a word from your custom dictionary

Oops! You've added a misspelled word to your custom dictionary. Now Word won't ever flag "dosn't" again. All is not lost. You can edit your custom dictionary right within Word. Here are the steps:

1. **Go to Office button → Word Options (Alt+F, I). In the list on the left, click Proofing.**

   Access to the custom dictionary is with the Spelling and Grammar tools.

2. **Roughly in the middle of the window, among the Spelling settings, click the Custom Dictionaries button.**

   The Custom Dictionaries box opens (Figure 6-8).

3. **In the list on the left, choose CUSTOM.DIC.**

   When you add words to your dictionary while checking spelling, Word stores them in the CUSTOM.DIC file. If you've added any additional custom dictionaries (page 150), you'll see them in this list too.

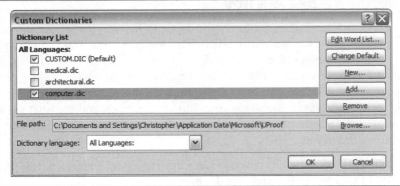

Figure 6-8:
Use the Custom Dictionaries box to manage your personal dictionary and add professional dictionaries to Word. Here's where you choose the dictionaries in use, add new dictionaries, and open your custom dictionaries for editing.

4. **Click Edit Word List to open the dictionary.**

   Yet another dialog box opens with CUSTOM.DIC in the title bar (Figure 6-9). Your custom words are in the list labeled Dictionary.

5. **Select the misspelled word, and then click Delete.**

   The list is alphabetized, so you can use the scroll bars on the right to find your misspelled word. As a shortcut, you can click the first word in the list, and then type the first letter of the word you want. Say you're looking for "dosn't"; press D, and the list jumps to words starting with D.

   Once you find the word, click it, and then click Delete at bottom.

6. **Close the windows by clicking OK.**

   You've opened three dialog boxes to get to edit your dictionary. Clean things up by clicking OK in each. Now the non-word "dosn't" officially earns a wavy line.

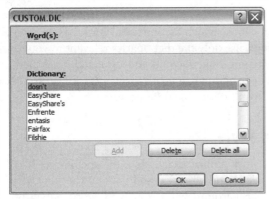

Figure 6-9:
You can add and delete words from your custom dictionary CUSTOM.DIC. To add a word, type it in the box at the top, and then click Add. Remove words from the list by selecting the word in the Dictionary button, and then clicking Delete. Be careful with that Delete All button—it really does delete all the words in your custom dictionary.

Adding professional dictionaries to Word

It seems that every profession, business, and industry has its own language, and often that means it has its own custom dictionary for Word too. You can find all sorts of custom dictionaries, either free or for a price. Search the Web, and you'll find dictionaries for everything from architecture to zoology. And if it's not out there, you can always create your own. Google is a good place to start the search. Just type "Microsoft Word" .dic dictionaries in the search box and see what pops up. If you want to zero in on a specific business like construction or computers, then add that word to your search.

Once you find a dictionary and download or copy it to your computer, you can add it to Word's dictionary list. Here are the steps:

1. **Open the Custom Dictionaries box (Figure 6-8), as described in steps 1–2 on page 148.**

2. **Click the Add button on the right to open one of Windows' standard file boxes.**

   A box labeled Add Custom Dictionary appears. You see the standard tools for navigating through your computer folders and hunting down files. Use the tools on the left and the drop-down menu on top to navigate to the folder containing your new dictionary.

3. **Double-click your dictionary file, or select it, and then, at the bottom of the window, click Open.**

   The Add Custom Dictionary box closes, and you're back at the Custom Dictionaries box. Your new dictionary is listed along with CUSTOM.DIC and all the rest.

4. **If you plan on using the dictionary right away, make sure there's a checkmark in the box next to its name.**

   Using the checkboxes, you can choose which dictionaries Word uses for its spell check. To minimize misspellings, use only the dictionaries relevant to your current document. A slip of the typing fingers could end up matching a medical term. Also, for each dictionary you add, it can take Word a little longer to check spelling, though you probably won't notice the difference.

Checking Grammar and Style

Word's grammar and style tools work almost exactly like the spelling tools. You have the same choice between background checking and manual checking. If you check grammar and style in the background while you type, word puts a wavy green line under suspect sentences and phrases. If you check grammar manually, you view problem sentences in the Spelling and Grammar dialog box (Figure 6-10).

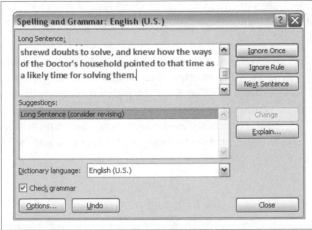

Figure 6-10:
If you check spelling and grammar manually, you see errors appear in the Spelling and Grammar dialog box. Text in the upper-left corner describes the error, and suggestions appear at bottom. For a more detailed description of the problem, click Explain.

You may feel that Word's grammar police are a little too strict for your personal style of writing. If that's the case, you can tinker with the settings (Office button → Word Options → Proofing). Here are some of the options you toggle on or off in the Grammar Settings box (Figure 6-4):

- **Capitalization.** Finds words that should be capitalized, (like *madame* DeFarge).

- **Fragments and run-ons.** Checks for complete sentences and flags overly long meandering sentences that seem to just go on and on and you can't wait for them to stop but they never do.

- **Misused words.** Looks for the incorrect use of adjectives and adverbs.

- **Negation.** Flags double negatives.

- **Noun phrases.** Checks for proper usage of "a" and "an" and finds phrases where the number doesn't agree with the noun. For example, it wouldn't like "A Tale of Two City."

- **Possessives and plurals.** Leave this option checked if you have a problem forgetting apostrophes in phrases like "the ships hold."

- **Punctuation.** Checks your usage of quotation marks, commas, colons, and all those other little marks.

- **Questions.** Checks for question marks, and flags questions with non-standard structure.

- **Relative clauses.** Finds errors in relative clauses, such as the use of "which" instead of "who" in a clause referring to people.

- **Subject-verb agreement.** Flags sentences where the verbs don't match the nouns, as in "All of the nobles has gone to the guillotine."

- **Verb phrases.** Finds errors in verb usages such as incorrect tense.

Style checking is even more subjective than grammar checking. If you feel there ain't no reason Microsoft should meddle when you say you're real mad at the congressman, you can turn this feature off.

You can tweak the Style checking settings in the Word Options dialog box (Office button → Word Options → Proofing). For example, the "When correcting spelling and grammar in Word" section has a Writing Style drop-down menu with two options: Grammar & Style or Grammar Only. If you choose Grammar & Style, Word hunts down problems such as clichés, passive sentences, and run-on sentences. It's always your choice though; turn on the suggestions that you find helpful and that match your own personal style.

Controlling AutoCorrect

The AutoCorrect feature packs more punch than you may expect, and it works across several of the Office programs, including Word, Publisher, and Outlook. With AutoCorrect, if you accidentally type *hte,* Word changes it to "the." The program doesn't ask you for permission (it comes with AutoCorrect turned on). You may not even notice when Word makes the change. Obviously, AutoCorrect is not a feature for control freaks. On the other hand, there's some surprising power in the concept. Have you ever tried to figure out how to type the © symbol? If you have AutoCorrect on, and you type (c), it magically turns into the copyright symbol. That's just the beginning. AutoCorrect lets you enter a lot of other symbols right from the keyboard, from math symbols to arrows to smiley faces. And just imagine, if you work for the *American Gastroenterological Association,* wouldn't it be great to type in *aga* and let AutoCorrect type in all those words, especially that middle one?

How AutoCorrect Works

AutoCorrect changes words immediately after you type them, so you see the change when it happens right behind your insertion point. If you don't like what AutoCorrect did, press Ctrl+Z to undo it. The text goes back to the characters you typed, and AutoCorrect won't mess with it again.

Fine-tuning AutoCorrect Options

Given that AutoCorrect's reason for being is to change the words that you write, it's important to know how to bring it under control. To adjust AutoCorrect settings, open the AutoCorrect dialog box (Office button → Word Options → Proofing → AutoCorrect Options). You can also jump to the AutoCorrect dialog box from any word in your text with a wavy red spelling line. Right-click the word, and then choose AutoCorrect → AutoCorrect Options from the shortcut menu. The AutoCorrect dialog box gives you access to a lot of settings, so it may take a few moments to sort out how all the options work. At the very top, the "Show Auto-Correct Options buttons" checkbox controls whether or not the little lightning-bolt menu buttons (Figure 6-11) show up in your text.

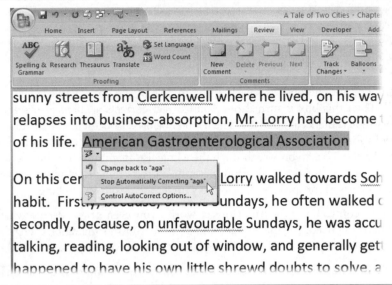

Figure 6-11:
If you see a hollow blue line under a character or you see a lightning bolt, AutoCorrect is at work. When you move your mouse cursor to the spot, you see a shortcut menu like this providing AutoCorrect options. Using this shortcut menu is the fastest way to make AutoCorrect stop autocorrecting something you don't want it to!

The checkboxes at the top of the AutoCorrect dialog box all deal with common typos and finger flubs (Figure 6-12).

Figure 6-12:
AutoCorrect likes to mess with your words as you type them. Fortunately, you can rein it in using this box. Use the checkboxes at the top to turn on (or off) AutoCorrect's fixes for some common typos. The box at bottom lists the changes AutoCorrect makes. By adding your own replacement pairs to this list, you can even use AutoCorrect as if it were AutoText.

Tip: As shown in this example, you can use the AutoCorrect feature as if it were AutoText. The difference is AutoCorrect automatically turns *aga* into American Gastroenterological Association. When you use Auto-Text, you need to press the F3 key after you type *aga*. So, it's your choice: AutoCorrect for fewer key-strokes, or AutoText for manual control.

The most important checkbox is smack in the middle of the box: "Replace text as you type." When this box is turned on, AutoCorrect corrects spelling errors and makes other replacements as you type. The list box below shows the text that Auto-Correct looks for (on the left) and the text that it uses as a replacement (on the right). Use the scroll bar to browse through the whole list. If you turn on the check-box at the bottom, AutoCorrect also automatically corrects misspelled words using the same dictionary as for spell checks. No wavy underline. Just fixed spelling.

In addition to controlling how AutoCorrect works, you even get to decide what errors it corrects—by editing the Replace and With lists in this dialog box. Here's how to add your own entry to the list of replacements AutoCorrect makes:

1. **Choose Office button → Word Options → Proofing. At the top of the Proofing panel, click the AutoCorrect Options button.**

   The AutoCorrect dialog box opens.

2. **Make sure the "Replace text as you type" checkbox is turned on.**

   This checkbox is AutoCorrect's master on/off switch.

3. **In the Replace text box, type *aga*, and then press Tab. In the With box, type *American Gastroenterological Association*, and then click Add.**

   You've just told Word to be on the lookout for the sequence of letters "aga," and to replace it with "American Gastroenterological Association."

4. **Click OK to close the AutoCorrect box, and then click OK to close Word Options.**

Note: If AutoCorrect is making replacements you don't like, you can fix this by deleting pairs from this list. Suppose every time you type *are*, AutoCorrect tries to replace it with "Association of Restaurant Entre-preneurs." To remove this annoyance, select the pair "are" and "Association of Restaurant Entrepreneurs," and then click Delete. If you choose "Stop Automatically Correcting" from the AutoCorrect Options button menu (Figure 6-11), Word deletes that entry from the list.

Autocorrecting Math, Formatting, and Smart Tags

AutoCorrect is more than a spelling correction tool. A better term may be *AutoRe-place*, since it can apply automatic formatting fixes to mathematical symbols and special text characters like quotation marks and dashes. The AutoCorrect feature also governs Smart Tags—those little "i" buttons that pop up and save you time by performing actions that you'd normally have to open other programs to do. (See the box on page 155 for more detail on Smart Tags.)

As on the AutoCorrect tab, the Math AutoCorrect, AutoFormat, and Smart Tag tabs let you turn certain kinds of fixes on or off. The Math tab also has Replace and With lists that let you type fancy math symbols by hitting a few letters on the keyboard.

- **Math.** Go to Office button → Word Options → Proofing → AutoCorrect Options and click the Math AutoCorrect tab to see how AutoCorrect gives you quick access to math symbols. Sure, you could hunt down some of these symbols with Word's symbol tool (Insert → Symbols → Symbol), but if you use the same math symbols frequently, AutoCorrect provides quicker, easier access. You can customize Math AutoCorrect by typing characters in the Replace and With boxes. It works just like the AutoCorrect tool for words.

- **Formatting.** Go to Office button → Word Options → Proofing → AutoCorrect Options, AutoFormat As You Type tab or AutoFormat tab. Have you ever wondered how Word's smart quotes feature works? You enter straight quotes (?), actually the symbol for inches, on both sides of a quote, yet Word automatically provides curly quotes, curled in the proper direction on both ends of the quote. That's AutoCorrect working behind the scenes. AutoCorrect can jump into action when you start making a numbered list or a bulleted list. It can provide a respectable em dash (—), every time you type two hyphens. The AutoFormat options are presented as checkboxes. Just turn on the ones you want to use.

UP TO SPEED

Smart Tags

As you're typing in Word, any number of little helpers pop up from time to time. There's the mini-toolbar, the Auto-Correct Options button, those wavy red lines that the spell checker lays down. And then there are Smart Tags (Figure 6-13). Microsoft's underlying idea is a perfectly good one—to let you share information and features among Office programs with fewer mouse clicks.

So, for example, when you type the name of an Outlook Contact in a Word document, the Smart Tag appears in your document, with a dotted purple line and a little "i" for information button that reveals a shortcut menu when you click it.

You can choose from the menu and send an email, schedule a meeting, or insert an address without the extra steps of launching Outlook and tracking down the contact's name all over again. When you're typing somebody's name, Word figures that you may be thinking of that person and puts a few typical options at your fingertips.

If you're one of those "shut up and let me type" types, you can turn off Smart Tags in the AutoCorrect dialog box. Just click the Smart Tags tab, and then turn off the "Show Smart Tag Actions buttons" checkbox.

- **Smart Tags.** Go to Office button → Word Options → Proofing → AutoCorrect Options, Smart Tags tab. Word's Smart Tags work behind the scenes as you type, looking for connections between your words and other resources. Type a name, and Smart Tags checks to see if that person is in your Outlook address book. If the person is, a dotted purple line appears under the name. Move your mouse over the word, and you see the Smart Tag "i" for information button. Click this button, and you can shoot an email off to your pal. Smart Tags

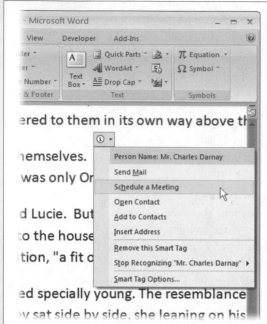

Figure 6-13:
If you let them, Smart Tags appear in your document as little shortcut menus that link to information in other Microsoft programs. Choose from the menu to perform tasks like sending email or scheduling meetings.

perform a number of other tasks, like converting measurements and adding dates to your calendar. You can adjust the settings in the Smart Tags tab of the AutoCorrect box: Click the "Label text with smart tags" box to turn Smart Tags on, and then use the other checkboxes to choose the type of words you want tagged.

Exploring Word's Research Tools

Word's Research panel provides links to a library shelf of Internet research tools that you can use from within Word. To open the panel, go to Review → Proofing → Research. The Research task pane opens at the screen's left (Figure 6-14).

Here's a list of the tools tucked away in the Research panel:

- **Encarta Dictionary.** Like any dictionary, Microsoft's version provides definitions, parts of speech, and pronunciation.

- **Thesaurus.** Provides synonyms and alternate word choices.

- **Encarta Encyclopedia.** Finds links to articles in the MSN Encarta Encyclopedia.

***

Note: Encarta started life as a CD-ROM product before everyone was connected to the Internet. Originally, Microsoft purchased the rights to contents of the Funk and Wagnall's encyclopedia and merged that content with other sources.

***

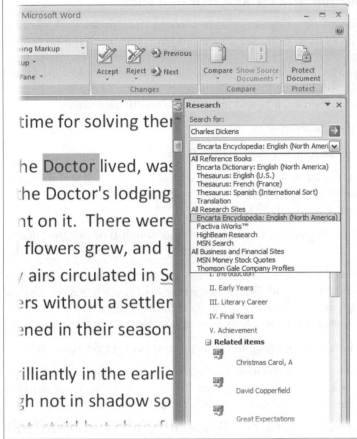

Figure 6-14:
Use the drop-down menu at the top of the Research task pane to choose references when you're searching for information. Word provides dictionaries, encyclopedias, Internet search tools, and business reference resources.

- **Factiva iWorks.** A service of Dow Jones & Reuters, Factiva provides business and news information.

- **HighBeam Research.** Finds references in newspapers, magazines, journals, books, photos, maps, encyclopedia articles, dictionaries, thesauruses, and almanacs.

- **MSN Search.** Microsoft's Internet search tool.

- **MSN Money Stock Quotes.** Microsoft's financial information service.

- **Thomson Gale Company Profiles.** Provides business and financial details of companies.

Note: If you're not connected to the Internet, obviously you can't use these online tools. Furthermore, their responsiveness depends on the speed of your connection. Some of the Proofing tools, such as the spell checker, thesaurus, and some of the translation tools, still work even if you're not connected. Encarta, Factiva, and the business research sites don't.

Finding Information with the Research Task Pane

For the most part, anyone with an Internet connection and a browser can use all of Word's research tools. You use the same panel and the same quick and easy search process whether you're looking for company information in Thomson Gale, researching a topic for a school paper in HighBeam Research, or looking up the pronunciation of a word in the Encarta Dictionary. You don't have to go hunting all over the Web, and then learn how to use the tools on different sites.

Here's how to research a topic:

1. **Go to Review → Proofing → Research (Alt+R, R).**

   The Research task pane opens to the right of your document. If you want, you can click the top bar and drag the Research task pane out of the Word window so that it floats independently like a palette.

2. **At the top of the Research task pane, type your search terms in the "Search for" text box.**

   If your search words appear in your document, there's a shortcut: Select the words in your document, and then choose Review → Proofing → Research. The search words appear automatically in the "Search for" box, and Word immediately begins to search for references using your last selected reference source.

3. **Use the All Reference Books drop-down menu to select your reference source.**

   Say you're looking for information on Bulldog Brewing Company but don't need the dictionary definition of an English canine. Choose Thomson Gale Company Profiles. The search begins as soon as you make a selection.

   Or, if you leave the menu set to All Reference Books, click the green Start Search button with the arrow. In this case, Word searches in all the reference books and lists the results in the Research pane.

   Be patient. This is, after all, an Internet search. Sooner or later you'll see the results in a large text box (Figure 6-15).

4. **If necessary, use a link to follow up in your Web browser.**

   Often the results include links to Web sites. If you want to continue your research, click the links, and your browser opens to the Web site, such as MSN Money or HighBeam Research.

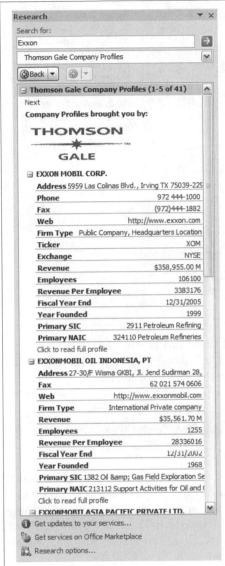

Figure 6-15:
Use Word's Research task pane to get access to Word's thesaurus, Encarta dictionary, encyclopedia, and translation tools. Clicking the arrow next to the Back button opens a menu where you can return to the results of your last few searches.

Accessing Word's Thesaurus

A well-thumbed thesaurus sits on many writers' bookshelves, somewhere between Strunk and White's *The Elements of Style* and Bartlett's *Familiar Quotations*. By providing synonyms and antonyms to common words, a thesaurus helps writers find what Flaubert called *le mot juste*—"the perfect word." Word's thesaurus (Figure 6-16) makes it so easy to look up a synonym that your hard-copy thesaurus may start gathering dust.

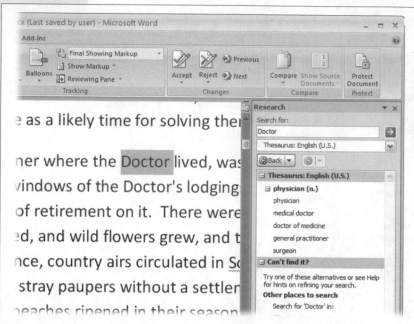

Figure 6-16:
To use Word's thesaurus, just right-click a word, and then choose synonyms from the shortcut menu. Choose a word from the list, or, if you need more research, at the bottom of the menu, choose Thesaurus to open a thesaurus in the Research task pane.

To use Word's thesaurus, just right-click any word in your document, and then point to Synonyms in the pop-up menu. A submenu appears with appropriate synonyms. If that's not enough for you, at the bottom of the menu, click the Thesaurus option to open the Research task pane, with your word entered in the "Search for" box (Figure 6-16). Click the green arrow to look up the reference.

Translating Text

Word's research tools include language translation. When you select a word in your text and click the Translate button on the ribbon (Review → Proofing → Translate or Alt+R, L), Word begins to look up the word using the last language selection for the translation (Figure 6-17). (Word speaks Arabic, Chinese, Dutch, English, French, German, Greek, Italian, Japanese, Portuguese, Russian, Spanish, and Swedish.)

Accurate translation is more of an art than a science. As a result, computer automation goes only part of the journey. Along with the translation of words and phrases, you get an offer to professionally translate your entire document for a fee (Figure 6-18). (Or, you can ask a friend who speaks the language for help.)

Translation ScreenTips

Translation screen tips are another pop-up helper you can turn on. Go to Review → Proofing → Translation ScreenTip, and choose a language from the drop-down menu. Screen tips are available in English, French, Spanish, and other languages.

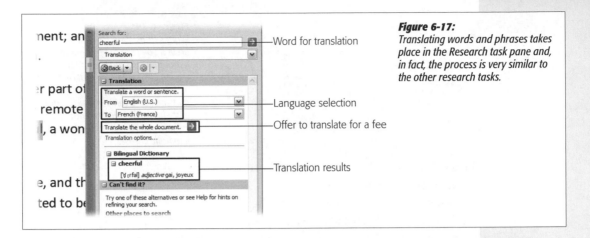

Figure 6-17:
Translating words and phrases takes place in the Research task pane and, in fact, the process is very similar to the other research tasks.

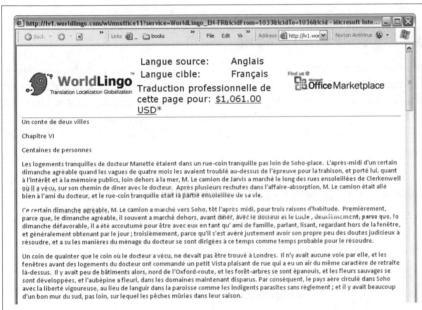

Figure 6-18:
When you ask Word to translate for you, you get a computer translation and a commercial offer to have a pro do the job. In this case, Lingo offered to translate a 4500-word chapter of A Tale of Two Cities for just over $1000.

Once you choose your language, all you have to do to see a translation and definitions for the word is to pause your mouse cursor over the word for a couple seconds (Figure 6-19). The multilanguage details are surprisingly complete.

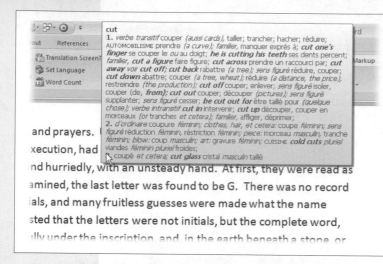

Figure 6-19:
Word's translation screen tips are great if you're in the process of learning a language or you're working in a language that isn't your first. Pause your cursor over a word, and you see a complete dictionary entry in two languages. Entries include parts of speech and idiomatic phrases.

Checking Your Word Count

It's often necessary to count your document's words, lines, paragraphs, and pages. Word keeps a running tab of pages and words in the status bar at the document window's lower-right corner (Figure 6-20). To see more details, double-click the status bar to bring up the Word Count box. Addressing gripes from earlier versions of Word, Microsoft has added checkboxes that let you include or exclude text boxes, footnotes, and endnotes from the count.

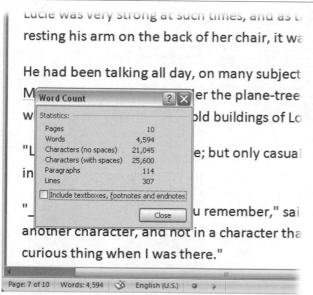

Figure 6-20:
Word keeps track of stats such as pages and word count in the lower-left corner of the window. Double-click this area, or go to Review → Proofing → Word Count to open the Word Count dialog box where you see stats on characters, lines, and paragraphs.

Printing Word Documents

At some point in their lives, most Word documents are headed for the printer. Even when you email a document or create an Adobe Acrobat (PDF) file, your recipient may want to print it. In fact, some people like to proofread a hard copy before sending off any document, believing they're more likely to catch mistakes that way.

Word puts a lot of printing power at your fingertips. This chapter shows you how to do things that would make Gutenberg drop his type, starting with the quickest and easiest ways to print your entire document. You'll learn how to choose and use the best printer for the job (say, your color inkjet for photos), a laser or fax for documents, and a PDF file for good measure. And if you're sending that document via snail mail, then you'll need to print an envelope or a label. Word's got you covered there too.

Quick and Easy Printing

When you first install Word, the shortest route to the printer is the Quick Print button. With a document open in Word, go to Office button → Print → Quick Print. With a couple clicks your complete document begins to spew forth from your printer.

Tip: To print with even fewer clicks, add the Quick Print button to the Quick Access toolbar, as described in Figure 7-1.

The Quick Print process does have its limitations; it prints one copy of the entire document, single sided, every time. If you want to print just a few pages, print multiple or collated copies, or print on both sides of the paper, you must take a couple extra steps. Perhaps the biggest limitation of one-click printing is that your printer must be set up properly. It needs to be turned on, it needs to have paper, and it needs to be connected to your computer and set to run. Otherwise, the Quick Print button does nothing except give you an error message once it's given up.

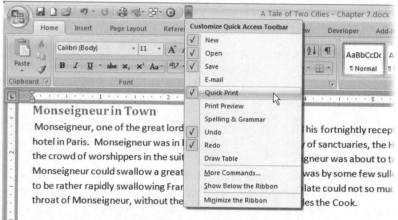

Figure 7-1:
You can customize the Quick Access toolbar to hold any command button. For the convenience of one-click printing, add the Quick Print button. On the right side of the toolbar, click the Customize Quick Access toolbar button, and then turn on the Quick Print option.

You can use another quick and easy printing shortcut—printing a document directly from Windows Explorer. Select a file in Explorer, and then choose File → Print from Explorer's menu (Figure 7-2). Yet another Explorer option is to right-click the file, and then choose Print from the shortcut menu. Windows opens the file in Word (launching Word first, if necessary), and Word then prints the document. (If Word wasn't already running when you gave the Print command, then it closes down when printing's done. If Word was already running, just the document closes.) Like the one-click print button, you can't specify any particulars when you print from Windows in this way, but it's a quick and easy way to spit out one copy of your document.

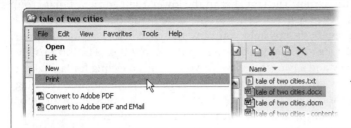

Figure 7-2:
You can print Word files directly from Windows Explorer by selecting your document in Explorer, and then choosing File → Print. Windows' Print command works for just about any printable document, including those created in Word. Windows finds and runs the program needed to print the file.

Print Preview

Old movies have that great image of the writer ripping paper out of the typewriter, wadding it up in a ball, and throwing it on the floor. If you're not interested in that much drama (or wasted paper) when you work, then get to know Print Preview. You find Print Preview with a couple of other print commands on the Office menu. To see them, go to Office button → Print (Figure 7-3).

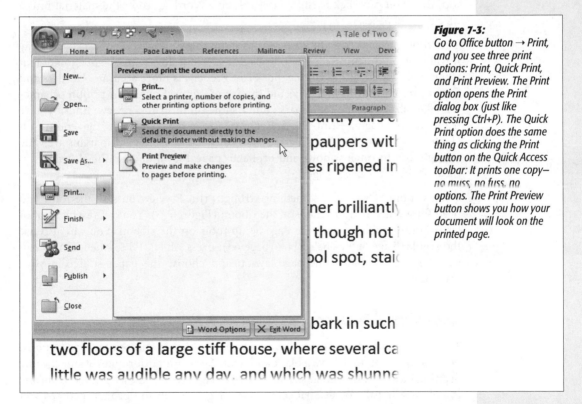

Figure 7-3:
Go to Office button → Print, and you see three print options: Print, Quick Print, and Print Preview. The Print option opens the Print dialog box (just like pressing Ctrl+P). The Quick Print option does the same thing as clicking the Print button on the Quick Access toolbar: It prints one copy—no muss, no fuss, no options. The Print Preview button shows you how your document will look on the printed page.

When you click Print Preview, your Word window changes quite a bit. You can't edit text in this view; it's just for reviewing your work before you print. Up at the top, a single tab appears on the ribbon: Print Preview. On the left, you find two buttons with printer icons—Print and Options. Some familiar-looking tools occupy the Page Setup group. The launcher in the lower-right corner of that group indicates that, with a click, you can bring up the Page Setup dialog box. The tools in the Zoom and Preview groups help you view the page before you go to press. Click the big magnifying glass, and you bring up the Zoom box. The buttons give you a single-page view and a two-page view, so you can get a feeling for facing page layouts. In the Preview group, you can toggle the page rulers on and off. The Magnifier checkbox appears. It works like a toggle and turns your mouse cursor into a Zoom tool. One click and you zoom in; click again and you zoom out.

In Print Preview, you can use the Next Page and Previous Page buttons to look through your document, but it's just as easy to use the scroll bar on the right side of the window. The most curious and confusing button in the group is the Shrink One Page button. You may think this button performs some kind of Alice in Wonderland trick on one of your pages, but no, it makes an attempt to reduce the overall number of pages in the document. This button performs this magic by slightly reducing the type size and reducing the letter spacing. For example, if you preview your document and find it's 11 pages long, but page 11 has just a few lines at the top, then you can click Shrink One Page, and Word squeezes the material into a nice even 10 pages.

The whole purpose of Print Preview is to show you your document exactly the way it will look on the printed page. Word's Print Layout does a pretty good job of that when you're writing and editing, but Print Preview is more accurate. Headers and footers are positioned precisely, and they're not grayed out. Non-printing characters like tabs and paragraph marks don't show up in Print Preview. And if you're using facing pages, Print Preview gives you a good feel for the end result (Figure 7-4). Print Preview's a great place to check to see if your margins are wide enough and to catch widows and orphans (page 105) and abandoned headers at the bottom of the page (page 76).

What's more, if you find something wrong, Print Preview puts all the tools you need for a quick fix right there on the ribbon (Figure 7-5). You can resolve a lot of last-minute problems with the Page Setup tools on the ribbon. You can also use the regular Page Setup dialog box (page 63); press Alt+P, PS to open it. You can adjust margins, change the page layout, and choose the paper source in your printer.

Choosing a Printer

These days, it's not unusual to have a couple of printers and printer-type options. For example, you may have a black and white laser printer for quickly and cheaply printing basic text documents. You may also have a color ink-jet printer for printing photos and the occasional color chart or graph. On top of that, perhaps you have a fax modem connected to your computer. (Windows thinks of fax machines as printers. When you think about it, they are sort of long-distance printers.) If you have the full-blown Adobe Acrobat program on your computer, Adobe PDF shows up everywhere you see your computer's printers listed. (Word considers creating PDFs, too, to be a type of printing.)

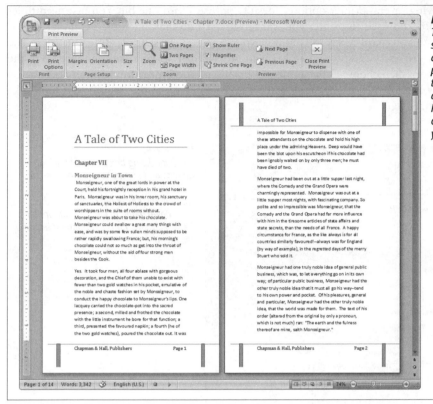

Figure 7-4:
The Print Preview window shows you how your document will look on paper. Using the Zoom tools, Preview controls, and checkboxes on the Print Preview panel, you can get a good look at your document.

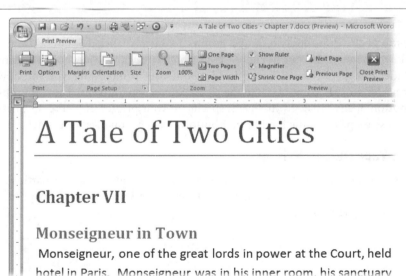

Figure 7-5:
If you find a problem when you're viewing your document in Print Preview, then you've got the Page Setup tools close at hand.

Having several printer options doesn't confuse Word one bit. You just need to let Word know which printer you want to use. To do that, open the Print dialog box, which in typical Microsoft fashion you can do at least three different ways. The quickest and easiest to remember is to press Ctrl+P. If you like to mouse up to the ribbon, then choose Office button → Print. For good measure, you can also use the new keyboard shortcut Alt+F, P. However you arrive at the Print box, it looks like Figure 7-6.

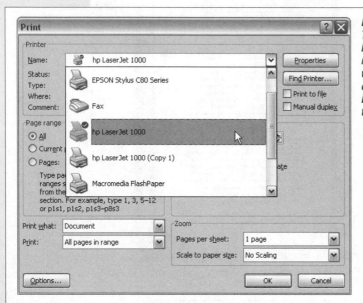

Figure 7-6:
The Print dialog box packs a bunch of buttons and menus that you can use to make your printer do exactly what you want. In the upper-left corner, use the drop-down menu to choose your printer. Details about your printer appear below the menu.

At the top of the Print box you find a group of controls labeled Printer. Use the drop-down menu at the top to choose the printer you want to use for this print job. Under this menu you see some details about your printer—its type and how it's connected to your computer. On the right, you see two buttons. The top Properties button opens a dialog with details specific to your printer. If you're on a network and share printers, the Find Printer button can help you locate a printer.

Setting Your Default Printer

If you don't specifically choose a printer, Windows always uses one particular printer—known as the *default* printer. You'll see a checkmark next to its printer icon in the list (Figure 7-6).

You can promote any of your printers to this exalted position, but you can't do it within Word. You need to use the Windows system for this job. Here are the steps:

1. **In your screen's lower-left corner, go to Start → Printers and Faxes.**

   Printers and Faxes is in the Start menu's lower-right corner. When you click it, the Start menu goes away, and the Printer and Faxes box opens in a window that looks remarkably like Windows Explorer—because that's exactly what it is (Figure 7-7). You're in a special location in Explorer that's devoted to printers.

2. **In the Printers and Faxes box, right-click the printer you want to use most of the time, and from the shortcut menu, choose Set as Default Printer.**

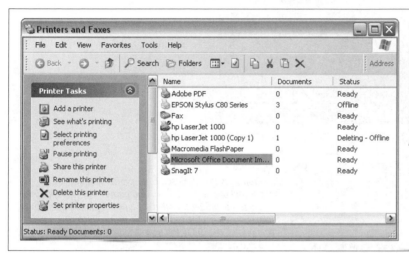

Figure 7-7:
Your Printers and Faxes dialog box probably looks different from this one, because it lists the printers and devices connected to your own computer. The Task Pane on the left gives you the tools you need to add and remove a printer from your computer.

Exploring Printer-Specific Properties

Different printers have different talents. Choose from color printers and black-and-white printers, printers that can print on both sides of the paper, printers that can use huge pieces of paper, and even computer thingys that behave like printers but aren't really printers. Adobe Acrobat and fax machines fall into this category. You need some way to get at the controls for these printers and, obviously, the controls are different for each one. You use the Printer Properties boxes to fine-tune the behavior of your printers and printing devices. For example, Figure 7-8 shows the properties for a black and white laser printer. Figure 7-9 shows the Properties box for a color inkjet printer. Figure 7-10 is the Properties box for the professional version of Adobe Acrobat. It's not really a printer at all; it just thinks it is.

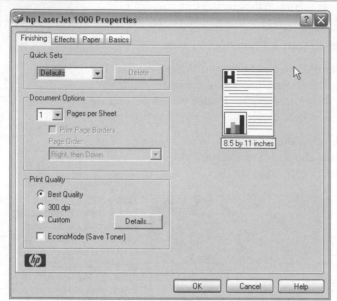

Figure 7-8:
This Properties box for a Hewlett-Packard LaserJet is simple and utilitarian. It gives you a little bit of control over the quality of the print, and under the Effects tab, you can scale your document to print at a larger or smaller size.

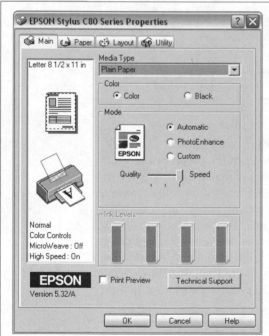

Figure 7-9:
The Properties for this Epson color printer give you lots of options that are helpful for printing photos. For example, you can adjust the printer for different types of photo paper, to make sure you get the best possible prints. Because it's an inkjet printer, the Utility tab provides tools to clean the print head and nozzles.

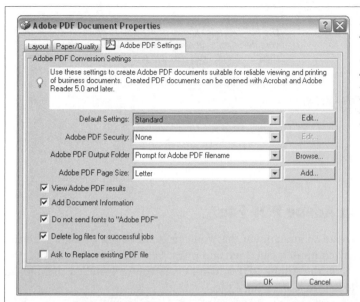

Figure 7-10:
Adobe Acrobat isn't really a printer, but when you install Acrobat Pro (the commercial program used to create Adobe PDF files), it creates a "printer" for PDF files. When you "print" your document, you're actually writing a PDF file. The Properties box lets you choose options for file security and paper size.

Adobe Acrobatics

The dawn of the personal computer revolution generated talk about the paperless office. Of course, that never happened. If anything, personal computers and printers brought about a quantum leap in paper consumption. Still, if any computer tool came close to realizing an alternative to paper, it's Adobe Acrobat or PDF (Portable Document Format). The idea was to create a computer file format that can perfectly capture what's printed on the page—text, graphics, the whole kit and caboodle. The files need to be compact so they can be sent over the Internet. And anyone should be able to read and print these files without paying for additional software.

Adobe created Acrobat to meet all these needs, and before too long, everyone was using this new Portable Document Format to distribute reports and booklets over the Internet. Folks started calling them PDF files, because the filenames end in .pdf (Figure 7-11). Now you'll find PDFs online for just about everything. You can probably download the manual for your TV, your cell phone, and your refrigerator from the manufacturers' Web sites as PDF files. The Census Bureau and many other government agencies provide the information they collect as PDFs.

Businesses are using PDFs more and more as a way to distribute reports, spreadsheets, and other documents. Unlike an Excel spreadsheet, you don't need Excel to open a PDF, since the Adobe Reader program comes on all computers (and if not, it's only a free download away). Furthermore, with a PDF, no one can inadvertently erase or change your information once your document is open.

Adobe's format was so successful that it spawned some imitators. It doesn't make much sense to imitate a standard by creating an incompatible format, but that's what happened. Microsoft launched it's own format called XPS, which stands for XML Paper Specification. And an open source format has similar properties and aspirations—the Open Document format. After some wrangling, Microsoft decided to provide support for *all three* of these formats in Word 2007. The XPS format is included with Word. To add either Adobe PDF or Open Document support, you need to download an add-in program to make it part of Word. To find the add-in that installs both PDF and XPS capabilities to your computer, go to *http://www.microsoft.com/office* and enter *pdf xps* in the search box at the top of the page.

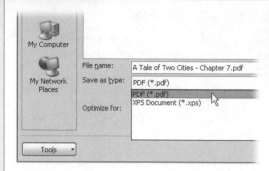

Figure 7-11:
*Use PDF files (also known as Acrobat) to distribute copies of
your documents via email or over the Web. People who
receive your files can view and print them using Adobe's free
Adobe Reader available at www.adobe.com/products/acrobat/
readstep2.html.*

Printing to an Adobe PDF File

Say you want to create an attachment that you can email or put up on a Web site
that anyone, on any computer, can open and print. First, read the box on the previous page and install the Adobe PDF add-in. Once you've installed the add-in,
creating a PDF file is as easy as saving a file.

Go to Office button → Save As → PDF or XPS. The Publish as PDF or XPS dialog
box opens. It looks just like a Save As dialog box. It has all the standard navigation
tools, so you can choose a folder to hold the file. In the "Save as type" drop-down
menu near the bottom, choose PDF, and then click the Publish button in the
lower-right corner (where you'd normally see a Save button). When you're done,
you've created a PDF file that you or anyone else can read and print with Adobe
Reader.

Faxing with Word

Think of faxing a document as a form of long-distance printing. You tell Word to
print a document, and it sends the pages over the phone lines and prints it out on
your friend's fax machine. You need to have a fax modem in your computer, and
the person on the other end needs a fax machine (see the box on page 174). Other
than that, it's a lot like printing. Here are the steps:

1. **With your document open in Word, press Ctrl+P or choose Office button →
   Print.**

   The Print box, as shown in Figure 7-6, opens.

2. **Use the drop-down menu at the top of the Print box to select your fax modem
   as the printer, and then click OK to start the Send Fax Wizard.**

   The Print box closes and the Send Fax Wizard opens (Figure 7-12). The Send
   Fax Wizard consists of several dialog boxes. The first box is stunningly useless.
   It does nothing but welcome you to the Send Fax Wizard and make you click
   the Next button an extra time. The next screen is more functional. You use it to
   tell your computer where to send the fax.

Figure 7-12:
The Send Fax Wizard walks you through the process of addressing and sending your fax. You start by entering names and fax numbers or choosing recipients from your Windows address book.

3. **Enter names (optional) and fax numbers into the Send Fax Wizard.**

   You can click the Address Book button to choose a name and fax number from your Outlook address book, or you can type into the "To" and "Fax number" text boxes. Click Add to add recipients to the list at the bottom. When your list is complete, click Next.

4. **Choose whether or not to include a cover page.**

   If you turn on the cover page checkbox, the wizard prompts you for a subject and a note. The wizard automatically fills in details that Word collected when you installed the program, such as your name and contact info. If you need to, you can review and change those details by clicking the Sender Information button at right. When you're done with the details about the cover page, click Next.

5. **Use the next wizard screen to schedule your fax.**

   You have three options for scheduling. You can send it now, or you can choose to send it when discount rates apply. Last but not least, you can enter a specific hour and minute. When you've scheduled your fax delivery, click Next.

6. **Check the details and preview the fax, and then click the Finish button to send it.**

   The last box of the Send Fax Wizard gives you one last chance to review your fax recipients and to preview the fax by clicking the Preview Fax button (Figure 7-13). A viewer pops up where you can inspect your fax page by page before you send it. When you're certain that everything is okay, click Finish to send your fax on its way.

Figure 7-13:
The last step in the Send Fax Wizard gives you a chance to preview your fax and double-check the names and numbers of the recipients.

Fax Modem vs. Fax Machine

In the days before everyone used email, fax machines took the world by storm. At first, people asked if you had a fax, and then they just asked for your fax number. If you don't have a fax machine, a computer with a fax modem is a pretty good substitute. Any document that you can print, you can send as a fax. Today, most modems also include the smarts to send a fax, and you can get one for only $50 or so.

To see whether your computer has a fax modem, go to Start → Control Panel → Printers and Faxes. When the control panel opens, you'll see Fax listed, but that doesn't necessarily mean you have a fax modem installed. In the list, right-click the word Fax, and then choose Properties from the shortcut menu to open the Fax Properties box.

Last, but not least, click the Devices tab. If your computer can send a fax, you'll see the name of the fax modem listed in the Devices panel.

You can receive faxes with a fax modem too, but if you plan on receiving a lot of faxes, you may want to get a phone line specifically for fax traffic—otherwise your friends are likely to be greeted with a fax screech when they call. If you want the complete capabilities of a fax machine, then you need to add a scanner to your setup. Then you can scan newspaper articles, comic strips, and other important documents and fax them to colleagues.

Changing Print Settings

Sometimes clicking Quick Print doesn't do the trick. Perhaps you want to make several copies of your document, or maybe you want to print only certain pages. To tackle those chores and others, you need to give Word and your printer more specific instructions. To do that, open the Print box (Figure 7-14) by choosing Office button → Print → Print (or pressing Ctrl+P).

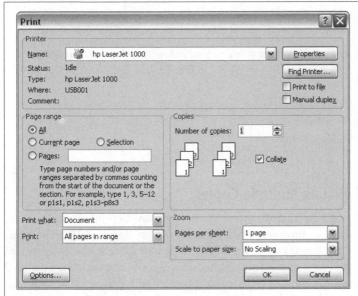

Figure 7-14:
*When your print job gets more
complicated, you need to use the Print
box. In addition to letting you choose a
specific printer, the Print box lets you
print multiple copies or print just a
portion of your opus. You can also get at
specific settings for your printer via the
Properties box.*

Printing Part of Your Document

Word is pretty flexible when it comes to printing bits and pieces of your document. You can choose to print specific pages, or you can select a part of your document, and then tell Word to print only what you've selected. You make your choices using radio buttons in the Print dialog box's "Page range" section:

- **All.** This option prints your entire document using the Print dialog box's current settings. You can choose to print and collate multiple copies of your entire document, if you want.

- **Current page.** This option is ideal for printing a test page. Word prints the page that's currently showing in the window (not the page with the insertion point).

- **Pages.** You can select consecutive pages, random pages, or a combination of the two. For example, if you type *7, 9, 12-15* in the Pages text box, then Word prints exactly those pages (Figure 7-15).

- **Selection.** Select the text you want to print before opening the Print box (Ctrl+P), and then click the Selection button. Word prints only the text that you've selected. This method helps you proofread a specific chunk of your text or print an individual element like a chart or a picture.

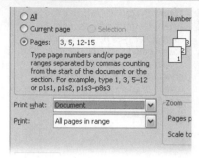

Figure 7-15:
In the "Page range" section of the Print box, you can choose to print your entire document or just a part of it. Using the Print drop-down menu, you can print your document, your document with reviewers' markup (page 365), or the document with its properties, paragraph styles, and other technical details.

Printing and Collating Multiple Copies

Open the Print dialog box (Ctrl+P) to tell Word you want to print multiple copies and provide details about how you'd like them served up (Figure 7-16). The Copies section of the Print box is on the right side. Type a number in the "Number of copies" box, and then turn on the Collate checkbox if you'd like each copy ordered in sequence. If you don't turn on Collate, your printer will spit out all the page 1s, then all the page 2s, and so forth.

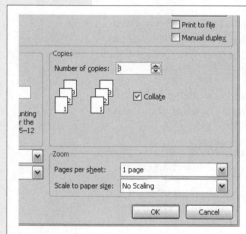

Figure 7-16:
On the right side of the Print box, you can tell Word how many copies to print and whether or not you'd like them collated. In the Zoom section at bottom, you can choose to print more than one page per sheet of paper; Word automatically shrinks everything to fit. The "Scale to paper size" drop-down menu shrinks or enlarges your document to fit a different size of paper.

Printing on Both Sides of the Page

Printing on both sides of the paper produces attractive, professional newsletters, reports, and brochures. Your subject matter can benefit from nice big two-page spreads. Or maybe you'd just like to cut down on the amount of paper you're using. Whatever the reason, you can print on both sides (also known as *duplex* printing).

Word gives you two ways to print both sides of the page—the easy way and the hard way. Unfortunately, the easy way is more expensive. It requires you to have a duplex printer that knows how to print both sides. Duplex printers vary, so you may need to explore your printer's Properties (Ctrl+P, Alt+P) to make sure it's ready for printing on both sides. If so, you'll also see some extra options in the Print dialog box to turn two-sided printing on.

If you don't have a duplex printer (most people don't), you can get the same result if you're willing to do a little paper juggling:

1. **Go to Office button → Print to open the Print dialog box. Turn on the "Manual duplex" checkbox.**

    This checkbox is on the right side, below the Properties button, as shown in Figure 7-17.

2. **Click OK to start printing.**

    Word prints all the odd-numbered pages on one side of the paper, and then it prompts you to remove the printed pages and place them back in the printer tray.

3. **Take the printed pages out of the tray, flip them over, and then click OK.**

    Word prints the even-numbered pages on the backs.

    You may want to experiment on five or six pages to get the routine down. The process is different for different printers. You need to watch for a couple of things with the second print run. First, you need to learn whether to place the pages face up or face down. You may also need to reorder the pages so they print properly. Hint: On the second run, page 2 prints first, so you want page 1 at the top of the pile.

Figure 7-17:
Even if you don't have a fancy duplex printer for printing both sides of the paper, Word will help you out. Turn on "Manual duplex," and Word first prints the odd pages, and then prompts you when it's time to reload.

Printing Envelopes

Computers have always been great for printing documents on standard-size paper, but envelopes present a little bit more of a challenge. Envelopes are oddly shaped and kind of thick. And on some machines, the text needs to print sideways. Fortunately, Word 2007 and most modern printers have overcome the hurdles presented by printing on envelopes.

The first step for successful envelope printing is to make sure that your return address info is stored in Word.

1. **Go to Office button → Word Options and click Advanced.**

   The buttons on the left side of the Word Options box show you different panels of Word.

2. **Scroll down to the General group.**

   Oddly, the General group is almost at the bottom of the Advanced options.

3. **Enter your information in the "Mailing address" box. Click OK when you're done.**

With your vital details stored in Word, you're ready to print an envelope. Here are the steps:

1. **On the ribbon, go to Mailings → Create → Envelopes (Alt+M, E).**

   Most of the tools on the Mailings tab are for mail merge and mass mailings. The Create group, with two buttons—Envelopes and Labels—is on the left side. Clicking Envelopes opens the Envelopes and Labels dialog box to the Envelopes tab, as shown in Figure 7-18.

2. **At the top of the Envelopes tab, in the "Delivery address" text box, type a name and address.**

   Just type in the information on different lines as you'd put it on an envelope.

   The little book icon above and to the right of the Delivery address text box opens your Outlook address book. Click it to select an existing contact. (Look, ma—no retyping!)

Note: The first time you click the Address Book icon, the Choose Profile box opens. There you can select a source for addresses, including your Outlook address book.

---

3. **In the bottom text box, inspect your return address and edit if necessary.**

   If you provided an address in your Word Options, as described in the previous steps, that information appears in the Return address box. If you want, you can change the details now. Just delete the existing address and type the new information. (If your envelopes have a preprinted return address, turn on the Omit checkbox to prevent your stored return address from printing on the envelope.)

4. **Check the preview window and take notice of the feed direction for your envelope.**

   The Preview panel shows you how the envelope will look with the addresses printed on it. The Feed panel gives you guidance for placing envelopes in your printer.

Tip: The Options button leads to another dialog box where you can choose a different envelope size (assuming your printer can handle it). You can also change the font and font size.

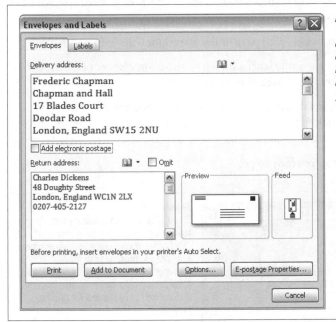

Figure 7-18:
The Envelope tab in the Envelopes and Labels dialog box provides a place to enter both a delivery and return address. The Preview and Feed icons in the lower-right corner show you how the envelope will look and the way to place your envelope in the printer.

Printing Labels

Word comes ready and willing to work with standard address labels. If you just want to print a single label, or if you want to print a bunch of the same label, then follow the steps in this section. (However, if you're printing labels, you're probably working on some kind of large mailing that would benefit from Word's automated mail merge feature. For details, go to page 289.)

Word is prepared to handle labels from Avery and many other manufacturers. Take note of the maker and model number of the labels you've bought, and follow the manufacturer's instructions for loading them into your printer. Then follow these steps to print one or more of the same label:

1. **Go to Mailings → Create → Labels.**

   The Envelope and Labels dialog box opens to the Labels tab.

2. **In the Address box at top, type the address you want to put on the label.**

   If you want to print a batch of your own return address labels, click the box in the upper-right corner labeled "Use return address."

3. **Click the Label section. (It's not just a preview—it's a button!)**

The Label Options dialog box opens, as shown in Figure 7-19. Choose your label manufacturer, and then choose your label's model number. This information tells Word how many labels are on a sheet and how they're spaced. Click OK when you're done.

4. **In the Print section, select "Full page of the same label" or "Single label."**

If you want to print the same label a bunch of times on a sheet of labels, choose the first radio button, "Full page of the same label."

You can print a single label from a sheet of labels, saving the rest of the sheet for another project. Click the "Single label" radio button, and then identify the row and column for Word, so it knows which label to print on.

5. **Click Print when you're ready to go.**

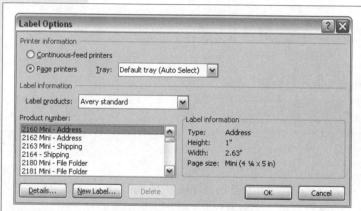

Figure 7-19:
Word's label printing tool is all set to work with a mind-boggling variety of label types. It also gives you some ways to make the most of your label resources. For example, using the Single label button, you can print one label on a sheet and save the rest for another project.

Setting Print Options

The Word Options window is where you tweak Word to make it behave the way you want. Some print settings worth knowing about are, somewhat oddly, tucked away on the Display panel. Go to Office button → Word Options → Display. The printing settings are at the bottom. A checkmark indicates the option is turned on. Here's what you find:

- **Print drawings created in Word.** The factory setting is to have this option turned on. Turn it off if you ever want to print a document without any graphics or floating text boxes.

- **Print background colors and images.** Page color and background images work better for Web pages than they do for printed documents. When you install Word, this option is turned off, but you can always toggle it back on.

- **Print document properties.** Turn this option on, and Word prints your document, and then prints the document properties—author, title, and so on—on a separate page at the end. (If you've never checked out your document properties, take a look by choosing Office button → Prepare → Properties.)

- **Print hidden text.** You can hide text in your document using a font style command (Alt+H, FN, Alt+H). With this box turned on, that text doesn't stay hidden when you print.

- **Update fields before printing.** Word fields include things like the date in a header (page 76) or a contact from your Outlook address book. It's usually a good idea to leave this box turned on because it makes sure you have the most up-to-date information before you print.

- **Update linked data before printing.** Like the fields option above, this option is turned on when you install Word, and it's good to leave it that way. If you link a table or chart from an Excel spreadsheet, this option makes sure it's using the most recent info.

Part Two: Creating Longer and More Complex Documents

2

Planning with Outlines

If your teachers kept hammering you about how important outlining is and made you do elaborate outlines before you tackled writing assignments, forgive them. They were right. Nothing beats an outline for the planning stages of a document. When you're facing writer's block, you can start listing your main topics in a Word document, and then break your topics into smaller pieces with some subtopics underneath. Before your know it, you're filling out your ideas with some essential bits of body text. You've broken through the block.

Word's Outline view is a fabulous outlining tool. It lets you move large blocks of headings and text from one part of your document to another, and rank headings and their accompanied text higher or lower in relative importance. In Outline view, you can even show or hide different parts of your document, to focus your attention on what's important at the moment. Best of all, Outline view is just another document view, so you don't have to outline in a separate document.

Switching to Outline View

Outline view is another way of looking at your document, like Draft view or Print Layout view. In other words, in Outline view, you're just looking at your document in outline form. When you switch into Outline view, your heading text (Heading 1, Heading 2, Heading 3, and so on) simply appears as different outline levels (Figure 8-1). Similarly, you can start a document as an outline—even do all your writing in outline form—and then switch to Print Layout view and have a perfectly normal looking document.

Tip: Jumping back and forth between Outline view and the other views can be very conducive to brainstorming. If you're working with your document in Print Layout view or Draft view and need to get a feeling for the way one topic flows into another, then pop into Outline view, collapse the body text, and examine your headings.

To switch views in Word, go to View → Document Views and click the button you want, or use the keyboard shortcuts in the following list.

- Use **Outline view** (Alt+W, U) to develop headings, establish a sequence for presenting topics, establish a hierarchy between topics, and jump from one section to another in long documents.

- Use **Draft view** (Alt+W, E) for writing rapidly when you don't want to worry about anything except getting ideas down on the page. In Draft view you aren't hindered by too many formatting niceties.

- Use **Print Layout view** (Alt+W, P) when you're putting the finishing touches on your document. In this view, you get a feel for the way your document looks to your readers.

When you switch to Outline view, a new Outlining tab appears on the ribbon. The Outlining Tools group at left has two parts, separated by a vertical bar. You use the controls to move paragraphs around and change their outline levels for (more on that shortly). The tools on the right side don't actually affect the outline—they just control the way it looks.

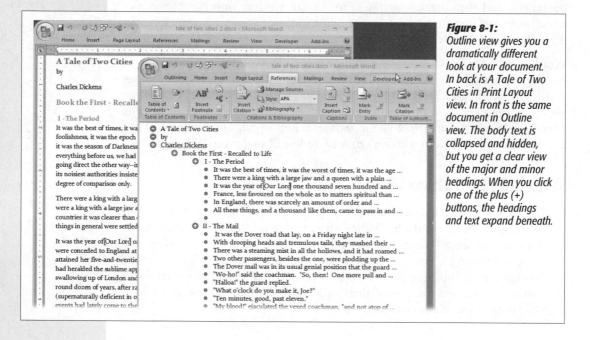

Figure 8-1:
Outline view gives you a dramatically different look at your document. In back is A Tale of Two Cities in Print Layout view. In front is the same document in Outline view. The body text is collapsed and hidden, but you get a clear view of the major and minor headings. When you click one of the plus (+) buttons, the headings and text expand beneath.

When it comes to outlining, Word divides your document into two distinctly different elements:

- **Headings or topics.** You can tell headings are the most important element in outlines by the big + or – button at their left. With headings, it's all about rank. Every heading has a level, from 1 to 9. More important headings have lower-level numbers and are positioned closer to the left margin. Level 1 starts at far left, Level 2 comes below it and is indented slightly to the right, followed by Level 3, 4, and so on.

  Each heading is called a *subhead* of the one that came before. For example, Level 2 is a subhead of Level 1, Level 3 is a subhead of Level 2, and so on.

- **Body text.** For outlining, body text takes the back seat. It just gets that little dot, and if it's in the way, you can hide it entirely, or you can view only the first line—just enough to give you a hint of what's beneath. Body text doesn't really get assigned to a level; it stays glued to the heading above it.

Promoting and Demoting Headings

Planning a document is a little bit like putting a puzzle together. You try a piece here and then over there. A topic you thought was minor suddenly looms larger in importance. When you're brainstorming and plotting, it's important to keep an open mind. Word's helpful because it's so easy to try things out, and you can Ctrl+Z to undo whenever you need to.

When you *promote* a topic, you move it toward the left margin. At the same time, it moves up a rank in the headings hierarchy; so, a Level 3 header becomes a Level 2 header, and so forth. For most documents that means the formatting changes too. Higher-level headers typically have larger or bolder type—something that distinguishes them from their less impressive brethren. To *demote* a heading is the opposite; you move a heading toward the right, usually making it a subordinate of another topic.

For you, these promotions and demotions are easy. In fact, you encounter a lot less complaining here than you'd find in promoting and demoting employees in your company. The easiest way to promote and demote is to click a header and move it to the left or to the right. When you move it a little bit, a vertical line appears, providing a marker to show you the change in rank, as shown in Figure 8-2.

Note: When you promote or demote a heading, the body text goes with it, but you have a choice whether or not the subheads move below it.

When you're brainstorming and pushing ideas around in your document, you don't want to get distracted by the mechanics. When it comes to outlines, you may be grateful that Word provides so many different ways to do the same thing. You get to choose the method that works best for you, and keep your focus on shaping

---

your document. Word gives you three ways to manipulate the pieces of your outline:

- **Dragging.** For outlining, nothing's more intuitive and fun than clicking and dragging. You can put some words in a heading, and then just drag them to another location. As you drag topics and text, Word provides great visual clues to let you know the end result (Figure 8-2).

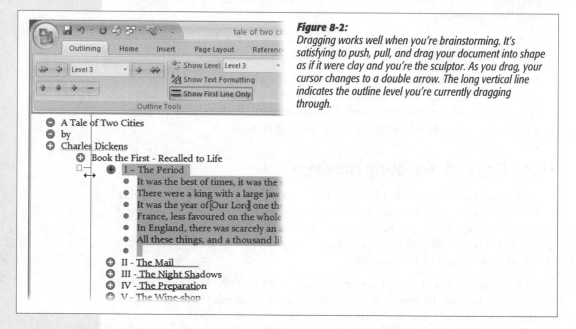

Figure 8-2:
Dragging works well when you're brainstorming. It's satisfying to push, pull, and drag your document into shape as if it were clay and you're the sculptor. As you drag, your cursor changes to a double arrow. The long vertical line indicates the outline level you're currently dragging through.

- **Ribbon.** The buttons on the Outlining → Outline Tools group give you quick, visual access to the commands for promoting and demoting headings and for showing and hiding all the bits and pieces of your document. It's a bit more mechanical than just clicking and dragging the pieces where you want them (Figure 8-3).

One potentially confusing thing about the Outlining tab are those two drop-down menus showing levels. They look almost identical and both give you a choice among the nine topic levels that Outline has to offer. Here's the key: The menu on the left promotes or demotes the current item, while the menu on the right shows or hides levels.

- **Keyboard shortcuts.** Keyboard shortcuts are ideal when your hands are already on the keys and you're typing away. During the planning stages, speed isn't as much of an issue, but if you took your teachers' advice to heart and do lots of outlining, keyboard shortcuts can really streamline your work. Just remember that all these commands use Alt+Shift plus another key, as shown in the table.

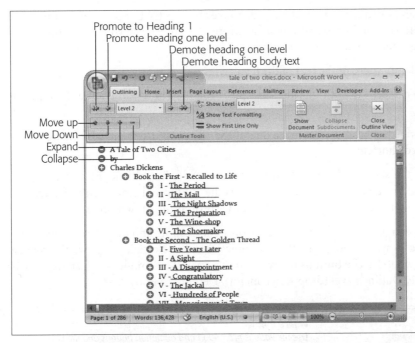

Figure 8-3:
The buttons on the Outlining tab provide a command central for promoting and demoting topics and showing just the right part of your document. The up and down buttons move topics forward and backward in the document, providing a great way to move big chunks of text.

Action	Keyboard Shortcut
Promote Heading Up a Level	Alt+Shift+Right arrow, or Tab
Demote Heading Down a Level	Alt+Shift+Left arrow, or Shift+Tab
Demote Heading to Body Text	Alt+Shift+5 (number pad), or Ctrl+Shift+N
Expand Outline Item	Alt+Shift++
Collapse Outline Item	Alt+Shift+_
Expand or Collapse Outline Item	Alt+Shift+A, * key (number pad)
Show *n* Level Heading	Alt+Shift+*n*, n=number key (top row, not the number pad)
Show Only First Line of Text	Alt+Shift+L

Tip: Another keyboard shortcut helps with outlining: the / key on the number pad. That one little key conceals any fancy character formatting you've applied so you can focus on your outline. See page 192 for more on the Show/Hide Text Formatting command.

Controlling Subheads During Promotion or Demotion

When you promote or demote an outline item, any subheads and subtopics below it move with that item, but only if you collapse the items below, so that they're hidden. In other words, when you move the header above, the subheads keep their relationships even though you can't see them. When you drag topics, the subheads go along, because when you select a topic, you automatically select the subtopics, too.

Word gives you a number of ways to move the header but leave everything else where it is. Here's a step-by-step description of the ways you can promote or demote a heading all by its lonesome:

1. **Click anywhere in the text of the header.**

   Don't select the entire header; just place the insertion point somewhere in the text.

2. **Change the header level using one of the ribbon buttons or by pressing a keyboard shortcut.**

   Use the shortcut keys Alt+Shift+Left arrow or Alt+Shift+Right arrow to promote or demote the header. As long as the subtopics below aren't highlighted, they won't move when you do the header promoting or demoting.

   You can use any of the ribbon controls that promote and demote headers in the same way. As long as the subtopics aren't selected, they won't change (Figure 8-4). The buttons that you can use include: Promote to Heading 1, Promote, Outline Level (drop-down menu), Demote to Body Text.

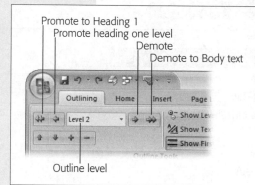

Promote to Heading 1
Promote heading one level
Demote
Demote to Body text

Outline level

Figure 8-4:
Use the various promotion and demotion buttons and the Level drop-down menu on the Outlining tab to organize your outline. If subheads are collapsed under a topic or they're selected, they maintain their relationships when you demote or promote the header. Otherwise, if only the header is selected, it moves and the subtopics stay put.

Note: Working with outlines is actually a lot simpler to do than it sounds. Want to test drive Word's outline features? To check out the screencast—an online, animated tutorial—of the examples in this chapter, head over to the "Missing CD" page at *www.missingmanuals.com*.

Moving Outline Items

Part of organizing your thoughts means moving them to an earlier or later position in the document, without changing their outline level. Say you decide a section you've typed in the middle of your document would make a great introduction. You can move it to the beginning of the document, without promoting or demoting it. Moving topics and items up and down in your document is very similar to moving them left and right. (Figure 8-5). If you want to take subtopics along with an item when you move it, make sure that they're selected (or collapsed) under the item that you're moving.

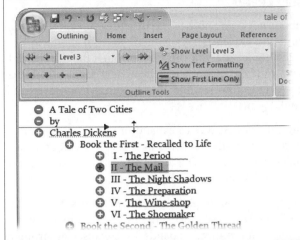

Figure 8-5:
*When you drag a header up and down, you see a
horizontal line that acts as a marker to show you
exactly where the heading (and connected text) will
appear when you let go of the mouse button.*

In addition to dragging, Word gives you two other ways to move topics up and
down in your outline. Select the heading you want to move, and then click the
Move Up or Move Down buttons on the Outlining tab (Figure 8-6). You can also
use the shortcut keys Alt+Shift+up arrow or Alt+Shift+down arrow.

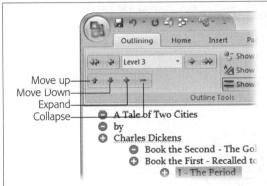

Figure 8-6:
*Use the Move Up and Move Down buttons to reposition a topic
before or after other topics in the sequence of your document.
Its ranking in the heading hierarchy doesn't change.*

Showing Parts of Your Outline

Outline view doesn't just let you see and organize the structure of your prose; it
also helps you zero in on what's important while you make decisions about the
shape and flow of your work. If you want, you can show your headings only so you
can focus on their wording with all the other text out of the way. When you want
to read inside a certain section, you can expand it while leaving everything else collapsed. (Or, if you're having trouble with a passage, you can collapse it so you
don't have to look at it for a while.)

Expanding and Collapsing Levels

You know that old saying about not being able to see the forest for the trees. On the Outlining tab, the Expand and Collapse buttons help you put things in perspective (Figure 8-6). Collapse a topic, and you can read through the major headers and get a feel for the way your document flows from one topic to another. When you need to explore the detail within a topic to make sure you've covered all the bases, expand the topic and dig in.

When you're mousing around, the easiest way to expand or collapse a topic is to double-click the + sign next to the words. It works as a toggle—a double-click expands it, and another double-click closes it. The topics with a minus sign next to them have no subtopics, so you can't expand or collapse them.

If you're interested in making grander, more global kinds of changes, turn to the Outlining → Outline Tools → Show Level menu. (It's the drop-down menu on the right.) Just choose a level, and your outline expands or collapses accordingly (Figure 8-7).

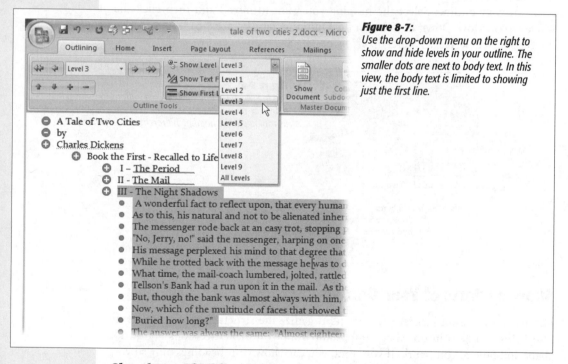

Figure 8-7:
Use the drop-down menu on the right to show and hide levels in your outline. The smaller dots are next to body text. In this view, the body text is limited to showing just the first line.

Showing and Hiding Text

Text takes a subordinate position when it comes to outlining and planning, so it's not surprising that Word provides a couple different ways for you to hide the body text (Figure 8-8). You can double-click the headings above the body text to expand and collapse the topic, just as you would with subheads. The + and – buttons on the Outlining tab work the same way. You can also use the keyboard shortcuts Alt++ to expand and Alt+− to collapse body text under a heading.

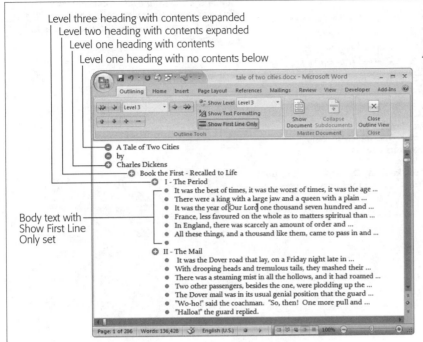

Figure 8-8:
Show and hide text by double-clicking the header just above the text. Click the Show First Line Only button on the Outlining ribbon to hide the paragraphs while leaving the first line to hint at the contents.

Showing Only the First Line

Because each paragraph of body text is like a sub-subtopic, Word's outline view lets you work with them as such. Click the Show First Line Only button, and all you see is the first line of each paragraph. That should be enough to get a sense of the topic that's covered. It's just another way that Outline lets you drill down into your document while you're in a planning and plotting phase.

Showing Text Formatting

Your document's character formatting—different fonts, font colors, and sizes that may bear no relation to the Level 1, Level 2 hierarchy—can be distracting in Outline view. The easiest thing is to turn the formatting off. You can click the Show Formatting button on the Outlining ribbon (Figure 8-9) to toggle formatting on or off, or you can use the shortcut key, which is the / (forward slash) on the number pad.

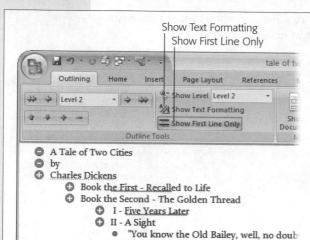

Show Text Formatting
Show First Line Only

Figure 8-9:
*Use the Show Text Formatting checkbox (or the / key
on the number pad) to hide text formatting, as
shown here. This picture also shows the result of
clicking the Show First Line Only button or pressing
Alt+Shift+L to show and hide all the paragraph text
except the first line.*

Working with Long Documents

Longer documents present bigger challenges to writers. The more pages there are, the more details you have to keep track of. Fortunately, computers are great with details, so Word can be a lot of help with your bigger projects. This chapter offers some tips on navigating long documents and dividing them into smaller sections. Voluminous documents also often require extras like tables of contents, indexes, hyperlinks, bookmarks, cross-references, footnotes, and bibliographic citations. Word has tools to make all these jobs easier and moderately less painful, and this chapter shows you how to use all of them.

Word offers a special feature—the master document—for very long documents, like books with multiple chapters. Master documents have a reputation for going bad, but this chapter shows you how to avoid problems. To wrap it all up, this chapter provides some good tips on moving around longer documents using tools like the Document Map and Thumbnails.

Navigating a Large Document

In documents of more than, say, 20 pages, that scroll bar on the right side is way too slow and inaccurate. Instead, it's faster to jump between specific points the document. You can always use the Go To box (Alt+H, G) to jump to a specific page, but what if you don't know the exact page number? Instead, you just know which heading you're looking for. Word gives you quite a few tools to navigate large documents, like bookmarks and browse buttons. Also, a couple of special viewing and navigation tools help you find your way around long documents: the Document Map and Thumbnails (Figure 9-1).

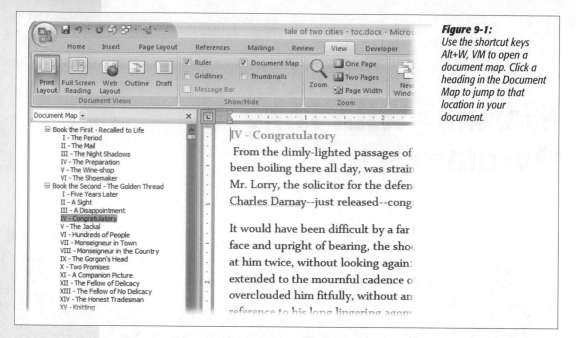

Figure 9-1:
Use the shortcut keys Alt+W, VM to open a document map. Click a heading in the Document Map to jump to that location in your document.

- **Browse buttons.** The Browse buttons at the bottom of the scroll bar are another great tool for navigating documents of any size. By clicking the circular Select Browse Object button, you can choose to browse by headings, endnotes, comments, bookmarks, or pages. Click the double-headed arrow buttons to browse forward or backward through your document.

Tip: When you want to return to a place in your text with nothing specific (like a caption or heading) for the browse tools to look for, just attach a comment to it (page 365) like "Come back and edit this," and then you can just browse by comment. Or, use a bookmark, as described next.

- **Bookmarks.** Bookmarks are versatile tools in Word and do much more than their humble name implies. Covered in detail on page 47, bookmarks are a great way to hop from place to place in your document. When you insert and name a bookmark to mark a page (or a range of pages) with the shortcut Alt+N, K, you can always jump to that spot using the Go To box (Ctrl+G or Alt+H, FD, G).

- **Navigate with the Document Map.** A document map shows you the headings and subheadings in your document. If you choose View → Show/Hide → Document Map (or use the shortcut Alt+W, VM), a panel opens on the left side of Word with an outline of your document. When you click a heading, Word scrolls to that part of your document.

- **Navigate with Thumbnails.** The Thumbnails panel is the document map for the visually oriented. Instead of words, you see mini-pictures of the pages in your document (Figure 9-2). You can't view the Document Map and Thumbnails at the same time. On the ribbon, if you check the box for one, the other disappears. You can use a drop-down menu in the upper-left corner of the panel to change the view from Document Map to Thumbnails.

Figure 9-2:
As a navigation tool, thumbnails work best for documents with graphics or pages that are visually distinctive.

Understanding Sections

The longer and more complex your document is, the more likely it is to contain different *sections*. Word's sections don't have anything to do with how you've divided your document with headings and subheadings. They're electronic divisions you create by adding *section breaks* to your document. Section breaks are a close cousin to page breaks, except that a section can contain any number of pages. More important, each section in a Word document can have its own page formatting.

Many people work with Word for years without ever really understanding Word's sections. After all, the majority of Word documents are only a single section. But sometimes Word adds section breaks behind the scenes. For example, when you add a table of contents or an index to a document, as described later in this chapter, or when you insert an envelope into the same document as a letter (page 289), Word uses a section break to separate the different page formats needed to create these features.

Other times, you break your document into different sections for your own reasons. For example:

- **To change the page orientation.** If you want to have some pages in portrait orientation and others in landscape orientation (charts or graphs, for example), you need to insert a section break where the format changes (Figure 9-3).

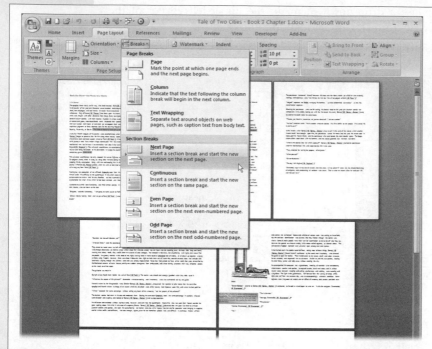

Figure 9-3:
Use section breaks to make major changes to your page format. For example, after you insert a Next Page break, you can change the page orientation or the paper size.

- **To use different sizes of paper in a single document.** If you want to insert some tabloid-size pages in the middle of a document that's the standard 8.5 x 11 inches, you need to use page breaks where the format changes.

- **To change the number of columns on the page.** Perhaps you want to change from a single column format to a double column format; you need to insert a section break where the format changes. You can even put the break right smack in the middle of a page.

- **To change page margins in a single document.** When you want to change page margins, not just adjust a paragraph's indentation, you need to create a section break where the margins change.

- **To restart automatic numbering for separate chapter.** Word uses automatic numbering for figures and other items. If you have a multichapter document, you may want the numbers to restart with each chapter. Not a problem when you insert section breaks between each chapter.

Inserting Section Breaks

As you can see from the list above, sections are all about page formatting, so it's not surprising that the section break commands are found under the Page Layout tab (Page Layout → Page Setup → Breaks or Alt+P, B). When you click the Breaks button in the Page Setup group, the menu is divided into two parts: Page Breaks and Section Breaks.

Note: When you use the Breaks menu (Figure 9-3), remember that the breaks shown at the top aren't section breaks. They're just text formatting breaks like page breaks and column breaks. The commands on the bottom are section breaks, as advertised.

Section breaks have two major distinctions. There are Next Page breaks, which create a new page for the new section, and there are Continuous breaks, which place a divider mark in the text with no visible interruption. Everything below that mark is in a new section. You use a Next Page break when you're changing the paper size or orientation. Or you can use a Next Page break if you want each chapter to start on a new page. You use the Continuous break to change the number of columns or the margins in your document in the middle of a page.

The other two options—Even Page and Odd Page—are just variations on Next Page. They create section breaks *and* start the new section on the next even or odd page. For example, you use this option to make sure that all your chapters begin on a right-hand page (like the ones in this book).

Here's how to insert a section break and change the paper orientation for the new section from Portrait to Landscape.

1. **Click within your text to place the insertion point where you want the section break.**

   You're going to insert a Next Page break, so click after the end of a sentence or paragraph. Also, make sure you're in Print Layout view, so you can see the results of the break.

2. **Choose Page Layout → Page Setup → Breaks, and then select Next Page from the drop-down menu.**

   If you're at the end of your document, Word creates a new empty page, and your insertion point is on the new page, ready to go. If you're in the middle of a document, Word creates a page break and moves your insertion point and all the remaining text to the new section.

3. **With the insertion point in the new section, click the Orientation button (Page Layout → Page Setup → Orientation), and then choose Landscape.**

   When you make Page Setup changes in your new section, they affect only the new section. So when you change the page orientation to landscape, you see pages before the break in portrait orientation and pages after the break in landscape orientation.

In Print Layout view, you see how your document looks with section breaks inserted. In Draft view, section breaks appear in your document as dotted lines. The line doesn't print, but it's visible on your computer screen (Figure 9-4).

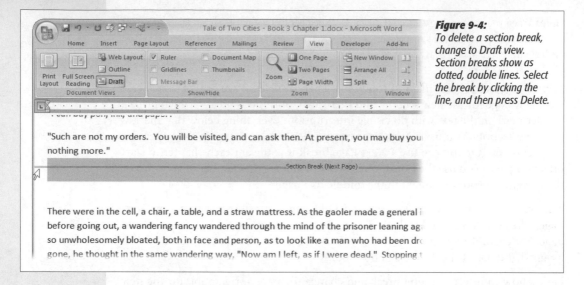

Figure 9-4:
To delete a section break, change to Draft view. Section breaks show as dotted, double lines. Select the break by clicking the line, and then press Delete.

Creating a Table of Contents

When you create very long documents in Word—like theses, annual reports, or even books—you may need to provide a table of contents. Your readers will be glad you did. What's more, if you did a good job of creating headers and subheads as described on page 76, then most of the hard work is done. Word generates the table of contents automatically from your headers, looks up the page numbers for each heading, and formats the whole table for you. All you have to do is tell Word where you want to place the table of contents, and then choose a predesigned format that compliments your document—all of which you do in the Table of Contents group on the References tab, or in the Table of Contents dialog box.

Tip: You can create your table of contents anytime you have headings in place, but it's usually easiest if you do it when you're finished writing and editing.

Here's how to insert a table of contents into your document:

1. **Place the insertion point where you want to put the table of contents.**

   The traditional spot for a table of contents is right after the title and before the main part of the text. It's best to put the insertion point on an empty line, so the table doesn't interfere with any other text. If you agree, click after the title, and then press Enter.

2. **Choose References → Table of Contents, and then choose one of the Automatic table styles from the drop-down menu.**

   The Table of Contents menu gives you a few choices (Figure 9-5). You can choose from two Automatic tables—*Contents* and *Table of Contents*. Or you can choose to create your table of contents manually. If you used custom headings in your document (instead of Word's standard Heading 1, Heading 2), you must create it manually, as described on page 81.

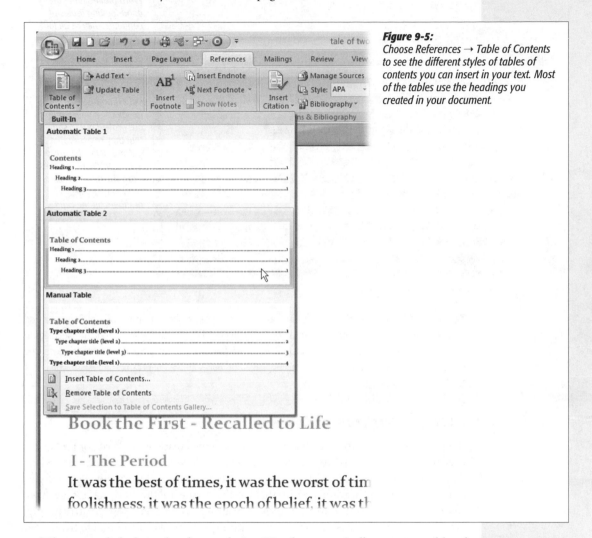

Figure 9-5:
Choose References → Table of Contents to see the different styles of tables of contents you can insert in your text. Most of the tables use the headings you created in your document.

When you click the style of your choice, Word automatically creates a table of contents and inserts the results in your document. To create the table, Word takes paragraphs you've formatted with heading styles, such as Heading 1, Heading 2, and Heading 3 (Figure 9-6).

3. **Review the table of contents.**

Don't forget to inspect the table of contents that Word created. You never know when something unexpected may happen. Maybe you forgot to format a heading with a Heading style, and it doesn't show up in the table. Or worse, some paragraph is mistakenly tagged with a heading style—oops, it's in your table of contents.

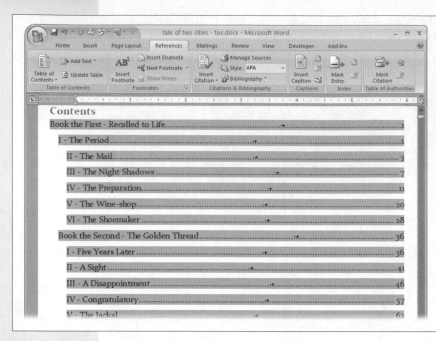

Figure 9-6:
Word makes some pretty good-looking tables of contents. They're all laid out very neatly with subheadings indented and leader characters marching off to the page numbers aligned on the right margins. The headings in your table are grayed out to show that they're generated by a Word field. The arrows in the middle of the lines show the tab characters used to align the numbers on the right.

Tip: If you'd like to reword the entries in your table of contents—shorten overly long headings, or add some descriptive text, for example—you can edit the contents directly, like any Word text. The headings in your document aren't affected. Remember, though, that if you update the table of contents (as described in the next section), be sure to update only the page numbers, not the entire table. Otherwise, you'll lose any hand-entered changes.

Updating Your Table of Contents

If you make changes to your document after you've created a table of contents, you need to have Word update the table to match. For example, if you've added or deleted any headings, the table of contents needs to reflect that change. Even if you didn't change any headings, edits that you've made to the body text may have changed the page numbering and moved headings to different pages. Surprisingly, Word doesn't make these updates automatically—it needs a little nudge from you. Here are the ways you can update your table of contents:

• Go to References → Table of Contents → Update Table.

• Press Alt+S, U.

• Right-click anywhere on the table, and then choose Update Field, as shown in Figure 9-7.

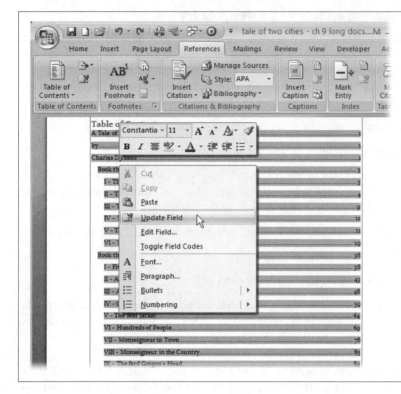

Figure 9-7:
The easiest way to update your table of contents is to right-click anywhere on the table, and then choose Update Field from the shortcut menu. Once it's in place, you can also use your table of contents to navigate. Just Ctrl-click one of the entries to jump to that heading in your document.

When you give Word the command to update the table of contents, a box appears asking you to choose exactly what you want updated (Figure 9-8):

- **Update page numbers only.** You can edit the words in your table of contents, but your changes will disappear if you use "Update entire table," as shown below. Use this option if you've edited the table and want Word to update only the page numbers in the table of contents, while leaving your customized table of contents intact.

- **Update entire table.** This option is the same as deleting the old table of contents and creating a brand new one in its place. Use it if you've made lots of changes to your document and just want to start fresh.

Figure 9-8:
When you update your table of contents, Word needs to know whether you want to update only the page numbers or whether you want to generate a brand new table of contents.

Manually Adding a Table of Contents Entry

Sometimes you have text that you wish to include in your table of contents, but it isn't formatted as a heading. Suppose you've finished your historical novel and decide that it needs an introduction. You don't want to format the word "Introduction" as a heading, but you want it included in the table of contents for the book.

Here's how to add an entry to an existing table of contents:

1. **Select the text you want to add to the table of contents.**

   Put the insertion point in the paragraph you want to add as a table of contents entry. Word uses all the text in the paragraph as an entry. If that's more than you bargained for, you can edit the text in the table later.

2. **Go to References → Table of Contents, and then click Add Text (Alt+S, A).**

   The Add Text drop-down menu appears.

3. **Choose a level for your new contents entry.**

   The menu gives you a choice for each level included in the table of contents. To add an entry, choose its level. For example, Level 1 entries are the major topics, the ones listed closest to the left margin in the contents.

Tip: The Not Shown in Contents option on this menu lets you remove a heading from the table of contents. Place the insertion point in a heading, and then go to References → Table of Contents → Add Text → Not Shown in Contents.

---

4. **Go to References → Table of Contents → Update Table (or press Alt+S, U) to update your table of contents.**

   After you make changes to your document—or specifically to the headings in your table of contents, as you've done here—you need to update the table. Use the ribbon command or the keyboard shortcut Alt+S, U.

Using the Mark Table of Contents Entry box

One more tool can help you manually add an entry to your table of contents. It's the Mark Table of Contents Entry box (Figure 9-9). Select some text that you want to add to the table of contents, and then press Alt+Shift+O to show the box. You can do most of the tweaks in this box from the Table of Contents menu or by editing the table of contents text. The main reason you'd use this box is if your document has more than one table of contents. Some very long documents may have a table of contents for each major chapter or section. If that's the case, the "Table identifier" option in this box lets you choose a specific table of contents.

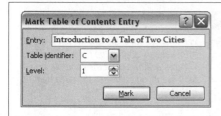

Figure 9-9:
*The Mark Table of Contents Entry box lets you edit the text that's used in the
table of contents. If your document has more than one table of contents,
use the "Table identifier" menu. The Level text box lets you set the table of
contents level for the entry.*

Formatting Your Table of Contents

You can select text in your table of contents and format it just as you would any
other text, but that's not the best way to change the look of your table. If you make
changes or update your table, you'll probably lose the formatting. It's better to
make changes to the table of contents styles using the Table of Contents dialog box
(References → Table of Contents → Table of Contents → Insert Table of Contents).
That way, when you add new entries or update your table, Word formats everything correctly.

Quick formatting for tables of contents

The Table of Contents box shown in Figure 9-10 lets you tweak some formatting
options of the table of contents. Here are your options:

- **Show page numbers.** Turn off this box to remove page numbers from your
  table of contents. You may not want page numbers if, for example, you're doing
  a very short document like a newsletter or brochure, and just want an "In This
  Issue" list.

- **Right align page numbers.** You can make your page numbers line up against
  the right margin, as shown in Figure 9-6, or they can follow immediately after
  the entry's text.

- **Tab leader.** You can choose from any of the standard tab leaders: dots, dashes,
  lines, or none.

- **Formats.** Choose table of contents formatting from several different standard
  styles. These options change the font sizes and styles (italics, bold, and so on).

- **Show levels.** Words standard settings create tables of contents from the first
  three heading styles. You can increase or decrease the number of headings used.

As you make changes, you see the results in the Print Preview box on the left side
of the Table of Contents dialog box (Figure 9-10).

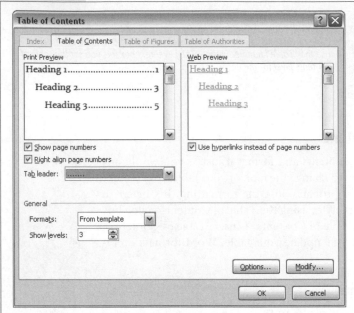

Figure 9-10:
The Table of Contents box shows two versions of your table. On the left is the print version, and on the right is the HTML version. It shows what the contents would look like if you published the document as a Web page.

Detailed formatting for tables of contents

Each line in the table of contents that Word creates has a paragraph style, just like any other paragraph in your document. For the table of contents, these styles not only set the font, font size, and type style, but they also determine the indent from the left margin and the tab leader. Because these styles are ordinary, everyday Word styles, you can fiddle with them all you want. The styles are called: TOC 1 for level 1 entries, TOC 2 for level 2 entries, and so on.

Here are the steps for modifying your Table of Contents styles:

1. **Go to References → Table of Contents → Insert Table of Contents.**

   The Table of Contents dialog box opens (Figure 9-10).

2. **In the lower-right corner, click the Modify button to open the Style box.**

   The Style box lists all the TOC entries 1 through 9. Click an entry, and you see a formatting description in the bottom of the box.

3. **Choose the TOC style you want to format, and then click the Style box's Modify button.**

   When you click Modify, yet another dialog box opens. If you've customized any paragraph styles or created your own, this box should look familiar.

4. **In the Modify Style box, choose from the Format menu at lower left to choose the formatting you want to change.**

Your choices include Font, Paragraph, Tabs, Borders, and more. For more details on paragraph formatting, see page 100.

You can change several different styles from the Modify Style box before closing it. Just choose a new style from the drop-down menu at the very top.

5. **Click OK to close each of the boxes and return to your document.**

Note: One of the entries in the Table of Contents menu is Manual Table of Contents. Choose this option when you just want to create your own table of contents without any help from Word. Word provides the basic format and some placeholder text to get you started. You replace the placeholders by typing your own entries, including the page numbers, which you have to look up yourself. A table of contents created in this way is just plain text. Word won't update it for you if you add new headings to your document or if the page numbers change.

Deleting a Table of Contents

To delete a table of contents, go to the Table of Contents menu (References → Table of Contents → Remove Table of Contents (it's at the very bottom of the menu). Word removes the entire table from your document. But don't worry, you can press Ctrl+Z immediately to bring it back, or just insert a new one.

Creating an Index

An index helps readers find the material that's most important to them. In many ways, indexing is an art, because you have to decide what is likely to be important to your readers. An index that's too cluttered is almost as bad as no index at all. Word can generate and format an index, but it's no help making the important decisions about what to index. That part of the heavy lifting is up to you. On the other hand, by building the index, keeping track of page numbers, and formatting the end result, Word takes a huge burden from you.

Obviously, you don't want to create an index for your document until you're ready to print or distribute it. When you're ready, making an index with Word is a two-step process. First, you mark your index entries in your document—that's the human job. Then, you generate the index—that's the computer's job.

Marking an Index Entry

The first phase of creating an index involves paging through your entire document and, using the Index group on the References tab or pressing a special keystroke, inserting electronic markers for the items you want listed.

As Figure 9-11 illustrates, three types of index entries are available:

- Individual words, phrases, or symbols.
- Entries that span more than one page.
- Entries that reference another index entry, such as "execution, *See guillotine.*"

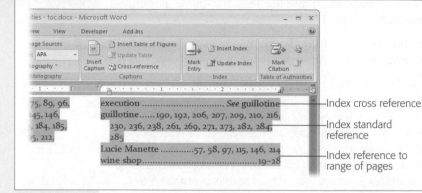

Figure 9-11:
Word automatically alphabetizes and formats your index. This example consists of two columns, with page numbers aligned to the right margin. You can format your index in a number of different ways.

Index cross reference

Index standard reference

Index reference to range of pages

WORD TO THE WISE

What to Index

Here are some tips to keep in mind when you mark index entries:

- **Take the reader's point of view.** This tip is the most important and perhaps the hardest for an involved writer. As you mark index words, ask these questions: Why are people reading this document? What questions did I have when I first approached this subject?

- **Avoid marking too many words.** It's way easy to mark too many words, especially when you know that Word is going to spare you the job of typing out the entire index. If you want a truly helpful index, take the time to consider every marked entry carefully.

- **Consolidate entries whenever possible.** For a professional quality index, it's important to consolidate entries under the most logical index listing. Text like "Miss Manette," "Lucie Manette," and "Lucie" should all be consolidated under "Manette, Lucie" in your index.

- **Make use of cross-references.** Cross-references help your readers find answers. For example, the entry for execution may appear: "execution, *See* guillotine."

- **Use page ranges to reduce clutter in the index.** The index entry for "Lucie Manette" could read: "Manette, Lucie…60, 70-78…" Using page ranges reduces the length and clutter of your index, which makes research easier for your readers.

Here are the steps to mark an index entry:

1. **Select the word or phrase you want to add to the index.**

   Word uses whatever text you select for the actual index listing (unless you make changes in the next step). When you select text, you're also marking its location so Word can identify the page number when it builds the index.

2. **Go to References → Index → Mark Entry (or press Alt+Shift+X).**

   The Mark Index Entry dialog box opens (Figure 9-12). In the "Main entry" text at top, your selected text appears, followed by its page number. You can edit or change this text. For example, you can change "Lucie Manette" to read "Manette, Lucie" so the index entry will be alphabetized under "Manette."

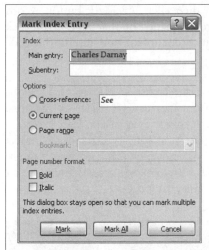

Figure 9-12:
Use the Mark Index Entry box to customize your index entry. The text in the Main entry box is used for the actual index listing. Use the three options in the middle to choose the type of index entry. With the buttons at the bottom, you can choose to mark a single entry or to mark every occurrence of the word or phrase.

3. **In the middle of the Mark Index Entry box, choose a radio button for the index entry type.**

   As mentioned at the beginning of this section, three types of index entries are available: Select the "Cross-reference" radio button if this entry refers to another index entry. (For example, if you select the word "execution," and then type "guillotine" in the cross-reference box, the index entry looks like this: "execution, *See* guillotine.") For individual words, phrases, or symbols, click the "Current page" option. For entries that span more than a page, click Page Range, and then select a bookmark from the Bookmark drop-down menu.

   Note: Before you can mark a Page Range index entry, you must create a bookmark. That's the only way Word can keep track of the page numbers. To create a bookmark, select the text, and then go to Insert → Links → Bookmark (or Alt+N, K). Detailed bookmark instructions are on page 47.

4. **Format the entry.**

   Use the checkboxes under "Page number format" to apply bold or italics formatting to the page numbers. Typically, the page that holds the most important information about an entry gets bold formatting, and page ranges get italics, but Word will do whatever you tell it. This kind of formatting is completely optional.

5. **Click Mark to create an entry for a single page, or Mark All to create entries for every instance of the selected words that Word finds in the document.**

   Word hides a special code in the text of your document to mark the entry or entries. Word reads all these hidden codes when it builds an index. (For details, read the box on page 210.)

Say you select the word "England," and then click the Mark button, Word places a single chunk of code after the word "England" on that page. If you click Mark All, Word looks through your entire document and inserts the code everywhere the word "England" appears.

Warning: It's easy to get carried away with the Mark All button because it's so tempting just to click it, and then let Word find every occurrence of a word or a phrase. The problem is, you can end up with too many index references. Instead of using the Mark All button, consider using the Mark Index Entry box in tandem with Word's Find tool. Use the Find box to search for words and phrases, but you can use your discretion when you mark items for the index. (The Mark All button has no discretion; it just marks the occurrence of a word or a phrase.) The Mark Index Entry box stays open, so it's easy to search and mark more index entries. When you want to close the Mark Index Entry box, click Cancel.

POWER USERS' CLINIC

Understanding Index Codes

Whenever you mark an index entry as described in the previous steps, Word inserts a code right within the text of the document. It's just hidden so you don't usually see it. Hidden text (page 379) doesn't show when the document is printed, but you can see it onscreen by going to Home → Paragraph → Show/Hide ¶.

An index entry marking the words Lucie Manette may look like this: { XE "Manette, Lucie" }. The code is within the curly braces, and the XE is how Word identifies the code as an index entry.

Here are examples of the code Word inserts in your document to mark pages for different index entries:

* **Basic Index Entry.** Example: { XE "Manette, Lucie" }. All the code is within the curly braces ({}), and the XE identifies the code as an index entry. Word adds the page where this code appears to the Manette, Lucie index listing.

* **Index Subentry.** Example: { XE "England:London" }. The colon in this code means it's a subentry. Word adds a London subentry, with the page number, under the England index listing.

* **Page Range Entry.** Example: { XE "Dover Road" \r "DoverRoad" }. The |r marks this entry as a page range entry. *DoverRoad* is the name of a bookmark (page 47) in the document that marks more than one page. The pages included in the DoverRoad bookmark appear as a range in the Dover Road index listing.

* **Index Cross-reference.** Example: { XE "execution" \t "See guillotine" }. The |t marks this entry as a cross-reference. Word lists "execution" in the index followed by the note "See guillotine."

To create an index, Word reads all the entries and alphabetizes them, and then removes duplicate entries. For example, five Lucie Manette entries are on page 94, Word lists the page only once.

Building an Index

Creating the actual index is a lot easier and faster than marking your index entries. You have only a couple decisions to make, and Word does all the rest. The first thing to decide is where you want to place the index.

Follow these steps to create the index:

1. **Press Ctrl+End to move the insertion point to the end of your document, and then press Ctrl+Enter to start your index on a brand new page.**

   Traditionally, an index goes at the back of a document, but Word puts it wherever you want.

2. **Type *Index* to give the section a title, and then choose Home → Styles → Heading 1.**

   Giving the title for the index a Heading 1 makes it look important and means that it shows up in the Table of Contents, to boot.

3. **Go to References → Index → Insert Index (or press Alt+S, X) to open the Index dialog box, where you make some choices about the appearance of your index (Figure 9-13).**

   At the upper-right corner of the Index tab, the Print Preview box shows you how your index will look on the page. Use the other controls to change its appearance. For Type, if you select Indented, then the index lists the subentries indented under the main entry. If you choose Run-in, then subentries and page numbers immediately follow on the same line as the entry.

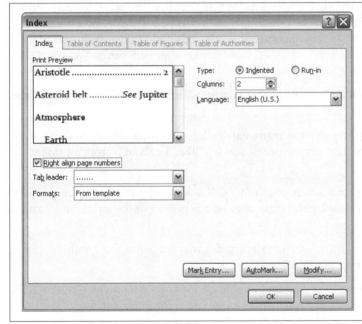

Figure 9-13:
Use the Index dialog box to create an index for your document. Make adjustments to the appearance with the Type, Columns, and other controls. The Print Preview box lets you see the results of your formatting on example text.

From the Columns menu, you can choose the number of columns per page (two or three columns usually work well). Below the Preview box, you find controls to align index page numbers on the right margin and to set the leader that links the entry to the page number. The Formats drop-down menu provides several formatting options that change the font size and style. If you want to customize the appearance of your index, click the Modify button, and then you can format your index using Word's standard style and text formatting tools (Chapter 4).

4. **When you're done formatting your index, click OK.**

Word builds the index and places it in your document at the insertion point. The process may take a few moments.

Tip: The Mark Entry button closes the Index box and opens the Mark Index Entry box (Figure 9-12). Click it if you decide you're not ready to create the index and want to go back to marking entries. Clicking the AutoMark button makes Word go through your document and mark entries for you, but only if you supply a concordance file.

Using AutoMark with a Concordance File

If you have a long document and a short amount of time to index it, then you may find Word's AutoMark feature appealing. Basically, you type a list of every word you can think of that should go into the index into a separate Word document—a *concordance file*, like the one shown in Figure 9-14. You don't have to mark each entry in the document; you don't even have to read the entire document if you're already family with what it contains. When you References → Index → Insert Index, and click the AutoMark button, Word reads your concordance file and creates an index based on those instructions. It sounds good in theory, but in practice it often creates *too many* entries because, unlike a human being, Word is indiscriminate about marking entries.

Here are the two major problems that pop up with both the Mark All button and the AutoMark tool:

- **AutoMark returns way too many entries for each topic.** Word has no way of telling an important occurrence of a word (like "England") from an unimportant one.

- **AutoMark does not create page ranges.** If a word appears on twelve consecutive pages, AutoMark puts twelve page numbers next to the index entry instead of a range.

Still, if you're in a hurry, an AutoMark index may be better than nothing. If you want to go this route, here are the steps:

1. **Go to Office button → New and double-click Blank Document. Create a table with two columns and as many rows as you need for index entries.**

This table holds your concordance file.

---

2. **For each entry, enter a search word in the left column and an index entry in the right column.**

   You'll probably want to gather a few search terms under each entry. For example, instead of separate index entries for "guillotine" and "Guillotine," you want Word to list the page numbers for both "guillotine" and "Guillotine" under the same entry—"guillotine"—"as shown in Figure 9-14. Save and close the concordance file when you're done.

3. **Follow steps 1 through 4 starting on page 208 to position and format your index. Then, in the Index dialog box, click the AutoMark and open your concordance file.**

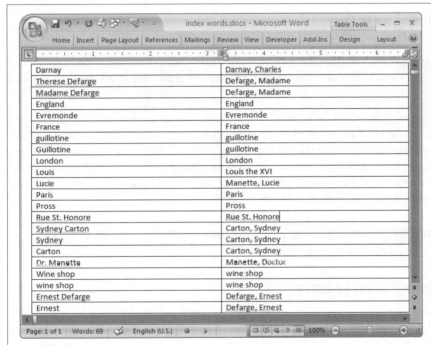

Figure 9-14:
In a concordance file, type words that you want Word to search for and mark for the index in the left column. Type the words that you want actually listed in the index listing in the right column. Several marked words can lead to the same index listing.

Updating an Index

What if you need to update an index? Perhaps you remembered and marked some additional entries after you built your index. No problem—Word gives you a quick and easy way to add those new entries to your index. Place your insertion point inside your index, and then press the F9 key or (Alt+S, D). Or, if you can't remember keystrokes, just go to References → Index → Update Index on the ribbon. It may take a moment or two, since Word rereads all the index entries, but you end up with a new index including any new entries you've created.

If you want to change your index's formatting, place the insertion point somewhere in the index, and then go to References → Index → Insert Index. Make your formatting changes, and, when you're done, click the OK button. An alert box pops up asking if you want to replace the selected index (Figure 9-15). Click OK, and the old index is gone and your all-new, improved index takes its place.

Figure 9-15:
If you try to create an index in a document that already has an index, you see this message. When you click OK, Word removes the old index and inserts a new one. When you click Cancel, Word leaves your old index in place.

Deleting an Index

You may have a couple reasons for wanting to delete an index from your document. Perhaps you decided not to have an index, or you want to make major changes to your index, so you're going to delete the current index and insert a new one.

The index looks like a lot of words on the page, but the entire index is represented by one relatively short bit of computerese known as a *field code*. With one command, you reduce your entire index to a field code of just a few characters, making it much easier to delete. Press Shift+F9, and your index disappears. What you see looks something like this: { INDEX \c "2" \z "1033"}. Select this text, including both brackets, and then press Delete. Good bye index.

Note: A different command is used for hiding field codes and displaying the results. If you've turned your index into a field code but want to change it back to the index text, press Alt+F9.

Deleting an Index Entry

It may seem odd, but it's easier to delete the entire index than it is to delete individual entries from your document. For one thing, you probably don't have to search for the index—it's big and it's usually at the end of your document. The marked index entries in your document could be anywhere, and if you're deleting every vestige of Lucie Manette index entries in *A Tale of Two Cities*, that's a lot of deleting.

If your plan is to have a document without an index at all, you may want to delete the index as described above and not worry about deleting each and every hidden index entry code in your text. Under normal circumstances, the hidden text doesn't show when you print or view your document.

To delete an index entry, you need to find the index code in your document, and then delete it, just as you would any text. Here are the steps:

1. **Go to Home → Paragraph → Show/Hide ¶ to view the hidden text in your document.**

   You're on a search and destroy mission, so the first thing you need to do is make sure you can see your target. When you turn on hidden text, you can see the index codes (along with other hidden characters like, well, paragraph marks). The index code looks something like this: { XE "Manette, Lucie" }.

   You can scroll through your document and scan for entries you want to delete, but it's faster to use the Find dialog box, as described in the next step.

2. **Press Ctrl+F to open the Find box to search for the index codes. In the "Find what" text box, type *XE*.**

   You can't search for the curly brackets, but you can search for some of the other text within. That way, Word searches for each index entry so you can inspect them one by one.

3. **Click Find Next, until you find the first index entry you want to delete. Select the entire code including the brackets, and then press Delete.**

   The entry is a goner. Of course, that's just a single entry on a single page. If you want to remove an item entirely from the index, you must keep clicking Find Next until you've found—and deleted—every marking of that entry.

Navigating with Hyperlinks

Hyperlinks are those bits of underlined text or pictures that, when you click them, take you to a new place, like another Web page. Most people never think of adding links to their Word documents, because they're thinking of them as printed documents. However, if some of your readers may read your work onscreen, consider adding hyperlinks (Figure 9-16).

Figure 9-16:
Word highlights hyperlinks with a different text color and an underline. When readers hold their cursor over the text, a screen tip pops up explaining that they can jump to another location using Ctrl-click.

Word's hyperlinks are identical to the hyperlinks on Web sites. They even use the same programming language (HTML). Hyperlinks you create in Word stay intact if you save the file in a format other than Word—like a PDF file or a Web page. And since other Office programs also use HTML, if you copy or cut the text and paste it in another document in a program such as Excel or PowerPoint, the hyperlink will work just fine in the new document.

Links aren't just for Web pages anymore. Word lets you make hyperlinks that go all sorts of places:

- **Locations in your document.** If your document refers to another section, add a link so your readers can jump right there instead of scrolling.

- **Other documents on your computer or network.** If you're working with a group of people on an office network, hyperlinks to related shared documents can be very effective. When you click the link to a shared document, Word opens that document even if it's not on your computer, as long as you have permission to open it.

- **Documents on the Web.** Whatever topic you're writing about, you can find related Web pages, photos, maps, news items, and blogs on the Internet. If you can find them, you can create hyperlinks for your readers.

- **Email forms.** You can give your readers an easy way to interact with you or your company by inserting email hyperlinks in your document. When they Ctrl+click the link, a properly addressed email form appears. All they have to do is fill in their comments (Figure 9-17).

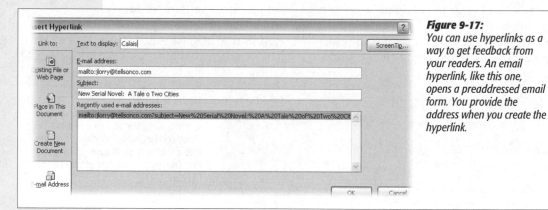

Figure 9-17:
You can use hyperlinks as a way to get feedback from your readers. An email hyperlink, like this one, opens a preaddressed email form. You provide the address when you create the hyperlink.

To create a hyperlink to any of the above places, the steps are almost the same. You select the text you want to turn into a hyperlink, and then, in the Insert Hyperlink box, you tell Word what to link it to:

1. **Select the text for the link.**

   Choose text that gives your readers a good clue to where the link goes. Two or three words is usually enough to catch your readers' attention.

2. **Go to Insert → Links → Hyperlink (Alt+N, I or Ctrl+K) to open the Insert Hyperlink dialog box.**

The Insert Hyperlink box looks much like a standard Windows Open file box, but there are some significant differences (Figure 9-18). In fact, the box is something of a chameleon and changes when you click the buttons on the left side.

3. **On the left, in the "Link to" box, choose the type of link you want to create.**

You have several options:

- **Existing File or Web Page** is the button to click if you want to link to another Word document on your own computer or network, or if you want to link to a Web page. Just to the right of the "Look in" drop-down menu, click the folder icon to browse your computer or network for documents (as shown in Figure 9-18). Double-click the document you want to link to. The Insert Hyperlink box closes, and Word creates the link.

  To link to a Web page, click the Internet icon in the upper-right corner (it looks like a globe under a magnifying glass) to open your Web browser and go to the Web page you wish to link to. After you've found the page in your browser, go back to the Insert Hyperlink box and once again click the Existing File or Web Page button. Word adds the address in your Web browser to the Address box. (It begins with *http://*, as do all good Web addresses.) Click OK to close the box and create the hyperlink.

- Click **Place in this Document** if you're creating a link to help readers jump around in a long document. Within a document, Word can create links to either headings or bookmarks, and shows you a list of your choices. (If you don't have anything for Word to attach the link to, click Cancel to close the dialog box and create a bookmark, as described in the next section.)

- **Create New Document** lets you create a hyperlink to a document you haven't even started yet. When you click Create New Document, the Insert Hyperlink box changes. Type the name of the new document you want to create in the "Name of new document" text box, and then click OK. Word creates and saves your new document on the spot. You can go back and add text to it later.

- **Email Address** creates a *mailto* hyperlink in your document. When you choose this option, the Edit Hyperlink box changes, as shown in Figure 9-18, so you can type the email address you want to link to. It's also helpful (but not necessary) to provide a Subject for the email. Click OK to close the box and create the link.

Tip: When you type some text in the ScreenTip box, Word displays it as a small, onscreen label whenever someone's mouse passes over the link, just like on a real live Web page.

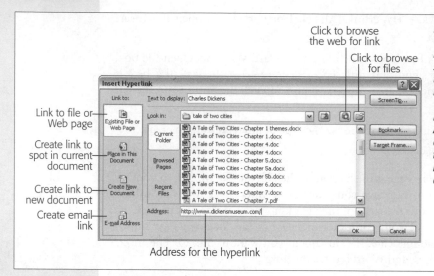

Click to browse the web for link

Click to browse for files

Link to file or Web page

Create link to spot in current document

Create link to new document

Create email link

Address for the hyperlink

Figure 9-18:
You can create four basic kinds of hyperlinks, as shown by the options in the "Link to" box: Existing File or Web Page, Place in This Document, Create New Document, or E-mail Address. Each time you click one of the options, the tools in the "Look in" box change to match your choice.

Inserting Bookmarks

Bookmarks, which mark a spot in your document, may seem like a somewhat mild-mannered Word tool, but more power is hidden under their Clark Kent exterior than you may expect. Bookmarks come in handy in long documents because so many other features depend on them:

- **Browsing by bookmark.** You give each bookmark a name when you create it, and you see those names listed in the Go To dialog box (Home → Editing → Go To). You can then use these bookmarks to hop from place to place in your document, as described on page 48.

- **Indexing.** Because bookmarks are based on selected text, you can create a bookmark that includes several pages. In this way, you can use bookmarks to create page ranges for building indexes, as described earlier in this chapter.

- **Hyperlinks.** When you create a hyperlink (page 216) to a specific point in your document, Word needs something to anchor the link to. That can be a heading or a bookmark that you've created at any point in the text.

- **Cross-references.** When you create cross-references in your documents, you can link to headings, but what if you want to link to specific text within a topic? You can create a cross-reference to any part of your document, by simply creating a bookmark first, and then referencing the bookmark. (More on cross-references in the next section.)

- **Macros.** These mini-programs that automate Word tasks also frequently use bookmarks. Say you create a macro that performs a task with the text from a particular part of your document; you need to be able to identify the text. You can do that by creating a bookmark. The macro uses the bookmark's name to do its magic. For more on Word's macros, see page 434.

Detailed tips on how to create and use bookmarks are on page 47, but in a nutshell, here's how to quickly insert one into your document: Just select some text, and then go to Insert → Links → Bookmark (or press Alt+N, K). Proceed as shown in Figure 9-19.

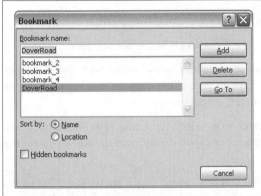

Figure 9-19:
The Bookmark dialog box gives you the power to both create and destroy. To delete a bookmark, select it in the list, and then click the Delete button (or press the Delete key). To create a bookmark, you need to select text before you open this box. Type a name in the text box at the top, and then click Add.

Cross-Referencing Your Document

Schoolbooks, business reports, and a variety of other documents use cross-references to refer to photos, figures, charts, tables, and other parts of the document. When readers view your document on a computer, they can Ctrl-click the reference to jump to that spot. For example, clicking the words "Chart A" takes the reader right to the chart in your document. You can turn this chore over to Word with confidence that it will keep track of the reference and the page number for you, even as you add or move material.

With Word you can create cross-references to the following items:

- **Numbered item.** Numbered paragraphs in your text created with the Home → Paragraph → Numbering command (Alt+H, N).

- **Bookmark.** Bookmarks in your text that refer to specific locations or ranges of pages. Bookmarks are inserted with the keyboard shortcut Alt+N, K.

- **Heading.** A paragraph you styled with a built-in headings such as Heading 1or Heading 2.

- **Footnote.** Word keeps track of your footnotes' locations and their numbers.

- **Endnote.** Endnotes are a little easier for a human to hunt down; still, Word keeps track of their locations and page numbers.

- **Equation.** For documents dealing with math, Word keeps track of all the equations created with the built-in equation editor.

- **Figure.** When you insert pictures and label them with a caption, Word keeps track of the "figure" number. For a step-by-step description of creating cross-references for figures, see page 220.

- **Table.** Tables with or without captions are tallied in Word, and you can create cross-references to them.

Here are the steps for adding a cross-reference to your document:

1. **In your document, type the text you'd like to go *before* the reference.**

   Usually, cross-references have some preceding introductory text, like *As shown in* or *For more details, see.* You have to type this part yourself; Word adds the cross-reference (the Ctrl-clickable text or page number).

2. **Go to Insert → Links → Cross-reference. When the Cross-reference dialog box opens (Figure 9-20), use the "Reference type" drop-down menu to choose the object that you're referring to.**

   Whichever type you choose, in the text box below, Word shows you a list of the specific items in your document (numbered items, bookmarks, headings, and so on) that are candidates for cross-referencing.

3. **From the "Insert reference to" menu, choose the text that describes the reference.**

   Here's where you select what appears in your document—the text that your readers can read and Ctrl-click. Your choices from this menu depend on what you've chosen from the "Reference type" menu. For example, if you're referring to a heading, you can choose to insert the heading text itself (Figure 9-20), or just the page number.

4. **If desired, turn on the "Insert above/below" checkbox.**

   In addition, you can insert either the word "above" or the word "below" to indicate where the item is relative to the cross-reference. For example, say you're putting the cross-reference "see Table 1," before Table 1 in your document. If you turn on this checkbox, the reference reads "see Table 1 below." If you happen to move Table 1 to before the cross-reference, Word changes it to "see Table 1 above." This way, if your readers print your document, they have a clue where to go looking for the cross-reference without the benefit of a hyperlink.

Tip: Of course, if your readers are hard-copy types, choose the page number from the "Insert reference to" menu (step 3), so they'll know exactly where to look.

---

5. **When you're done, click Insert to close the Cross-reference dialog box.**

   Back in your document, you see your newly minted cross-reference.

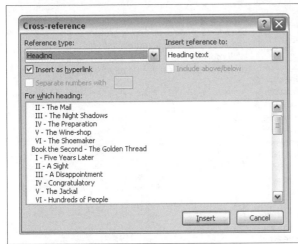

Figure 9-20:
In the Cross-reference box, use the "Reference type" drop-down menu to choose the type of item you're referring to and the "Insert reference to" menu to choose what actually appears in your text. For example, you could choose a page number, a figure number, or the text from a caption.

Deleting cross-references

You can delete a cross-reference as you'd delete any text; just select it, and then press the Delete or Backspace key.

Cross-Referencing Figures

Figures—those photos, drawings, and other graphics—help convey information that would be hard to describe in text. They help break up that vast sea of words as they illustrate your point. In academic papers, magazine articles, and business documents, figures usually have numbers to make it easier to refer to them (Figure 9-21).

Tip: For details on how to add captions and figure numbers to your graphics, see page 287.

To create a cross-reference to a figure, you use the Cross-reference dialog box, as described in the previous section. However, since figures have a figure number and a caption as well as a location in your document, you have a few more options when creating the cross-reference, so the process is a bit more complicated.

First, of course, you need some text to introduce the figure, like *The guillotine, as shown in.* Remember to type only the words that come before the cross-reference, not the cross-reference itself, and then choose Insert → Links → Cross-reference to open the Cross-reference dialog box. From the "Reference type" drop-down menu, choose Figure. The text box below lists the figures in your document. Select the one you want to reference, and then, from the "Insert reference to" drop-down menu, choose the text that describes the reference to the figure.

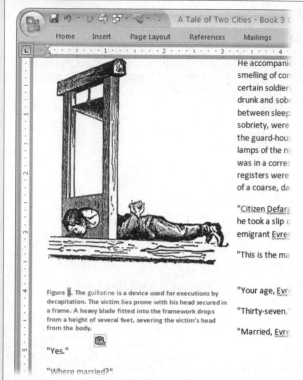

Figure 9-21:
Use figures, photos, and other artwork as an opportunity to provide more details for your readers. With captions and an image, you can explain complex subjects in a very small amount of space.

Captions have three parts: a label, (like the word "Figure"), a number, and the caption text. Your cross-reference can include any one of those items, or all three. It can also show the page number and state whether the figure is above or below the reference in the text (Figure 9-22). For example, if you turn on all of these options, you may end up with something like this: *The guillotine as shown in Figure 1 on page 1 above.*

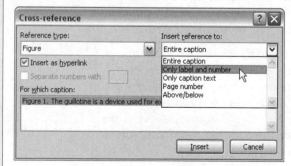

Figure 9-22:
To insert a cross-reference for a figure, choose Figure as the reference type. Use the "Insert reference to" drop-down menu to select the text that appears in the reference.

Making a Table of Figures

In addition to keeping track of figures and their captions, Word can create a table that lists the figures, shows their captions, and shows the page numbers. Inserting a table of figures is similar to inserting a table of contents. Go to References → Captions → Insert Table of Figures (Alt+S, G) to open the Table of Figures box (Figure 9-23). Use the Formats drop-down menu to choose a style for your Table of Figures. Word can take its style cue from your template, or you can use one of several predesigned styles from the menu.

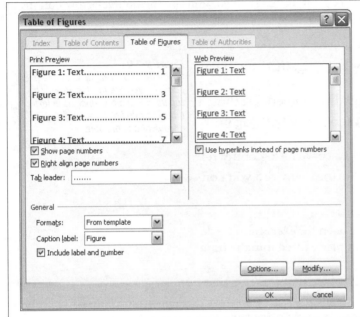

Figure 9-23:
The Table of Figures box gives you a preview of the printed table on the left. On the right you see a Web preview. Check the box below to use hyperlinks on the Web page instead of page numbers. Use the other tools such as the "Show page numbers" and "Right align page numbers" box to format your table.

Creating Footnotes and Endnotes

If you've ever read—or written—a term paper, thesis, or book of a scholarly nature, you've encountered footnotes or endnotes. Typically, writers use these notes for background or explanatory information that may be of interest to some, but not all readers. *Footnotes* and *endnotes* are the exact same thing, except footnotes appear at the bottom (foot) of each page, and endnotes come all together at the end. (*Citations* are similar to footnotes, but in Word, you create them with a separate tool; see page 227.) A footnote or endnote marker in the text, usually a superscript number, indicates that a note with a matching number is at the bottom of the page or at the end of the document (Figure 9-24).

When you create footnotes and endnotes using Word's tools, the program keeps track of the numbering for you. If you add and remove notes, Word renumbers the rest automatically. When you print the document, Word places the footnotes and endnotes in their rightful places at the bottom of the pages or at the end of the document, just as if you'd typed them there yourself—but a whole lot easier.

Onscreen, Word provides some helpful navigation techniques. You can double-click a note to jump to its partner reference mark and vice versa. When you're working with the notes themselves, a right-click brings up a context menu that includes "Go to endnote" or "Go to footnote" options. Click these options to jump from the note to the reference in your text. You can also use the Browse buttons (page 46) at the bottom of the scroll bar to move between footnotes and endnotes. First, click the round Select Browse Object button and choose either footnotes or endnotes from the pop-up menu. Then you can use the double-arrow buttons to jump from note to note.

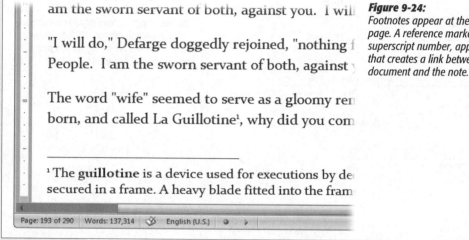

Figure 9-24:
Footnotes appear at the bottom of the page. A reference marker, usually a superscript number, appears in text that creates a link between the document and the note.

Inserting Footnotes and Endnotes

Footnotes are easier than endnotes for readers because they require less page flipping to find the note. Different types of documents have different standards, and more often than not it's a teacher or a professor who dictates the preferred style. Back in the typewriter era, endnotes were much easier to create, because you didn't have to worry about leaving space at the bottom of the page for the notes. Fortunately, Word makes it equally easy to create footnotes and endnotes.

Just follow these steps:

1. **Click to place the insertion point in your text where you want the reference mark.**

    You may want to put the mark at the end of a sentence or paragraph. But if the note pertains to the meaning of a specific word, click-right after that word.

2. Go to References → Footnotes → Insert Footnote (Ctrl+Alt+F or Alt+S, F) or Insert Endnote (Ctrl+Alt+D or Alt+S, E).

Word places the reference mark at the insertion point and takes you to the bottom of the page (where the footnote will appear) or the end of the document (where the endnote will appear). You see the note's reference mark, immediately followed by the insertion point, so you can start typing the note.

Tip: You can also press Alt+S, Q (or click the dialog box launcher at the bottom of the Footnotes group) to insert notes using the Footnote and Endnote dialog box. Use this method if you'd like to change the numbering scheme from the usual 1, 2, 3.

---

3. Type the text for the note.

After you type the note, right-click your footnote, and then choose Go to Footnote. Your insertion point jumps back to your original location, where you can continue work on the main body of your document.

Tip: If you want to change the text of your note later, you can edit it as you would any other text.

Formatting Footnotes and Endnotes

You can format your footnotes and endnotes just like any other text, using the methods described in Chapter 2. For example, if you want to make a word bold or italics, just select it, and then press Ctrl+B or Ctrl+I. However, to edit the reference marks—say, change them from superscript numbers to letters—you need to open the Footnote and Endnote dialog box. Press Alt+S, Q or, on the ribbon, click the dialog box launcher in the lower-right corner of the Footnotes group.

Using the Footnote and Endnote box (Figure 9-25), you can choose where your notes appear, and you can customize the style of the reference mark. Reference numbers can be Arabic numbers, Roman numbers, lowercase Roman numbers, letters, or other symbols. The Numbering drop-down menu lets you choose whether the numbers apply to the whole document or they start with each new section. Change the number in the "Start at" text box if you want to start at a reference other than 1 or the first symbol. For example, if your book or thesis is split between more than one document, you can make the numbering in the second document pick up where the first document left off.

Tip: If you decide (or your instructor tells you) to convert all your endnotes to footnotes or vice versa, you can do that in the Footnote and Endnote box, too. At the top of the box, click the Convert button, and then choose one of the options from the Convert Notes box.

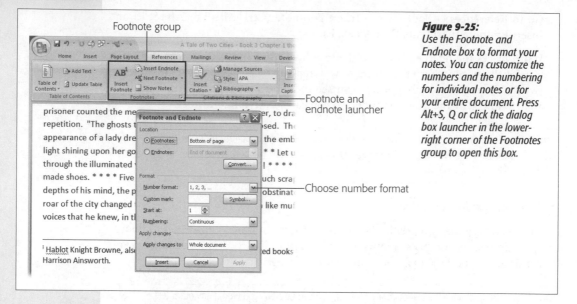

Footnote group

Figure 9-25:
Use the Footnote and Endnote box to format your notes. You can customize the numbers and the numbering for individual notes or for your entire document. Press Alt+S, Q or click the dialog box launcher in the lower-right corner of the Footnotes group to open this box.

Footnote and endnote launcher

Choose number format

Deleting footnote and endnotes

It's easy to delete unwanted footnotes and endnotes. Select the reference mark in your text, and then delete it by pressing the Delete or Backspace key. Not only does the reference mark disappear, but the note does too.

Inserting Citations and Creating a Bibliography

Citations are similar to endnotes in that they're listed at the end of the document, and you can click a reference link in the text to go see them. The difference is that they refer specifically to a source, such as a book, an article, or a Web page. And, instead of a superscript number, a citation uses an abbreviation, like the author's last name, to refer to the source in the text.

The list of sources at the end of a document is called a *bibliography*, which is simply Latin for "list of books." You could create a simple bibliography by hand, by simply typing the list of books, articles, and Web sites you got your information from. Often, however, bibliographies must follow a specific format. For example, high schools often require students to use APA or MLA style for bibliographies. Different professional fields have their own specific styles, such as those of the American Psychological Association or the American Medical Association. All these styles have complicated rules for where the titles, authors, punctuation, and other information goes, making bibliographies incredibly tedious to produce. Fortunately, Word is familiar with all the popular style sheets, and assembles, alphabetizes, and formats the bibliography automatically from information you provide. The program can even help you with your research: Word 2007's reference tools (page 156) are integrated with the citation feature. You may just finish your term paper without that third pot of coffee.

Tip: You can create a bibliography without citing the sources in your text, but Word 2007 puts the tools for Citations & Bibliography all in one spot (Figure 9-26).

Figure 9-26:
On the References tab, the Citations & Bibliography group provides the tools to give credit where credit's due. Word's Sources and Bibliography tools help you collect the details while you're doing your research.

Adding a Citation

You need to know three things to add a citation to your document. You need to decide on a style for your citations and bibliography. You need to know where you want to place your citation. And, of course, you need the details, such as author, title, and publisher.

Here are the steps for adding a citation to your document:

1. **Using the Style drop-down menu (References → Citations & Bibliography → Style or Alt+S, L), choose a style for your document.**

   On the list, you see several standard styles for citations, like the one recommended by the Chicago Manual of Style; it's a style that many universities and publishing companies prefer. To use that one, choose Chicago from the list. When in doubt, ask your instructor or publisher.

2. **Place Word's insertion point where you want to place the citation.**

   Citations usually come at the end of the sentence, but you may want to place one mid-sentence if that's where the referenced information is.

3. **Go to References → Citations & Bibliography → Insert Citation (or press Alt+S, C).**

   The Citation drop-down menu opens, giving you three options:

   Choose **Add New Source** if you're ready to provide the details for your bibliography. For example, for books you need to include the publisher, the publisher's city, and the date. For Web sites, you must have details about the site's home page, the date of the material, and the date the material was referenced. If you're not ready to provide the details, you can choose to **Add a Placeholder**, and then update the citation later. The last option, **Search Libraries**, opens the Research task pane (page 158) where you have access to Word's Web-based reference tools like the Encarta encyclopedia and research and financial Web sites. (For more details on Word's research resources, see page 156.)

4. **Choose Add New Source, and then fill out the details for your citation.**

Word's Create Source box opens with lots of blanks for you to fill. It looks like a lot of work, but it's not difficult. Just start at the top and work your way down. First, in the drop-down menu at the top, select the Type of Source. You have choices such as Book, Article in Periodical, Web site, or Report. When you choose one that suits your source, the text boxes and the labels in the Create Source box change. Type the details providing information about the author, publisher, date, and, in the case of Web sites, the Internet address also known as the URL.

5. **Click the OK button to close the Create Source box.**

Word closes the Create Source box closes and places a reference in your text, usually just the author's name. Word keeps track of all the other information you entered in the Create Source box to use for the bibliography. Best of all, if you want to refer to this source again, you just choose it from the ongoing list of sources on the Insert Citation menu (Figure 9-27).

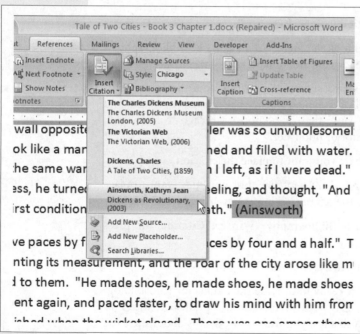

Figure 9-27:
The Insert Citation menu gives you several choices. You can choose a source that you've already used, or you can add a new one. If you're not ready for either of those options, you can mark the spot with Add New Placeholder and fill in the blanks later. The Search Libraries option takes you to Word's Reference task pane with sources like Microsoft's Encarta online encyclopedia.

Adding a Bibliography

If you've already added all your sources and marked your citations, adding a bibliography to your document is a breeze. It's very similar to adding a table of contents or an index, as described earlier. Place the insertion point at the end of your document (or wherever you want your bibliography). Then go to the References → Citations & Bibliography → Bibliography menu, and choose the style that you want. Word inserts the bibliography into your document, completely formatted (Figure 9-28).

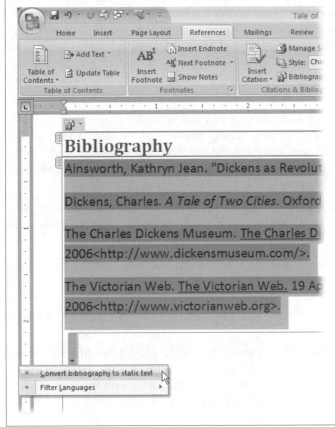

Figure 9-28:
Your bibliography appears in your document formatted in the style of your choice. Word uses a content control (page 340) to create the bibliography. You can use the drop-down at upper-left to update the bibliography or to convert it to regular text.

When Word creates your bibliography, it inserts it as a Word field, just like a table of contents (page 200). It's just a chunk of computer-generated text that you can update at any time by clicking somewhere in the field, and then pressing the F9 key. When you print your document, the bibliography looks like normal text, but if you share your document as a computer file, you may want to convert the field to regular text. That way, no one using the document onscreen can accidentally cause damage by, say, deleting the field. To convert the bibliography from field to text, click any place in the bibliography, and then look for a menu button in the upper-left corner. Click it, and then choose "Convert bibliography to static text" from the pop-up menu. Now you can edit the bibliography just like any text in your document.

Warning: Remember, once you've converted it to text, Word can no longer update the bibliography.

Working with a Master Document

The term *master document* has a kind of ominous ring to it, and maybe with good reason. This feature has given a lot of people headaches. Here's the idea behind master documents. Suppose you and a team of coworkers are writing a manual for the new Ferrari that's hitting the streets in October. To complete the manual in time, each of you is writing a chapter. Your master document is the complete manual. The chapters are subdocuments, and each chapter is a complete Word document in its own right (Figure 9-29). Word's master document feature acts like a binder that holds the subdocuments and handles some housekeeping chores like page and chapter numbering, tables, and indexes. It sounds great in theory, but it has happened that the Word files get fouled up to the point that they're unreadable.

A few solutions are available. First of all, you may want to figure out another way to work. Perhaps you don't need a master document at all. You can break your work into chapters, and then assemble the chapters into one large Word document when you're all done. If you decide to use a master document, use these safety measures:

• **Keep the master document and subdocuments in one folder.** It's easier for both you and Word to keep track of the subdocuments when they're all in the same folder.

• **Bring sufficient computer power to the project.** Computers working on a master document need to have plenty of memory (that is, random access memory, usually referred to as RAM). The minimum RAM required to run Word is 256 megabytes (MB). Try to have at least twice that, 512 MB, if you plan to use master documents.

• **Back up early and often.** All people working on the project should back up their work regularly. Keep copies of the last two or three versions by saving them with different names. Also, regularly back up the folder with the master document and the subdocuments, keeping the past two or three versions.

Creating a Master Document

To create a master document, you start with a regular Word document, switch to Outline view, and then add subdocuments. For this example, say you've already created a few chapters and want to gather them up in a master document.

First, as recommended earlier, make sure all your soon-to-be-subdocuments are in the same folder. Then, follow these steps:

1. **For the master document, create a new file with Office button → New → Blank Document, and then save it (Office button → Save).**

    It's a good idea to give it a name that identifies it as the master document, like *Master – A Tale of Two Cities.docx*. And, of course, make sure to save it in the same folder as your subdocuments.

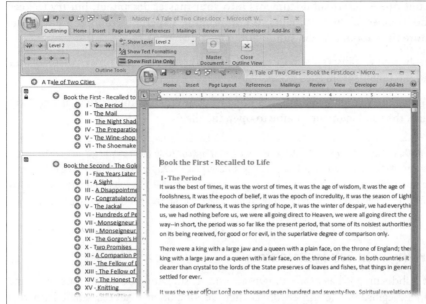

Figure 9-29:
*The master document is
in back, and in front of it
is the first subdocument.
The padlock in the
master document shows
that the subdocument is
currently open, so no one
else can make changes
to it.*

2. **With your master document open, go to View → Document Views → Outline
   or press Alt+W, U.**

   When you switch to outline view, the Outlining tab appears on the left side of
   the ribbon. One of the groups in the Outlining tab is the Master Document
   group.

3. **On the Outlining tab, click the Show Document button (Outlining → Master
   Document → Show Document) to expand the Master Document group.**

   Not many options appear in the Master Document group until you click the
   Show Document button. Then you see additional buttons for Create, Insert,
   Unlink, Merge, Split, and Lock Document.

4. **Click the Insert button, and then, when the Insert Subdocument dialog box
   opens, find and double-click a file to insert it into the master document.**

   It shouldn't be hard to find your subdocuments…they're all in one folder,
   right? Once you find the file, you can double-click it, or you can select it, and
   then click the Open button.

   If the document you're inserting and the master document have the same paragraph styles—for example if both have a Heading 1 style—you'll see a message
   box that asks if you want to change the style names of the subdocument. If you
   need a different Heading 1 style in your subdocument, click Yes. Otherwise, you
   can click No, and all your Heading 1 styles will match.

5. Continue to insert subdocuments into your master document, but try to keep the number of subdocuments to a minimum. Experts recommend having no more than about a dozen subdocuments.

   Each time you insert a subdocument, Word creates section breaks that separate subdocuments from each other.

6. When you're done, you can open one of your subdocuments for editing. Ctrl-click the subdocument's name to open the file.

Tip: If you don't have any subdocuments to start with, you can create them as you go. Just create a master document, as described in step 1, and then go to Outlining → Master Document → Create. You see a box in your master document, similar to the subdocuments in Figure 9-30, except it doesn't have any text. Use the icon in the upper-right corner to open the subdocument. You can open the subdocument you created, add text, and save it with a name.

Working with Subdocuments

Each subdocument has a box drawn around it, showing you where one ends and another begins. In the upper-left corner, subdocuments have a small icon that looks like a menu, or at least like a box with some horizontal lines. Double-click this icon to open your subdocument for editing. When a document is open, a small padlock also appears in the upper-left corner of the subdocument, to show that it's locked (Figure 9-29). No one else can edit it while someone has it open.

A master document is just an outline that connects to other documents. When you reopen your master document, it may look like Figure 9-30. To see the contents of the subdocument, instead of the filenames and paths, click the Expand Subdocuments button (Outlining → Master Document → Expand Subdocuments or Alt+U, X).

Locking subdocuments

Locking the subdocuments prevents other people from editing them or changing them in any way. When you open a subdocument, it's automatically locked. If you want to lock a subdocument without opening it, click the subdocument icon to select it, and then choose Outlining → Master Document → Lock Document.

Unlinking subdocuments

Unlinking a subdocument does two things. As you can guess, it breaks the link between the subdocument and the master document. Surprisingly, it inserts the text of the subdocument into the master document before it breaks the link. To unlink a subdocument, go to Outlining → Master Document → Unlink. The unlink option is available only when the master document is expanded.

Deleting subdocuments

To remove a subdocument from the master document, click the subdocument icon, and then press the Delete or Backspace key. The subdocument disappears from the master document, but the subdocument file still exists on your computer.

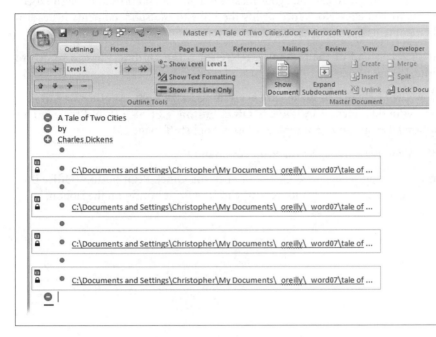

Figure 9-30:
Master documents are files that point to other documents known as subdocuments. This view shows the location of the subdocument files. To view the contents of those files right in the master document, click the Expand Documents button in the Master Document group.

Formatting Your Master Document

You can format the text and the paragraphs in your master document using all the usual suspects. Expand your subdocuments, and then change to Draft or Print Layout view, so that you can see the full result. You can select text and apply bold, italics, or other character formatting. If you want to change the paragraph formatting, like increasing the font size for a heading style, you can modify the style as you would in any Word document. For example, you can right-click the style in the Styles menu (Home → Styles), and then choose Modify from the pop-up menu. When you save the changes in your master document, the changes are saved in the subdocument too.

Printing Your Master Document

If you've successfully managed a master document to the point that you're ready to print—congratulations. Many people have never made it this far. But now that you have, printing a master document is pretty easy.

1. **Expand the subdocuments using Outlining → Master Document → Expand Subdocuments or Alt+U, X.**

   If you try to print your master document without expanding it, Word shows an alert box asking whether you want to open the subdocuments before printing. If you click Yes, Word expands your master document and prints all the subdocuments. If you click No, Word prints the links to the subdocuments instead of their contents.

2. **At the right end of the Outlining tab, click Close Outline View to return to Print Layout view.**

3. **Now's your chance to make sure everything looks right. Another way to preview your document is by going to Office button → Print → Print Preview. This option lets you use Zoom tools and other cool stuff (page 23).**

4. **When you're ready, select the Print command.**

   In Print Layout view, press Ctrl+P or click the Quick Print button (Office button → Quick Print). In Print Preview, click the Print button on the ribbon.

Organizing Your Information with Tables

If you think of tables as an ugly grid for holding numbers in place, something more suited to a spreadsheet than a Word document, think again. Or, better yet, talk to someone who's done some Web design. Tables are incredible tools for page design, both the printed page as well as a Web page. With tables, you can group related text and pictures so that they stay together no matter how your document changes. You can use background and border colors to give your words a visual splash and to draw attention to important parts of your message. If you're presenting numbers to your readers, you need the rows and columns that tables offer to line everything up and provide totals. Once you're comfortable creating and modifying tables, you'll probably find all sorts of ways to use them.

Word's table feature has grown stronger and more versatile with each passing version. For example, you can choose from a few different ways to create tables and multiple ways to modify them by inserting or deleting rows, columns, and individual cells. You can also get really creative and add color and other formatting. If you're a number cruncher, you can use tables as a simplified spreadsheet right in your document. Word 2007 also offers Quick Tables, preformatted tables for things like calendars and other common uses.

Creating Tables

If you've never created a table in a Word document before, don't worry—it's remarkably easy and even fun, especially if you use the drawing-with-the-mouse method.

You can create tables by:

- **Pointing at and clicking a mini table map.** Chose Insert → Table and click the grid that appears to size and create a table.

- **Filling in numbers and clicking button in a dialog box.** Choose Insert → Table → Insert Table or press Alt+N+TI to open the Insert Table dialog box.

- **Drawing your table on the page with your mouse.** Choose Insert → Table → Draw Table or press Alt+N+TD to turn your cursor into a table-drawing tool.

Creating a Table from the Ribbon

As always, the ribbon approach to the job is very visual, and it may seem vaguely familiar. It's a variation on the way you'd create tables in the last few versions of Word, where you'd click a button and drag out a grid that represented the table. Word's new method is even a little easier for newcomers to grasp. The drop-down menu presents a 10 x 8 grid. You click to select the number of boxes you want in your table, as shown in Figure 10-1.

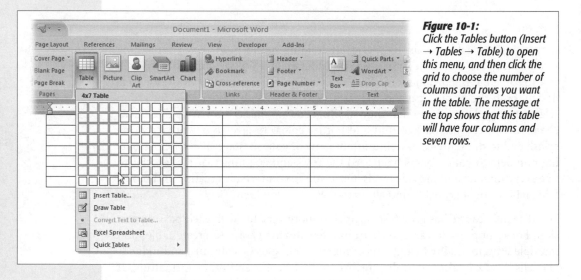

Figure 10-1:
Click the Tables button (Insert → Tables → Table) to open this menu, and then click the grid to choose the number of columns and rows you want in the table. The message at the top shows that this table will have four columns and seven rows.

Note: A column is a group of cells running vertically, while a row is group of cells that run horizontally.

---

1. **On the ribbon, choose Insert → Tables → Table.**

   A menu appears with what looks sort of like a bunch of boxes or a piece of graph paper (Figure 10-1).

2. **Point to a box on the grid to create a table with the number of rows and columns you want.**

   As you move your mouse over the grid, the boxes in the grid are highlighted, and you see the table appear on your page. (Tables use Microsoft's Live Preview feature that shows you what will happen if you click the mouse button.) A message above the grid on the menu keeps tally of the number of columns and rows. You don't have to be exact; it's easy enough to create or delete columns and rows later.

3. **Click the grid to create the table and place it in your document for real.**

   The Tables menu disappears, and your table is right there in your document with evenly spaced columns and rows.

Using the Insert Table Box

The Insert Table dialog box is a more traditional—and boring—way to create a table. Choose Alt+N, TI to open the Insert Table box (Figure 10-2). The box is a simple affair. Just type numbers in the text boxes at the top for the columns and rows you need in your table. This dialog box also lets you choose the AutoFit behavior, as explained below:

- **Fixed column width.** Use this option if you want to limit columns to a specific width. Enter a number in the box next to this option to set the width of the columns. Or, if you choose Auto instead, Word creates a table that fits in your current margins, with the number of columns specified above, each of equal width.

- **AutoFit to contents.** With this option, the column width adjusts automatically to accommodate the amount of text you type in the cells. Use this option if you're not sure how much space your text will take up until you type it.

- **AutoFit to window.** This option is more suited to Web pages than printed documents. It makes the table expand and contract to fit a browser window. Web pages are designed to work on all different types of computers, PDAs, cell phones, TV sets, and who-knows-what in the future. AutoFit tables like these help Web designers create pages that work for screens and browsers with dramatically different capabilities.

If you're going to create similar tables in the future, turn on the "Remember dimensions for new tables" checkbox, and Word keeps the settings in the Insert Table box for your next visit.

Drawing a Table

As you can guess, the least mechanical and most creative way to make a table is to draw your own. It's a great technique if you need an irregularly shaped table. With Word's table tools you can draw tables, and divide them into columns and rows in just about any configuration imaginable. As you can see from Figure 10-3, you can do just about anything except make a curve.

Here's how to use the table drawing tools to draw a fairly traditional table:

1. **Choose Insert → Tables → Table → Draw Table.**

   Your mouse cursor changes into a pencil, inviting you to start drawing.

Figure 10-2:
The Insert Table box gives you a more traditional but less artistic way to create tables. The advantage of using this box is that you can specify exact column widths for precise layout. The AutoFit to window option is helpful if your document is going to end up as a Web page.

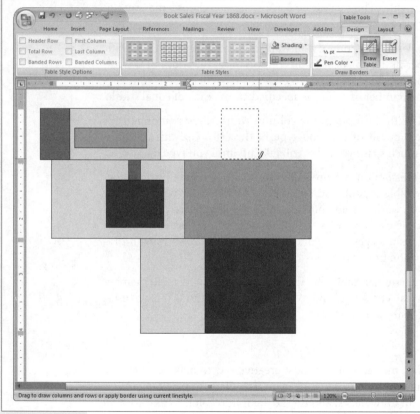

Figure 10-3:
You may be surprised how flexible tables are, especially if you use the Draw Table option (Alt+N, TD). Using the cell shading and border tools, tables become strong graphic elements in your document.

2. **On an empty place on the page, drag diagonally to draw your first rectangle (Figure 10-4).**

   The rectangle that appears on your page marks the borders for your table. Soon you'll divvy it up, creating columns and rows inside. Word adds paragraphs, adjusts margins, and generally does whatever's necessary to place your table exactly where you draw it.

The moment you release the mouse button, the Table Tools contextual tab appears on the right side of the ribbon. Two tabs appear in this contextual tab: Design and Layout. You're now on the Design tab, where you see tools for formatting your table. On the right side, the Draw Table button is highlighted, indicating that you're in Draw Table mode.

3. **Next, drag to draw a vertical line to divide your table in half.**

   Your line separates the table into two cells. You can draw lines wherever you want to divide your table into cells of just about any shape. When you drag diagonally, you create rectangles instead of lines. Rectangles turn into cells, or if they're far enough from the original table, they're new tables.

   Experiment to get a feeling for creating tables and cells. If you make an error, undo it with Ctrl+Z.

   Next to the Draw Table button you find an Eraser button (Table Tools | Design → Draw Borders → Eraser or Alt+JT, E). If you click the button to highlight the eraser, then your mouse cursor changes to an eraser icon. Dragging it over lines in your table erases them.

4. **Draw a horizontal line on the left half of your table.**

   When you draw the horizontal line, you divide one of the cells into two cells, creating a new row. You can draw the line to the vertical divider or you can continue onto the right side of the table. This horizontal line creates two rows in your table.

   You can continue to divvy up your table into additional cells.

5. **When you're done, click the Draw Table button (on the right side of the ribbon), to turn off the Draw Table mode.**

   The Draw Table button loses its highlight glow, and the cursor changes from the pencil back to its familiar I-beam.

Note: Drawing a table is actually a lot simpler to do than it sounds; for a screencast—an online, animated tutorial—of the steps you've just read, head over to the "Missing CD" page at *www. missingmanuals.com*.

Choosing Quick Tables

If three ways to create tables aren't enough, you can always choose from one of Word's predesigned tables. Choose Insert → Tables → Quick Tables to see a menu full of pre-rolled tables that you can drop into your documents. The choices range from calendars to periodic tables (Figure 10-5). Of course, you don't have to keep the content that Microsoft's put in there. If you like the look of one of the tables, you can always insert it and then delete the text and fill the space with your own words and graphics.

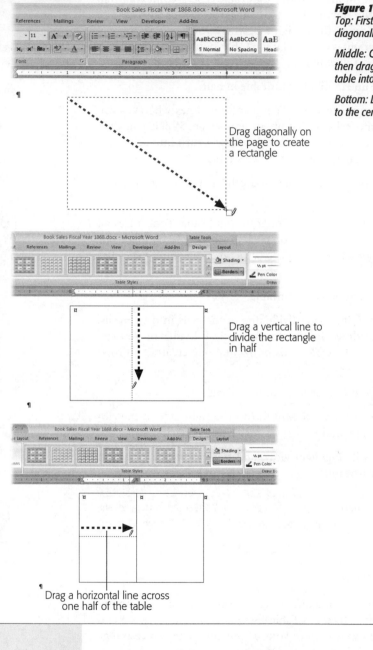

Figure 10-4:
Top: First click and then drag the pencil cursor diagonally across the page to create the table.

Middle: Click at the top of your table, and then drag down to draw a line that divides the table into two cells.

Bottom: Draw another line from the left side to the center to create two rows on the left.

Drag diagonally on the page to create a rectangle

Drag a vertical line to divide the rectangle in half

Drag a horizontal line across one half of the table

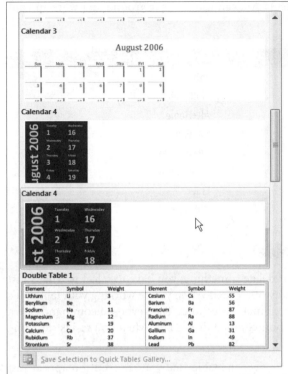

Figure 10-5:
If you're in a hurry, you can choose one of the predesigned Quick Tables (Alt+N, TT). The large menu gives you a good view of the different tables available. Once it's in your document, you can edit it and alter it for your own purposes.

Moving Around a Table

Working with tables, columns, rows, and cells is different from working with plain text. Still, you want to do the same things, such as select bits and pieces so that you can copy, move or delete them. And when you type in text and numbers, you want to be able to move around the table, preferably without taking your hands off the keyboard.

If you're rapidly entering text in an empty table, the best way to move from cell to cell is with the Tab key. Just hit Tab when you're finished typing in a cell. Word selects the next cell, and you can continue typing. It's important to note that the cursor doesn't just move to the next cell; everything in the cell is selected, so if text is already in there, Word deletes it when you start typing. If you want to move backward, use Shift+Tab.

The arrow keys work pretty much as you'd expect, moving the insertion point one character at a time through your document. When you get to the point between two columns, the insertion point hops over to the next cell. The up and down arrows behave in a similar way. The up arrow moves the insertion point to the next line of text above it; that line may be in the same cell, or it may be in the row above.

Here are some keyboard shortcuts you can use to move around and work in your table:

Command	Keyboard Shortcut
Select next cell	Tab
Select previous cell	Shift+Tab
Move to first cell in a row	Alt+Home
Move to last cell in a row	Alt+End
Move to last cell in a column	Alt+PageDn
Move to first cell in a column	Alt+PageUp
Create new paragraphs in a cell	Enter
Insert tabs in a cell	Ctrl+Tab

Selecting Parts of a Table

Before you can copy, format, or delete something, you have to select it. That's just as true with tables as it is with any other text. When you're working with tables, it's often easiest to use your mouse to make selections. The keyboard commands are a little cumbersome, and the ribbon commands are best when you're just learning your way around.

- **Select table.** Hold your mouse over the table, and you see a button appear just off the upper-left corner. The Select Table button is a square, inside of which is a cross with arrows pointing in four directions. That's a hint that you can grab this button and drag the table wherever you want it. Clicking that button selects the entire table.

- **Select column.** Move the cursor to the top of a column, and the cursor changes to an arrow pointing down (Figure 10-6). One click and you select the column the arrow points to. Drag to select more than one column.

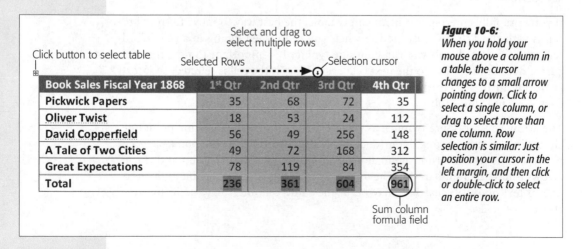

Click button to select table

Select and drag to select multiple rows

Selected Rows

Selection cursor

Book Sales Fiscal Year 1868	1st Qtr	2nd Qtr	3rd Qtr	4th Qtr
Pickwick Papers	35	68	72	35
Oliver Twist	18	53	24	112
David Copperfield	56	49	256	148
A Tale of Two Cities	49	72	168	312
Great Expectations	78	119	84	354
Total	236	361	604	961

Sum column formula field

Figure 10-6:
When you hold your mouse above a column in a table, the cursor changes to a small arrow pointing down. Click to select a single column, or drag to select more than one column. Row selection is similar: Just position your cursor in the left margin, and then click or double-click to select an entire row.

- **Select row.** When your cursor is at the left edge of the table, it changes to a small dark arrow, angled up slightly. (It's different from the hollow arrow you see if move your cursor into the left margin.) One click selects the first cell in the row. A double-click selects the entire row. If your table happens to be on the left margin, you can select a row just like you'd select a line of text, with a single click in the margin.

- **Select cell.** Move the cursor to the lower-left corner of any cell, and the cursor changes to a small dark arrow, angled up slightly. One click and you select the cell and any text, graphic, or other object in the cell. A highlight color fills selected cells. Drag to select more than one cell. If you want to select cells that aren't next to each other, select the first cell, and then press Ctrl while you click and select more cells.

A quick triple-click is another way to select a single cell. Keep your finger down on that last click, and you can drag to select multiple cells. Press Ctrl as you triple-click to select random cells that aren't next to each other.

If you're working on text that's inside a cell, the basic selection and editing commands work as always. You can select text and format it, or move it around using all your favorite tools and commands, like Ctrl+C to copy and Ctrl+V to paste.

Command	Ribbon Command	Keyboard Shortcut
Select table	Table Tools | Layout → Select → Select Table	Alt+JL, KT or Alt+5 (on the number pad, with Num-Lock off)
Select column	Table Tools | Layout → Select → Select Column	Alt+JL, KC or Alt+Shift+PageDN
Select row	Table Tools | Layout → Select → Select Row	Alt+JL, KR
Select cell	Table Tools | Layout → Select → Select Cell	Alt+JL, KL

Merging and Splitting Cells

The cells in your table don't have to be a perfect grid, so don't be afraid to get creative with your table layouts. Maybe you want to have a single "1st Quarter" heading centered over three columns of sales figures. To merge cells, select two or more adjacent cells, and then use Table Tools | Layout → Merge → Merge Cells or the shortcut Alt+JL, M.

Command	Ribbon Command	Keyboard Shortcut
Merge cells	Table Tools | Layout → Merge → Merge Cells	Alt+JL, M
Split cells	Table Tools | Layout → Merge → Split Cells	Alt+JL, P
Split table	Table Tools | Layout → Merge → Split Table	Alt+JL, Q

To split cells, make sure the insertion point is in the cell you want to divide, and then use either the command Table Tools → Layout → Merge → Split Cells or the

shortcut Alt+JL, P. A dialog box appears, asking you to specify exactly how you want to divvy up the real estate (Figure 10-7).

Figure 10-7:
The Split Cells dialog box lets you be quite specific about how you want to divide the territory. Enter the number of columns and rows you want in the text boxes. If you select more than one cell before you give the Split Cell command, you have the option to merge the cells before you break them into smaller parts.

Adjusting Column Width and Row Height

Once you have your table in place, you may want to make some adjustments. Tables can shape-shift in a number of ways to work with whatever you decide to toss into them. Even though tables can automatically change shape to accommodate the contents, it's still good to know how to adjust them manually. You can change the width of individual columns and the height of the rows in your table.

To adjust the width of a column, move your mouse cursor over one of the vertical lines in the table. The cursor changes to a two-headed arrow (Figure 10-8). Drag the line where you want it. The entire line from top to bottom of the table moves in one motion. If, for some reason, just one piece of the line moves, that means you selected a cell or two before you dragged the line. When a cell is selected, your modifications affect only the selected cell.

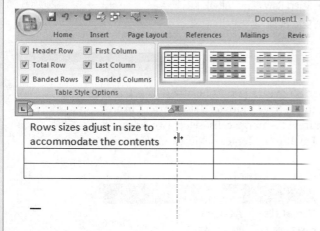

Figure 10-8:
When you hold the cursor over a line, the cursor changes to a double-headed arrow. Drag one of the lines in your table to resize a row or column. The dotted line helps you line up the edges of the cell with other objects in the table or on the page.

Changing the height of a row is similar. Just click to grab one of the lines, and then drag it where you want. You'll probably find that it's less necessary to change row height than it is column width, since rows automatically adjust to accommodate the lines of text. As you type into a cell and your words create a new line, the row height increases to make room.

Inserting Columns and Rows

Often when you're first creating a table, it's difficult to know how many rows and columns you'll need. It's not a major issue, because it's easy enough to add and delete rows and columns. You can make these changes using buttons on the ribbon, with keyboard shortcuts or with the handy pop-up menu that appears when you right-click within the table.

When you're inserting rows or columns, the first step is to click somewhere in the table to position the insertion point. Clicking in the table does two important things. First, the Table Tools contextual tab doesn't make an appearance unless the insertion point is inside a table. Second, the insertion point serves as a reference point so you can tell Word to add the row or column before or after that spot.

With the insertion point in place, you can choose one of the commands from the Table Tools | Layout → Rows & Columns group. The menu commands and their icons present a clear picture of the options (Figure 10-9): You can delete individual cells, or rows, or columns, or the entire table.

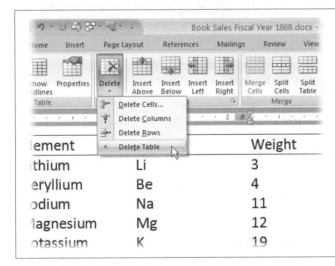

Figure 10-9:
The commands to insert and delete rows and columns are neighbors in the Table Tools | Layout → Rows & Columns group. Make sure you click within a table, or you won't see the Table Tools contextual tabs.

All the options shown on the ribbon have keyboard equivalents. Here's a table of the commands and the ways to use them:

Command	Ribbon Command	Keyboard Shortcut
Insert row above	Table Tools	Layout → Rows & Columns → Insert Above	Alt+JL, A
Insert row below	Table Tools	Layout → Rows & Columns → Insert Below	Alt+JL, E
Insert column left	Table Tools	Layout → Rows & Columns → Insert Left	Alt+JL, L
Insert column right	Table Tools	Layout → Rows & Columns → Insert Right	Alt+JL, R

A right-click within a table makes a shortcut menu appear, and as usual Word's pretty smart when it comes to figuring out what you're trying to do. So, if you've selected an entire row before you right-click, then the shortcut menu gives you options to insert or delete rows, as shown in Figure 10-10. Just take your pick from the list.

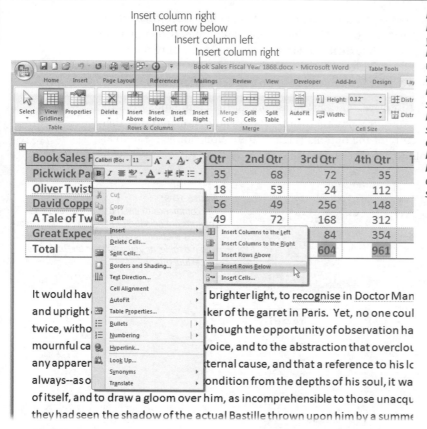

Figure 10-10:
If you've already got your mouse in hand, here's an easy two-step way to add a row. Move the mouse into the left margin, and then click to select an entire row. Right-click to display the shortcut menu, and then choose Insert → Insert Rows Below or Insert Rows Above. You can create columns with a similar technique.

Deleting Cells, Columns, Rows, and Tables

The techniques to delete columns and rows pretty much mirror the ways you insert them. Deleting individual cells is a little trickier, since plucking cells out of the middle of your table tends to shift things around. Easiest of all is deleting the entire table. As long as your insertion point is somewhere in the table, you can use Table Tools | Layout → Delete → Delete Table or the shortcut Alt+JL+DT.

Using the Delete menu (Table Tools | Layout → Rows & Columns; see Figure 10-9), you can delete any element of a table from the entire table down to groups of rows and columns on down to a single cell. Just select the bits and pieces you want to remove, and then choose the command. You can select several rows, and then delete them all at once. Keyboard shortcuts are also available for deleting table parts:

Command	Ribbon Command	Keyboard Shortcut
Delete table	Table Tools	Layout → Rows & Columns → Delete → Delete Table	Alt+JL, DT
Delete columns	Table Tools	Layout → Rows & Columns → Delete → Delete Columns	Alt+JL, DC
Delete rows	Table Tools	Layout → Rows & Columns → Delete → Delete Rows	Alt+JL, DR
Delete cells	Table Tools	Layout → Rows & Columns → Delete → Delete Cells	Alt+JL, DD

Deleting cells

Deleting cells is sort of like pulling a brick from the middle of a wall. Other bricks have to move in to take its place. But it doesn't happen at random: Word lets you choose how you want cells to fill in the space. When you give the command to delete a cell or a group of cells (Alt+JL, DD), Word shows a dialog box asking whether you want to pull cells up or bring them over to the left (Figure 10-11).

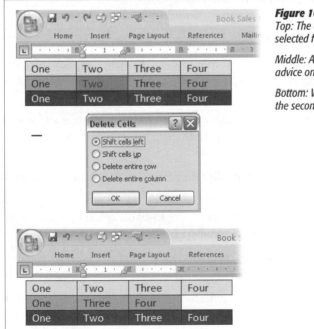

Figure 10-11:

Top: The cell second from the left and second from the top is selected for deletion.

Middle: After invoking the Delete command, Word asks for advice on how to shift the rest of the cells.

Bottom: With the "Shift cells left" button selected, the cells in the second row shift over from the right.

Note: Selecting a cell and then pressing Delete on the keyboard deletes the contents of the cell but not the cell itself. And that's just fine, because most of the time that's exactly what you want.

Formatting Tables

The Table Tools contextual tab has two tabs devoted to Design and Layout, indicating that formatting is a big part of working with tables. In fact, these two tabs are so close to each other in function that it's easy to forget which tab holds certain commands. The Design tab holds commands related to color and borders, while the Layout tab relates more to the structure of the table: inserting and deleting rows and columns, aligning text, and adjusting cell size.

Using Table Styles

For a quick and easy way to add color to your table, nothing beats Table Styles (Table Tools | Design). Word provides dozens of styles using a variety of colors, fonts, and font styles. When you design tables, try to look at them from your readers' point of view. What information is most important to them? Do you want to emphasize headings on the top row or in the left column? Is it important for readers to compare numbers along a horizontal row? Answering these questions will help lead you to good table design decisions (Figure 10-12).

The Table Styles are on the Table Tools | Design tab. Use the two groups on the left side to modify and select a table style. The Table Style Options group (far left) is pretty nifty. As you make choices and check off options, the styles in the Table Styles menu change per your specs. Here are your options:

- **Header Row** puts an emphasis on the top row, either with a color or a strong border. This option works best when your top row contains headings.

- **Total Row** puts an emphasis on the bottom row. As the name implies, this style is ideal for emphasizing the totals at the bottom of columns when your table is a spreadsheet.

- **Banded Rows** uses alternating row colors to help readers track text and numbers horizontally. It's useful for wide spreadsheets, but you can also use it for design effect.

- **First Column** puts an emphasis on the first column, like when your left column holds a list of categories.

- **Last Column** puts an emphasis on the last or right-hand column. It's particularly useful when you sum up rows of numbers in the right column.

- **Banded Columns,** like banded rows, help guide your reader's eye, but you can also use them strictly for design purposes.

The toughest thing about applying table styles is choosing one from the many that the menu presents you (Alt+JT, S):

1. **Click within your table so that Word knows where to apply the style.**

   You don't have to select the entire table; it's enough to have the insertion point in the table you want to format.

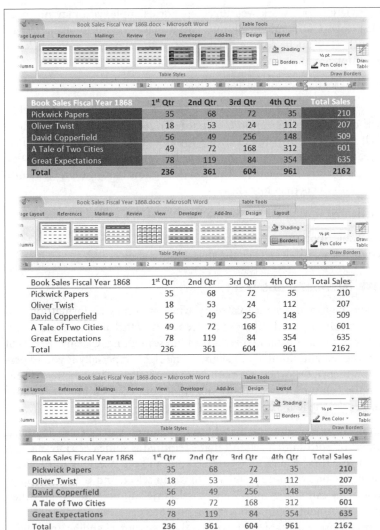

Figure 10-12:
Three different table styles give this one table a dramatically different look.

Top: This style, called Colorful Grid Accent 1, sets the numbers off from the headings and the totals at bottom and right.

Middle: This table, using the Basic style, looks more mundane, but if you're making multiple photocopies, it's best to avoid cell shading, which tends to get splotchy.

Bottom: The bottom table, Light Shading style, has alternating cell shading, making it easier for readers to track numbers across rows.

2. **Choose Table Tools | Design to show the Design tab.**

   With the Design tab selected, on the left end of the ribbon you see the two groups that apply to Table Styles: Table Style Options and Table Styles. You want to tackle them in order from left to right.

3. **Adjust the Table Style Options to match your needs.**

   As you turn the Table Style Options checkboxes on and off, you see the Table Styles on the right change to match your desires. (Everything in life should work like this.)

Not all the Style Options work well together. For example, you may not need both Banded Rows and Banded Columns. So, it may be good to take a less-is-more approach. Try unchecking everything, and then, one by one, click the options you think are most important for your table.

4. **Preview the different styles on the Table Styles menu.**

   Move your cursor over one of the Table Styles to see how it fits your table. About a half-dozen styles appear on the ribbon. To see more, use the scroll button, or click the drop-down menu in the lower-right corner. With Live Preview, you see your table change as the cursor hovers over different styles. You can go back and forth between the Table Style Options and the preview until you come up with the perfect format.

5. **Select the style that works best for your table.**

   To choose a Table Style and modify your table, on the Table Styles menu (Table Tools | Design → Table Styles), click the style of your choice.

Aligning Text, Numbers, and Data

Tables are in the high-maintenance category when it comes to formatting and other housekeeping chores. With all those different bits of text and numbers in different boxes, it seems you constantly need to realign something. Usually, you want text to align on the left and numbers to align on the right (especially if you're performing math on them). Or, when no math is involved, it may look better to center numbers in the columns. Also, usually you want your column headers to have the same alignment as the items below.

And that's just horizontal alignment. To add to the choices, you can also align text to the top, center, or bottom of a cell. All that's required is some decision making. Fortunately, applying this formatting is easy, so you can keep tweaking until everything looks right. It's one of those standard "first you select, and then you apply" formatting jobs. You can speed things up by selecting multiple items, and then applying a single alignment command to them all. (See page 242 for the selection techniques you can use with tables.) Here are the steps for changing text alignment inside table cells:

1. **Select the cells you want to align.**

   Often you can apply alignment to a column or more at a time. To select a column, hold the cursor at the top of the column. The cursor changes to a dark arrow pointing down. Click to select the column, or drag to select multiple columns.

2. **Choose Table Tools | Layout → Alignment and select the alignment option.**

   On the left side in the Alignment group, click one of the buttons to apply an alignment format to the selected cells (Figure 10-13).

You have nine alignment options. You can choose to have text horizontally aligned left, center, or right. With each of those options, you can also choose the vertical alignment: top, center, or bottom.

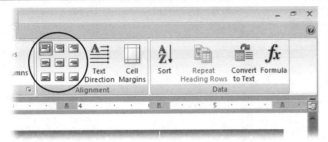

Figure 10-13:
Nine buttons help you align text within your table cells. If you can't quite make out what the icon means, hold your mouse cursor over a button, and a screen tip appears, explaining the command.

Applying Shading and Borders

Word's Table Styles primarily apply to a table's shading and borders. You can customize your table with these settings too. Or, better yet, you can apply one of Word's styles, and then make modifications to fit your needs.

Here's an example of manually changing the shading and border for the top row in a table. In this example, you'll highlight your table's top row with nice light blue shading and a double line along the bottom of the row. You'll also delineate the top of the table with a dark blue, 1.5-point line. Here are the steps:

1. **In the lower-left corner of the first cell of your table, double-click to select the entire top row.**

    Before you apply shading and border styles, you need to select the cells that you want to change. When you move your cursor to the lower-left corner of a cell, the cursor changes to a dark arrow angled upward. A single click selects the cell, and a double click selects the entire row.

2. **Choose Table Tools | Design → Shading, and then select a light blue color from the drop-down menu (Figure 10-14).**

    The Shading drop-down menu is in the Table Styles group of the Design tab. You see a menu with colors that match your theme at the top. Bold, standard colors are near the bottom, along with a button that removes colors from the selected cells.

3. **Choose Table Tools | Design → Table Styles → Borders, and then select the Borders and Shading option at the bottom of the menu.**

    The Borders and Shading box opens to the Borders tab. At left are preformatted options. In the middle, you can choose different line styles, colors, and widths. On the right side is a preview box, but this box does more than just show you the results; you actually use it to format your borders.

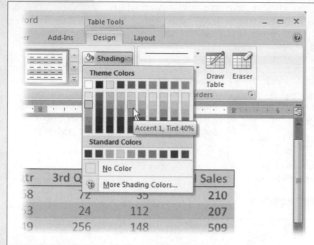

Figure 10-14:
The Shading button in the Borders and Shading dialog box shows colors that match your document's theme. When you point to a color chip, a screen tip describes the color. Click the chip to apply the color to the selected cells.

4. **At left, click the None button to clear all borders from the selected cells.**

   By clearing all the borders, you can start from scratch to create a new look.

5. **In the middle of the dialog box, scroll down through the Style box, and then select the double line from the list.**

   You see a variety of solid and dotted lines, as well as different types of multiple line options. When you choose the double line, you see a double line in the Width box below.

6. **In the Color box, select a dark blue color.**

   Click the button on the right side of the Color box to show the menu. The color chips at the top match your document's theme. Click one of the chips to select a color. The menu closes, and the color you selected shows in the box.

7. **In the Width box, choose 1.5 points for your line width.**

   You can't enter your own number in the width box; you must select one of the preset line widths.

8. **In the Preview box on the right, click the border at the bottom of the preview example.**

   At first, no borders appear in the example, because you cleared all the borders in step 4. When you click the bottom border, the thick double line appears along the bottom of the example. Clicking the border elements in the preview is how you tell Word where to apply borders.

9. **In the Style box, click the single line, and then choose "3 pt" on the Width menu. In the Preview box, click the top border to apply this line style.**

   When you've made your changes, the preview box looks like Figure 10-15. (You can, if you wish, continue to design border styles and apply them to different parts of the selected cells.)

10. **When you're done, click OK to close the Borders dialog box.**

Using these tools and techniques, you can apply shading and borders to any of the cells in a table.

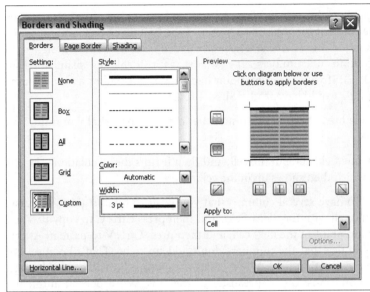

Figure 10-15:
The Borders dialog box gives you the tools to format border styles for the cells in your table. This dialog box is Word's standard tool for applying borders to paragraphs, around pictures, and around text boxes.

Doing Math in Tables

When presenting numbers in your document, whether it's a budget, or sales figures, or an inventory tally, you probably want to total some of the columns. Sure, you could add up the numbers on a calculator, and then type the totals into the cells. That's fine if you know the figures aren't going to change, and you're certain you won't transpose any figures between your calculator and the table. A better (though, admittedly, not necessarily easier) way is to insert one of Word's fields with instructions to sum the column above. Use the Formula button (Figure 10-16) on the Layout tab to insert the field into your table.

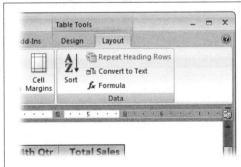

Figure 10-16:
Use the Formula button (Table Tools | Layout → Data → Formula) to insert a math field into your table.

Here are the steps for adding a SUM field that totals the number in the column above:

1. **Click to place the insertion point in the bottom cell of a column with numbers, and then go to Table Tools | Layout → Data → Formula.**

   The Formula dialog box opens (Figure 10-17). Word makes some assumptions based on the fact that the insertion point is at the bottom of a column of numbers. For example, the Formula box is preloaded with a formula designed to total the column of numbers. It's almost as readable as plain English: =SUM(ABOVE). If your insertion point had been at the end of a row of numbers, the formula would have read: =SUM(LEFT).

2. **In the Formula box, check to make sure the formula does what you want, and then click OK.**

   Word inserts the field code in the cell, and then it runs the calculation—in this case, a sum, which then shows up in the cell.

It's not unusual to have several columns that you want to total. If that's the case, you can select the cell with the SUM field, and then press Ctrl+C to copy it. Then move the insertion point to the next cell, and then press Ctrl+V to paste it. At this point, you may notice that the numbers don't add up right. That's because you need to update the function field. Word tables may look a little like spreadsheets, but unlike Excel and most other spreadsheet programs, Word doesn't automatically recalculate formulas when you edit cells. If you change numbers in a row or a column that's summed with a field, you need to update the SUM fields just like any other Word field (page 76). Click to place the insertion point in the field, and then press F9. Word runs the math again, and then places the correct number in the cell. To update all the fields in a table, select the entire table (Alt+JL, KT), and then press F9.

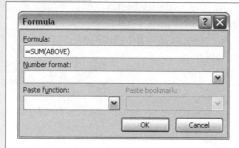

Figure 10-17:
If all you're doing is summing a column of numbers, the Formula box is pretty easy to manage. In the top text box, you see the actual formula that Word uses to create the text it places in the cell. Use the "Number format" box if you want the total to show as currency. The Paste function box leads to other formulas such as average, round, and count.

UP TO SPEED

Other Table-Like Options

When you need to organize parts of your document separate from the body text, you have a few different options. You can use either tables or text boxes to separate blocks of text from the body of your document. If you're working with numbers, you can use a table, or you can insert an Excel spreadsheet into your document. When you're working with columns of newspaper-style text, you can use Word's columns or you can use a table. So the question arises, when should you use tables for these jobs and when should you use an alternative? Here are some rules of thumb:

- For a pull quote or a sidebar, it's better to use a text box than a table to hold the text. The end result may look pretty much the same no matter which you use, but text boxes provide easier, quicker formatting options. The details for creating and using text boxes begin on page 343. The only time you can consider using a table is when you need multiple columns. You can't do multiple columns in a text box, but you can fake multiple columns in a table by placing text in two different columns of a table, and then hiding the border lines.Use tables to create grid-like charts and for simple text-based projects. You can also use tables for simple projects like budgets and reports that total columns and rows of numbers.

- However, if you need to do more complicated math formulas, it's easier to insert an Excel spreadsheet into your Word document. The printed page will look the same, but it's easier to create and update the formulas in a spreadsheet. Find more details on embedding Excel spreadsheets and other objects on page 281.

- Word's columns are fine for text that flows evenly and predictably from one column to another, but they're murder if you're trying to organize a page with irregularly shaped text. So, for example, if you're creating a newsletter with blocks of text of different shapes and sizes, it's probably easier to create a table with a few cells, and then place blocks of text inside the cells. Tables are great for accurately positioning items next to each other.

- Last but not least, if you're pulling your hair out while trying to align items with tabs and paragraph marks, it's time to consider using a table for the job. Tables give you much better control when you're aligning items. What's more, you can automatically turn that text with the tabs into a table with the command Insert → Tables → Table → Convert Text to Table or the keyboard shortcut Alt+N, TE.

Adding Graphics, Video, and Sound to Your Documents

A striking graphic helps you capture your readers' attention and cement your message in their memories. A chart or graph helps clarify complex topics better than words can say. Even in text-heavy documents, graphic elements like pull quotes and drop caps help lure readers into your words.

Word's here to help. It lets you embellish your documents with photos, drawings, charts, clip art, and a new Word 2007 graphic type called SmartArt that combines text with graphic shapes. (See the box on the next page for a full rundown on all the graphic types.) Word gives you a whole range of tools to place graphics in your document. You can use a slew of options for positioning them, applying borders and special 3-D effects. This chapter shows you the whole gamut of tools and techniques you can use with photos, drawings, and other graphics. It also shows you how to add video and audio files, so you can give your readers a multimedia presentation right there in your Word document.

Tip: Although graphics and other objects add pizzazz, it's important to understand your audience and keep the graphics appropriate. For example, you don't want to get too cutesy if you're presenting a budget to the Board of Directors.

Drop Caps, Text Boxes, and WordArt

Drop caps, text boxes, and WordArt let you turn text into a design element. Although these elements lose their impact if you overdo them, putting a little pizzazz in your text can direct your audience's attention to important information.

In Graphic Terms

People use the word *graphic* to mean any kind of visual representation or illustration, whether they're thinking of a photograph, a line drawing, a chart, or what-have-you. Word works with several types of graphics, each of which looks and acts a little differently in your document. Here's a guide to what all these graphic terms mean:

- **Pictures.** With the Insert Picture command, you can find photos and drawings you've created or saved on your computer and place them in a Word document. As long as it's in a computer graphic file format—like .jpg, .tif, or .emf—Word thinks of it as a picture. You insert pictures, along with the following four items, from the Insert → Illustrations group.

- **Clip art.** Word comes with a huge library of photos and pictures that you can add to your documents for free. Also, although they're not technically clip art, you can find media files like movies, music, and other sounds in the Clip Art task pane. Some of these files are on your computer and others are in libraries on the Internet. The task pane lets you search for just the right image, video, or audio out of the thousands available. (Obviously, you'll use the video and audio files in documents destined for the Web or email rather than print.)

- **SmartArt.** Part graphic and part text, SmartArt is a new type of graphic introduced in Word 2007. All you have to do is type text into a box and SmartArt handles all the formatting and placement chores, creating a great looking graphic image. When you make changes to the words, SmartArt is smart enough to make everything fit.

- **Shapes.** Word includes a library of simple shapes, lines, arrows, and common icons. They're easy to size, position, and format. You can use them to create your own charts and illustrations.

- **Chart.** Charts are different from other images in that data is behind the graphic. Charts take numbers and translate them into lines, bars, or pie charts. You tell Word what kind of a chart to create, and then you provide the labels and numbers.

- **Drop caps, text boxes, and WordArt (Insert → Text).** These graphic elements are a little different from the other items in this list because they're character-based; but when it comes to sizing and positioning them, they behave much like photos and drawings.

For example, you can use a text box to create a pull quote that highlights your company's stellar performance.

Drop caps, text boxes, and WordArt take color, font, and design cues from the theme you've selected for your document. When you see color choices, the theme colors are usually presented at the top of the menu. Later, if you decide to change the theme for your document, the accent colors and font styles in your graphics change to match.

Note: To work with pictures, drawings, and SmartArt, you need to be in Print Layout or Web Layout view. In Draft or Outline view, your graphics appear as placeholder boxes. In these views, you can position the placeholder boxes, but you can't modify the graphics. (If you don't see a placeholder box in your document, just click the empty space where the graphic should be. You then see a box that you can drag to a new location.)

Adding a Drop Cap to a Paragraph

Drop caps are a decorative feature with a practical purpose. They give a paragraph an added sense of importance as the beginning of a chapter or document. Drop caps attract readers' attention and draw their eyes to the beginning of the text, inviting them to start reading (Figure 11-1). With Word you can easily add a drop cap to any paragraph, and if you're in the mood, you can fiddle around with it to create your own special effect.

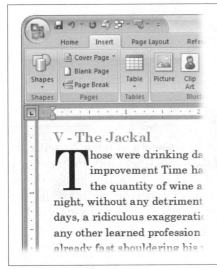
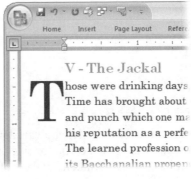

Figure 11-1:
Word provides two styles of drop caps.

Top: Dropped is the most common style and fits within the body of the paragraph.

Bottom: The In Margin style places the drop cap by itself in the left margin.

Here are the two simple steps for creating a drop cap:

1. **Click within the paragraph you want to have a drop cap.**

   You don't have to select the letter. Word knows that a drop cap is going to be the first letter of the paragraph.

2. **Choose Insert → Text → Drop Cap, or use the shortcut Alt+N, RC, and then choose from the three styles on the menu.**

   The choices available are: None, Dropped, and In Margin. Dropped, as shown at the left of Figure 11-1, is the most familiar style. The In Margin style places the oversized initial in the left margin.

   When you click your choice, the menu disappears. Word changes the initial cap in the paragraph to about three lines tall and positions it according to the option you chose. That's all there is to it.

Modifying a drop cap

When you create a drop cap, Word places the initial character in the paragraph in a frame of its own and positions it either in the paragraph or in the margin, but you can do lots of things to modify the design. Word provides a Drop Cap dialog box where you can make some changes (Figure 11-2), but it's just as easy to edit the drop cap right in the document.

Figure 11-2:
Using the Drop Cap box, you can choose one of the three styles and adjust the font, size, and position of the initial.

Because the cap is in a frame, you can drag it anywhere you want. To resize the drop cap, simply drag on a corner or side of the frame. Click inside the frame, and then select the letter to format it. Use any of Word's font formats to modify the letter. The color, shadow, emboss, and engrave options are great for drop caps. You can even add letters to the Drop Cap frame, so you can create a drop word, as shown in Figure 11-3.

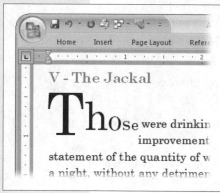

Figure 11-3:
To create a drop word like this, first insert a drop cap, and then type the rest of the word. In this example, each letter was also selected individually and resized using the Home → Font → Font Size command. Then the drop word was positioned by dragging the frame.

Removing a drop cap

Use the same menu—Insert → Text → Drop Cap—to remove a drop cap from your paragraph. Just select the None option, and the drop cap and the frame disappear. The paragraph goes back to its regular shape, with the initial letter back in line and sized like its compatriots.

Inserting a Text Box

Text boxes are another element that's designed to capture readers' interest and lure them into reading the text (Figure 11-4). Text boxes often contain an intriguing quote from the text designed to pique interest. Sidebars are another common use for text boxes. Like a footnote, but much more attractively formatted, sidebars provide additional, specific information that's not included in the text.

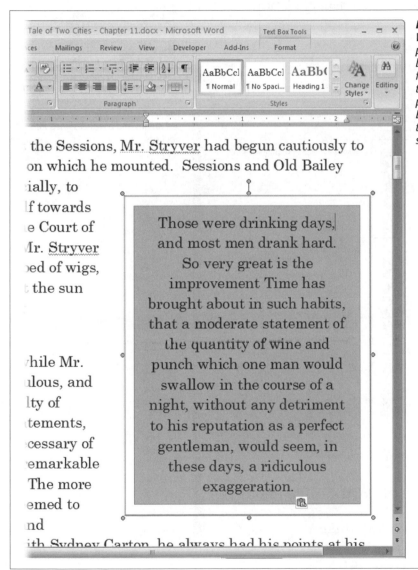

Figure 11-4:
Word's text boxes are preformatted with a background shade, border, font, and font style. Either type into the box, or copy and paste from your document. Either way, Word formats the text to match the text box style.

Whether it's a pull quote or a sidebar, you create the text box the same way:

1. **On the ribbon, choose Insert → Text → Text Box (Alt+N, X), and then select a text box style (Figure 11-5).**

   The menu shows you good-sized thumbnails of the different styles, making it easy to choose one for your document. Make your decision based on the general appearance of the text box; don't worry about positioning or even the size. You can modify those details later.

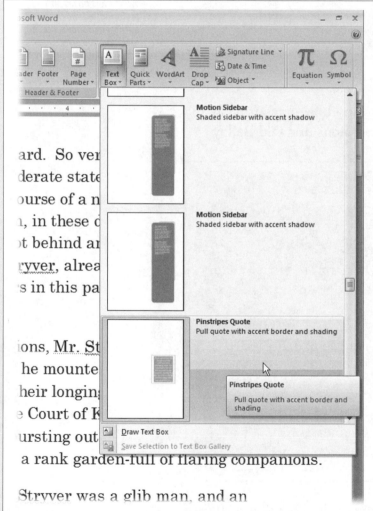

Figure 11-5:
The Text Box menu is in the ribbon's Text group with WordArt and Drop Caps. Use the scroll bar on the right to view the preformatted text box styles. You see two types: boxes designed for pull quotes and boxes designed for sidebars.

2. **Click in the box and begin typing.**

   If the text box is a pull quote, you can copy text from your document (Ctrl+C), and then click in the box and paste it (Ctrl+V). The box formats the text you enter to match the style.

3. **Size the box to fit your text by dragging the corners or borders.**

   You may need to adjust the box to fit your material. If you have big empty spaces in the text box, you can shrink it, or, if you don't have enough room for your text, drag an edge to make it bigger.

4. **Position the text box by dragging it or by using the Position drop-down menu.**

   To drag a text box to a new position on the page, hover the mouse over a part of the text box where there isn't any text, and your cursor changes to the "move" icon (a cross with four arrows). Drag the text box to a new position.

   The other way to position the text box is with a ribbon command. When you click the text box, the Text Box Tools contextual tab appears. Choose Text Box Tools | Arrange → Position to open the Position menu (Figure 11-6).

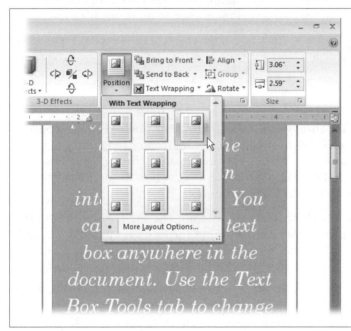

Figure 11-6:
Use one of the options from the Position menu to place your text box on the page and set the text wrapping behavior.

Customizing your text box

When you select a text box in your document, the Text Box Tools contextual tab appears on the right side of the ribbon (Figure 11-7). Using the commands on the Format tab, you can make all sorts of changes to your text box. The colors and effects make use of your document's theme. Here are some of the ways you can change the look of your text box:

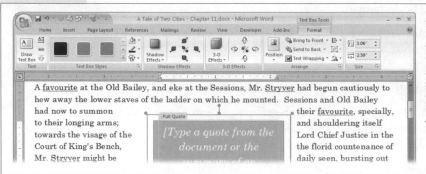

Figure 11-7:
Use the tools in the Text Box Tools contextual tab to fine-tune the look of your text box. The ribbon groups include Text, Text Box Styles, Shadow Effects, 3-D Effects, Arrange, and Size commands.

- **Text Direction, Alt+JX, G.** With a click of a button, you can change the direction your text runs. For example, for a heading or a special effect, your text can run up from the bottom of the page.

- **Create Link, Alt+JX, C.** You can create sidebars where the text continues from one page to the next. Select the first text box, click the Text Box Link button (Layout → Text → Text Box Link), and then click the second box. Text flows from one box to the next, just like normal text flows from page to page. Just keep an eye on the end of your text in the last box to make sure it's a good fit.

- **Text Box Styles, Alt+JX, K.** Click one of the colors in the Text Box Styles group to change the highlight colors for your box. Choices include solid colors and blends. Using other options in the styles box, you can adjust the fill and outline colors and even the box's shape.

- **Shadow Effects, Alt+JX, V.** Most of the text box styles include drop shadows. Use the tools in the Shadow Effect group (Text Box Tools | Format → Shadow Format → Shadow Effects) to modify the types of shadow and the direction. The drop-down menu (Alt+JX, D) provides preformatted effects (Figure 11-8). The tool to the right of the menu gives you controls to turn the drop shadow effect on and off and to change the shadow's position.

- **3-D Effects, Alt+JX, U.** The 3-D effects work like the shadow effects. They change the background of the text box, but the text stays put. Use the drop-down menu (Alt+JX, 3) to choose predesigned effects, or use the tool to the right of the menu to create your own custom effect.

- **Arrange, Alt+JX, P.** Use the tools in the Arrange group (Text Box Tools | Format → Arrange) to position your text box in relationship to the page and other items. The Position drop-down menu (Figure 11-6) automatically places the text box on the page and sets the word wrap options. As an alternative, you can use the separate Align (Alt+JX, AA) and Text Wrapping (Alt+JX, TW) tools.

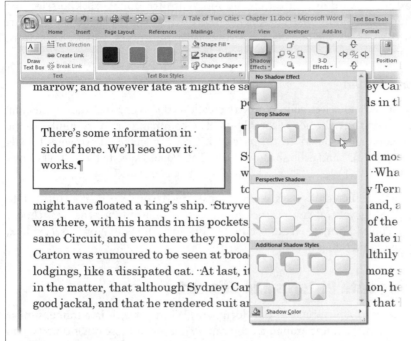

Figure 11-8:
The Shadow Effects and 3-D Effects are set up the same way in the Text Box Tools ribbon. The drop-down menu on the left provides preformatted designs. With the tools to the right of the menu, you can customize the position of the drop shadow or the rotation of the 3-D effect.

Bending Words with WordArt

WordArt is a lot more fun than it is useful. How often do you really need arched headlines in your documents? On top of that, you can waste a lot of time fiddling with all the options to see the cool effects you can produce (Figure 11-9).

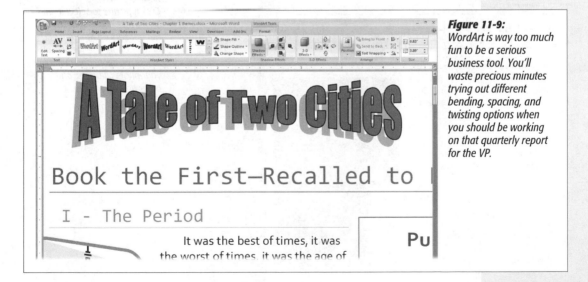

Figure 11-9:
WordArt is way too much fun to be a serious business tool. You'll waste precious minutes trying out different bending, spacing, and twisting options when you should be working on that quarterly report for the VP.

To transform a word in your document into WordArt, double-click to select the word, and then choose Insert → Text → WordArt to see the menu of WordArt designs. If you click the one that suits your artistic purposes, you see your word transformed.

Modifying WordArt

When you click to select your WordArt creation, the WordArt Tools contextual tab appears on the right side of the ribbon. The commands are very similar to the text box commands described on page 264. You can make adjustments to 3-D effects (Alt+JW, U) and drop shadows (Alt+CW, V) and specify the text wrapping options (Alt+JW, TW).

In spite of the incredible ways you've transformed your word, it's still text to Microsoft. So if you catch a misspelling or need to make other changes, choose WordArt Tools | Format → Text → Edit Text to open the Edit WordArt Text box, where you can fix things up.

Working with Pictures and Clip Art

When you insert a picture into your document, Word places it in a frame, similar to a text box or the frame around a drop cap. And as with those other objects, you can resize it, move it, and wrap text around it. As far as Word's concerned, if it's a graphic file—like a .JPG, .TIF, or EMF file—then it's a picture. The contents can be a photo or a drawing; it's all the same to Word. Once you've placed a picture in your document, you can edit it using any of the Picture Tools (Figure 11-10).

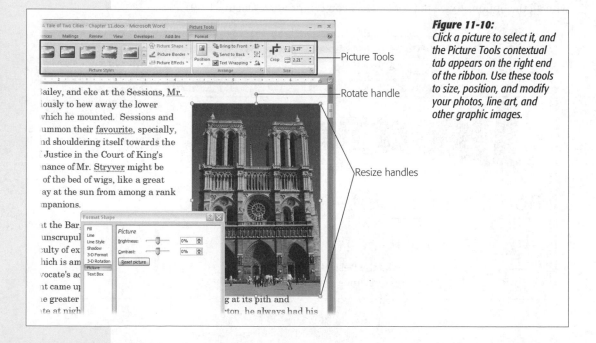

Figure 11-10:
Click a picture to select it, and the Picture Tools contextual tab appears on the right end of the ribbon. Use these tools to size, position, and modify your photos, line art, and other graphic images.

Note: As explained in the box on page 258, Word's clip art collection also includes photos and drawings. The main differences between clip art and pictures are the source of the images and how you insert them into your document. Use the Insert → Illustrations → Picture command to find pictures on your computer and place them in the document. Use the Insert → Illustrations → Clip Art command to search for photos in your clip art collection, including libraries of stock photos and artwork on the Internet.

Inserting Pictures into Your Document

To get some practice with Word's picture tools, in these steps you'll insert a picture into your document and then adjust its formatting and positioning.

1. **Click to place the insertion point where you want to insert the picture.**

   Don't worry about putting the insertion point exactly where you want the photo. You'll be able to fine-tune the placement after it's on the page.

2. **Choose Insert → Illustrations → Picture or use Alt+N, P to open the Insert Picture dialog box.**

   The Insert Picture dialog box starts out showing you the contents of your My Pictures folder. You can use the tools along the left side and top of the box to navigate to any folder on your computer or network that contains image files. For example, if your computer is connected to a network, and you have a photo library on one of the other network computers, click the My Network Places button in the lower-left corner.

3. **When you find the picture you want to use, double-click it to place it in your document.**

   Double-clicking does the same thing as selecting the photo, and then clicking the Insert button in the lower-right corner. The Insert Picture box closes, and you see your photo in your document.

4. **To resize the picture, Shift-click, and then drag one of the corners.**

   When you close the Insert Picture box, your newly placed picture is selected, as you can see from the frame and sizing handles around the image. (If your picture isn't selected, click it.) You can resize your picture by dragging any of the sizing handles on the corners or edges of the picture. As you resize the picture, while you're still pressing the mouse button, you see both the full-sized image and a faint copy of the new size. Release the mouse button when the copy is the size you want.

   Usually, when you resize, one edge or corner of the image moves and the other edges remain in place. If you'd rather keep the center anchored while all the edges adjust to the new size, press Ctrl as you drag a sizing handle. Use the handle that's sticking out of the top to rotate your image (Figure 11-11).

Tip: To avoid squashing or stretching the image, press Shift as you drag, and your picture keeps its handsome proportions.

5. **On the right side of the Picture Tools | Format tab, click the Position menu, and then choose one of the positions for your photo.**

Generally, it's good design practice to place a picture in one of the corners or at one of the edges of your document. Occasionally, you'll want to place a picture smack dab in the middle. If one of these options works for you, you're in luck. Word's Position menu can place your picture in one of these typical locations, and automatically wraps the text around it.

Figure 11-11:
Rotating a photo—or just about any other object in Word—is simple. A handle extends from the top center of the photo. Drag this handle around in a circle, and you see a ghost image of the photo rotating. When the image is in the position you want, let go of the mouse button.

Finding and Using Clip Art

Once you insert clip art into your document, it's really no different from any other photo or drawing. The difference between pictures and clip art in Word is all in the finding and inserting. Any photo or image file you store on your computer and insert into a Word document is a *picture. Clip art* refers to the tens of thousands of graphics and other media files in online libraries on the Internet and in libraries Word installs on your computer.

Since you have such a wealth of images to sort through, you need a quick way to search those images and filter out the ones you don't want, so you can focus on a few good candidates for the job. Fortunately, that's exactly what the Clip Art task pane does (Figure 11-12).

Here's how to find clip art and insert it into your document:

1. **Make sure you're on the page where you want to insert the clip art.**

It's not important to position the insertion point carefully because you can always position your picture later.

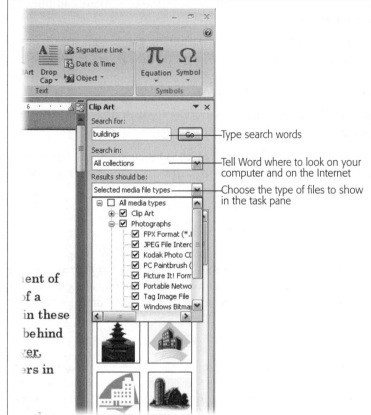

Figure 11-12:
When you click the Clip Art button (Insert → Illustrations → Clip Art), the Clip Art task pane opens at your document's right. Answer three questions, and Word shows you clip art examples that meet your specifications. Word needs to know what to look for, where to look, and what type of files to show you (like JPEG, MP3, and AVI).

Type search words

Tell Word where to look on your computer and on the Internet

Choose the type of files to show in the task pane

2. **Choose Insert → Illustrations ▸ Clip Art or use the shortcut Alt+N, F.**

   The Clip Art task pane opens at your screen's right.

Tip: If you want to, you can click the top bar of the task pane, and then drag it out of the Word window, like a separate palette (Figure 11-13).

---

3. **In the "Search for" box at the top of the Clip Art task pane, type a word or phrase that describes what you're looking for.**

   For example, if you're looking for pictures of buildings, type *buildings* or *architecture*. If you want to reduce the number of images Word shows you, narrow it down by typing, say, *buildings France* or *buildings England*. The more specific you can be, the fewer images you'll have to look through.

---

4. **From the "Search in" drop-down menu, choose the collections and libraries you want Word to search.**

   Click the checkboxes to select libraries for the search. Some of the libraries have different subdirectories of images—you can tell by the square button with a + sign next to their names. Click the button to expand the list, and then you can choose specific subdirectories for your search.

5. **From the "Results should be" menu, choose the types of files you want to see in the Clip Art task pane (Figure 11-12).**

   Another way you can narrow down the search is by choosing the type of files you're looking for. Clip art includes photos, drawings, audio files, and video files. If you aren't interested in audio and video clips, open the "Results should be" menu, and then turn off checkmarks from the Movies and Sounds boxes.

6. **Click the Go button to start the search.**

   When you click Go, a message appears in the clip window to tell you that Word's searching for clip art. When it finds art that matches your search, the results of your clip art search appear as thumbnails in the main box in the Clip Art pane. (You see a small globe in the lower-left corner indicating art that's stored on the Internet.)

7. **Review the results and, if necessary, adjust your search terms.**

   If Word can't find any images to meet your criteria, you see a message that says "(No results found)." You can do a couple things if your search fails. Double-check to make sure your computer is connected to the Internet. If it's not, Word can access only the limited number of clip art files on your computer.

   If you're connected to the Internet and still get no results, try expanding your search by changing your search words. For example, if *cathedrals Paris* didn't bring up any results, then try *buildings France* and see what pops up. If you limited the collection and libraries used for the search by using the "Search in" box, try expanding your search to include more sources.

8. **When you find an image you want to use, double-click to place it in your document.**

   Once you find the perfect picture, the easiest way to pop that image into your document is to double-click the thumbnail. Or, when you click once to select an image, a drop-down menu button appears on the right side. When you click to open this menu, you see several options:

   - Choose **Insert** to place the image in your document.

   - Choose **Copy** to place a copy of the image on Word's clipboard.

   - Click **Delete from Clip Organizer** if you don't want to see the clip in future searches.

   - Click **Make Available Offline** to copy and store the image on your computer.

Once the clip art image is inserted into your document, it's like any other picture or drawing. When you click to select the picture, the Picture Tools contextual tab appears on the right side of the ribbon. You can use all the usual formatting tools and commands to resize, position, and format your clip art, just as you would any other picture.

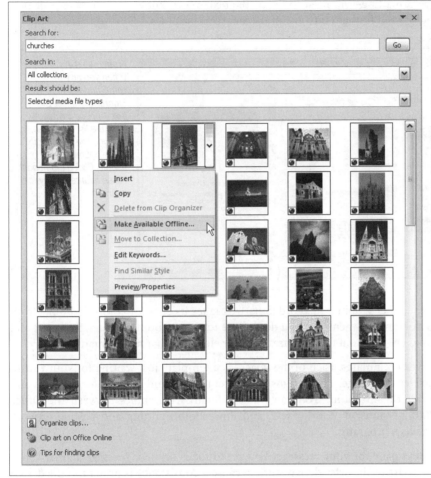

Figure 11-13:
If you'd like a little more room to inspect all the pictures in your Clip Art task pane, drag it out of the Word window by the top bar. Then you can drag any of the borders to resize the Clip Art pane to give you a better view. Each thumbnail has a drop-down menu that lets you insert or copy the clip. (If you're connected to the Internet when you search for clip art, Word shows you results from online libraries, indicated by a tiny globe icon.)

Working with SmartArt

SmartArt is another new Word 2007 feature designed to help busy people create and format a strong, graphic message. It's a boon to non-artistic business types faced with the challenge of creating a sleek, professional looking PowerPoint presentation. Maybe the designers at Microsoft decided the world had seen enough white slides full of black, square bullet points. Still, take the "Art" in SmartArt with a grain of salt. SmartArt isn't Rembrandt, Gauguin, or even Andy Warhol. It's the kind of art that an MBA loves—relationship trees, pyramid charts, and matrices.

Say you have a list of bullet points: a few main topics, each with a few subtopics. Rather than just present them as bullet points, you want to create a graphic that helps tell the story with impact, so you peruse the SmartArt library (Figure 11-14). Once you choose your graphic, you simply type the text you want to add. Word does all the formatting, sizing, and arranging. If you don't like the finished product, you can choose another graphic. Word swaps in the new design and does all the reformatting—no need to retype the text. Word knows how to take your bullet points and fit them into any of the SmartArt graphics.

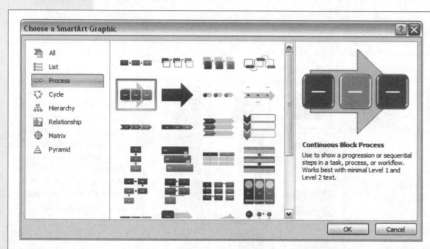

Figure 11-14:
When you give the command to insert SmartArt, you see this box. Choose a category from the list on the left, and you see thumbnails of the options in the middle. Click a thumbnail to see a large preview on the right.

Like the other graphics in Word, SmartArt takes its cues for colors and fonts from your document's theme, so you don't have to worry about clashing. SmartArt and Themes are a natural fit. Here are the other elements that make SmartArt smart:

- **Layout templates.** Each of the images is a template just waiting for your text to deliver a message. The designs are contemporary and suitable for business and other organizations. You can transfer SmartArt graphics between the Office 2007 versions of Word, Excel, and PowerPoint, cutting and pasting artwork between programs.

- **A text pane for your message.** You get to focus on your message and let Word take care of the artsy design stuff. Because a consistency is present in the design of the templates, Smart-Art can reformat and reconfigure your text to work with many different graphics and layouts.

- **Automatic sizing and positioning of shapes and text.** One of the most time-consuming issues when it comes to developing graphics for business presentations is the endless tinkering you have to do every time you change a word. SmartArt removes this problem. Just edit your text on the text pane, and SmartArt takes care of the font size and the graphic's shape and size.

Choosing a SmartArt Graphic

SmartArt graphics are divided into categories, each of which arranges information in a particular way. When deciding what kind of SmartArt to use, think of *how* you want to present your material:

- **Lists.** Great for individual facts, outlines, procedures, and other, well...lists.

- **Processes.** Used to track the changes in a project or goal, like harvest, production, distribution, sales, and consumption.

- **Cycles.** Suited to presenting processes that end back at the beginning. Think Winter, Spring, Summer, and Fall.

- **Hierarchies.** You've seen this type of organizational chart, where bosses proves they really *are* in charge.

- **Relationships.** The graphics in this group provide different ways to show the connections between items. For example, you find concentric circles, vertical tabs with arrows connecting them, and more.

- **Matrices.** This MBA favorite helps businesses make better decisions or at least understand why things aren't working.

- **Pyramids.** These graphics are good for illustrating proportions. For example, the U.S. Food and Drug Administration uses a pyramid chart to prove that you're not eating enough fruits and vegetables.

Inserting SmartArt into Your Document

SmartArt is a little more complicated than your average drawing, so it takes a few more steps to insert it into your document.

1. **Click to position the insertion point on a page of your document.**

   You don't have to be exact when you position the insertion point. You'll be able to move SmartArt later, just like any picture.

2. **Choose Insert → Illustrations → SmartArt or press Alt+N, M.**

   The Choose a SmartArt Graphic box opens (Figure 11-14). It displays categories on the left side, thumbnails in the middle, and a preview panel on the right.

3. **On the left side, click to choose a category.**

   Choose from one of the general categories described earlier in this section. Or, if you want to see all your options, leave the category set to All. Thumbnails appear in the middle of the box. If you need to, use the scroll bar to check out all the possibilities. When you click a thumbnail, the image in the preview on the right shows a larger, color version of your selection.

   When you've made your selection, click OK to insert the SmartArt into your document.

The dialog box closes, and the SmartArt of your choice appears in your document. A text pane opens next to the SmartArt, as shown in Figure 11-15.

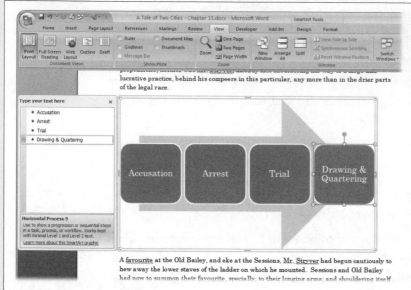

Figure 11-15:
The large arrow in the background of this graphic suggests a process or sequence of events. As you type in the text pane, your words appear in the SmartArt graphic. To add elements to a SmartArt graphic, simply press Enter, and then keep typing. This SmartArt started with just three boxes. The fourth box was added by pressing Enter, and then typing Drawing & Quartering.

4. **In the text box titled "Type your text here," do what it says.**

   The text box can vary depending on the SmartArt graphics you choose. Almost always, you see a bulleted list and prompts for you to start typing away.

5. **Promote and demote items in your text pane.**

   You can promote and demote items in your bulleted list, just like you do with an outline. While you're working in the text pane, use the keyboard shortcut Alt+Shift, Left arrow to promote items, and Alt+Shift, Right arrow to demote them. The left side of the SmartArt Tools | Design tab (Figure 11-16) also has Promote and Demote buttons.

6. **Close the text pane to finish your graphic.**

   When you're finished, click the X button in the upper-right corner of the text pane to close it, or—faster still—just click within the text of your document. You see your SmartArt graphic formatted and in place.

Modifying SmartArt

When you click to select a SmartArt graphic, you don't see the usual Picture Tools contextual tab. Also, the frame around SmartArt looks different from the frame around other kinds of pictures. That's because you have a different set of SmartArt tools to use. Two tabs are located within the SmartArt contextual tab—Design and Format. Use the Design tab to fine-tune layouts and overall styles. Use the Format tab to apply specific colors and WordArt styles.

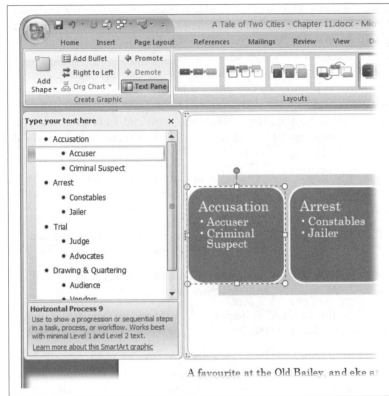

Figure 11-16:
*The SmartArt Promote and Demote
buttons help you position and rank
the bullet points in the graphic.*

The frame around a SmartArt graphic, although it looks different, lets you move and resize the graphic just like any other picture. Hold the mouse over the edge of the frame. When you see a cross with four arrows, you can drag the art to a new place. Hold the cursor over a corner or an edge, and you see a double-arrow that you can drag to resize the image.

Tip: The little dots on the edges of a SmartArt graphic's frame indicate a handle that you can drag with the mouse.

On the left side of the frame you see a tab with two triangle-shaped arrows. Click this tab to open the text pane, where you can edit and add to the text in your SmartArt.

Working with Shapes

Word's Shapes don't have SmartArt's IQ, but they're much more flexible. SmartArt knows what it wants to do and can be stubborn if you try to change its ways. Shapes let you push and pull them into just about any size or shape. The drawback with shapes is that you must insert, position, and format each one individually.

To open the Shapes menu, choose Insert → Illustrations → Shapes or use the short-cut Alt+N, SH. You see dozens of shapes, arrows, lines, and icons. Down at the very bottom of the menu you find the New Drawing Canvas command. The draw-ing canvas is a rectangular work area where you can arrange several shapes, and then treat them like a single graphic. If you're inserting a single shape, you can simply insert it, format it, and then flow the text around it. If you're working with several shapes, it's better to place a drawing canvas in your document, and then work with your shapes on the canvas. That way, you can have your text flow around the entire canvas instead of fine-tuning it to flow around several individ-ual shapes.

In the following tutorial, you'll place a canvas in your document and add shapes to it. In the process, you'll explore some of the myriad possibilities for positioning, sizing, and formatting shapes.

1. **Position the insertion point in your document where you want to place the canvas.**

   It works best if you have the insertion point on a blank line because Word ini-tially creates a canvas that runs from margin to margin.

2. **Choose Insert → Illustrations → Shapes → New Drawing Canvas, or use the keyboard shortcut is Alt+N, SHN.**

   The drawing canvas appears in your document—a large rectangle bounded by a dashed line and solid black resize handles at the corners and the middle of each side. When you pass the mouse over the canvas, it turns into a clear arrow instead of an insertion point.

3. **If you wish, click a corner or edge to resize the drawing canvas.**

   If the edges of your canvas aren't visible, click anywhere on the colored area of the canvas to select it. When you hold the mouse cursor over one of the resize handles, the cursor changes shape, indicating that you can drag.

   If you hold the cursor over one of the canvas borders without resize controls, it turns into a cross with arrows pointing in four directions—so you can drag the entire canvas to move it.

4. **Open the Format Drawing Canvas dialog box.**

   You can open the Format Drawing Canvas box three different ways. Right-click the canvas, and then choose Format Drawing Canvas from the shortcut menu. Press the keyboard shortcut Alt+JD, FA, or go to Drawing Tools | Format → Shape Styles → Advanced Tools.

   The Format Drawing canvas box has tabs along the top, labeled Colors and Lines, Size, Layout, and Alt Text. For now, you use the first tab to change the canvas's color and transparency.

Tip: You can ignore the Alt Text tab unless your Word document is destined to become a Web page (Chapter 13). It lets you add some text describing the image. Folks who have images turned off in their Web browser see this text instead, and so get an idea of what the image shows. Alt text also benefits visually impaired people whose browsers read Web page text aloud.

5. **On the Color and Lines tab, in the Fill section, choose a color for the canvas, and then set its transparency so that text or other objects show through the canvas.**

   The Fill Effects button leads to yet another dialog box where you can adjust the shading and the gradations of color for your canvas (Figure 11-17).

6. **When you're through, click OK to close the dialog box, and then return to your document.**

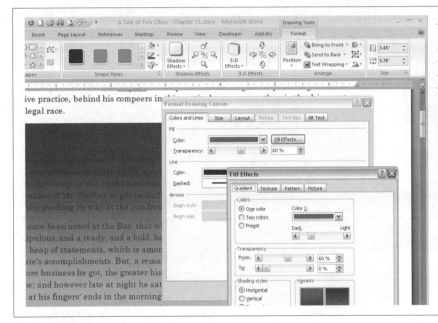

Figure 11-17:
You use nearly identical tools to format the drawing canvas and the shapes that you insert into your documents. Once you're comfortable working with colors, borders, and transparency for the canvas, you can apply everything you know to the shapes and lines in your graphics. Other formatting tabs let you specify the canvas's size and position and the way that text wraps around the object.

7. **Go to Insert → Shapes and click to choose a shape (Figure 11-18).**

   On the Drawing Tools ribbon, use the scroll buttons to see more shapes, or click the button at bottom to see them all at once on a menu.

8. **Drag on the canvas to position and size the shape on the canvas.**

   After clicking one of the shapes, click somewhere on your canvas, and then press the mouse button as you drag diagonally across the canvas. You see an outline of the shape drawn on the canvas as you drag the mouse. When it's roughly the size and shape you want, release the mouse button.

If you want to move or resize the shape, you need to click to select it. When the shape is selected, handles appear around the edges. The handles for different shapes can have slightly different functions, but controlling them is very similar. Drag the corner or edge handles to resize the shapes. The handle sprouting out from the top is used to rotate the shape; just drag to spin the shape around.

Tip: You may also see diamond-shaped handles on a shape. These handles have special functions depending on the shape. For example, on a rectangle, they let you round the corners. Don't be afraid to experiment and try out all the handles. You can always get back to square one with the wonderful Ctrl+Z undo keystroke.

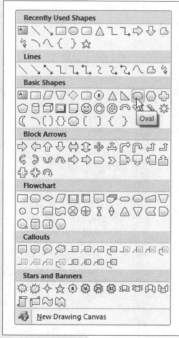

Figure 11-18:
On the Shapes menu, click to choose one of the shapes, and then drag to create a drawing canvas. The selected shape appears on the drawing canvas in your document. You can add other shapes to the canvas. For example, you can create an organizational chart using a combination of boxes and arrows.

9. **To add color to the shape, go to Drawing Tools | Format → Shape Styles and choose a style.**

The quickest way to apply formatting to shapes, lines, and your drawing canvas is with one of the Shape Styles shown on the Drawing Tools ribbon. Seventy variations are available using your documents Theme colors with different borders and shades. When you click one of them, Word applies the formatting to the selected shape.

As an alternative, you can add color, borders, and shades to your shapes just like you formatted the canvas using a dialog box. In fact, you can use the same command (Drawing Tools | Format → Shape Styles → Advanced Tools) or shortcut (Alt+JD, FA) to open the Format AutoShape box.

Next, you'll add a second shape and shape-adjust its position with the Send to Back and Bring to Front commands.

10. **Choose a different shape from the Insert Shapes menu. Drag to place it on the canvas, making sure that it overlaps the first shape.**

Notice that each shape exists on its own layer. It's like placing one piece of paper on top of another. Every time you add a shape or a line to your drawing, Word puts it on a layer above the existing shapes. You can change the layer order of your shapes using the commands in the Drawing Tools | Format → Arrange group. Under the Bring to Front and Send to Back drop-down menus, several variations let you move the selected shape one layer at a time or to the top or bottom of the heap.

Next, you'll draw a line between the two shapes.

11. **Choose one of the lines from the Insert Shapes palette (it doesn't matter if it has arrows on the end or not).**

The cursor changes to a cross, but when you hold it over one of the shapes, it changes, looking a little more like a crosshair, and the shape shows handles at the edges.

12. **Click one of the shape handles to attach one end of your line to that shape. Click a blank spot on the canvas to place the other end of the line anywhere that's not connected to one of the shapes.**

Lines have some special talents. They can be independent, just like any of the shapes, or they can connect to a shape on either end. Word provides visual hints as you're drawing to let you know exactly how the line will behave.

Now, if you move the shape, you see the line stays attached and moves along with the shape. The unattached end of the line moves freely.

When you click to select the line, handles appear in the middle and on both ends. You can move the line by clicking just about anywhere except the ends and dragging it. You see the familiar move icon that looks like a cross with four arrows. Hold the cursor over one of the end handles, and the cursor changes to the cross without the arrows (Figure 11-19).

13. **Click the line's free end handle and drag it over to one of the handles on the other shape.**

Word attaches the line to the shape. With the line attached to the two shapes, you can move the shapes around the canvas, and the line shrinks, grows, and repositions itself to remain attached to both shapes.

14. **Format the line using the tools of your choice.**

Lines don't have to be dull black affairs. You can format lines using the same tools and commands that you use for the other shapes. You can apply Shape Styles (Drawing Tools | Format → Shape Styles), or you can fine-tune the formatting with the Format AutoShape box (Alt+JD, FA).

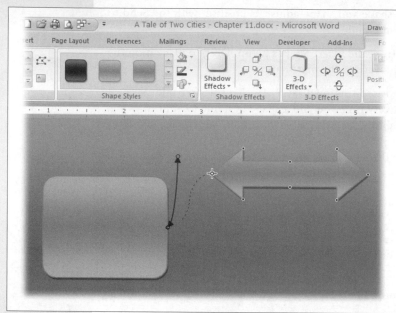

Figure 11-19:
Lines have some pretty clever AutoShape behaviors. When you attach lines to the handles of shapes, they'll stay attached even when you move the objects around the drawing canvas. This makes it easy to create organizational charts and other graphics that show relationships.

At this point you have three objects, each on its own layer above or below the other objects. The line connects one shape to another and stays connected if you move either object. Sometimes when you're working on more complicated graphics, it's helpful to group several objects together as if they're a single object. Next, you'll group the drawings and the line.

15. **Click to select one of the shapes. In turn, Ctrl+click the line, and then Ctrl+click the second shape.**

With each click, selection handles appear on the shapes and the line.

16. **With all three objects selected, go to Drawing Tools | Format → Arrange → Group → Group.**

Now instead of lots of little handles, the trio of shapes and lines sport a simplified set of handles. You can position, size, and rotate the three objects as one. When you select the group as a unit, you can also apply formatting commands such as color to all the objects at once. If you want to apply formatting to just one of the objects, select the group first, and then click to select the object within the group.

17. **Go to Drawing Tools | Format → Arrange → Text Wrapping or Alt+JD, TW and set the text wrapping behavior for the canvas and drawings.**

Several options are available for wrapping text around your graphics or around the canvas. The different commands let you position the drawing above or below the text and choose how tightly the text wraps around the shapes or the canvas. Figure 11-20 explains how Word decides what to wrap the text around.

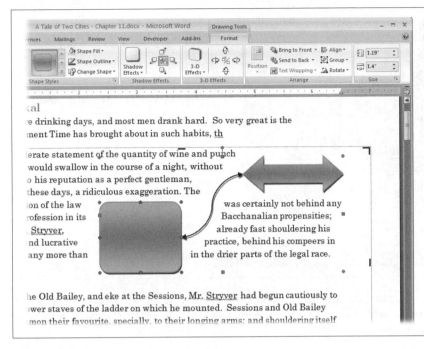

Figure 11-20:
If your shape isn't on a canvas or if you didn't apply color to the canvas, you can choose to wrap the text tightly around the shapes. If your graphics are on a canvas with a color fill, the text wrap commands apply to the entire canvas.

Inserting Charts and Graphs

Charts and graphs are different from other graphics because they're backed up by data. Word reads the numbers from a data chart or an Excel spreadsheet and uses those figures to show bars, plot lines, or to divvy up pieces of the pie. Your job is to provide the numbers and choose the best type of chart to represent the data. To get a feel for how it works, you'll create a bar graph that shows the number of executions in Paris and London over a four-year period.

Note: The Insert Chart command behaves differently depending on whether or not your have Excel 2007 installed on your computer. You can create snazzier charts if Excel is installed, as the following example shows.

If Excel is not installed when you create a new chart in Word, Microsoft Graph opens with some simpler options. A chart appears with a table called a data sheet. You type numbers in the data sheet to create the chart.

1. Go to Insert → Illustrations → Chart.

   The Create Chart box opens (Figure 11-21).

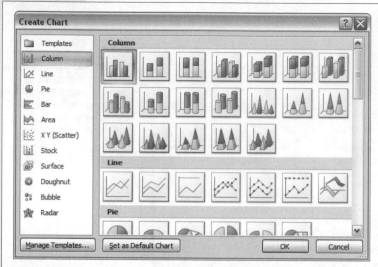

2. **In the panel on the left, click Column for chart type, and then click the example with two rows of cylinders. Click OK to insert the chart into your document.**

   You can choose from many types of charts, and one of the arts of chart making is to pick the right style to present your story. Pie charts are great for showing proportions, line charts for showing trends over time, and bars are good for comparing fixed numbers (like dollars…or executions).

3. **Edit the labels in the top row and first column of the data table to match your project, and then remove unneeded data from the example chart.**

   Immediately, after you insert the chart in your document, Word opens an Excel worksheet. You see a table with example text and numbers already entered. To create your chart, you replace the example text with your labels and your numbers.

4. **In the top row, leave the first column as is, type *Paris* in the second column, and then type *London* in the third column.**

   The fourth column is not needed, so you can delete it. (Click just above the column to select it, and then press Delete (or right-click and choose Delete from the shortcut menu). The text and numbers in the selected column disappear.

   The two columns show the number of executions in Paris and London over a period of four years (Figure 11-22). Now, change the headings in the rows to show the years 1789 through 1792. Leave the first row in the first column as it is, and type *1789* in the second row of the first column. Type *1790* in the third row, and continue moving down, entering *1791* and *1792* in the next rows.

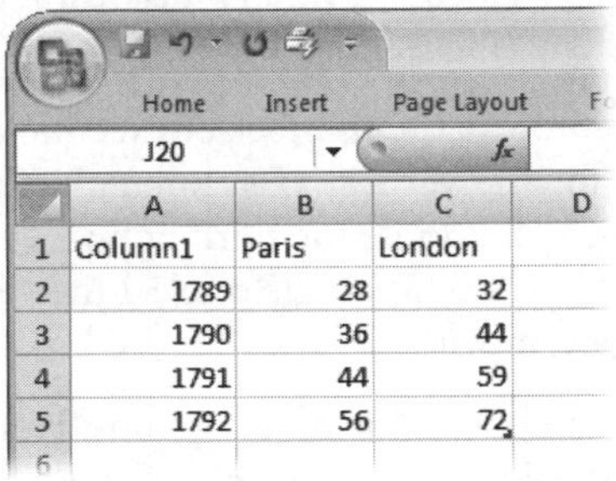

Figure 11-22:
Here's the data table with the edited labels and numbers filled in. The names of the cities appear at the top. The years 1789-1792 are listed on the left. The (made-up) numbers in the middle represent the number of executions in the cities each year.

Tip: If you need to add more data to a data table, you can add rows or columns just by typing the labels and numbers. Your chart automatically reflects the data table.

---

5. **Type the numbers for your chart data.**

   With the labels in place, you can enter your numbers. For this example, just type random numbers between 20 and 100. Fill the eight cells below the Paris and London headings.

6. **Close the data sheet.**

   To close the data sheet, just click your Word document. If you're using Excel to enter data, choose Office → Close or just switch from Excel to Word using the shortcut Alt+Tab.

   With the data sheet out of the way, you can see your chart. It looks pretty good but can still use some formatting and tweaking.

7. **Choose Chart Tools | Layout → Labels → Legend → None to remove the legend.**

   Legends are important for some charts, but for this chart, the city names are already shown and the legend isn't necessary. Removing the legend provides more room for the rest of the chart.

8. **Choose Chart Tools | Layout → Labels → Axis Titles → Primary Horizontal Axis Title → Title Below Axis to label the axis at the bottom of the chart.**

   The numbers at the bottom of the chart represent years, but that may not be obvious to all readers. Being specific with your axis titles eliminates all possibility for confusion. After you choose the ribbon command Title Below Axis, a text box appears below the chart with the words "Axis Title." Select those words, and then type the word *Years* to replace them.

---

9. Choose Chart Tools | Layout → Labels → Axis Titles → Primary Vertical Axis Title to label the axis on the left side of the chart (Figure 11-23).

The numbers on the left side of the chart represent the number of executions. You can choose from three text directions for the vertical axis: Rotated Title, Vertical Title, and Horizontal Title. For this chart, choose the third option Vertical Title. Replace the words in the text box with *Executions*. (To select the vertical text, simply drag from top to bottom. Hey, it works!)

If you don't like the look of the vertical title, try one of the other options. Horizontal Title takes up a lot of room, while Rotated Title leaves plenty of room for the chart and is still easily readable. You don't have to retype the title; just choose a different option from the menu, and Word reformats the title.

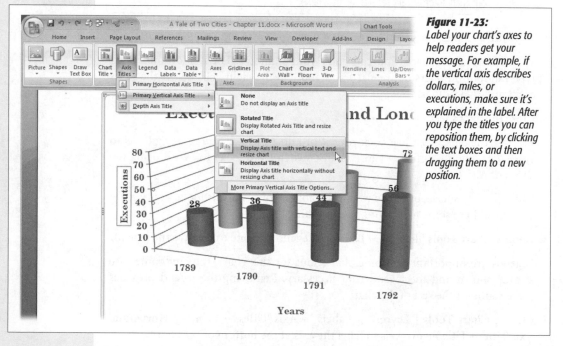

Figure 11-23:
Label your chart's axes to help readers get your message. For example, if the vertical axis describes dollars, miles, or executions, make sure it's explained in the label. After you type the titles you can reposition them, by clicking the text boxes and then dragging them to a new position.

10. Choose Chart Tools | Layout → Labels → Chart Title and then select Above Chart from the drop-down menu.

A text box appears above your chart. Select the text and replace it with *Executions in Paris and London*. Your finished chart should look like Figure 11-24.

Inserting Sound, Video, and Other Objects

If this chapter proves anything, it proves that your document is a container for more than just text. You can insert photos, drawings, and even sound and movie clips into your document. In fact, you can place dozens of different objects in your

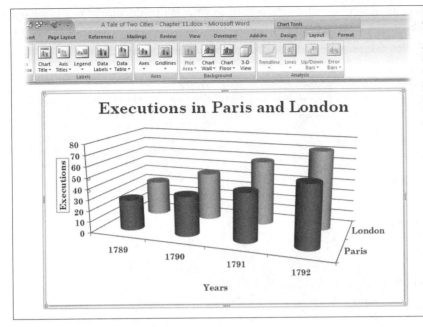

Figure 11-24:
The finished chart looks something like this. You can tweak your chart in plenty of other ways by adding background colors, gridlines, and so on. If your chart has 3-D effects like this one, try clicking the 3-D View button (Alt+JA, 3) to change the view angle.

document (Figure 11-25). If you can save it as a file, chances are you can pop it into a Word document using the insert object command: Insert → Text → Object → Object. Here's a list of some of the objects you can insert into your Word documents:

- Adobe Photoshop image files (.psd, .eps or .tif)

- Flash animations (.swf, or .png)

- Excel charts and worksheets (.xls, .xlsx, .xlsm, or .xlsb)

- Visio drawings (.vsd, .vss, or .vdx)

- Audio files (various formats, including .mp3, .wav, and .aif)

- Video clips (various formats, including .avi, .mov, and .divx)

Once you insert an object in your document, Word can treat it in a variety of ways. In some cases, Word becomes a media player for the object. In other cases, Word acts more like a container. When you save your document, the object gets saved along with it. If you copy the file and give it to friends or coworkers, they can read the document and enjoy the object you inserted, provided their computers have the right stuff to handle that kind of object. For example, if you put an MP3 music file in your document, your recipients need iTunes, Windows Media Player, or some other program that knows how to play MP3 files. If you've plugged in a Video for Windows file (AVI), then your pals need a program that can play videos. Windows Media Player does the trick, and it's installed on most computers along with Internet Explorer.

Inserting an object—a video clip, say—into your Word document is a two-stage affair. First, you insert a placeholder into your document to show Word where you want your object to go, and then you replace the placeholder with the object.

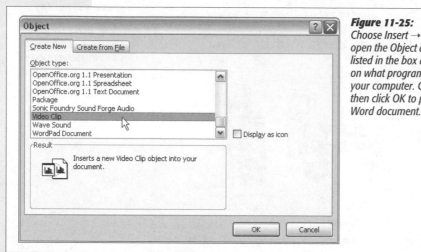

Figure 11-25:
Choose Insert → Text → Object → Object to open the Object dialog box. The Object types listed in the box at the top vary depending on what programs you have installed on your computer. Choose an object type, and then click OK to plop the object into your Word document.

1. **To open the Object box, choose Insert → Text → Object → Object from the ribbon, or use the keyboard shortcut Alt+N, JJ.**

   The object types listed in the Object box match the programs that are installed on your computer.

2. **Scroll down the list until you can see Media Clip in the list, and then double-click to place a media clip icon in your document.**

   The media clip icon appears in your document and the media player control appears where you'd normally see the ribbon. All the media player buttons are grayed out because you haven't chosen a particular media file to play; you've just put a placeholder in your document.

3. **In the menu bar at the top of the window, choose Insert Clip → Video for Windows. Then choose a video file to insert into your document.**

   The Insert Clip menu has several options. For example, you can insert a video clip by choosing the Video for Windows option, or you can insert an MP3 song by choosing the Sound option. In either case, you see a standard Windows file box to help you find a media file to load into the media player. When you choose a video file and click OK, the placeholder icon changes into a window in your Word document where the video will play. Double-click the video window, and the movie plays right there in your document (Figure 11-26).

4. **Resize and format the video window.**

   You may want to resize or format the video window once it's in your document. It's easy to do. In fact, it's just the same as formatting any picture. Click

Two Cities - Chapter 11.docx - Microsoft Word

days, a ridiculous exaggeration. The learned profession
any other learned profession in its Bacchanalian prope:
already fast shouldering his way to a large and lucrativ
this particular, any more than in the drier parts of the

A favourite at t
Sessions, Mr. S
away the lower
mounted. Sess
summon their f
arms; and shou
the Lord Chief
the florid count
seen, bursting (

sunflower pushing its way at the sun from among a rar

It had once been noted at the Bar, that while Mr. Stryv

Figure 11-26:
*To play a video that's
inserted in a document, just
double-click the video
window. You see some
basic media player controls
like Stop and Pause along
with a progress bar. The
video plays within its
window in your Word
document.*

to select the video placeholder window, and handles appear around the edges.
Drag one of the corner handles to resize your video while keeping the proportions the same. (If you drag one of the edges, you'll stretch or squash your
image. It'll still play, but people will laugh.)

Tip: It you've got more serious formatting in mind, you can bring up the standard picture-formatting box
by right-clicking the video window, and then choosing Format Object from the pop-up menu. From there,
you can fine-tune the size, layout, and position of the video window.

The steps to insert an MP3 song or a WAV sound file are almost identical to the
video steps. It's a little easier, because you don't need to worry about visual issues.
The sound clip appears as a small icon in your file. Double-click the icon, and
you'll hear sweet music.

Note: Inserting a video clip is much simpler than it sounds; for a screencast—an online, animated tutorial—of the steps you've just read, head over to the "Missing CD" page at *www.missingmanuals.com*.

Adding Captions and Figure Numbers to Graphics

Pictures, charts, and clip art help get your message across, but they can often benefit from a few extra words that identify the image, point out specific details, or provide additional information (Figure 11-27). You can add a caption to pictures, clip art, SmartArt, charts, and shapes that use a drawing canvas. To add a caption to a graphic, right-click it, and then choose Insert Caption from the shortcut menu. The Caption box opens (Figure 11-28). Once you've entered text for your caption and made some formatting decisions, your caption appears in all its glory.

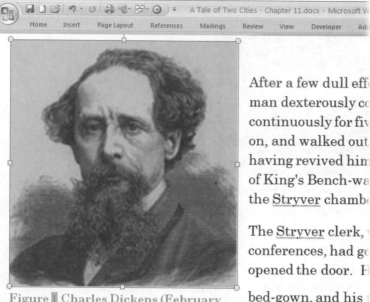

Figure 11-27:
Your document's theme determines the font and text color the caption uses. Using Word's formatting options, you can place the caption above or below your picture (as shown here).

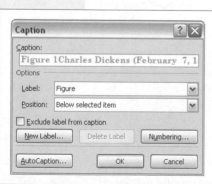

Figure 11-28:
Type your text in the Caption box. Choose Figure (or Equation or Table) from the Label drop-down menu. Or, if none of those three strike your fancy, create your own label (Picture, Image, Photo, or whatever) by clicking the New Label button. Use the Position menu to place your caption above or below the graphic.

Mass Mailing with Mail Merge

When you need to write to 650 of your closest friends with a personal message that you know will be of the utmost interest to them, it's time to dust off Word's *mail merge*. The "merge" part is where this feature gets exciting. In a mail merge, you write your letter in Word, and then merge it with personal information (name, address, and so on), from another document or even another program (like Excel or Outlook). When Word prints out the 650 copies of your letter, the first one reads: Dear Charles; the second reads: Dear Sydney; the third reads: Dear Lucie; and so on. And you can use the same tools to print envelopes or labels or even non-mail-related chores. (Now, if only Word could lick the envelopes.)

In this chapter, you learn how to make mail merge jump through hoops. Some of this gets kind of geeky with the talk about fields and lists, but you get a big payoff in how much time you save when you use mail merge. This chapter starts out easy with the basics and the Mail Merge Wizard. You go through the whole step-by-step process of creating and printing a mail merge letter. The end of the chapter digs deeper into customizing mail merge for other projects and controlling mail merge using conditions you set up (*rules*).

Understanding Mail Merge Basics

Mail merge consists of two parts: a document and a list. The document is like a form with placeholders, such as "Dear <<FirstName>>" or "We are certain that <<CompanyName>> will quadruple its annual profits by using our widget." When you initiate a merge, words from the list fill in the blanks on the form. These blanks, shown here (and in Word) by the double brackets, are called *fields* in mail-merge lingo. So, a person's first name is a field, the Zip code is another field. When you insert a field into your letter, it gets filled in automatically from your list.

Common Types of Merge Documents

You can see the most common types of mail merge documents in the Start Mail Merge menu (Figure 12-1). Go to Mailings → Start Mail Merge → Start Mail Merge or use the keyboard shortcut Alt+M, S.

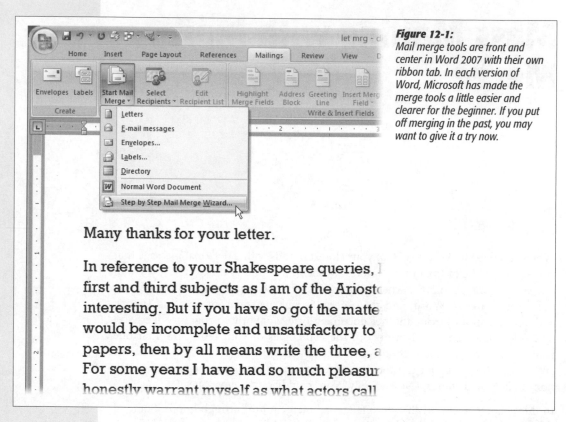

Figure 12-1:
Mail merge tools are front and center in Word 2007 with their own ribbon tab. In each version of Word, Microsoft has made the merge tools a little easier and clearer for the beginner. If you put off merging in the past, you may want to give it a try now.

- **Letters.** Create form letters that begin with a real name instead of Dear Resident. For example, they can begin, "Sydney Carton. You may already be a winner!"

- **E-mail messages.** Form letters aren't just for snail mail anymore. You can use Word to automate the creation of email messages. All you need is a list of names and email addresses.

- **Envelopes.** Most printers can handle letter-sized envelopes, and some of the fancier ones can manage large envelopes. If your printer can handle them, Word can address batches of envelopes at a time.

- **Labels.** The solution for large envelopes is often labels. Mail merge reads your list of recipients and prints out sheets of labels for large envelopes or boxes.

- **Directory.** Outlook and contact managers are all well and good when you're sitting at your computer, but sometimes you need a printed list of names and addresses. You can use the mail merge directory feature to create a list that includes phone numbers, fax numbers, email addresses, and anything else you like.

You aren't limited to letters and envelopes when you use the mail merge tool. In fact, you can be creative and make a merge document that doesn't have anything to do with mail. For example, you can generate a catalog of your favorite CDs by making a list with merge fields that include Album Title, Musician, Record Label, Genre, Year of Release, and Short Critique. Then just use Word to design the pages and place the fields to hold the list items.

Mail Merge Recipient Lists

The lists used in mail merge have more in common with the tables discussed in Chapter 10 than they do with your everyday shopping list. In fact, when Word gives you a form to edit your list, it's a simple Word table (Figure 12-2). For the typical mail merge job, each row (or *record*) holds information about one recipient. The individual bits of information (*fields*) in each row may include details such as First Name, City, and Zip code. So, if you do a mail merge for envelopes, Word uses the name and address in the first row to print the first envelope. The name and address in the second row go on the second envelope, and so on.

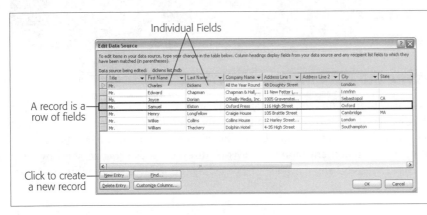

Figure 12-2:
The lists used for mail merging look suspiciously like Word tables or Excel spreadsheets. In fact, many of the same commands that you use for tables work with the Edit Data Entry box. For example, use the Tab key to move from one cell to another.

The Six Phases of a Mail Merge

A mail merge consists of six overall phases. Before you begin, look over the following list and gather the information you need. If you use the Mail Merge wizard, it will ask you to answer the following questions:

- **Decide what type of document you're creating.** Is mail merge going to create letters, envelopes, labels, or some other type of document?

- **Select the starting document.** Are you using an existing document or starting from scratch?

- **Choose the recipients or list that you're using for the merge.** Does this list exist or do you need to create it?

- **Add merge fields to your document.** Where do you want to insert words from your recipient list, such as Dear <<First Name>>?

- **Review the results.** Before you run off 650 letters, you want to ask: Is the merge working as expected?

- **Print to paper, email, or your screen for further editing.** Where is this merge headed? Is it being printed? Is it creating email? Or do you want to see all the letters in a Word document so you can edit each letter a little bit more?

POWER USERS' CLINIC

Decoding Merge-Speak

If you're familiar with databases, you may be inclined to translate Word's mail merge terminology into more familiar database language.

- **Recipient list.** Actually, just a very simple, bare-bones database.

- **Data source.** The computer file that holds the recipient list. When you create a list inside Word, it saves the list in an Access file that ends in .mdb (the filename extension for the Access format).

- **Recipient.** In database terms, one recipient (that is, one row in the recipient list) is the same as a *record*.

- **Merge field.** For the most part, a merge field is just like a field in any database.

- **MergeRec.** The special field MergeRec is a counter that keeps track of the records that are actually used in a merge.

Running the Mail Merge Wizard

If you're new to mail merges, the Mail Merge wizard is a fine way to start. You can watch how Word sets up your documents, and then later, you may want to forgo the wizard and strike out on your own. The wizard appears in the task pane to the right of your document and takes you through the process step by step (Figure 12-3). As you answer questions posed by the wizard, Word edits your document to match.

Note: If you opt to work without the wizard, you don't see the Wizard task pane, and it's up to you to edit your document. You must also insert fields manually, as described in the box on page 298.

In many ways, it doesn't matter if your merge is creating letters for a mass mailing, printing envelopes, or cranking out multiple business proposals. Each of the wizard's steps follows the same pattern. Answer the questions and do the tasks at the top, and then at the bottom, click Next to move on to the next step.

Tip: If you need to change something you did in an earlier step, you can backtrack. Just click the Previous button at the bottom.

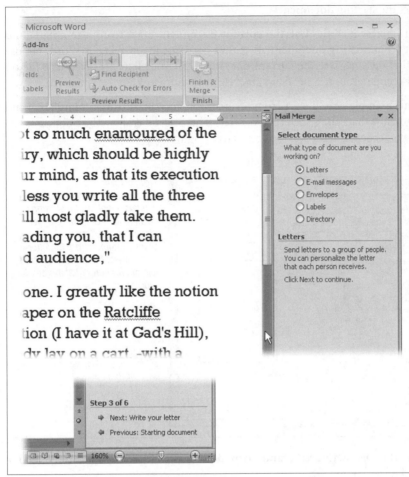

Figure 12-3:
*Top: Start the Mail Merge
Wizard (Alt+M, SW), and a
panel opens to the right of
your document. Word walks
you through the mail merge
process, making sure you
provide all the details and
make all the decisions
necessary for a successful
merge. The first step is to
choose the type of document
you want to create.*

*Bottom: After you complete
each step, click the Next
button to move on.*

The tutorial on the following pages takes you through the steps for a typical mail
merge letter.

Select Document Type

As mentioned earlier, you can merge into all sorts of documents: letters, envelopes, labels, and even brand-new documents of your own choosing. For this
example, you'll use one of Word's templates designed to create a mail merge letter.

1. **Go to Mailings → Start Mail Merge → Step by Step Mail Merge Wizard.**

   As shown in Figure 12-3, you have the choice of: **Letters, E-mail messages,
   Envelopes, Labels,** or **Directory** (as in a phonebook).

   For this example, choose Letters, and then at the bottom of the wizard pane,
   click "Next: Starting document."

2. **Select the starting document.**

   Your choices include: **Use the current document, Start from a template,** and **Start from existing document.** If you've got your letter open in Word, choose the first option: "Use the current document." If your letter is saved in a file on your computer, use "Start from an existing document."

   In this example, you'll start from scratch, so click "Start from a template," and then below that, click "Select template." The Select Template box appears, letting you choose a template for your letter (Figure 12-4).

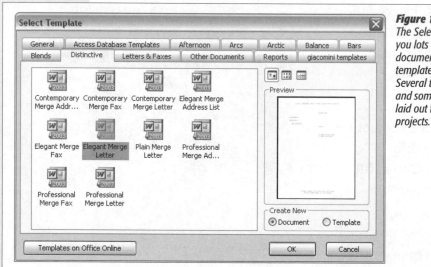

Figure 12-4:
The Select Template box gives you lots of options for starting a document. Click the tabs to see templates in different styles. Several templates are for letters, and some of them are specifically laid out for other mail merge projects.

3. **Click the Distinctive tab, and then double-click the Elegant Merge Letter template.**

   Sounds perfect—you're an elegant individual (Figure 12-5).

Note: If you can't find that template on the Distinctive tab (it may not have been included when you installed Word), choose one of the other Merge Letter templates.

The template opens in Word, and it's ready for you to begin filling in the blanks. For example, at the top between the square brackets it says "[Click here and type company name]." You see a prompt where the body of the letter should appear: Type your letter here and at the end of the letter you see prompts to add your name and title to the closing. At the very bottom, prompts appear for your address and other details that complete the template's letterhead.

4. **Click between each pair of square brackets, and then replace the boilerplate
text with your own.**

In this step, you're filling in the letterhead for the letter that you'll later use in
the mail merge. When you're finished, at the bottom of the Mail Merge pane,
click "Next: Select recipients."

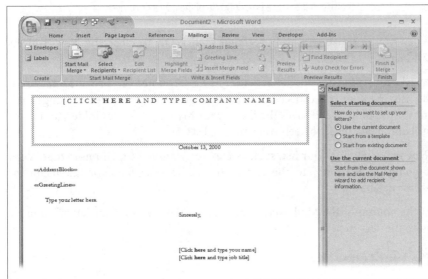

Figure 12-5:
*The Elegant Merge Letter
template lives up to its
billing. It has a simple,
classic look with letter-
spaced type at the top
and bottom. What's
more, the
<<AddressBlock>> and
<<GreetingLine>> merge
fields are already in
place where they'll show
details from your
recipient list. The items
inside square brackets
([ ]) are typical template
prompts asking you to fill
in words such as your
company name for the
letterhead.*

Select Your Recipients

In this step you choose or create the recipient list for the mail merge.

1. **On the next wizard screen, tell Word where to find your recipient list.**

The wizard gives you three options to choose from: **Use an existing list**, **Select
from Outlook contacts**, or **Type a new list**. If you've done a previous mail
merge, you may have a saved list you can use. Or, you can choose names and
addresses that are stored in Outlook. The last option, "Type a new list" is the
one to click for this example.

2. **Below, click the Create to open the New Address List box.**

Except for the way the title looks, this dialog box looks exactly like the Edit Data
Source box shown in Figure 12-2. Each row holds details about one person such
as first name, company, and city.

3. **Fill in the boxes in the first row, with first name, last name, company name,
and so on, to create a complete address.**

When you're done with one recipient, click the New Entry button in the
bottom-left corner, and then enter details for another recipient.

Tip: Most of the shortcuts and techniques that you use with tables (Chapter 10) work in the New Address List box. For example, use the Tab key to move forward to the next cell or Shift+Tab to move backward. When you're at the end of the last row, Tab creates a new row (which does the same as clicking the New Entry button). If it's hard to see all the text for some of the longer fields, mouse up to the top of the box and position it between two field names. The cursor changes to a cross with two arrows pointing left and right; drag to adjust the column width. A double-click automatically adjusts the column to fit the contents. To adjust the size of the whole box, drag one of the edges or corners.

4. **When you've finished adding recipients, click OK to close the New Address List box.**

   Word opens a file box titled Save Address List. You need to provide a name for the list, and then you can save it wherever you want. If you don't change folders at this point, Word saves the file in your My Data Sources folder, and that's probably a fine place to keep your mailing lists.

5. **Type in a name for your list, such as *Dickens Mailing List*, and note that Word is going to add .mdb to the end of the name—the filename extension for Access databases.**

   At the bottom of the Mail Merge pane, click "Next: Write your letter" to move on to the next step.

Write Your Letter

Writing your letter is the easy part; Just click in your document and start typing. In addition to writing the actual letter you're going to mail, the other important task at this point is to make sure your merge fields are in place. Back in step 3 on page 294, you chose the Elegant Merge Letter template. The merge letter templates already have the merge fields in place. For example, the top picture in Figure 12-6 shows two merge fields: AddressBlock and GreetingLine. When you run the merge, Word replaces these fields with words from your recipient list.

You can see the results by clicking Mailings → Preview Results → Preview Results or Alt+M, P. This button works like a toggle, so you can click back and forth between the preview and the field code. Use the arrow buttons to the right of Preview Results to see other copies of your letter to other recipients. The template puts the name and address merge fields in a logical place, but at times you may want to customize a template. You can cut, copy, and paste merge fields just as you do any text. You can also select fields and drag them to a new spot. (Just don't delete them!)

When you're finished editing your letter and inserting merge fields, at the bottom of the Mail Merge pane, click "Next: Preview your letters."

Note: This particular step has different names depending on whether you're creating a letter, an email, or envelopes. If you're working on a merge to print addresses on envelopes, the wizard prompts you to "Arrange your envelope."

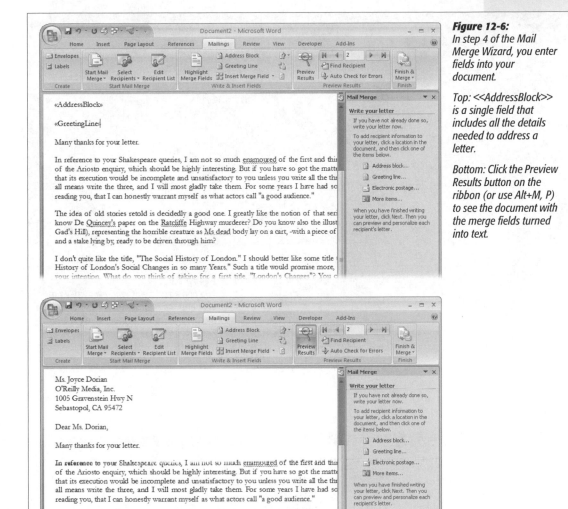

Figure 12-6:
*In step 4 of the Mail
Merge Wizard, you enter
fields into your
document.*

*Top: <<AddressBlock>>
is a single field that
includes all the details
needed to address a
letter.*

*Bottom: Click the Preview
Results button on the
ribbon (or use Alt+M, P)
to see the document with
the merge fields turned
into text.*

Preview Your Letter

In this step, you look over your document in the Mail Merge pane to make sure everything looks right. It's not unusual to discover a couple gotchas at this point. The key to success usually depends on the consistency of your recipient list. Like most computer programs, mail merge doesn't like special cases. So things may look off kilter if, say, one of your recipients doesn't have a street address or goes only by one name. (You *do* write to Madonna, Bono, and The Rock, don't you?)

POWER USERS' CLINIC

Adding Your Own Merge Fields

Granted, it's convenient that the merge letter templates come with merge fields in place, but it's not difficult to place a merge field into the body of the letter yourself. Say you want your letter to begin "Many thanks for your letter from <<City>>," where you mention the name of the recipient's city.

First, make sure the Preview Results button is turned off so that you see merge fields. For example, you should see the <<AddressBlock>> merge field in your document instead of an actual address.

Type *Many thanks for your letter from*, leaving the insertion point positioned just after the word "from." Then, choose Mailings → Write & Insert Fields → Insert Merge Field → City (Figure 12-7). The menu closes, and you see the <<City>> merge field in the text of your letter.

Click the Preview Results button, and you see the name of a city merged into the text. If you thumb through your recipients with the Next Record button (Alt+M, X), you see different city names to match each recipient.

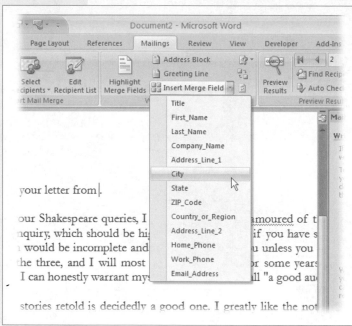

Figure 12-7:
You can insert fields wherever you want in your document simply by selecting them from the Insert Merge Field menu.

Use the buttons in the Mailings → Preview Results group to browse through your letters (Figure 12-8). If you've got a long list and want to search for a particular recipient, click "Find a recipient" to open the Find Entry box. Type the name of the person you want to find, and then click Find Next.

To remove one of the letters from the merge, click "Exclude this recipient" in the Mail Merge pane.

When you're through with your review, click "Next: complete the merge" at the bottom of the Mail Merge pane.

Complete the Merge

If everything looked great in the preview, you're ready to print your letters. Click the Print button in the Wizard task pane, and the Merge to Printer box pops up. You have three options:

- **Print all of the records.** Make sure you have plenty of paper in your printer.

- **Print the current record.** The *current record* is the letter showing in Word's window.

- **Print a range of records.** If you want to print a range of letters, say from letter #3 to letter #5, type those numbers in the text boxes. Sometimes, it helps to use Preview Results (Mailings → Preview Results) to get a handle on the records in a specific range. The record number shows in between the Previous Record and the Next Record button (Figure 12-8).

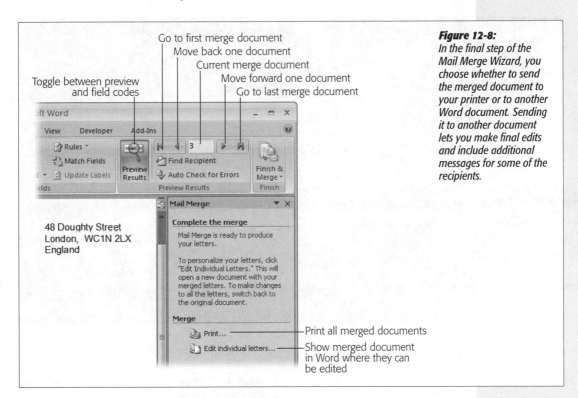

Figure 12-8:
In the final step of the Mail Merge Wizard, you choose whether to send the merged document to your printer or to another Word document. Sending it to another document lets you make final edits and include additional messages for some of the recipients.

If you want to tweak your letters a bit before you send them off, click "Edit individual letters." This option offers a couple of advantages. First, it merges all the letters, creating one new Word document. So, say you start with a one-page letter and 650 recipients. You click "Edit individual letters," and then click "All" in the Merge to New Document box. A new 650-page Word document opens where each page is a letter to a different recipient. You can save this document, and you can go in and make changes to each letter. Notice that these letters lack an <<AddressBlock>>

merge field. All the fields have been converted to text. Second, this option gives you a chance to add an extra personal note or paragraph to some of the recipients. You get the best of both worlds: the convenience of a mass mailing, with the opportunity to personalize your message to some of your contacts.

When you're finished reviewing and editing the merged document, you can click Print to send the job to the printer. Like any document, you can print some or all of the pages.

Tip: You can save both the initial letter and the merged document, just as you'd save any Word files. To save the initial letter, before the wizard step 6 ("Complete the merge"), go to Office button → Save As and save your document. To save all the merged letters as one file, in step 6, select "Edit individual letters." Word creates a new file containing all the letters with the fields merged. Save this file with Office button → Save As.

Speedy Addressing with the Address Block

Because letters and labels are such a natural for mail merge, Microsoft created the *address block*, a sort of super data field that includes the typical details that belong on a complete address, so you can work with the address as just one field instead of a bunch of little ones.

Word creates the address block from several separate fields like the recipient's name, street address, and so on. When you use the address block, you simply insert the one field in your document, and mail merge gathers all the necessary bits of information from the following individual fields:

- <<First Name>> <<Last Name>>

- <<Company Name>>

- <<Address Line 1>>

- <<Address Line 2>> (if needed)

- <<City>>, <<State>> <<Zip Code>>

The address block even adds the comma between the city and state. Even more impressive, if gaps appear in the address, such as no second address line, Word doesn't show an empty line in the address block.

The Greeting Line merge field is similar to the address block. It's a pre-rolled bit of field code specifically for use in letters. It has some built-in smarts too. The greeting line enters Dear <<First Name>> into your document, but if the record in the recipient list doesn't include a first name, Word inserts "Dear Sir or Madam" instead.

Merging to E-Mail

Merged documents aren't limited to snail mail. Word's merge tools play well with email too. All you need is your document and your recipients' email addresses, which you probably have in Outlook. As mentioned in the previous section, you can choose Outlook as the source for your recipient list. That way, you can use Outlook fields to insert merge codes in the body of your document and, even more important, you can use the address in Outlook to address your email messages.

Tip: If you're using Outlook as the source for your recipient list, create a single Outlook folder especially for the mail merge, and put all your recipients in it. Depending on the way you organize your contacts, you can either copy contacts into the mail merge folder or move them right into it.

You can use the Mail Merge Wizard to create email, as described in the previous section, but this tutorial shows you a do-it-yourself email merge. First, before proceeding, raise your right and hand and repeat: I promise to use email merge for good purposes only and will never contribute to the evil spam threatening the citizens of the World Wide Web.

1. **Open a blank document, and then choose Mailings → Start Mail Merge → E-Mail Messages or press Alt+M, SE.**

   Because this message is intended for email, Word shows it to you in Web Layout view. For example, there are no margins. Lines of text run from the left side of the window all the way to the right. If that makes it hard to read, you can make it more readable by adjusting the size of the entire Word window.

2. **Create the body of your message.**

   You can type text of your message into the blank document you just created. Or, if you have a preexisting document that you want to use, open it now. (You can always paste text into your open document too.)

   When you're done with your message, select your recipients.

3. **Choose Mailings → Start Mail Merge → Select Recipients → Select from Outlook Contacts or Alt+M, RO.**

   The Select Contacts box opens, displaying your Outlook folders. Some of these folders are mail folders that hold messages, and some are Contacts folders.

4. **Choose one of your contact folders. (If you followed the Tip above, you have a single folder with all your email merge recipients in one spot.)**

   The Mail Merge Recipients box opens. All the contacts in the folder have a checkmark, indicating that they're selected to receive your email.

5. **In the Mail Merge Recipients box, review, and, if desired, cull the recipient list.**

   To take a person off the list, click the box to remove the checkmark. When you're happy with your list, in the lower-right corner, click the OK button.

6. **Insert merge fields in your letter using the Mailings → Write & Insert Fields → Insert Merge Field command.**

   When you use Outlook as the source for your recipient list, you get a whole slew of merge fields (Figure 12-9). Assuming you entered the information into Outlook, you can use fields like Assistant, Spouse, Birthday, Hobbies, Nickname, and Profession.

If you want your email to look like a more formal letter, you can insert the Address Block and GreetingLine fields just like in a business letter. Buttons for both commands are in the Mailings → Write & Insert Fields group.

For a more informal email approach, insert the First or Nickname merge field to insert your Contact's first name (Mailings → Write & Insert Fields → Insert Merge Fields or Alt+M, I).

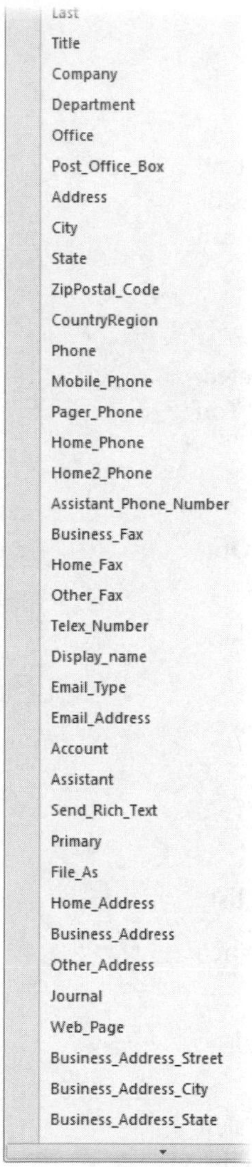

Last
Title
Company
Department
Office
Post_Office_Box
Address
City
State
ZipPostal_Code
CountryRegion
Phone
Mobile_Phone
Pager_Phone
Home_Phone
Home2_Phone
Assistant_Phone_Number
Business_Fax
Home_Fax
Other_Fax
Telex_Number
Display_name
Email_Type
Email_Address
Account
Assistant
Send_Rich_Text
Primary
File_As
Home_Address
Business_Address
Other_Address
Journal
Web_Page
Business_Address_Street
Business_Address_City
Business_Address_State

Figure 12-9:
Outlook Contacts come with dozens of precreated fields. You can use the standard address, phone, and email fields, but if you've gone to the trouble to add other details, you use those in merge too.

Tip: As an alternative to using the Insert Merge Fields command, you can use these same fields with the mail merge rules described at the end of this chapter (page 310) to choose recipients and customize the text in your merge.

7. Go to Mailings → Preview Results → Preview Results (or press Alt+M, P) to review your document.

Word translates your merge codes into text from your Outlook contacts. Use the arrow buttons to see results with different recipients.

8. **When you're ready to merge your document to email, select Mailings → Finish → Finish & Merge → Send E-Mail Messages.**

The small Merge to E-mail box pops up.

9. **In the To drop-down menu, make sure the "E-mail address" option is selected, and then, in the text box in the middle, type a subject line.**

Your recipients will see this subject when your message arrives in their inbox.

10. **Use the drop-down menu at the bottom to choose the format for your email: attachment, plain text, or HTML. Click OK to start the email merge.**

Figure 12-10 describes your alternatives.

Figure 12-10:
In the drop-down menu at the bottom of the Merge to E-mail box, you can choose the email formatting. If you send it as HTML, the formatted text and inserted photos appear in the body of the email message, like a Web page. If you send it as plain text, the email gets minimal formatting but has the advantage of being readable by virtually any email program. If you send your message as an attachment, the letter arrives as an attachment and opens in Word.

You're likely to see a couple of warnings after you click the OK button to send your email (Figure 12-11). The first message warns you that a program other than Outlook is trying to access your contacts' email addresses. The second message notifies you that a program other than Outlook is trying to send email. You must click Allow in both of these boxes to send your email merge on its way, traveling the Internet to reach the recipients.

Editing Your Recipient List

One of the keys to running a successful merge is getting your recipient list in shape for the merge. If anything fouls up a mail merge, it's usually because the recipient list is missing some details. Time spent massaging your list is time well spent, because you can then use the list for one successful mail merge after another.

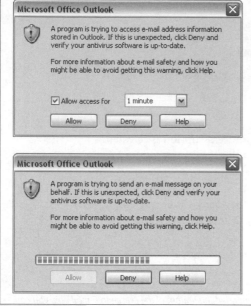

Figure 12-11:
Top: This warning lets you know that a program other than Outlook is trying to access email addresses. If see this message when you're running an email merge, you can safely click Allow. Use the drop-down menu to set a time limit so that other programs (read: viruses) can't send email after the merge is done. If you're not aware of a legitimate reason for a program to be looking up email addresses, click Deny.

Bottom: A second warning box appears if a program other than Outlook is trying to send an email message.

Editing Your Recipient Lists

If you use the same list frequently, sooner or later you'll want to add a new person to the list or update the address of someone who's moved. Editing a list saved from an earlier merge is simple:

1. **Choose Mailings → Start Mail Merge → Select Recipients → Use Existing List.**

   The Select Data Source box opens, showing the contents of your My Data Sources folder. (By the way, it's a good idea to store your recipient lists in this folder, where Word and other Office programs have easy access to them.)

2. **In the Select Data Source box, double-click your recipient list to open the file.**

   At first it may seem like nothing happened, but behind the scenes Word opened your recipient list in preparation for using it in a mail merge. Just look at the ribbon: In the Start Mail Merge group, the Edit Recipient List button, which was grayed out until this point, is available.

3. **Click Edit Recipient List, or press Alt+M, D.**

   The Mail Merge Recipients box opens (Figure 12-12). It may look like a box where you can edit your list, but it's not. It's for selecting recipients during a merge (by turning on the checkmarks next to the names).

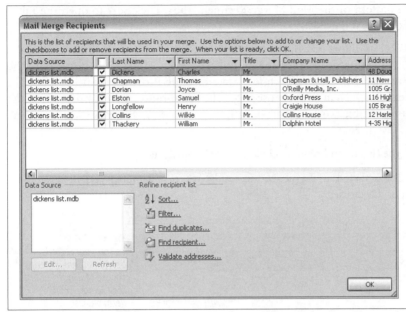

Figure 12-12:
In the Mail Merge Recipients box, you choose those lucky souls who get your letter. This box also leads to some other merge management tools. For example, you can select a Data Source and edit the entries. Before you do a merge, you can sort the list or filter it, to select specific recipients.

4. **In the lower-left corner, in the Data Source box, click to select the filename of your recipient list, and then click Edit.**

The Edit Data Source box should look familiar from Figure 12-2. It gives you all the tools that you used to create the list. You can edit the text in any of the fields. Use the New Entry button to add names to your list. To delete a name, click anywhere in the row, and then click Delete Entry at lower-left.

5. **When you're finished, click OK to close the Edit Data Source box, and then click OK to close the Mail Merge Recipients box.**

Sorting Your Recipient List

There are lots of reasons why you may want to sort your recipient list before you do a merge. If you're sending a letter as bulk mail, you need to sort letters by Zip code to get a discount from the post office. If you're printing up a directory of clients, you may want to sort the list by state and then by city. Whatever the reason, if you need your letters to be in a specific order at the *end* of the merge, you need to sort your recipient list at the *beginning*. Assuming that you've already started your merge and selected a recipient list, here's how to sort the list first by state, and then by city:

1. **Choose Mailings → Start Mail Merge → Edit Recipient List, or press Alt+M, D to open the Mail Merge Recipients box (Figure 12-12).**

At the top, the Mail Merge Recipients box lists all the individuals who are part of the merge. If you don't want to send a letter to someone, click to remove the checkmark. At the bottom of the box, several options appear under the heading "Refine recipient list."

2. **At the bottom of the Mail Merge Recipients box, click Sort to open the Filter and Sort box (Figure 12-13).**

   The Filter and Sort box opens showing the Sort tab. You see three rows in the box, each with a drop-down menu, followed by a couple radio buttons. In the first row, labeled "Sort by," choose State or State/Province from the menu. In the next row, "Then by," choose City. The radio buttons are used to order the sort as Ascending (A to Z or 1 to 100) or Descending. For this sort, Ascending works just fine.

3. **Close the two open boxes by clicking the OK buttons.**

   Your list is sorted, and you see the results when you merge your letters, envelopes, or directories.

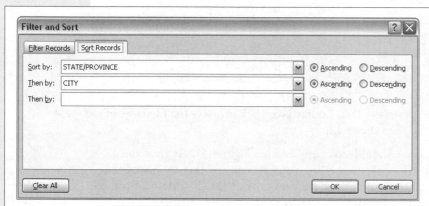

Figure 12-13:
To sort your records before you run a merge, choose Mailings → Start Mail Merge → Edit Recipient List, and then choose the Sort button at the bottom. In the "Sort by" box, choose a field to sort by, and then select whether you want the order to be ascending or descending.

Filtering Your Recipient List

Filtering is an indispensable tool if you work with large mailing lists. Imagine that you're the publicist for the author of an historical novel about the French Revolution. The author's doing a book tour in the western U.S. and wants you to send copies to book review editors. You've got a list of all the book review editors for the whole country, but you need to filter out just the editors in the western states.

No problemo. The steps are nearly identical to the previous ones for sorting a recipient list:

1. **Go to Mailings → Start Mail Merge → Edit Recipient List or press Alt+M, D.**

   At the bottom of the Mail Merge Recipients box you have several options that help you clean up and select recipients for your mail merge.

Note: You can use one of your own lists for this exercise, or, if you don't have a list, go to *www.missingmanuals.com*, and then click the "Missing CD" logo at the top of the page. You'll find the *editors.mdb* contact database listed on this book's page.

---

2. Under "Refine recipient list," click Filter to open the Filter and Sort box (Figure 12-14).

   The Filter Records tab presents drop-down menus in logical order. You use them to narrow down the selection of recipients used in the merge.

3. **In the Field drop-down menu, choose State. Then under Comparison, choose "Equal to." Finally, under "Compare to," type in** *CA* **for California.**

   Your merge will include any recipient with CA in the State field.

   You also want the book reviewers in Arizona. On the left, in the second row of the Filter Records tab, you see a new option: a drop-down menu with two choices—And and Or.

4. **Choose Or because you want book reviewers that are in California or Arizona.**

   "And" won't work because no one can be in two places at the same time. (However, if you were zeroing in on a particular city, you could specify recipients in California *and* Glendale.)

5. **After making your "And/Or" decision, select "State" as the Field, and "Equal to" as the Comparison, and then type** *AZ* **for Arizona in the "Compare to" box.**

   Repeat these steps for every state you want to add to the mailing.

6. **Close the Filter and Sort box by clicking the OK button.**

   Word does the filtering as soon as you click OK. Your Mail Merge Recipients box shows the list of book reviewers who are lucky enough to be on the list to receive that best seller.

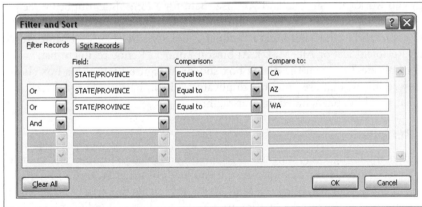

Figure 12-14:
The Filter Records tab shares a box with the Sort Records tab.

Choosing a Comparison option

The Comparison option is an important factor in filtering your recipient list. Word provides several options (that may bring back memories of a math class long ago), which you use to determine *how* Word decides which recipients to filter from your list relative to the selected field. Much of the time you'll use the first option, "Equal to," which is why it shows up automatically at the top of the list. Here's the complete list of Comparisons you can choose:

* **Equal to.** Finds a perfect match. For example, if you're working with states, "Equal to CA" finds California.

* **Not equal to.** Use "Not equal to" when you want to exclude part of your list. "Not equal to CA" removes California recipients from your list.

* **Less than.** Usually used for numbers, less than can also be used alphabetically where A is less than Z. If you're filtering by Zip code, "Less than 99987" includes 99986 and smaller Zip code numbers.

* **Greater than.** The opposite of "Less than," also for both letters and numbers. In an alphabetical list, "Greater than Smith" includes, for example, Smithy and all names that come after it alphabetically.

* **Less than or equal to.** This example is just like "Less than," except it includes the number used in the comparison. So, "Less than or equal to 99987" includes 99987 *and* all smaller Zip code numbers.

* **Greater than or equal to.** The cousin of "Less than or equal to." For example, to include all recipients who have a first name, use "Greater than or equal to A."

Find Duplicates

When you work with big lists and you use them for a long time, duplicate recipients seem to pop up. You can help to minimize the problem with the "Find duplicates" command in the Mail Merge Recipients box (Mailings → Start Mail Merge → Edit Recipient List or Alt+M, D). At bottom, under "Refine recipient list," click "Find duplicates" to open the dialog box shown in Figure 12-15. This box shows you any recipients that are potential duplicates. All you have to do is uncheck the ones that shouldn't be included in your mailing.

Find Recipient

If you're maintaining a very long list of recipients and need to jump in and change, say, a street address, a search tool can save you loads of time. To zero in on a specific recipient in your list, open the Mail Merge Recipients box (Alt+M, D). Then, at the bottom of the box under "Refine recipient list," choose "Find recipient." The Find Entry box opens (Figure 12-16). It's easy to use the box to search for a specific word or even just a group of letters or numbers. If the first record that pops up isn't the one you're looking for, click the Find Next button.

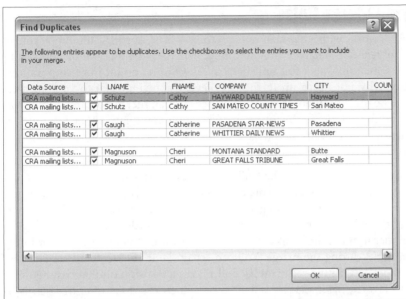

Figure 12-15:
*The Find Duplicates box hunts
down recipients that are
suspiciously similar. Turn off
the boxes next to duplicates
that you don't want to include
in the merge. Eliminating
duplicates is an important
part of maintaining large
mailing lists. It's also helpful
to use Find Duplicates when
you're combining a couple of
lists for a merge.*

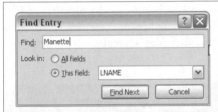

Figure 12-16:
*Open the Find Entry box to search for a specific recipient in your list. Type
the words for your search in the Find box. Click "All fields" to search
everywhere in your list, or use the drop-down menu to select a specific
field. This search looks for "Manette" only when it appears in the LNAME
field.*

UP TO SPEED

Creating Non-Mail Merges

If you think of mail merge as a multipurpose tool, you can really get creative. You can merge any list of words or things into any type of Word document. The shape and form of the document and what's in the list are entirely up to you. You can use mail merge for projects that have absolutely nothing to do with mail. Perhaps you're making presentations to several different companies; you can use mail merge to create customized marketing pieces. Imagine your massive sales force blanketing the nation with customized proposals in hand that say:

"We guarantee that **Apple** will quadruple its profits by using our EZ-Clipper for its next **iPod** promotion. Just give us a call and we'll give you a personal presentation in **Cupertino**."

"We know that **Microsoft** will quadruple its profits by using our EZ-Clipper for its next **Xbox** promotion. Just give us a call and we'll give you a personal presentation in **Redmond**."

Applying Merge Rules

When you work with the mail merge tools—lists, sorting, filtering—you've entered the realm of database programming. Whether you know it or not, you're doing the same things that full-time database developers do for huge corporations every day. Why not move up to the next level—applying *rules* to your merges. Rules are like mini-programs that help you set up mail merge documents that you or someone else will use in the future. So, when you don't have all the information you need when you set up the merge document, you can create a rule to help the person running the merge to correctly fill in the blanks.

For example, when you insert the "Fill in" rule into a document, it makes a message pop up during the merge. This box asks a question and provides a text box where you, or whoever's running the merge, can type the answer. Word then places the typed answer into the document. In other words, the "Fill in" field acts as a reminder to fill in the blanks at the time of printing. In other cases, Word may not need input during the merge. You can set up your rule so that Word simply looks at the details in the recipient list and makes a decision on that basis. So, if a recipient's favorite baseball team is the Yankees, then you don't offer free tickets to Fenway Park.

Rules are an advanced type of field that you insert into your document just like ordinary merge codes. When you run the merge, Word reads these fields, and then does something. The Rules drop-down menu provides several tools to help you create your own rules.

POWER USERS' CLINIC

Who'll Lick the Stamps?

So, you've got Word printing all those personalized letters and the envelopes. You still need to get some postage on the envelopes. Word can help there too—for a fee. Go to Mailings → Create → Envelopes to open the Envelopes and Labels box. In the lower-right corner, you see the E-postage Properties button. If you've never heard of E-postage, then it's probably not installed on your computer. In that case, you'll also see a message saying "You need to install electronic postage before you can use this feature," along with an invite to the Office Online Web site (*www.microsoft. com/office*).

Click Yes when you see the box with the invitation to visit Office Online. Your browser opens to a page with a Print Postage Overview. Links on the page take you to sites such as Stamps.com. The upshot of all this: For about $15 a month, you can print postage on envelopes and labels. For a small office, this arrangement may be less costly than getting postage meter. For a home office, though, it may be too pricey. It all depends on how frequently you need postage and how far away the post office is.

Note: The Rules shown in the Mailings tab are actually fields that are available to any document, not just mail merge documents. To use them, choose Insert → Text → Quick Parts → Field. You'll often encounter these fields in templates because they provide a way to make decisions and to insert text into documents when they're printed or distributed. For this same reason, they're great for mail merge projects.

Here's a brief rundown on how the Rules shown on the Mailing tab work with your documents:

- **Ask…** This field stops the merge and presents a dialog box asking for a response. Word places the response in a bookmark (page 218) that a field (specifically, a REF field) later in the document can reference. Therefore, the Ask field is the perfect tool when you want to use the response several times in the document. If you need to use the response only once, the Fill-in field, described next, is a better option.

- **Fill-in…** Stops the merge and presents a dialog box asking for text that's then inserted into the document. Figure 12-17 shows the dialog box you use to create a "Fill in" field.

Figure 12-17:
Use this text box to set up a "Fill in" field. Type a question into the Prompt text box, and then type the most common answer to the question in the "Default fill-in text" box. The checkbox at the bottom determines whether the pop-up box appears for every recipient in the mail merge or if it just appears once at the beginning.

- **If…Then…Else…** Makes a decision based on the contents of the recipient list. For example: **If** the recipient's state is California, **then** Word inserts the words "the Golden State" into the document, **else** (that is, if the recipients state is *not* California), it inserts "your state."

Tip: Don't be afraid to use whole paragraphs of text with your If…Then…Else statements. If you manage a technical support department, then you can create statements that make it easy to answer the most frequently asked questions and merge them into email messages using rules.

- **Merge Record #.** When you merge a document to the printer or to another document, Word gives each recipient a Merge Record number. If you insert the Merge Record # field in your document, it shows that number in the text. This field may not be useful for letters, but it can come in handy when you're creating a directory of people.

- **Merge Sequence #.** Similar to the merge record, with one significant difference. The Merge Record # takes into account all the recipients whether they're included or excluded from your merge. The Merge Sequence # is based only on those recipients that are shown in the merge.

- **Next Record.** Go to the next record (that is, the next row in the source list). If any other merge fields are in the document, Word fills them in using data from the next row in the recipient list. Use this option to create a directory or a page of address labels, where you want details from several recipients to appear on the same page.

- **Next Record If.** Similar to the Next Record rule above, except that it applies a condition. For example, the rule could be: Go to the next record *if* the City field equals Chicago.

- **Set Bookmark.** Sets a bookmark in the text that you can use as a reference. For example, the rule can place a bookmark named TaxRate with a value of .0775 in a document. Other fields or macros can then use this field to calculate the tax for a sale. (You can display the bookmark's contents in your document using a REF field.)

- **Skip Record If.** Excludes a record from the merge based on a condition.

Part Three:
Sharing Documents and Collaborating with Other People

3

Creating Web Pages and Blogs

You can save any document you created with Word as a Web page. Need to make a report available to everyone in your company and all your customers? Save it as a Web page, and then anyone with a Web browser, such as Internet Explorer or Firefox, can view it.

This chapter shows you how to save your Word documents as Web pages. You'll learn how to use tables to organize your pages and how to create hyperlinks so that Web visitors can jump from one place to another. Access a list of design and style tips to help you create Web pages that your visitors will love. And for good measure, if you're interested in life in the blogosphere, you'll find details on creating and posting blog entries with Word.

Note: You won't find many Web designers who place Word near the top of a list of their favorite Web design tools. There are a few reasons for this. First and foremost, Word wasn't created to design Web pages; its primary job is to produce printed pages. (See the box on page 317.) Most documents designed for the printed page need some tweaking to become respectable Web pages, so it's worthwhile to learn how to use the tools Word offers for creating Web pages, as this chapter explains.

Saving Word Documents As Web Pages

You create Web pages with Word in two steps. First you design the page including the text, headings, and pictures, and then, instead of saving the file as a standard Word file, you save the page as an HTML file. HTML stands for *hypertext markup language*, the code underlying Web sites. Web browsers, like Internet Explorer and Firefox, read HTML files, and then display the pages on your computer screen.

Most Web pages have both text and pictures. The HTML file contains the Web page's text, along with formatting instructions, and the photos, graphics, and sound and video clips are in separate files. Instructions in the HTML file link to the photos, in effect telling the browser, "Show that picture in this spot on the Web page," or "If someone clicks here, play this video." So, a single Web page is usually more than a single computer file; it's a combination of files that a browser assembles into a page to show on your screen.

Saving your document as a Web page isn't much different from saving it in any format. Start by opening the Save As box with Office → Save As or the keyboard shortcut (Alt+F, A). Word gives you three ways to save HTML files (Figure 13-1):

- **Single File Web Page (*.mht; *.mhtml).** This format saves all the files that make up a Web page in one package. Designed originally as a way to archive files, the MHTML format has limited acceptance among browsers. It works in Internet Explorer 5 and later, and Opera 9 and later, but in Firefox 2, you need the help of an add-in to display MHTML pages.

- **Web Page (*.htm; *.html).** Use this format if you're saving a file that you plan to edit with Word in the future. It creates a larger file because it includes codes that Word uses to work with your file.

- **Web Page, Filtered (*.htm; *.html).** Use this format when you're finished with editing and design, and you're ready to post your page on the Internet. This format strips the Word-specific code from the document, creating smaller files that show up more quickly in your visitors' browsers.

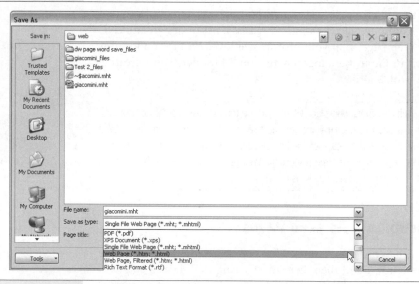

Figure 13-1:
To save a Word document as a Web page, use Office → Save As, and then choose one of the HTML-type options: Single File Web Page, Web Page, or Web Page, Filtered. Any Word document can be saved as a Web page, but to create attractive, readable Web pages, you need to do more than hit the Save command.

It's always a little surprising when Microsoft reduces the number of features in a program, but that's what's happened with Web-related functions in Word. Word 2003 and previous versions had a Web Tools toolbar, where you'd find widgets—such as text boxes, drop-down menus, and buttons—that you could pop into your Web pages (Figure 13-2). The toolbar is gone in Word 2007 and there's no special ribbon to replace it. In addition, some of the Web viewing and the online Web collaboration tools have been removed. Other options are buried deep within the Word Options settings. The overall message is that Web page creation is a less important feature for Word 2007 than it was for previous versions.

Figure 13-2:
Microsoft giveth and Microsoft taketh away. Several Web-related features were removed from Word 2007, including the Web toolbar that was included in previous versions of Word.

UP TO SPEED

Word Puts Extra Junk in Web Pages

One of the perennial complaints about Microsoft Word and Front Page is that they place lots of unneeded junk into Web page files (HTML). Microsoft doesn't consider all the code and commands it puts into HTML "junk," but the fact is that plenty of other programs create smaller, neater HTML files than Microsoft's do.

Consider a typical starting point for a Web page. You start a document and center a table in the middle of the page. The table serves as a container to hold text and images that you'll add later. Adobe's popular Dreamweaver Web-design program creates a trim, 812-byte HTML file.

Word's equivalent is 3,986 bytes, nearly five times the size. File size is less of an issue for folks who have high-speed cable modems, but leaner Web pages are still better, since some people still have slow, phone-line Internet connections, and others use cell phones, Blackberries, and similar small-screen devices to surf the Web.

Acknowledging this complaint, recent versions of Word provide a special Save As option that strips Word-specific codes out of the file. Microsoft recommends using the "Web Page, Filtered" option when you're finished editing your page in Word (page 316).

Creating a Web Page from Scratch

As shown above, you can save any Word document as a Web page, but everyone knows some serious differences exist between printed documents and Web pages. Most of the time, if you simply save a paper document as a Web page, the results are less than stellar. The best Web pages and Web sites are designed from the ground up to be viewed in a Web browser. For example, most Web pages are part of a Web site where the pages all have a similar look and feel. They're designed to help the visitors find the information they need quickly. People don't usually read Web pages from front to back like a novel. They jump from place to place, quickly snatching up the information they need.

You can use Word to create Web pages with a professional look and feel; it just takes some extra planning and a few easy-to-learn Web designer tricks (Figure 13-3). In the next few sections, you'll create a Web page starting from a blank document, lay it out with the help of Word's table feature, and create the links that connect it to other Web pages on the same Web site. Plus, you'll learn how to save your Web page file as a template to make it easier to create all those other pages.

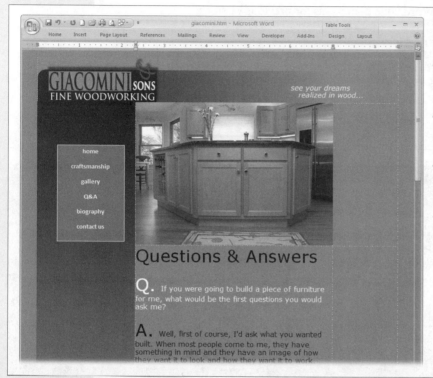

Figure 13-3:
It's certainly possible to create attractive Web pages, like this one, with the tools provided by Word 2007. That doesn't mean it's likely to be a professional Web designer's favorite tool for the job. Traditional Web design tools such as Adobe Dreamweaver and Microsoft's FrontPage are better choices if you plan to spend a lot of time creating Web pages.

Serious Web Design Tools

If you're planning to work on a lot of Web pages, you should get a program that's specifically designed to create Web pages, move pages to a Web site, and organize all the files. Adobe's Dreamweaver is one of the most popular programs used by the pros, but it costs about $400.

Microsoft's FrontPage comes with some of the Office suites and, under $200, it costs less than Dreamweaver as a standalone product. Homesite is a popular program that you can download from Web sites, such as *www.download.com*. It's free to test drive and costs $100 if you want to continue using it. MoreMotion Web Express is another program that you can download. It's free to use.

Creating the Web Page Document

Imagine you're creating a new Web site all about the novel *A Tale of Two Cities*. You want to provide information on the book, the author, and the historical events detailed in the book. Most Web sites have several pages, each containing a different kind of information—to make it easier for visitors to find what they're looking for, and to keep each page from getting too long. There's always a home page that welcomes visitors and provides links to all those other pages. You start by creating a Word document for the home page.

1. **Open a new Word document, and switch to Web Layout view: Go to View →
   Document Views → Web Layout or press Alt+W, L**

   As you design your page, you probably want to see it as it will look in a Web browser. For example, you no longer see the edges of a page because your document isn't headed for a sheet of paper. When you start with a new document, the margins are at the extreme edges of your screen.

Tip: Another quick way to switch views is the view buttons in Word's lower-right corner. Click the middle button (with the globe icon) to change to Web Layout view.

---

2. **Use the keyboard shortcut Alt+F, A to open the Save As box. Name your document *index.htm*.**

   The file name index.htm is the conventional name for a Web site's home page, which is exactly what you're about to create.

Tip: You may want to create a new folder to hold all your Web pages and folders for a Web site. You can do that by clicking the button near the top-right corner of the box (the folder with a starburst on it). After you name the new folder, double-click it to save your new *index.htm* document in it.

---

3. **At the bottom in the box labeled "Save as type," choose Web Page. Click Save
   when you're done.**

   As explained on page 316, you can use three different HTML file formats to save your document. Web Page is the format to use when you're going to continue working on a page.

Create a Table for Your Page's Layout

Web designers use tables to organize text and pictures on the page. By placing text in a table cell, you can control the line length. You also use cells to hold pictures and to keep the pictures next to relevant text.

1. **Go to Insert → Table or Alt+N, T. Create a table with three rows and three
   columns.**

   See page 235 if you need a refresher on creating tables in Word.

2. **When you hold your mouse over your table, you see a button on the upper-left side. Click the button to select your entire table. Choose Table Tools → Design → Table Styles → Borders → No Border.**

   If the borderlines around each table cell appeared on your Web page, it would look very cluttered. But if you hide the borderlines in the table, visitors won't even know they're there.

   On the other hand, while you're designing the Web page, it's nice to have some guidelines that show you the cells.

3. **Go to Table Tools → Design → Table Styles → Borders, choose View Gridlines.**

   Word places dotted lines on the screen when you're viewing the pages in Word. Visitors to your Web site don't see the gridlines when they're viewing your page in their Web browser.

4. **Add some color to your table using Table Tools → Design → Table Styles.**

   When you select the table, you see the Table Tools contextual tab appear on the right side of the ribbon (Figure 13-4). Beneath are two tabs that you use to change the look of your table. When you click the Design tab, you see several colorful table styles in the middle of the ribbon.

5. **On the left side, under Table Style Options, turn on Header Row and First Column, and leave the other boxes turned off.**

   Word highlights the top row, which you'll use for a heading, and highlights the left column where you'll place navigation buttons for your page.

6. **Choose a table style that you think will work for your page.**

   Scroll through the table styles, or click the button at lower-right to open the menu so you can see several styles at once. As you hold your mouse cursor over a style, you see your table take on the colors of the style.

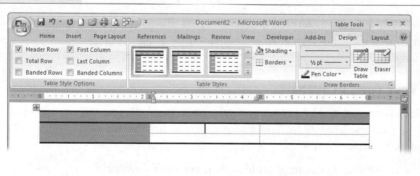

Figure 13-4:
Use Word's table styles to automatically format your table with background colors. In this example, the top row and the left column are highlighted. The top row will hold the heading for the page, and the left column will hold navigation buttons that link to other pages.

7. **Go to Page Layout → Themes → Themes to choose a color and font theme for your document. The keyboard shortcut Alt+P, TH opens the Themes drop-down menu.**

   You have lots of choices on the Themes palette. You can go with Microsoft's corporate blue. The Paper theme has a nice muted khaki look. Some of the others are bright and lively. Choose a color that matches the content of your Web page and that you think will please your visitors.

   When you choose one of Word's themes for your document, you define a consistent set of colors and fonts that are used. These colors appear at the tops of all the palettes, and they're used in graphics and headings.

Tip: You can select any colors you want, but if you're design-challenged, you know you'll be safe using the theme colors.

---

8. **Choose a background color for your Web page with Page Layout → Page Background → Page Color.**

   Time to put that theme to action by choosing one of the theme colors as a background color for your page. You'll be placing relatively small-sized text on this page, so choose a color that won't fight with the letters on the page. If you're using a light page color, plan on using black text. If you're using a dark page color, plan on using white text.

9. **Select the table by clicking the button at the table's upper-left, and then press Alt+H, AC to center it on your page.**

   The content for Web pages is usually aligned on the left side or in the center of the page. By aligning your table in the center, you can minimize the appearance of empty space by having an equal amount of space on either side of your text.

10. **Drag across the three cells in the top row. With all three cells selected, choose Table Tools → Layout → Merge → Merge Cells to make one big cell that goes across the top row.**

    This merged cell will hold a heading that identifies all the pages in your Web site. Most Web sites use the same header on every page. That way you always know when you're on the CNN Web site. It reinforces the brand and visitors know who's responsible for the information they're viewing.

11. **Type your heading—*A Tale of Two Cities*, for example.**

    At first, the text will be too small for a proper heading, so use the Font Size command (Alt+H, FS) to bump it up to a generous 36 points. Center the heading with the command Alt+JL, TC. If necessary, you can change the color too. Choose Home → Font → Font Color. Pick a color that contrasts well with the background color of the cells.

Add a Navigation Bar

It's helpful to your visitors to provide navigation tools on every page of your site. Most Web sites place consistent navigation bars either on the left side or on the top of the page. In this design, you'll create a navigation bar on the left (Figure 13-5).

1. **Drag to select the two bottom cells in the first column, and then press Alt+JL, M to merge the cells. While the cell is still selected, choose Home → Paragraph → Center.**

   Type some words that will lure visitors to explore the other pages: *Home, The Story, Main Characters, French Revolution, Dickens Bio, FAQs, Contact Us*. Use the Line Spacing button (Alt+H, K) to put some space between your navigation words. About 2.5 or 3.0 lines should look good.

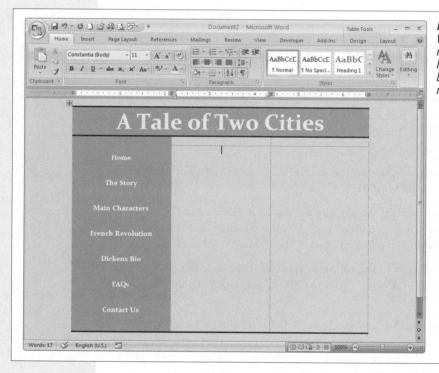

Figure 13-5:
With a heading and a navigation bar along the left side, your page begins to look like a respectable Web site.

2. **Select the second item in your navigation bar (*The Story*), and then use Insert → Links → Hyperlink or Alt+N, I to open the Insert Hyperlink box (Figure 13-6).**

   The story page doesn't exist yet, so you'll create it now.

3. On the left side of the box, choose Create New Document. In the "Name of new document" box, type *story.htm*. At the bottom of the box, select "Edit the new document later," and then click OK.

(You're not going to work on the story page yet.) When you close the Create New Document box, Word creates a new, empty HTML file named *story.htm* and, back in your document, creates a link from the words "The Story" to the new file. Notice that the words The Story are underlined and in a different color to show that they're not just text—they're a link to another location.

Tip: If you don't like your link's new look, you can change it using the standard formatting tools found at Home → Font.

---

4. **Repeat the previous step to create links for the rest of the items in your navigation bar.**

The Home item will link to the page you have open. So, in the Edit Hyperlink box, choose the first option in the panel on the left—Existing File or Web Page—instead of Create New Document. Then, in the Address box at the bottom, type *index.htm*.

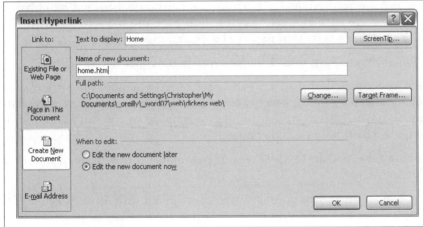

Figure 13-6:
The Insert Hyperlink box gives you several ways to link to documents on the Web or on your computer. You can even create links that connect to a different a part of the same Web page.

Create a Copyright Line

Web designers often put some standard information at the bottom of every Web page such as a date and copyright notice, contact information, and sometimes the name of the company that designed the Web site.

The area below the heading and to the right of the navigation bar is divided into four cells. You'll adjust the two bottom cells to hold a copyright line for your Web page. After all, you want to protect all your hard work from intellectual property theft.

1. **Above the two cells at your table's lower-right, drag the horizontal gridline toward the bottom of the table. Select the two cells, and then press Alt+JL, M to merge them.**

   You should have just enough room for one or two lines of text.

2. **Type your copyright notice © *Copyright 2007, Charles Dickens*. Press Enter to add a new line, and then type *Web Design: Pickwick Productions*.**

   AutoText (page 58) can help you create a copyright symbol by typing *(c)*. When you hit the space bar, the three characters turn into the copyright symbol. (If you don't like the change, press Ctrl+Z to undo it.)

   You want people to be able to find this information when they need it, but you don't want it to detract from the message of your Web pages.

3. **Select the text, and then reduce the font size to 8 or 9 points (Alt+H, FS).**

   It looks best if you center the notice, so while it's still selected, use the shortcut Alt+H, AC to center the text in the cell.

Save Your Page as a Template

The work done so far makes a great template for your other Web pages. You've got a page that's empty except for a heading, a navigation bar, and a copyright notice—these are all things you want on each page of your site (Figure 13-7). Now's a good time to save your page as a template for your other pages.

1. **Choose Office → Save, or click the Save icon in the Quick Access toolbar**

   Web designers follow the "save early, save often" philosophy. That way, you don't lose all the hard work you've done so far if there's a mishap or power failure. Next, you'll save your document as a template so you can use this table design as a basic layout for other pages.

2. **Choose Save As (Alt+F, A). Save your page under a new name, like *dickens template.htm*.**

   You don't want to mess up your template, so close it with Alt+F, C before you press another key.

To use the template in the future, open the template *dickens template.htm*, and then immediately choose Office → Save As to save the file under a new name. After you Save As, Word opens your new document, and the template file remains closed and unchanged where you can use it again.

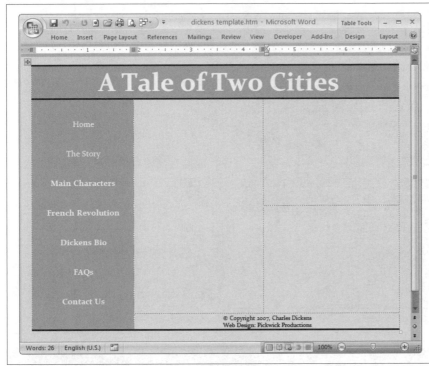

Figure 13-7:
Good Web sites have a consistent design from page to page, and you have an incredibly easy way to do it. Simply create a template that includes items common to all the pages like a heading, navigation bar, and basic contact or copyright details.

Add Text and Images to Your Web Page

To get back to work on your Web page, reopen *your home page* by choosing Office button → Recent Documents → *index.htm*. From here on, your work is exactly like creating any other Word document. Type directly into the cells to add words. You can use any of the formatting commands that are available to text and tables. If you need to adjust the size of the cells, just drag the gridlines. (Chapter 8 has the full story on working with tables.)

Pictures and graphics are an important part of any Web site. If you have the choice between delivering your message with a picture or with words, choose the picture. You can insert a photo from your computer by clicking Insert → Illustrations → Picture. Or you can look for clip art on your computer and on the Web (page 268).

Note: It's always important to respect copyrights. You can't copy photos, artwork, or text from other Web pages and publish them on yours unless you have permission from the copyright holder.

The last step for this page is to save and close it. Choose Office → Close and answer yes when Word asks if you want to save the file. At this point you have a finished page that looks something like Figure 13-8.

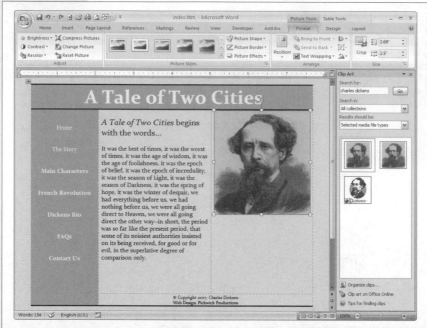

Figure 13-8:
Here's the end result of all the page design steps in the previous sections. Word's Clip Art panel is open on the right with a couple Dickens images.

Posting Your Pages on the Web

Once you've created Web pages, the next step is to move those pages from your computer to a site on the Internet where the whole world can admire your work. Getting Web sites online is beyond the scope of Word (and of this book). Here are some good books to get you started: *Creating Web Sites: The Missing Manual, Dreamweaver 8: The Missing Manual,* and *FrontPage 2003: The Missing Manual.*

It's not too hard to find free Web space where you can create a small Web site. Check with the company that gives you access to the Internet. Often, in addition to giving you an email address, they provide space for a Web site.

Web Page Design Tips

Having a quill pen can't make you write like Charles Dickens, and the same is true for designing Web pages. Having the tools to make a Web page and having the skills to create an attractive page that keeps visitors coming back are two different things. Here are some design tips to help you become a master Web designer:

• **Use tables to organize your Web page.** Tables are the all-purpose tool used by most Web designers to organize text, graphics, and other elements of a Web page. Place your text inside tables to control the line length and keep important graphics aligned with the text.

- **Avoid lines of text with more than 50 characters.** If you don't rein it in, Word tends to give you extremely long lines of text. Long lines are difficult for readers to follow. Most readers don't even tackle text that looks hard to read. Even if they do, they'll stop reading if it's too difficult

- **Avoid common body text faux pas.** Text is harder to read on a computer screen than it is on the printed page, so it's important to make it as easy as possible for your Web site visitors. If you use 10-point type for body text on the printed page, you won't go wrong using 11- or 12-point type for your Web pages.

- **Avoid clutter.** A common mistake made by amateur Web designers is to cram too much into a page. One of the great pleasures of Web design is that real estate doesn't cost a thing. It's better to add a new page than to force too much into a single page. By keeping clutter to a minimum, you can be certain that visitors to your page focus on the graphics and headings you think are most important.

- **Use common fonts such as Arial, Helvetica, Verdana, Times and Times Roman.** You don't have any control over the fonts on your visitors' computers. If they don't have the fonts that you used to design your page, then it's going to look very different on their screen. You can be pretty sure that they have a few basic fonts including the ones listed above.

- **Use Word's Themes to choose complementary colors.** One great tool that Word 2007 adds to the Web design mix is Themes. When you choose a theme for your document, you can be certain that you've got a good collection of complementary and contrasting colors for designing your Web page. Use these colors for backgrounds, body text, headings, and graphics.

- **Use headings, pull quotes, and short blocks of text to engage your visitors.** Web pages aren't novels. Edit your text to reduce the amount of text on your pages, and use headings, pull quotes, and other devices to draw readers into the body text.

- **Use a consistent navigation tool on each page.** If you're designing a series of Web pages, you'll do your visitors a great favor if you have a single, consistent tool for moving from one page to another. Place it at the top or on the left side where experienced Web surfers expect to find a navigation bar.

- **Use pictures and graphics to deliver your message.** People don't read Web pages the same way they read a book. They decide quickly whether your page is worthy of their valuable time. They'll absorb the message in a photo, a drawing, or some other graphic much more quickly than they'll read text. Hook them with your graphics, and then entice them with headings or strategic pull-quotes from your text.

- **Remember, hyperlinks don't *have* to be blue and underlined.** The geeky standard for hyperlinks is blue, underlined text. For most well-designed Web pages, this look is too jarring. Create a consistent design for your hyperlinks. You can use any of the font formatting on the ribbon (Home → Font). Once you have a style you like, you can save it as a style, and then apply it to all your hyperlinks. To create a new style, select your formatted text, and then go to Home → Styles → Save as New Quick Style.

Blogging from Word

Blogs are taking the media world by storm. *Blog* is a contraction of "Weblog," which is simply a journal or diary in Web page form. Blog has become a verb as well as a noun: "I've got to get home and blog this." People even refer to the *blogosphere*—the blogging community where information is rapidly shared, issues are vented, and opinions run wild.

Blogs are usually focused on a specific topic or a particular interest, but it's an open forum and can accommodate anyone's ramblings. A blog from a courtroom reporter may include reports on a trial with updates every half hour. A blog from a programmer on the Word 2007 development team may discuss new features that are being added to the program, and it may be updated every few weeks. When you visit a blog, usually you see notes, comments, and meanderings posted in reverse order, with the most recent entries at the top (Figure 13-9). Often, visitors to the blog have an opportunity to post their own comments and questions. Most blogs are primarily text, but you'll also find blogs that include photos and sound and video clips.

In Word 2007, you find some easy-to-use tools that help you write blog entries and post them on a site like Google's Blogger or Microsoft's Live Spaces.

Managing Blog Accounts

To become a blogger, you need to have a blog account somewhere on the Web. Don't pull out your wallet yet; you'll be pleased to know that you can get blog space for free. If you're new to blogging, try *www.blogger.com* or *http://spaces.live. com*, or search for other free blog providers. To create your account, you need to provide a user name and a password. The service asks for this name and password whenever you send a new post to your blog, which keeps strangers from hijacking your blog space.

Once you have an established account, you need to give Word your user name and password. Then when you want to publish a blog post, Word automatically contacts the blog site, provides your login details, and sends out your words of wisdom.

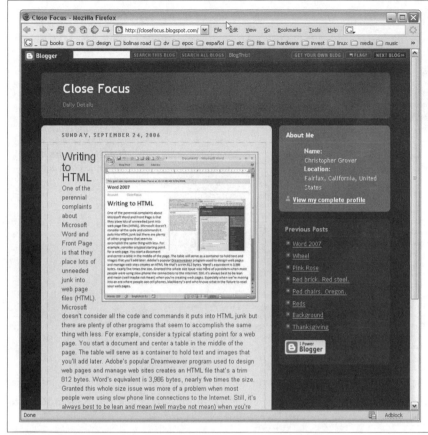

Figure 13-9:
You'll find blogs posted all over the Internet. Journalists often publish blogs on the Web sites maintained by their broadcast networks or publications. For the general public, sites are available such as Google's Blogger or Microsoft's Live Spaces.

Follow these steps to give Word details about your blog account.

1. **Go to Office button → New → New Blog Post.**

   A new window opens, and you see the Word's stripped down blogging environment with simplified formatting options (Figure 13-10). On the ribbon, the Blog Post tab takes the place of the Home tab. It provides the usual text tools like cut and paste. Over on the left, in the Blog group, the tab gives you tools for publishing blog posts and managing your blog accounts.

2. **Choose Blog Post → Blog → Manage Accounts to open the Blog Accounts box.**

   The Blog accounts box is where you work with one or more of your blog accounts. You can add and remove accounts from different blog services. You can change details, like your password.

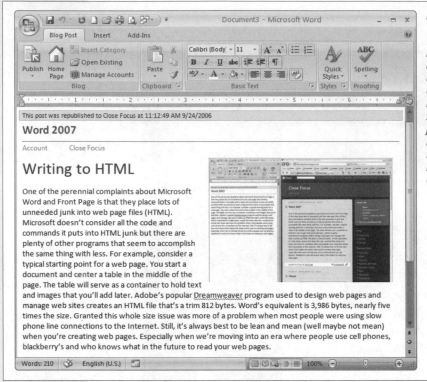

Figure 13-10:
To start blogging with Word, choose Office → New → New Blog Post, and you see the trimmed down blogging environment. Because blogs are relatively simple text-based journals, the tools are limited to some basic formatting options and buttons to post your entries.

3. **In the upper-left corner of the Blog Accounts box, click the New button to open the New Blog Account box (Figure 13-11).**

    Click the drop-down menu to choose your blog service. If your service isn't listed, then click the Other option. After you select your service, click the Next button to go to the next step.

Figure 13-11:
Blog accounts are usually pretty simple. Word is set up to communicate with some of the most popular blog services. Even if your service isn't listed, click the Other option. You'll need to provide the Web address for the service along with some other details, but it's not very complicated.

4. **In the text boxes, type in your user name and your password (Figure 13-12).**

   Fill in the details. If you're using a desktop computer and trust the other folks that have access to the computer, check the Remember Password box, and then you won't have to provide a password each time you post to your blog.

   Click OK to go to the next step.

Figure 13-12:
Word walks you through the steps to register a new account. The most important step is where you provide the user name and password you gave the blog provider when you set up your account.

5. **Click the Picture Options button to open the Picture Options box and then choose an option from the drop down list.**

   If you aren't going to post pictures on your blog, leave the option set to "None - Don't upload pictures." Otherwise Word needs to know where to send photos so they can show in your blog. If you're using a SharePoint site for your blog, leave the Picture Options set to "SharePoint blog." Word will send image files to the SharePoint site and create links to show pictures in your blog. For other blog sites use "My blog provider" if it's listed as an option.

   If none of these options are available, it gets a little more complicated. If you have already have a website that let's you post pictures, choose "My own server." Two new text boxes appear in the Picture Options box. In the Upload URL box type the Internet address you use to upload your pictures. In the Source URL box type the location where you view your pictures. If none of the above options work for you, you may be able to manual post photos to your blog using your web browser and tools provided by your blog. Once you've made a select, click OK to close the Picture Options box.

Note: The photo handling abilities of Word's Blogging tool are still a gem in the rough. Expect them to shine a bit more in the future as Microsoft makes improvements and some of the more popular blogging sites provide support for Word 2007.

---

6. **In the Choose a Blog box, select the blog you want to use.**

   After you've provided information on your blog account, Word displays the Choose a Blog box that shows the titles of your blogs. Choose the one that you want to work on from the drop-down menu, and then click OK.

7. **Check to make sure your registration was successful.**

When you register a new account with Word, you're simply providing the user name, password, and other details that Word needs to communicate with your blog service. At the end of the process, Word checks whether the service accepts your user name and password. If all goes as planned, you see a box that says "Account registration successful." Click OK, and you're all ready to post to your blog.

Posting to Your Blog

Compared to setting up an account with a blog provider and then registering that account with Word, posting to your blog is an absolute breeze. It's really just a matter of typing in the document, and then clicking Blog Post → Blog → Publish (Alt+H, P). The Publish button is actually two buttons in one. Click the bottom half, and you see a drop-down menu with the two options shown in Figure 13-13. Click Publish to immediately post your blog entry where the whole wide world can see it. When you click Publish as Draft, Word uploads your post to a private area on your blog site. It'll be there later for you to edit and post when it's ready for prime time.

Figure 13-13:
Click the Publish button to post your document as a blog entry. Click the Home Page button to open your blog in your Web browser. Use the Open Existing button to see previous blog entries and to open them for editing.

Setting Web Options

One of the frustrating facts of life on the Internet is that everyone shows up with different tools, including computers, screens, and browsers. Even if some of your visitors have exactly the same computer and browser as you, chances are they've set it up differently. The bottom line is, you never really know how your page will look on someone else's computer. Still, you need to make some educated guesses about the tools your visitors will use. Ask yourself: What kind of browser are they likely to use—a new browser or an old one? What size screen do they have? Once you make your best guesses, you can change Word's settings so that the Web pages Word writes match your visitor's Web browsing tools.

You can find the settings in the Word Options box (Office button → Word Options). After you open the Word Options box, click the Advanced button, and then scroll down to the bottom. Click the Web Options button to open the Web Options box (Figure 13-14).

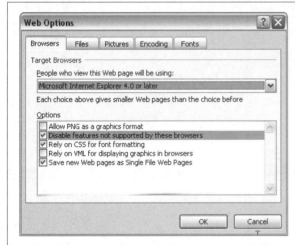

Figure 13-14:
Use the settings in the Web Options box to fine-tune the way Word creates Web pages. You set the options to match the Web browsing tools you expect your visitors to have.

The first three tabs are the most critical for setting up your Web pages to work with your visitors' browsers and computer setups.

• **Browsers.** Use the "People who view this Web page will be using" drop-down menu to choose the type of browser you think your visitors use. If you expect most of your visitors to be using Microsoft's Internet Explorer (which comes free on Windows PCs), you can select the Explorer-only options; otherwise, choose one of the Explorer and Navigator options. If you expect everyone to be using a fairly current browser, choose one of the 6.0 or more recent browser versions. When you make your choices with the drop-down menu, Word sets the checkboxes below to the correct options.

- **Files.** Under the Files tab, you can fine-tune the way Word stores files for your Web pages. Most Web pages consist of an HTML file and graphics files (.jpg, .gif, or .png). They can also include other files that relate to formatting and other technical details. If you turn on the "Organize supporting files in a folder" checkbox, Word creates a folder and stores the support files inside. If your page is named *dickens.htm*, then the folder is named *dickens_files*.

- **Pictures.** Web sites look dramatically different on different computer monitors. Using settings on the Pictures tab, you can choose the options for a "Target monitor." In effect, you're making a guess about the type of monitor your visitors will use. If you think most of your visitors have fairly new desktop and laptop computers, you're probably safe using 800x600 are your target monitor. Things will look okay on a bigger monitor, and folks with smaller monitors may need to scroll around to see everything on the page. If most of your visitors use Windows PCs, as in many corporations, set the "Pixels per inch" number to 96. If you think most of them will use Macs to view your Web site (in a school setting, for example), change this number to 72.

Creating Forms with Word

Apply for a job, driver's license, or bank account, and you have to fill out a form. Forms collect information, and every day it seems there's more information to collect. If you need to create a form to collect information, Word can help. With Word, you can create forms to print and hand to someone on paper, as well as computer-based forms that you can distribute by email or display as a Web page.

This chapter shows you how to create both paper- and computer-based forms, which you can do using the tools you've already learned in this book. (If you're not familiar with tables, you may want to review Chapter 10 first, since tables are a big help when making forms.) The second part of this chapter shows you how to make computer-based forms using *content controls*—objects you insert into Word documents to make it easier to collect information. Content controls let your audience fill in the blanks, while protecting the permanent text from changes or deletions.

Creating a Paper Form

Most forms have the same basic elements—permanent text and blanks. Permanent text includes things like the heading at the top of the page, labels, and perhaps tips on how to fill out the form. The blanks collect information from the people filling out the form. Take the IRS 1040 Income Tax form, for example. On second thought, scratch that—too depressing. Suppose you're a magazine distributor creating a subscription form, and as incentive you're running a sweepstakes so new subscribers get a chance to win a Porsche (Figure 14-1). This form has the two basic elements: permanent text and blanks to hold the subscription information. You also want your form to have some checkboxes for folks to choose which magazines they want. The entire form can fit on the back of a postcard, which is great since it's easy for people to fill out the form and mail it in.

Using a Table to Design Your Form

When you design a form, your primary concern is making it easy to use. If it's difficult or hard to fill out, chances are you'll get incomplete and incorrect information. Spend most of your time organizing and arranging the elements on your form. Tables are a great tool for the job. Using tables, you can keep the labels and the blanks next each other. You can organize text, pictures, and other elements with precision. As icing on the cake, you can format the cells in the table to provide visual clues. For example, you may have cells with a white background color for labels, and cells with a blue background color for blanks that need to be filled in.

In the following steps, you create a postcard-sized form that collects information for magazine subscriptions and entries in the Porsche sweepstakes (Figure 14-1). To lay out this paper-based form, you use a Word table.

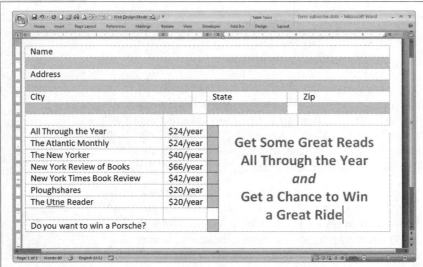

Figure 14-1:
Tables are great tools for organizing the information in a form. Use separate cells for labels and the blanks that need to be filled in. It's helpful to give cells that need to be filled in a different background color from the permanent text.

1. **Starting with a blank document, change the page size to Post Card using the command Page Layout → Page Setup → Size → Post Card. Open the Orientation menu (Alt+P,O), and then choose Landscape.**

   Post Card is one of the standard sizes provided in Word. The dimensions are 5.83" wide by 3.94" high. It's a good size for a postage-paid return card. Like most postcards, you lay this one out in Landscape (horizontal) orientation.

2. **Open the Margins tab in the Page Setup box with Page Layout → Page Setup → Margins → Custom Margins. Enter .25 inches for all the margins: top, bottom, left, and right.**

   Word's standard 1" margins eat up too much space on a tiny postcard.

3. Save the document with the name *form_subscription.docx.*

   Of course, you can name the document anything you want. Using the word *form* at the beginning of the name can help you identify it later.

4. **On the ribbon choose Insert → Tables → Table → Insert Table to open the Insert Table box. In the "Number of columns" box, enter *4*, and in the "Number of rows" box, enter *16*. Click OK.**

   The table appears in your document. The four columns are all the same width. You can adjust them later to fit the information you're collecting in the form. Tables are a great way to separate permanent text from the blanks that you want filled in. You separate the text from the blanks by placing them in different cells and formatting those cells with different background colors.

5. **Select the table. Remove the cell borders (Alt+JT, BN), and then turn on Gridlines (Alt+JL, TG).**

   In this step, you're applying basic formatting to the entire table. To select the table, move your mouse cursor over it. A button appears near the upper-left corner of the table. Click the button to select the entire table.

   Borderlines make the printed form look too busy, so you remove them with the shortcut Alt+JT, BN. On the other hand, it's helpful to have non-printing gridlines as you design your form, so you turn on the gridlines.

Tip: You can toggle gridlines on and off as needed. Just use the View Gridlines button on the left side of the Table Tools | Layout tab (Alt+JT, TG).

---

6. **Drag to select the four cells in the first row, and then merge cells to create a single cell with Table Tools → Layout → Merge → Merge Cells or Alt+JL, M. Type *Name* in the first row.**

   This step lays out the Name field for your form. The first row holds the label "Name," and the second row is a blank where people will write their name.

7. **In the same way, select and merge the cells in the second row, and then format the single cell with a light shade of blue (Alt+JT, H).**

   The results should look something like Figure 14-2.

   Repeat steps 6 and 7 in the third and fourth row to create a field for the street address. After you merge the cells, type *Address* in the third row. Use the same color to shade the fourth row where subscribers will write in their street address or P.O. box.

8. **Click within the cell in the third column on the fifth row, and then press Alt+JL, P to open the Split Cells box. In the "Number of columns" box type *2*, and then click OK.**

   You've split this cell into two cells to make room for more pieces of information.

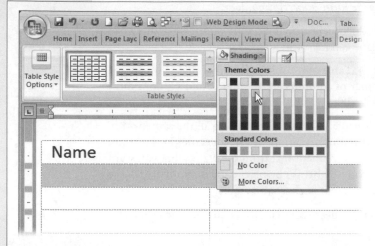

Figure 14-2:
Each field in this magazine subscription form has a label that describes the contents of the field and a blank shaded area where a subscriber provides details like name, address, and choice of magazine.

9. **On the fifth row, type** *City, State,* **and** *Zip code* **in the first, third, and fifth cells.**

   The empty cells between each of these fields keep them from running together and make it easier for subscribers to enter their information.

10. **Create matching blank cells below City, State, and Zip code, where subscribers will enter their details.**

    Split the third column as you did in the step above (Alt+JL, P). Shade the first, third, and fifth cell under the labels. Adjust the column widths to provide the right amount of space for each of the fields City, State, and Zip code (Figure 14-3).

11. **In rows 8 through 14, create seven fields with the names of magazines for subscribers to choose from.**

    In the first column, type the magazine names. Then, in the second column, type a subscription rate. The third column serves as a checkbox, so shade it with your fill-in-the-blank blue (Alt+JT, H). Put a border around each of the checkboxes (Alt+JT, BA) so subscribers can clearly understand how to use them.

12. **In the left margin, drag to select the rows with magazine names, subscription rates, and checkboxes, and then adjust the column widths (Figure 14-4).**

    For example, drag the vertical gridlines so that the magazine titles fit on one line. You can also reduce the column width so that the checkboxes actually look like boxes instead of rectangles.

13. **In the bottom row, type** *Do you want to win a Porsche,* **and then create a checkbox exactly as described in step 11.**

    In other words, adjust and format one of the cells in the bottom row to match the checkboxes in the rows with magazine names.

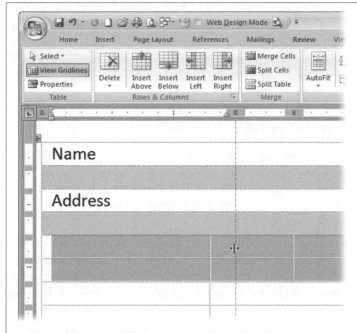

Figure 14-3:
To make adjustments to the width of the cells, select both rows. Move the mouse cursor to the left margin, and then drag to select the two rows. Drag the vertical gridlines to adjust the column width. The columns for both rows move independently of the rows on the form.

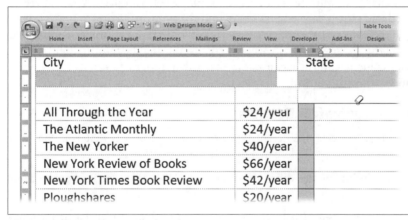

Figure 14-4:
In addition to boxes where subscribers enter their information, this form has checkboxes where they select magazines. If necessary, use the Eraser (Alt+JT, E) and the Draw Table (Alt+JI, D) tools to clean up the borders around the checkboxes.

14. Select and then merge the cells (ALT+JL, M) in the lower-right corner of the form, and then create a big, bold message to entice subscribers.

Type a message that you think will encourage people to subscribe. Big and bold is always good for a sales pitch, so bump up the font size (Alt+H, FS) to make your message fill the space (between 14 and 18 points should do the trick). For bold type, click Home → Font → Bold (Alt+H, 1). Change the color to something catchy with Alt+H, FC. Center the text in the cell both horizontally and vertically to set it off from the rest of the form. Use the command Table Tools | Layout → Alignment → Align Center or Alt+JL, CC.

When you're done, your form should look like Figure 14-1. It should be easy for subscribers to give you the information you need to sign them up. There's no confusion about the information you need and how they should give it to you. The form works great as a postcard—especially with the reply address and postage on the other side. (You can mail the postcard as fits in an envelope, or it can be tucked into a magazine or newspaper.)

Creating a Computer Form

Printed forms are fine, but they have a drawback: Sooner or later, someone has to manually take the information from the form and transfer it to address labels or a database to use it. This process is time-consuming and subject to error. If your subscribers in the example above filled out a computer form, then you wouldn't have to retype the information to use it.

You can email your form to subscribers and have them fill it out in Word, but the problem with that is obvious. Anybody with Word can also edit your form, even deleting important information and returning you something useless. (Or worse, what if they change your subscription rates?) You can solve this problem by using Word's content controls.

With content controls, you can lock up your form so bumbling or ill-intentioned folks can't change it, but they can type the information you need. You can create customized and clearly labeled text boxes and drop-down menus to make it easy for people to fill in just the information you're looking for. Content controls do other useful things, too, especially when it comes to using the information you collect. (Each content control has a name that other programs can use to extract information from your form.)

Understanding Content Controls

Microsoft provides several different types of content controls that you can plug into your documents—each designed to collect information in different ways.

Here's a description of the different content controls you can insert into your documents:

- **Rich Text.** Text boxes that hold a paragraph of formatted text. Great for areas where people need to fill in information. For example, use a text box for the Name field in a form. The main advantage of the Rich Text control over the plain text content control (mentioned next) is that the typist can apply different formatting to the text within the text box. For example, you can type "The *Missing* Manual."

- **Text.** For most forms, you should use the plain Text box. Use the Rich Text content control when the content needs elaborate formatting. You can format the words in a Text content control, but all the words are formatted the same. One major advantage of plain text boxes is that they can hold more than one paragraph. Rich Text content controls permit only one paragraph.

- **Picture.** A content control that holds pictures, which can be anything from a photo to a chart to a company logo. Suppose you are creating an employee form with contact information for each employee in your company. With the Picture control, you can include a photo as well.

- **Combo Box.** Shows a list of options and includes a text box for entries not on the list. Use a combo box to provide suggested options and still permit someone to enter their own information.

- **Drop-Down List.** This content control lets you show your readers a list of options, just like those real-live drop-down menus on Web sites and computer programs. Drop-down lists limit the options someone can choose from. For example, you give people two choices: either yes or no. Or you give them a choice of 50 states. Drop-down menus also help eliminate incorrect or misspelled entries.

- **Date Picker.** A calendar tool that lets your readers easily enter a date in a format that Word understands, without typos.

- **Building Block Gallery.** Building blocks are predesigned, preformatted chunks of text, pictures, and other content that people can insert into documents.

- **Legacy Tools.** These are controls and tools that were used in previous versions of Word. They don't have the same capabilities for sharing information as Word's new content controls, so unless you need to edit a form developed in an older version of Word, avoid the legacy controls.

Displaying the Developer Tab

When you create a computer form for other people to use, you graduate from the ranks of a mere Word worker bee to a Word developer. But don't worry—you don't have to don a propeller beanie yet. Your first step on the developer path doesn't involve learning a programming language or delving into your PC's innards. Instead, you're going to learn how to make Word do more of the work for you. To do so, you use ribbon menus and buttons just like the ones you've been using all along.

But first, you have to make those tools appear on the ribbon—by adding the Developer tab. This tab has the tools for inserting content controls into your documents. The Developer tab also lets you record macros, edit Visual Basic code, and work with XML documents (as described in the next chapter).

Since most people rarely use these tools, you don't see the Developer tab when you first install Word. Here's how to bring it out of hiding:

1. **Choose Office button → Word Options.**

   You can also use the shortcut Alt+F, I to open the Word Options box. You can locate several buttons on the left side of the box. You find the Developer tab settings in the Popular panel. (If it's not selected, then click the Popular button at the top of the list.)

2. **Near the top of the window, turn on the "Show Developer tab in the Ribbon" checkbox.**

   Several checkboxes at the top of the window turn the described settings on and off.

Tip: While you're here, take a look at the "User name" box near the bottom. Your name is probably in the box; if not, enter it now. Word uses the name in this box for the Author field in every document.

---

3. **Click OK to close the Word Options box.**

   When you close Word Options, you see the new Developer tab on the ribbon (Figure 14-5). When you click the tab, you meet some geeky-looking tools in the following groups: Code, Controls, XML, Protect, and Templates.

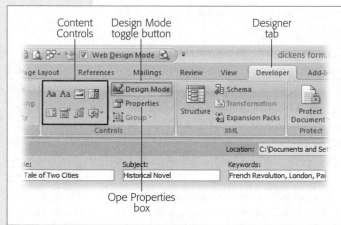

Figure 14-5:
Most of the tools you use for forms reside in the Developer tab's Controls group. The small icons to the right are the content controls used for forms. The Design Mode button is a toggle. In Design Mode, you can change the settings and properties of the content controls in your document. The Properties button opens the selected control's Properties dialog box (see Figure 14-7).

Adding Content Controls to Your Form

Earlier in this chapter you created a form destined for the printer. Subscribers fill in the blanks on paper and return the form to you physically. Then you use that information to sign them up for magazine subscriptions. In this section, you take the paper-based form and modify it to work as a computer-based form. You add content controls and protect the form, so subscribers can fill in the blanks but can't mess with the rest of it. The content controls also make it easy for a database or some other program to retrieve the information from the Word form.

In this tutorial, you insert content controls in each of the spots on the form that had blanks or checkboxes—text boxes and drop-down lists, respectively. Finally, you use the Developer → Protect settings to restrict the kinds of changes your potential subscribers can make to the document.

Adding text boxes to your form

Text boxes let your readers truly fill in the blanks with their own information. Or you can restrict what they can enter using the Protect settings, as you see later in this tutorial. But first, you must add the text box to your document using the Developer → Controls tools.

To get started, open the postcard form you created on pages 336–339 (or create it now). Or make a form that pertains to one of your own projects. Then follow these steps:

1. **Click within the second row of the table (under the Name label), and then choose Developer → Controls → Text to insert a Text content control (Figure 14-6).**

   Two types of Text content controls are available: Rich Text controls that readers can format and plain text controls, which simply store the characters without formatting. Plain text controls take on the formatting of the paragraph. For this example, you just want to collect the raw information, so you use plain text controls throughout this example, since formatting isn't an important part of the job. Plain text almost makes it easier for other programs such as FileMaker and or CGI script to read the information.

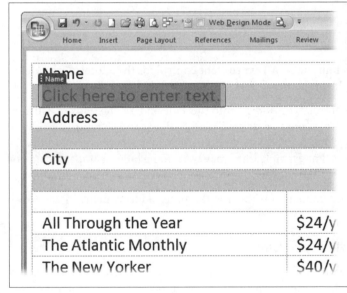

Figure 14-6:
Content controls look like text boxes, with a tab that displays the control's title. Don't fret if the box appears to be too small for the content it will hold. Word's text controls automatically adjust to fit the text typed into them.

2. **With the content control still selected on the ribbon, choose Developer → Controls → Properties or press Alt+L, L.**

   The control's Properties box opens (Figure 14-7).

3. **In the Title text box, type *Name*. In the Tag text box, type *Subscriber*.**

   Often, you use the same word for the title (which is what you call the control) and the tag (which is what software programs call the control behind the scenes), but it's not a requirement.

4. **Turn on the "Content control cannot be deleted" checkbox but leave the other boxes turned off.**

When people use your form, they won't be able to inadvertently or purposely delete the control, but they will be able to type in new text.

Figure 14-7:
Using the Content Control Properties dialog box, you can change the appearance and the behavior of your form's text boxes, drop-down lists, and other controls. For example, you can choose whether controls allow multiple paragraphs and whether they can be changed or deleted. You can find different options for different types of controls, as described in much greater detail on page 340.

5. **Similarly, in row four, insert a Text content control for the address line (Alt+L, E), and then set the properties (Alt+L, L).**

For the address control, type *Address* into the Title and Tag text boxes. Turn on the "Content control cannot be deleted" and "Allow carriage returns (multiple paragraphs)" checkboxes. The latter option lets subscribers enter multiparagraph address lines. For example, they may want to include a company name or a suite number with their address.

In the same way, add content controls for the other address items in the form: City, State, and Zip code.

Adding drop-down lists to your form

Drop-down lists give your subscribers much less leeway. The only way they can enter information with a drop-down control is by choosing one of the items on the list—or not. On the other hand, drop-down lists can make everyone's life easier by guiding your readers toward expected responses and eliminating the possibility of mistyped entries. Adding drop-down lists is just like adding text boxes, although the properties are, of course, different.

Tip: The properties for all of Word's content controls are described later in this chapter. To insert a different content control, like a date picker, follow the steps outlined here, and then flip to page 348 to find out how to set the properties.

Like the previous tutorial, these steps assume you've already created the postcard form on pages 336–339.

1. **For each magazine and the Porsche sweepstakes, add a drop-down list (Alt+L, O).**

   Use the keyboard shortcut or Developer → Controls → Drop-Down List to insert the controls. At first, the newly inserted controls may bend your table out of shape. You can change that as you set the properties for the controls.

2. **Open the properties box (Figure 14-8) for the drop-down list (Alt+L, L).**

   When you first open the properties box, only one Display Name appears in the list: "Choose an item." For the subscription form, you want subscribers to choose "Yes" or "No" to tell you whether they want to receive a magazine.

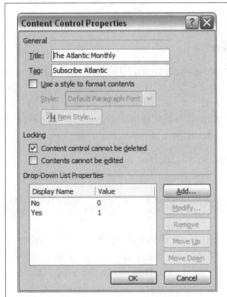

Figure 14-8:
When you create a drop-down menu, you define the items shown on the menu in the Content Control Properties box. This box contains two menu items: Yes and No. If Yes is selected, the content control stores the value 1. If No is selected, the control stores 0.

Each display name can also have a value assigned to it. The *value* is the data computer programs use when they process the information collected by the form.

3. **In the box at the bottom of the Content Control Properties dialog box, click the Display Name "Choose an item," and then click the Modify button on the right.**

   The Modify Choice box opens where you can change the Display Name and the Value.

4. **In the Display Name box, type** *Yes,* **and in the Value box, type the number** *1.* **Click OK to close the box.**

When your subscribers say "Yes," they want to receive a magazine, the drop-down list records the information as the value 1. Since you're using a numerical value instead of just Yes or No, another program like a database can do cool things like add up how many magazines you've sold.

Next, you need to add the No option to the drop-down list, and to do *that* you have to add another name to the Display Name list.

5. **Click the Add button to open the Add Choice box.**

Apart from the name, it looks identical to the Modify Choice box. In the Display Name box, type *No,* and in the Value box, type the number *0.*

Repeat the steps to create Yes/No drop-down lists for the rest of the magazines and to enter the Porsche sweepstakes.

Protecting Your Computer-Based Form

When you create a form for others to use, you want them to fill in the blanks and provide information. You don't want them to delete the explanatory text or the content controls you've carefully placed in the form. You have different ways to protect a document, but the most common method is to lock the entire document so that the only thing people can do is provide information in the content controls.

Open the form you created in the previous two tutorials, or any Word document you want to protect before you distribute it, and then follow these steps:

1. **Choose Developer → Protect → Protect Document → Restrict Formatting and Editing.**

The Restrict Formatting and Editing panel is divided into three numbered groups (Figure 14-9). In the first group, "Formatting restrictions," you limit the way other people can format your document. Leave this alone for now. The second group, "Editing restrictions," has a checkbox and a drop-down menu.

2. **Turn on the "Allow only this type of editing in the document" checkbox, and then choose "Filling in forms" from the drop-down menu.**

This setting makes it so people can type into text boxes and make selections from drop-down lists, but they can't, say, change the text or the structure of your document's table.

3. **In the third group, click the "Yes, Start Enforcing Protection" button to protect your document from changes.**

The Start Enforcing Protection box appears giving you the opportunity to password-protect your document. If you password-protect the document, only you or someone with the password can make changes to the document's protection settings. (Password protection doesn't prevent anyone from filling in the text boxes or using the other content controls.)

4. A password isn't necessary for this example, so just click OK.

The Restrict Formatting and Editing panel changes, showing one button that reads Stop Protection. You can use this button to stop protection at any time, so *you* can edit the form. For now, close the panel by clicking the X in the upper-right corner.

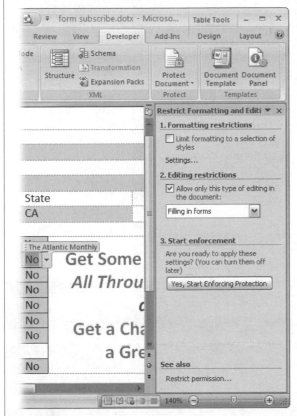

Figure 14-9:
The Restrict Formatting and Editing panel is divided into three parts. The first part lets you limit the way people can format your document. The second part lets you limit the way they can edit your document. The third part provides a button that lets you turn on the protection.

5. Save the form as a template Office button → Save As → Word Template with the name *form_subscription.dotx*.

By saving the form as a template, you can create new documents from the template, while leaving the original untouched. Templates are great for forms like this one. You can send each potential subscriber a new document to fill in, while your template remains bland and unchanged, ready for the next happy customer (Figure 14-10).

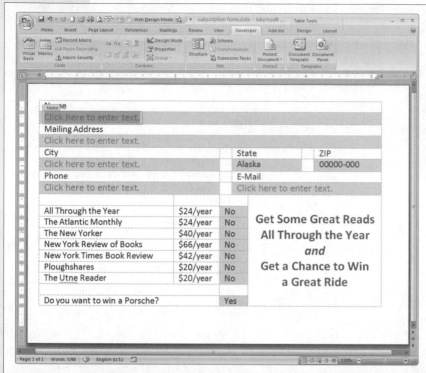

Figure 14-10:
The completed computer-based form looks very similar to the paper-based subscription form. The difference is that it has content controls instead of blank boxes. The content controls help to manage the information you collected and give you a way to protect the form from unwanted changes.

The InfoPath Alternative

If you're really serious about creating forms and working with information that's collected through forms, consider using Microsoft's InfoPath. One of the programs in the Office family, InfoPath is designed to create forms that collect data for use by databases and other programming tools. InfoPath can import and convert forms you've already created in Word or Excel. InfoPath is more powerful than Word because it has an extensive set of tools specifically for creating forms and checking the information people type in. For example, you can create a phone or Zip code content control that accepts only numbers.

You can create a date picker for people's date of birth that won't accept a date that's in the future. InfoPath is also set up to create forms that can collect information on Web pages or via email.

With Office 2007, Microsoft has shifted form creation responsibilities from the traditional Office programs onto the shoulders of InfoPath. Part of the reason for this shift may have to do with beefing up security and preventing people from using macros and controls to create malicious programs in Word, Outlook, and Excel.

Setting Properties for Content Controls

Word's new content controls are remarkably powerful tools, especially when you combine them with the XML features that are built into Word's new file formats. You determine how a control looks and acts by editing its properties. If you used

Visual Basic for Applications (VBA) in previous versions of Word, you're probably familiar with fine-tuning a control's properties, but you may be surprised when you open the Properties box for one of the new content controls. You find fewer properties, and most of the settings won't look familiar.

Microsoft is phasing out the old controls, in part, for security reasons. Earlier versions of Visual Basic for Applications combined with ActiveX controls were a playground for the folks who create computer viruses and other nasties. (If necessary, you can still insert the old VBA-style tools on the Legacy Tools menu.) The new content controls also work seamlessly with XML code—which is a new standard for documents and exchanging information. This arrangement makes it easy for another computer system to read the information collected in your form.

One of the best things about controls is that you can lock them (using two checkboxes in the Properties box) to prevent people from deleting them or editing the contents. In addition, each content control has its own specific properties. For example, the Date Picker control lets you specify a display format to show dates such as 10/1/2006; Sunday, October 1, 2006; and just about every variation in between. For the plain text control, you have an "Allow carriage returns (multiple paragraphs)" option, as a way to let readers create multiple paragraphs within a single text box.

To open the Properties box for a content control, switch to Design Mode (Developer → Controls → Design Mode). Select the control, and then go to Developer → Controls → Properties. The Content Control Properties box opens. Different controls have different properties that you can tweak. Here's a quick rundown:

- The **Title** appears in your document on the content control's tab. If you don't give your content control a name, Word leaves the tab—and the Title field—blank.

- The **Tag** may sound like just another name to you, but it's important to computer programs. They use the Tag to identify and then read or write to the contents in your control.

- Use the **Content control cannot be deleted** box to keep people from deleting the controls in your form when they fill in the information.

- Use the **Content control cannot be edited** if you don't want people to change the contents of the control. It's unlikely you'd use this for a form, but for other types of documents, you may want to show someone information in a control without letting them change it.

- Use the **Allow carriage returns (multiple paragraphs)** box to permit people to put several paragraphs in a Text control.

- Turn on **Remove content control when contents are edited** to create prompts in your documents. After someone types in text, the content control disappears, and the text takes its place in the document.

- Both the Combo Box and the Drop-Down List have **Drop-Down List Properties** where you provide words and options for the lists.

- The Date Picker has several unique properties including **Display the date like this** where you choose the format for the date (12/25/2006; Monday, October 1, 2006; and so on). **Locale** and **Calendar type** are also used to control the way dates are shown in different regions and languages. The **Store XML contents in the following format when mapped** option is used to communicate date information to other programs.

- The Building Block Gallery control uses **Gallery** and **Category** properties to select specific building blocks that can be inserted in the document.

The following table has a complete list of the available properties for each control.

Content Control Property:	Rich Text	Text	Picture	Combo Box	Drop-Down List	Date Picker	Building Block Gallery
Title	✗	✗	✗	✗	✗	✗	✗
Tag	✗	✗	✗	✗	✗	✗	✗
Use a style to format contents	✗	✗		✗	✗	✗	✗
Content control cannot be deleted	✗	✗	✗	✗	✗	✗	✗
Contents cannot be edited	✗	✗	✗	✗	✗	✗	✗
Allow carriage returns (multiple paragraphs)		✗					
Remove content control when contents are edited	✗	✗					
Drop-Down List Properties				✗	✗		
Display the date like this						✗	
Locale						✗	
Calendar type						✗	
Store XML content in the following format when mapped						✗	
Gallery							✗
Category							✗

Testing Your Form

The final step for any form, whether it's a printed form or computer-based, is to test it in the real world. When you've created a form yourself from the ground up, you probably think everything looks perfectly clear and self-explanatory. But what's clear to you, the creator, may not be clear to someone else.

Testing Your Printed Form

Hand out copies of your printed form to friends and coworkers to fill out. Listen to their questions and see if they fill out everything as you expected. Ask them if there's any way you could change the form to make it easier for them. Do they understand what's being asked for in each field? Is there enough room for them to write in their response? Are there parts of the form that are confusing? Do you need to provide more detailed instructions?

The answers to these questions will help you find the weaknesses in your form as well as places you can make improvements. Then, it's back to Word to make the changes. Ideally, follow all your changes with another round of testing.

Testing Your Computer-Based Form

You need to test your computer-based forms in the same way. But even before you turn your computer forms over to your guinea pigs, you need to test them to make sure everything is in working order. Can you type in the text boxes? Can you choose items from the drop-down lists? Does the protection prevent you from making changes to the permanent text? Is the template working properly, letting you open copies of the document while leaving the original intact?

After you've tested the computer-based form on your computer, copy it to another computer or ask a coworker to test it out. It's important to test your project on several different computers including desktops and laptops and any other device your target audience may use.

Word's XML Connection

XML is one of those warm and cozy computer acronyms that the pocket protector set seems to love. The fact that *XML* stands for eXtensible Markup Language doesn't make it sound any friendlier.

If you use Word to write letters to your aunt or to write the Great American Novel, you probably don't have to worry too much about XML. On the other hand, if you work in an office or with groups of people and need to share information, XML can help. If the previous chapter on forms caught your interest, then you definitely want to learn XML basics. Used by computers and companies big and small, XML is an industry-wide standard that breaks through the Babel of incompatible computer data and files. XML isn't a Microsoft creation; it's a standard language used to describe information. and it's growing in popularity.

This chapter won't turn you into an XML Xpert, but it will acquaint you with the ideas behind XML. You also learn about the connections between XML and Word 2007. Office 2007 has new document file formats for Word, Excel, and Power-Point, all of which are based on XML. In this chapter, you have a chance to see these formats from the inside. You learn how to insert XML tags into your document and how to decipher some of the mysteries inside an XML document file.

What's XML and Why Should I Care?

Almost 400 years ago, the English poet John Donne proclaimed, "No man is an island." What would he think today with everyone tethered to each other over computer networks? Yet, in spite of all the connections, it's still hard to share information. Different computers and different programs speak different languages. Expert programmers have spent years trying to make Macs and PCs communicate, and they still haven't fully succeeded. So imagine how much more of a challenge it is to get PCs to talk to those big computers at banks, insurance companies, and airline reservation desks. XML offers a way for all these machines and their programs to pass bits and pieces of information back and forth.

How XML Works

The basic idea behind XML is pretty simple. In XML, descriptive tags are placed around a piece of information, like so:

<TITLE>A Tale of Two Cities</TITLE>

That way, any program (or even a perceptive human) can see that the information inside the tags is a title. So, a program at a bookstore may plug this title information into a sales and inventory database, while a Word document at a publishing house may insert the same information into a press release to promote the book. (See the box below for a quick course in tags.)

UP TO SPEED

XML & HTML's Common Ancestors

If the XML tags such as this one, <title>A Tale of Two Cities</title>, look familiar, you've probably dabbled in HTML, the language that's used to define pages on the Web. There's a good reason why XML and HTML documents look similar—they share a common ancestor, SGML (Standard Generalized Markup Language). All these languages use similar tags to mark up documents, but they were created for different jobs. SGML was designed to do just about anything, but it's so complicated and difficult that it doesn't see much use.

XML and HTML have more modest goals, so they're not only easy to use, but they're also being used more and more all the time. HTML is designed to format information sent over the Internet so that it can be viewed as pages. XML was developed for sharing information between different computer systems and programs.

- **HTML** stands for Hypertext Markup Language. In computer lingo, hypertext is text with links. By clicking these links, you travel from one document to another. HTML is the language that defines the links in hypertext. It also describes formatting for the text and links pictures and other media to Web pages.

- **XML** serves a different function. Instead of describing the way a document looks, XML describes the information within a document. For example, markup tags in XML wrap around a word, a number, or a paragraph. They say, "This is the company name," "this is the telephone number," "this is a stock quote," and "this is a rhinoceros." Of course, you know what, say, a telephone number looks like, but XML's purpose isn't to tell humans about the telephone number; its purpose is to tell other programs and other computers about the telephone number. XML describes the parts of a document so that another program can identify those parts and then use them.

The Advantages of XML

As a way of sharing information between people and computers, XML has a lot of advantages over the files created by a specific program like Word, Excel, or Access. Here are some of the advantages:

- **XML can be read by humans.** There's no real mystery behind XML documents—they're based on standard text. So, if you need to, you can read a document with XML code and figure out what kind of information it contains. If you're so inclined, you can even make simple edits using a program like Notepad or Wordpad.

- **XML documents can be easily sent over the Internet or over a business network.** Because they're just text files, it's just as easy to send an XML document over the Internet or an internal company network as it is to send a Web page.

- **XML files aren't tied to a particular operating system or any particular program.** It's not difficult to write a program that can read an XML file and use the information inside. (Well, it's not difficult for people who know how to write programs.) Programs are available for just about every type of computer around today. Equally important, years from now programs will exist for Windows 2027 and Mac OS XXX that can read and use XML files and information.

- **XML isn't owned by any one company.** Microsoft doesn't own the XML standard and neither does any other company. It's free to use XML in a new program or to use it on your computer network.

XML and Word's New File Format

Office 2007 uses XML in a big way. Word, Excel, and PowerPoint each have a new document file format that's based on XML. The file formats, like Word's .docx and .dotx files, are smarter, smaller, and tougher than the previous document files.

- **Why are the new files smarter?** Your Word 2007 document file is essentially a package that contains several XML files, as shown in Figure 15-1. Each XML file describes a different part of the Word document. For example, one part of an XML file describes images, another part that describes headers, and another part that describes the main body of the document. If you create custom XML elements in a Word document, they're stored in a special datastore folder. As a result, other programs can reach in and use parts of your Word documents. Now that's smart.

- **Why are the new files smaller?** All these XML files are stored in a single Word file that's compressed to make it smaller. Smaller files travel faster when you send them over the Internet, which is a big advantage in today's world. Microsoft adopted the well-known Zip standard to combine all the files and then compress the whole shebang. Any other program—even a non-Microsoft program—that can open Zip files can easily open and work with the innards of a Word file. (Feeling brave? See the box on page 358 to learn how to take a peek inside one of your Word files.)

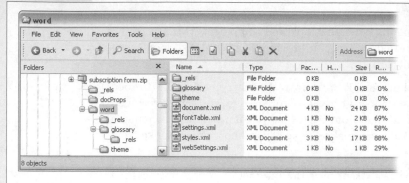

Figure 15-1:
The new file format for Word documents (and other Office documents) consists of XML files combined in a Zip file. This figure shows what a Word file looks like on the inside. The XML files describe different parts of the document. The document.xml file holds the text for the document. The fontTable.xml file has details about the fonts used in the document.

Note: You may be familiar with Zip compression if you've used programs like WinZIP. Just how much Zip shrinks a file depends on the content. In some cases, if the stars are aligned properly, Zip can reduce a file to about a quarter of its original size.

- **Why are the new files tougher?** These new-format files are more reliable than their predecessors, because even if part of the file gets corrupted, there's a good chance you can use the rest of it. Chances are, only one of the several files that make up a Word document will get corrupted at a time. The other files will be fine. So, if a picture or a sound clip that's embedded in your document gets fouled up, you can still read, retrieve, and save the text.

Reading XML Tags

As mentioned in the box on page 354, HTML and XML both use tags between angle brackets. The tag at the end includes a slash mark. For example, a tag can describe a bit of information as a title:

<TITLE>A Tale of Two Cities</TITLE>

Another program looking at the document understands that the words between those tags are a title. In fact, since XML uses basic English words, some humans can figure it out too. Now, when you tag your information with XML, you don't know exactly how another program may use the information. But that's part of the beauty of XML. It gives you a way to use and reuse information now and in the future. Imagine a city newspaper keeping track of every story it publishes with XML tags—a tag for the title, the author, and the date. Another tag encompasses all the text for the story. Tags also categorize the story as business, crime, or politics. (And sometimes all three at once.)

Over time, the newspaper creates a great library of all the stories they've published. People can search for articles by specific authors who cover specific topics.

By simply storing the story and the details about the story inside XML tags, the newspaper creates a versatile, searchable library of newspaper articles that can continue to grow. They can even add new tags as time goes on (like Dateline: Mars), and that won't bother XML a bit. Today, businesses are storing information in the XML language. Letters, memos, proposals, reports, and sales transactions are stored using XML, making the information accessible to coworkers and clients.

A pair of XML tags, including the information between them, is called an *element* in XML lingo. End tags in XML, like those in HTML, have a slash that distinguishes them from beginning tags. Elements can be nested inside other elements to establish relationships and create more complex objects. For example, here's a more detailed chunk of information describing a book:

```
<BOOK>
<TITLE>A Tale of Two Cities</TITLE>
<AUTHOR>Charles Dickens</AUTHOR>
<PUBLISHER>Chapman and Hall</PUBLISHER>
<PUBLICATION DATE>1859</PUBLICATION DATE>
<FICTION>Yes</FICTION>
<GENRE>Historical Fiction</GENRE>
<ILLUSTRATED>Yes</ILLUSTRATED>
<PAGES>358</PAGES>
</BOOK>
```

In this example, the TITLE, AUTHOR, and other tags are nested within the BOOK tags, making it clear that these are parts of the information regarding a book. XML tags are called *extensible,* which is computer lingo meaning that they can be extended to describe any type of information or data. HTML, by contrast, has a limited number of tags, and everyone agrees on just what they mean. With XML, you can create your own tags to describe your information. But that raises the question, if you create your own tags, how will someone else or some other computer program know what your tags mean? That's where different types of *helper files* come into play.

Unzipping a Word File

In the past, Microsoft's file formats were somewhat mysterious and proprietary. Those days are over. With Office 2007, the document formats for Word, Excel, and PowerPoint are an open book. They use the information-sharing XML language to describe their contents, and Zip technology to combine and compress the files. Both XML and Zip are well documented and freely available, so anyone can write a program that can read and write to Word files.

To see what the XML innards of a Word file look like, follow these steps:

1. Using Windows Explorer, copy (Ctrl+C) one of your Word (.docx) files, and then paste (Ctrl+V) a copy back into the same folder. Windows creates a new file with a name that begins "Copy of" to distinguish it from the original.

2. Right-click the new file, and then choose Rename from the shortcut menu. Then change the ending of the Word file from .docx to .zip. With this change, your computer will recognize the file as a file that's been compressed using the Zip standard. Notice that the icon for the file has changed from the big "W" Word icon to a folder with a zipper or, if you have WinZIP, a folder that looks like it's being squashed by a C-clamp.

3. Right-click an empty spot in the folder, and then choose New → Folder from the pop-up menu. A new folder appears, and your cursor is poised for you to type in a folder name, say, *Word Innards*.

4. To open your newly renamed Zip file, right-click it, and then choose Explore from the pop-up menu.

   Windows Explorer knows how to open up Zip files, and it shows them as if they were ordinary files and folders. When you *explore* a Zip file, you see its contents. In this case, that includes both folders and files. You see folders named *_rels*, *docProps*, and *word*. You also see an XML document called *[Content_Types].xml*.

5. Drag over all the files and folders inside the Zip file to select them. Then, with everything selected, drag the whole bunch to your Word Innards folder. Windows copies the files to the Word Innards folder.

6. Double-click to open the folders inside Word Innards.

   You can browse and explore to your heart's content, checking out the mysteries of Word's new file format. Double-click to open folders and to see what's stored inside them. In the *glossary* folder, you see XML files with names like *fontTable* and *webSettings*. (Almost all the files in the folders are XML files.)

7. Double-click to view the contents of the XML files.

   You can view the insides of XML files using a Web browser like Internet Explorer, as shown in Figure 15-2. So, double-click any file you want to view, and your browser opens, displaying the XML file like a Web page. Everything's formatted nicely in different colors to show the XML tags. You may be able to recognize some of the text in your document if you view the *document.xml* file inside the *word* folder.

   You can see how easy it would be for a program to open and edit the contents of a Word file, and then Zip everything back up. You could do it yourself with the tools that Windows provides. You can't edit and save an XML file with Internet Explorer, but Wordpad or Notepad will do the job.

   When you're done you can reverse the process and create a Word file. Just select all the files in the Word Innards folder, and then right-click to show the popup menu. Choose Send to → Compressed (zipped) Folder. Rename the new file *word innards.docx*. If you made changes to the text in *document.xml*, you see them when you open *word innards.docx* in Word.

Figure 15-2:
*You can use Windows Explorer to view the
contents of an XML file. Explorer formats the text
neatly and uses colors to separate tags from
content. Click the + and – buttons to the left of the
text to expand and collapse elements. This file
shows the address label and tag at the top. The
address text is shown below.*

The Files That Make XML Work

An open-ended system for tagging information with descriptions and making that
information available to other programs is all well and good. But how do those
other programs know how to interpret your tags and use your information? In
addition to an XML file that stores the tagged information, there's often a file
called a *schema*, which explains the tags in a way that makes sense to other computer programs. For example, the schema will explain that a telephone number
should be ten numbers and shouldn't include letters or punctuation. Another type
of file called a *transformation* (or *transform* for short) can take the information in
an XML file and turn it into a different type of document, like a Web page or a
Word document.

Here are some of the types of files related to XML documents:

• **Data files** (.xml) are the files that contain the information held within tags.

• **Schema files** (.xsd) describe the contents of an XML file so that other programs
 know what's inside specific tags. Figure 15-3 shows what a schema looks like on
 the inside.

• **Transform files** (.xslt) are used to transform an XML file into a different type of
 document, like a Web page or a database file.

• **XPath** is the language used to find information inside an XML file.

Figure 15-3:
This schema file describes the information inside a purchase order. If you look carefully, you can identify some of the elements you'd expect in a purchase order, such as poNum for purchase order number and poDate for the date. The details after "type=" explain the type of information that's expected: a string of characters for the PO number and a date for the PO date.

```
Purchase Order.xsd - Notepad
File  Edit  Format  View  Help
<xsd:complexType name="generalType">
 <xsd:sequence>
  <xsd:element name="poNum"    type="xsd:string"/>
  <xsd:element name="poDate"   type="xsd:date"/>
 </xsd:sequence>
</xsd:complexType>

<xsd:complexType name="orderType">
 <xsd:sequence>
  <xsd:element name="companyName" type="xsd:string"/>
  <xsd:element name="address"     type="xsd:string"/>
  <xsd:element name="city"        type="xsd:string"/>
  <xsd:element name="stateProv"   type="xsd:string"/>
  <xsd:element name="zipCode"     type="xsd:string"/>
```

Tagging Information with Content Controls

The previous chapter, on creating forms, describes how to insert content controls into your documents. In the example, the content controls are used to hold address information such as name, address, city, state, and Zip code. You can adjust the settings using the Content Controls Properties box (Figure 15-4).

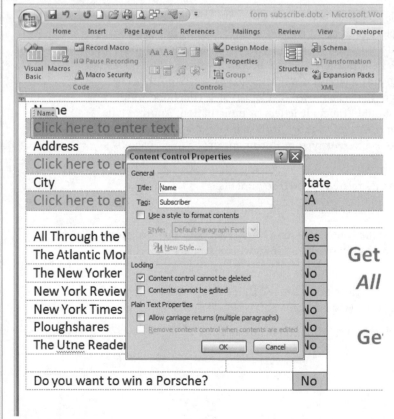

Figure 15-4:
When you insert content controls into a document, you're creating XML elements. Use the Content Control Properties box to name the XML tags. Other programs can extract information from your files using the tag names.

To open the box, go to Developer → Controls → Properties or use the shortcut Alt+L, L. The properties boxes vary for different types of controls, but each has two text boxes at the top—Title and Tag. These two settings seem suspiciously similar, but they actually serve different functions for programmers. The Title is the name a programmer uses to refer to the control in a macro or a program. The Tag is the name a programmer uses to refer to the XML element.

Whenever you insert a content control into your document and provide the tag with a name, you're creating an XML element. Other programs can use the element to access parts of your document. For example, a program can read the subscription forms and add that information to a database or spreadsheet. Content controls share information in two directions, too, so documents can be savvy enough to go out and collect information from other sources. Imagine a realtor has a fact sheet on a house that's for sale. One of the content controls on the fact sheet contains the price. Each time the fact sheet is opened, the content control that holds the price checks the current price for the house and displays the up-to-date price in the document.

Attaching an XML Schema to Your Document

The word *schema* sounds a little nefarious or at least seriously geeky. But a schema is simply a document that acts as a Rosetta stone for XML files describing the content. For an example, see Figure 15-3. Don't panic; you may never have to create a schema on your own. It's more likely that some day you'll want to *attach* a schema somebody else created to a Word document. For example, suppose you're a realtor who wants to tap into a database of homes that are on the market. You could create a document listing all the homes, along with details such as the number of rooms and the number of baths and the price. The folks who created the database could give you the name and location of a schema on the Internet. When you attach that schema to your document, you can display the information from the database in content controls in your Word document.

Here's how to attach a schema to your Word document:

1. **Open the document you want to use with the XML information with the command Office → Open.**

   The Open dialog box shows on your screen. Use it to find and open your file.

2. **Choose Developer → XML → Schema to open the Templates and Add-ins box (Figure 15-5).**

   The Templates and Add-ins box has several tabs at the top. When you open it with the Schema command, it automatically shows the XML Schema tab. The Available XML schemas box shows any schemas that are currently attached to your document.

Note: If the Developer tab isn't showing on your ribbon, go to page 341 for instructions on how to make the Developer tab visible.

Figure 15-5:
Use the XML Schema tab on the Templates and Add-ins dialog box to attach schemas to your document. The available schemas appear in the large box. Click to place a checkmark next to a schema and to attach it to your document. You can attach more than one schema to a document.

3. **Click the Add Schema button to open the Add Schema box.**

   The Add Schema box looks like any standard Windows file box. Using the buttons on the left and the drop-down menu at the top, navigate to the location with the schema you're adding to your document. If the document is located on a network, use the My Network Places button in the lower-left corner of the Add Schema box.

4. **Navigate to the schema file, and then double-click to select the .xsd file.**

   The Add Schema box closes, and the Schema Settings box opens. Most likely, the URI and Location boxes are already filled in with details that tell Word where to find information about the schema. You can fill in a name for the schema in the Alias text box.

5. **Click the OK to close the Schema settings and to return to the XML Schema tab of the Templates and Add-ins box.**

   The Schema you just attached appears in the "Available XML schemas" box. Make sure a checkmark appears next to the name so you can use it with your document. You can have several schemas installed and available in Word. Just use the checkboxes to attach a specific schema to your document.

6. **Click OK to close the Templates and Add-ins box.**

   Once the Template and Add-ins box closes, it probably looks like nothing has changed in your document. However, a change has taken place behind the scenes. Because a new schema is attached to your document, you can see the available tags in the XML Structure pane, as shown in Figure 15-6.

Once you've attached a custom XML schema to your document, you see a list of
the XML elements that are defined by the schema in the XML Structure pane. To
open the pane, go to Developer → Structure or use the keyboard shortcut Alt+L, T.
You use the elements listed in the XML Structure pane to apply custom tags to the
text in your document. To apply a tag, select the text you want to tag, and then
choose an element from the XML Structure pane.

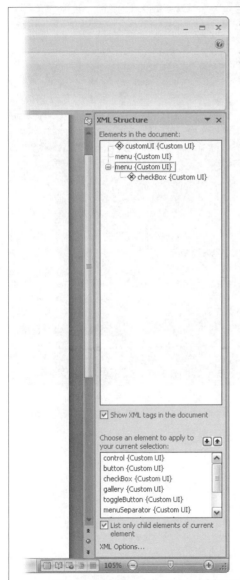

Figure 15-6:
*The XML Structure pane keeps track of the XML tags that are used in
your document in the box at the top and gives you a list of the available
tags in the box at the bottom.*

XML Primer for HTML Writers

This chapter makes it clear that XML serves a much different purpose than HTML. In spite of that, their method for marking up documents is much the same. They use tags that look similar. But if you're familiar with HTML and want to take a crack at creating some XML documents, there are a few gotchas to watch out for.

In many cases, the rules for creating XML are strict, while the rules for HTML are flexible. If an XML document doesn't conform to the rules, it's considered an *invalid* document, and programs designed to use XML simply ignore it. Here's a short list of some of the differences between HTML and XML:

- **XML code is case-sensitive.** When you write HTML code, it really doesn't matter if the characters inside the tags are uppercase or lowercase. A bold tag can be <b> or <B>. Browsers don't care a bit. With XML, there's a big difference. To a program reading XML, the tags <TITLE>, <Title>, and <title> are three entirely different tags.

- **Tags must be used in pairs, with one exception being the empty tag.** HTML writers get a little freeform with tags. Even though paragraphs should have a beginning tag <p> and an end tag </p>, many Web pages simply use the beginning tag, and most Web browsers don't seem to mind that the closing tag is missing. XML isn't as forgiving.

Because it's important to know where data begins and ends, you need to use both beginning and end tags. The exception is what's known as an empty tag—a type of tag that never has any content. Empty tags use a special form, with a slash before the last angle bracket. So, an empty tag may look like this: <nothingness/>; it means the same thing to XML programs as this: <nothingness></nothingness>.

- **Tags must be properly nested.** Another area where HTML coders get a little footloose is the order in which they place tags, for example: <outside> <inside>Great American Novel</outside></inside>. Technically, the closing </inside> tag should be next to the text, just like the opening one is. Most browsers forgive this kind of error, but XML programs doesn't. Tags must be properly nested, or XML programs will consider them invalid.

- **In XML, white space is considered intentional.** Web browsers don't pay much attention to tabs, line breaks, and paragraph marks unless they're told to with special instructions such as <pre> tags. XML takes a different approach. If you have 45 space characters between each word in your book title, XML assumes that you put them there on purpose.

Collaborating with Other People

Whether you're collaborating with a coauthor or reviewing someone else's manuscript, Word makes it easy to communicate as you edit. In precomputing days, editing a paper document resulted in a jumble of red pen marks, crossed out text, and notes scrawled in the margins. If several people reviewed a document, figuring out who said what was a nightmare. Word resolves those issues by keeping track of all changes and all reviewers. Word stores everything in the document file and, with a click of your mouse, you can show or hide the comments and edits.

This chapter looks at the reviewing process from all angles. You learn how to insert comments into a document and how to manage comments made by reviewers. The chapter covers the entire process of tracking changes and accepting or rejecting changes made by others. You even learn how to record voice comments with your document. Finally, you'll learn how to combine and compare two documents so only the right parts make it to the final draft.

Adding Comments

Collaborating is all about clear communication, so Word lets you attach easy-to-read comments directly to the text you're referring to. What could be clearer? Even better, for documents with several reviewers, Word keeps track of who said what, when (Figure 16-1). That makes it a breeze for authors to follow up on a comment and get more details.

When you select text and add a comment, Word marks it with the date, time, and your name or initials, and connects it to the selected text. Word lets you (and your readers) choose how you want to see these comments: as balloons, marked up in the text itself, or in the separate Reviewing Pane. See Figure 16-2 for details.

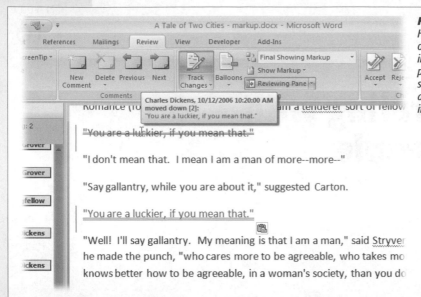

Figure 16-1:
Hold your mouse cursor over a comment or a change in your document and a pop-up note appears, showing who added the annotation and when—even if that's you.

Three Views for Review

Microsoft is seldom content giving you a single way to do anything, and this philosophy holds when it comes to reviewing comments and changes to a document. Depending on the amount of edits and your personal preferences, you can choose to display them in one of three ways:

- **Balloons** are like notes written in the margin. Show balloons by choosing Review → Tracking → Balloons → Show Revisions in Balloons. Comments and changes show up in the right margin preceded by the reviewer's initials. A line from the balloon creates a visual link to the highlighted text.

- **Inline revisions** appear with the text itself, as if inserted with a colored pen. To see inline revisions, choose Review → Tracking → Balloons → Show All Revisions Inline. With Track Changes on (Review → Tracking → Track Changes → Track Changes), each change and comment creates a highlight or a mark in the document.

When you hold your mouse cursor over a comment or a change, a pop-up note appears with the name of the reviewer and the time and date of the change (Figure 16-1).

- **The Reviewing Pane** shows comments and changes in a more formal, all business-style panel. This view lets you read comments and simultaneously see your document in its pristine, unmarked-up state. To display the Reviewing Pane, choose Review → Tracking → Reviewing Pane. From the drop-down menu, you can choose between a vertical pane that appears on the left of your document, and a horizontal pane that appears at the bottom. In the document, comments are highlighted and initialed. The actual comment appears in the Reviewing Pane.

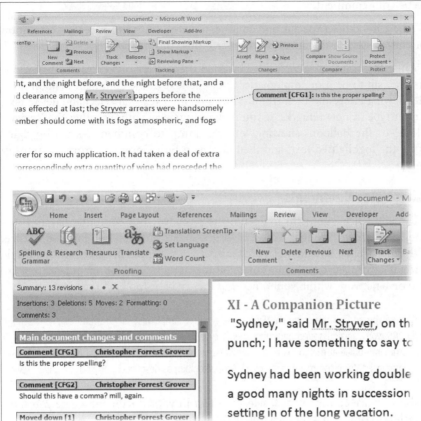

Figure 16-2:

Top: Balloon notes are like when you circle text, and then draw a line to a note in the margin.

Bottom: The Reviewing Pane opens either on the left or on the bottom of your document. When you click the highlighted text that indicates there's a comment, the Reviewing Pane scrolls to show the related comment.

Each comment you enter into a document is anchored by a word or a group of words. Here are the steps to insert a comment into a document:

1. **Select the part of the document you want to comment on by dragging to select the text.**

   You can select as much or as little text as you want. If you don't select anything, Word automatically chooses a word near the insertion point.

2. **Choose Review → Comments → New Comment, or use the shortcut Alt+R, C to insert your comment.**

   Word highlights the selected text and links it to a comment on the Reviewing Pane and in a balloon on the right margin. (You can choose which way you want to see comments and edits, as shown in Figure 16-2.)

   Comments from different reviewers appear in different colors, making it easy for you to quickly pay special attention to the VP's comments while ignoring the comment from the crazy guy in the cubicle next to the copy machine.

3. **Type your comment.**

It's best to be both specific and concise, to avoid losing your readers' attention or cluttering your document with superfluous commentary.

You can edit comments after you've inserted them. Say you've decided to reword your criticism to be more diplomatic. Click the text in the comment balloon or in the Reviewing Pane, and then edit just like any other text. Or select and delete text, and then type in new remarks. If you're working away without either the Reviewing Pane or the Balloons showing, you can jump to comment editing by right-clicking the highlighted text, and then choosing Edit Comment from the pop-up menu.

Adding Voice Comments

You can add voice comments to documents provided your computer has a microphone. Be warned, though: Voice messages make a document increase in size, quickly and steeply. For example, even a brief voice comment can easily quadruple the size of a five-page document. Voice comments work well for documents that are shared on a network within your office, but they may be too big to send by email.

Note: When you add a voice comment (Figure 16-3), you're simply inserting a sound clip. As described on page 285, you can add sound and other media clips to any document using the Insert → Text → Object command, but that method is a little cumbersome when you're reviewing a document. To save time, add the Insert Voice command to the Quick Access toolbar, as described in the box on page 370.

To insert a voice comment, first select the text in your document where you want to attach the comment, and then follow these steps:

1. **Click the Insert Voice command on the Quick Access toolbar to open the Sound Object box.**

The Insert Voice icon looks like a folder with a microphone on it. If you have trouble telling one icon from another on the Quick Access toolbar, just mouse over an icon for a couple seconds. A text box pops up with the name of the command.

2. **In the Sound Object box, click the Record button, and then speak your message.**

The Sound Object box sports control buttons that may remind you of a VCR or DVD player. Click the round Record button on the far right to record your message. The square button next to Record stops the recording. Use the triangle button in the middle to listen to your comment.

3. **Review and edit your comment if necessary.**

A sound graph of your message shows in the black box in the middle of the box. The vertical bar shows the location in the sound clip. You can use the bar and the buttons to edit and add to your sound clip until you're happy with the message.

---

4. **In the upper-right corner of the Sound Object box, click the X button to close the box.**

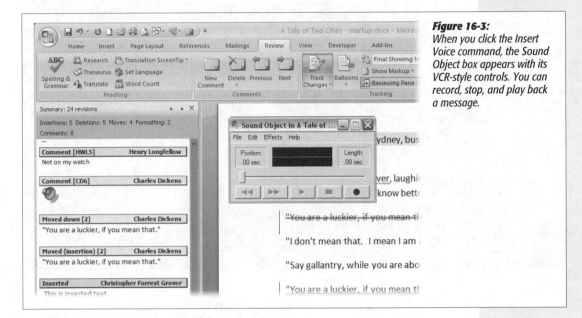

Figure 16-3:
When you click the Insert Voice command, the Sound Object box appears with its VCR-style controls. You can record, stop, and play back a message.

Voice comments show up in the balloons and the Reviewing Pane as icons that look like an audio speaker. To listen to a comment, just double-click the speaker icon. (Naturally, anyone who wants to listen to the comments needs to have a sound card and speakers connected to their computer.)

Deleting Comments

It's easy to delete a single comment. Just right-click the comment, and then choose Delete Comment from the shortcut menu. You can also click a comment's text, and use the same shortcut menu command. The keyboard shortcut to delete a single comment is Alt+R, DD, and the corresponding ribbon command is Review → Comments → Delete (Figure 16-4).

Notice that the Delete command on the Comments ribbon is actually a drop-down menu giving you two more handy ways to remove those helpful suggestions from your precious manuscript. You can remove all the comments in one fell swoop: Review → Comments → Delete → Delete All Comments or Alt+R, DO. Or you can remove only the comments that are currently showing: Alt+R, DA.

This last option gives you an easy way to remove the comments from a specific reviewer while leaving comments from others in place. It's a two-step process: First, display the comments you plan to delete and hide the others. Then, choose the Delete All Comments Shown command.

Setting Up Word to Insert Voice Comments

To make voice comments quick and easy, you need to add the Insert Voice command to your Quick Access toolbar. The Quick Access toolbar always appears in the upper-left corner of the Word window, so its commands are available no matter what ribbon tab is showing. Follow these steps to add the Insert Voice command to your Quick Access toolbar:

1. Choose Office → Word Options → Customize to show the panel where you customize your Quick Access toolbar.

   The panel has two large boxes with lists of Word commands. The box on the right lists the commands that appear in the Quick Access toolbar. The box on the left lists the commands you can add.

2. In the "Choose commands from" drop-down menu at the top left, choose All Commands.

   The left box shows every available Word command in an alphabetized list.

3. Scroll down the list, and then double-click the Insert Voice command.

4. When you double-click the command, it is automatically added to the list on the right.

5. Click OK to close the Word Options dialog box.

   After the Word Options box closes, you see the Insert Voice icon in the Quick Access toolbar in the upper-left corner.

Figure 16-4:
The Delete Comment drop-down menu lets you delete the selected comments, the visible comments, or all the comments in a document.

Here's a more detailed step-by-step:

1. **Go to Review → Tracking → Show Markup → Reviewers and choose your reviewers. Put a checkmark next to a name, and you see that reviewer's comments and edits in your document.**

   The comments of reviewers without checkmarks are hidden. You can show or hide any combination of reviewers.

2. **Choose Review → Comments → Delete → Delete All Comments Shown to remove the comments.**

   The comments that were visible in your document are deleted. They're gone now, and they're no longer a part of your document.

On the other hand, the comments from any reviewers that you hid in step 1 are still part of your document. You can view them by going to Review → Tracking → Show Markup → Reviewers and checking their names. If you have second thoughts after clicking Delete All Comments, you can undo it with Ctrl+Z.

Highlighting Text

When you insert a comment in a document, you do two things: You select the text, and then you type the attached comment. But sometimes, all you need to do is call attention to some words in the text, just like you'd use a highlighter pen on a paper document. You can find Word's highlighter equivalent on the Home ribbon: Home → Font → Text Highlight Color. You can either select text and then click the command, or you can click the command and then drag your cursor over the text that you want to highlight. It works either way. If you want to get fancy, you can use different highlights colors for different issues. Word gives you a palette of 12 colors to choose from (Alt+H, I).

Tracking Changes While Editing

When you're editing a document that someone else wrote, it's only fair to let the author see your changes. In the world of paper documents, the process can be rather lengthy. You get out your red pencil and mark up the document, crossing out words you want to delete and writing in words you want to add. Sometimes you draw a vertical line in the margin to draw attention to places where you've made edits. When you're through with your markup, you shoot the pages back to the original author. The document may go back and forth a few times before someone has the honor of typing up a new copy with the agreed upon changes. Fortunately, Word gives you a way to streamline the process.

Tracking and Viewing Changes

To begin tracking changes, just turn on the feature by clicking Review → Tracking → Track Changes or by pressing Alt+R, GG. The Track Changes button on the Review ribbon sports a highlight to signal that you're in Track Changes mode. In this mode, Word remembers every change you make and shows it in the Reviewing Pane or in balloons. Word also marks up your text by striking through deleted text and underlining added text.

Tip: By the way, you can change these settings. Suppose, for example, you want added text to appear in italics instead of underlined. See "Customizing your markup view" on page 374 for the details.

As you can imagine, your document gets pretty busy and hard to read after you've made a lot of edits. Fortunately, you can choose to show or hide the marked changes. You can also choose where you see those changes:

- **To see edits in your document,** go to Review → Tracking → Display for Review (Alt+R, TD), and choose either Final Showing Markup or Original Showing Markup from the drop-down menu (Figure 16-5). If you want to edit your document without the markup getting in the way, choose Final from the drop-down menu.

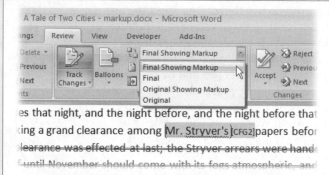

Figure 16-5:
Use the Display for Review menu to choose whether to show or hide edits in your document. Choose Final Showing Markup to see only the most recent edits. Choose Original Showing Markup to see all the edits that were tracked since the document was created. Final shows the most recent version with no markup. Original shows the version before any tracked changes.

- **To see edits in the Reviewing Pane,** click Review → Tracking → Reviewing Pane. The button works like a toggle, showing or hiding the annotations. Click the arrow button to see a menu with additional options. You can choose between a vertical reviewing pane that appears on the left side of your document and a horizontal reviewing pane that appears below your document. The Reviewing Pane provides more detail than the balloons, including a running tally of the number and the type of revisions.

- **To see edits in Balloons,** go to Review → Tracking → Balloons → Show Revisions in Balloons. An area opens on the right side of your document, displaying balloons with both comments and edits. Balloons show a clearer, simpler view of the changes in a manuscript than the Reviewing Pane. If the clutter of the Reviewing Pane distracts you, try working with balloons. On the other hand, if the comments are so extensive that the balloons are confusing, use the Reviewing Pane, where there's more room for long comments.

Modifying Your Markup View

Word has accommodations for documents that trudge a long path before they're final. These weary travelers endure multiple rounds of review and edit, and they come under the scrutiny of more than one reviewer. When you work with documents like this, it's important to be able to control what appears on the screen, or you're likely to get lost in the markup.

Choosing your markup view

If you need help recalling what your document said before anyone changed it, you don't have to undo all the changes. Word lets you sort of turn back the clock and see your document in its unedited state. By the same token, Word can hide the markings and show you the clean, edited result—what your document would look like if you accepted all the changes now (page 376).

You can use four different ways to show or hide the comments and changes that reviewers have in store for your precious manuscript:

- **Final Showing Markup.** This view shows the final document with all the comments and tracked changes showing. Word displays all inserted text in a different color and packs away deleted text into balloons or the Reviewing Pane.

  When you first open a document in Word, it's set to this view to prevent you from unintentionally distributing a document with comments and edits.

- **Final.** This view shows the edited version of the document with no markup showing. You see how your document looks if you accept all the changes. The Final option is great when you want to edit your document without the markup getting in the way.

- **Original Showing Markup.** This view shows the original document along with tracked changes. It's the reverse of Final Showing Markup, as deleted text appears in your document marked with strikethrough lines. It's as if the reviewer is only suggesting the change instead of making it for you.

- **Original.** This view shows your document before all the other cooks were invited to spoil the broth. If you reject all changes, your document will look like this again.

Showing and hiding types of changes

Reviewers make a lot of different types of changes when they mark up your document. They make insertions and deletions, they change formatting, and they insert comments. When you want to focus on a specific type of change, use the Show Markup menu (Review → Tracking → Show Markup or Alt+R, TM) to show and hide different types of changes (Figure 16-6). Checkmarks on the menu indicate which items are visible:

- **Comments (Alt+R, TM, C).** Shows or hides comments in balloons and the Reviewing Pane.

- **Ink (Alt+R, TM, K).** Shows or hides comments that were handwritten on tablets.

- **Insertions and Deletions (Alt+R, TM, I).** Shows or hides insertions and deletions.

- **Formatting (Alt+R, TM, F).** Shows or hides notes related to formatting changes.

- **Markup Highlight Area (Alt+R, TM, H).** Shows or hides the background color for the balloons.

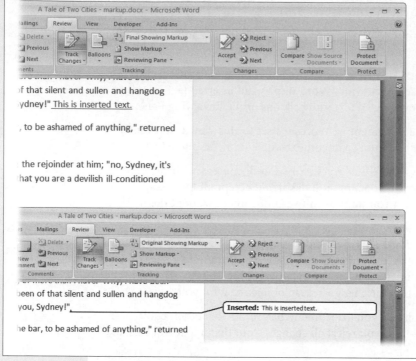

Figure 16-6:
Two views show reviewers' markup from different perspectives.

Top: Final Showing Markup shows edits in place in your text.

Bottom: Original Showing Markup shows your document how it originally appeared, with changes noted in the margins, as if they're suggestions, not a fait accompli.

Showing and hiding reviewers' markup

When several reviewers have worked in a document, you may want to filter out some of the opinions so you can concentrate on others. Use Review → Tracking → Show Markup → Reviewers to show or hide a reviewer's markup. To see edits from a reviewer, place a checkmark next to his name, as shown in Figure 16-7.

Tip: If you're ever editing a document on someone else's computer, you can change the user name so that your name appears in the markup. Choose Review → Tracking → Track Changes → Change User Name, and then enter your name and initials in the text boxes. Be kind—put their name back in place when you're done.

Customizing your markup view

Word gives you lots of ways to customize the appearance of your edits and markup, but the factory settings are hard to beat:

- Deleted text shows with a line through it, and insertions are underlined, so there's no doubt which is which.

- Moved text gets a double strikethrough where it was deleted, and a double underline where it was inserted.

- A vertical line appears in the margin next to any changes. Individual reviewers' edits and comments are color-coded.

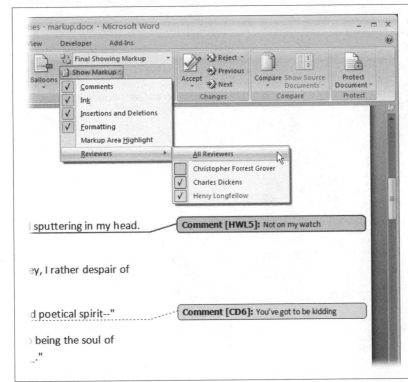

Figure 16-7:
Each comment or edit in your document bears the name or initials of the reviewer. Use the Show Markup menu to show or hide the edits and comments of different reviewers. Clicking the menu toggles a checkmark, indicating that the reviewer's edits are showing.

Word also keeps track of changes made to tables, including deleted and inserted cells. Formatting changes are listed in the Reviewing Pane and in the balloons, but they aren't marked in the text. If you're not happy with the factory settings, you can fiddle with them to your heart's content in the Track Changes Options box, as shown in Figure 16-8 (Alt+R, GO).

Printing Edits and Markup

Sometimes you need printed pages that show a document was edited—just ask any lawyer. The first step is to show the markup in your text, as described on page 373. You can choose either Final Showing Markup or Original Showing Markup from the Display for Review menu (Review → Tracking → Display for Review). Then, go to Office → Print to open the Print Dialog box, as shown in Figure 16-9. From the "Print what" drop-down menu at the lower-left corner, choose "Document showing markup," and then click OK. Your document prints slightly reduced in size to provide room to print the balloons in the right margin.

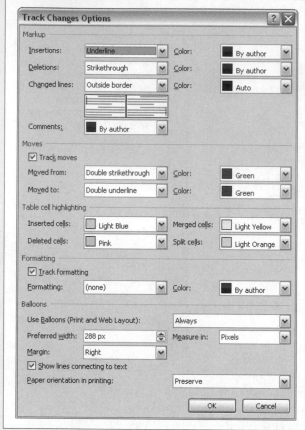

Figure 16-8:
The Track Changes Options box looks pretty intimidating at first, but most of these drop-down menus let you choose only colors for edits and comments. In the Markup section, if you leave the color and comment options set to "By author," each reviewer's comments and edits show in a different color.

Accepting and Rejecting Changes

You may or may not agree with some of the changes other people make in your meticulously crafted text. In any case, you should review each edit to make sure the document is getting better, not worse. Word makes reviewing changes a quick and easy process.

Here's the step-by-step procedure for reviewing the changes and edits in your document:

1. **Move the insertion point to the beginning of your document by pressing Ctrl+Home.**

   Most of the time, you want to start at the very beginning of your document to make sure you don't miss any of the changes.

2. **Choose a view, either Print Layout or Draft.**

   You see changes and comments in all of Word's five views except for Full Screen Reading. It's easiest to work in either Page Layout or Draft view.

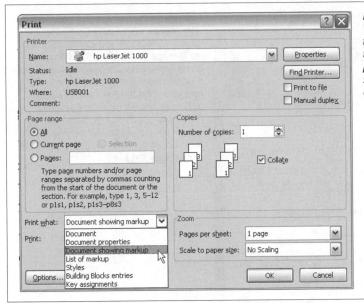

Figure 16-9:
The option to print edits and markup is tucked away in the lower-left corner of the Print dialog box. You can choose to print the document with the markup showing, or you can choose to print just a list of the edits and comments.

3. Go to Review → Tracking → Display for Review, and choose one of the options that displays markup.

   For example, choose Final Showing Markup to see the most recent changes, or choose Original Showing Markup to see all the changes.

4. Go to Review → Tracking → Show Markup → Reviewers to choose the reviewers whose changes you want to see.

   A menu appears, listing the reviewers who have commented on or edited your document. When you place checkmarks next to the names of reviewers, their edits show in your document.

5. Click the Review → Changes group on the ribbon, and then click the Next button. Then click the appropriate button to accept or reject the change (Figure 16-10).

   Repeat, reviewing all the edits until you reach the end of your document.

Removing All Comments and Tracked Changes

Before you send your quarterly sales report to the Board of Directors, you probably want to remove all the comments and corrections that you and your colleagues made while writing the document. *Hiding* tracked changes, as described on page 373, doesn't delete them from the document. Anyone with a copy of Word can see them by turning on one of the "Show markup" views. If you're passing a document to others, you probably want to make sure all the comments and tracked

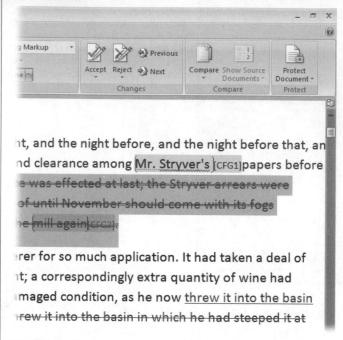

Figure 16-10:
After reviewers have edited and commented on your manuscript, you can quickly assess the damage they've done. The Changes group on the Review tab provides one-stop shopping when it comes to reviewing the reviewers. Click the Previous and Next buttons to jump through the edits and comments. Use the Accept button to make the edit permanent, or click the Reject button if you don't like the change. (See the box on page 380.)

changes are removed before you distribute it. In Word 2007, you can use a new feature called the Document Inspector (Figure 16-11) to find and remove all types of hidden details from your documents such as personal information, comments, and revisions.

You can use the Document Inspector (Office button → Prepare → Inspect Document or Alt+F, EI) to search and destroy the following items listed below. Turn on the checkboxes next to the type of items you want to find:

- **Comments, Revisions, Versions, and Annotations.** As explained earlier, when you collaborate with other people, your document collects comments and marked revisions.

- **Document Properties and Personal Information.** Some properties, known in geek-speak as metadata, store information such as the author's name (that's you), the subject, and the title. Documents can contain other personal information and details you may not want to share with others.

- **Headers, footers, and watermarks.** Headers, footers, and watermarks aren't quite as private and personal as some of the other items found by the Document Inspector, but in some cases they may be proprietary, and you may want to remove them before saving and distributing your document.

- **Hidden text.** One of Word's font formatting effects creates hidden text (Alt+H, FN). If you hid text in the first place (personal comments, notes to yourself, alternate text that you may reveal later), you probably don't want to share it with others.

- **Custom XML data.** Your office may use custom XML data that isn't visible when you simply look at the document. Use the Document Inspector to find this data. You then have the option to remove it.

To remove all the comments and edits from a document, follow these steps:

1. **Choose Office button → Prepare → Inspect Document to open the Document Inspector box.**

    The Document Inspector box appears, showing several types of items you can search for, including: comments, revisions, personal information, custom XML data, headers and footers, and hidden text.

2. **Make sure the checkbox next to Comments and Annotations is turned on, and then click Inspect.**

    If you're checking only for comments and edits, you may want to turn *off* most of the other checkboxes. For example, if you know your document has headers and footers, you may want Word to leave them alone.

3. **Review the results. Click the Remove All button (Figure 16-11) next to the items you want to delete from your document.**

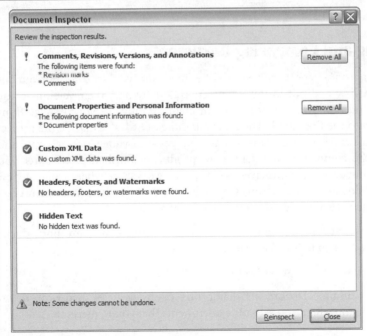

Figure 16-11:
After you run the Document Inspector, you see this box that shows details about the comments, revisions, and personal information contained in the document. Click the Remove All button next to items you wish to remove.

The Accept and Reject Buttons

When a reviewer or a collaborator makes tracked changes to your document, you're not stuck with them. You have a choice of whether to accept or reject every single one. The Review → Changes group gives you Accept and Reject buttons, which let you deal with edits either individually or in one fell swoop. Each of these buttons has two parts. Click the top part of a button to accept or reject the change and move to the next edit. Click the bottom part for some additional options:

- **Accept (or Reject) and Move to Next.** Use this option to accept or reject a change and automatically jump to the next edit. It's a great tool for quickly checking the changes that have been made. (Simply clicking the top half of the button does the same thing.)

- **Accept (or Reject) Change.** Use this option to accept or reject the change without moving to the next edit. This way, you can inspect the command's results before you move on.

- **Accept (or Reject) All Changes Shown.** This command is a little different from the following one, in that it accepts or rejects all the changes showing—which may or may not be all the changes in the document. Use this command when you want to accept or reject only changes from a single reviewer. Use Review → Tracking → Show Markup → Reviewers to choose which reviewer's changes appear. Then, when you click Accept or Reject All Changes Shown, the other reviewers' hidden changes remain intact.

- **Accept (or Reject) All Changes in Document.** Use this command to accept or reject all the changes in a document, from all reviewers, whether they're showing or not.

Combining and Comparing Documents

You're working on a report with your colleagues, and you send a draft out for everyone to review and put in their two cents. One by one, their versions come back to you, and now you have the chore of incorporating everyone's suggestions and changes into the final draft. The quickest and easiest way to tackle the project is to merge each reviewer's comments and changes into your working copy, and then review the comments and changes to produce a finished piece. After you combine two documents, Word gives you a special workspace where you can view the combined document with changes, as well as both the original and the revised document. Figure 16-12 shows the somewhat busy result.

To combine two documents and view the changes, first make sure both documents are closed. Then follow these steps:

1. **Choose Review → Compare → Combine.**

   When the Combine Documents dialog box opens, you see two drop-down menus at the top where you select the documents that you're merging.

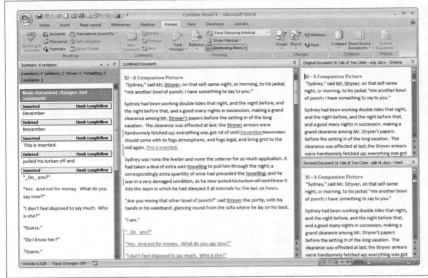

Figure 16-12:
After you combine two documents, Word shows you the changes as a marked up document in the center window. The original and the revised document are shown in small windows on the right. The revision panel on the left provides details about the differences between the two versions and other tracked changes.

2. **In the Original Document drop-down menu, select the name of your document (the one without the edits).**

   If its name is not on the list, click the little icon that looks like a folder. It opens a standard Windows file box where you can navigate to your document. In the "Label unmarked changes with" text box below the drop-down menu, type your name (or whatever name you want associated with the original document).

3. **In the Revised Document drop-down menu, select the name of your coworker's document (that is, the edited copy that you want to merge into the original).**

   If necessary, click the folder icon to navigate to the directory where the file resides. In the text box below the drop-down menu, type your reviewer's name.

4. **To see more options, at the bottom of the Combine Documents box, click the More button (Figure 16-13).**

   The Compare Documents box expands to provide additional options and settings, and the More button morphs into a Less button.

5. **If you wish, choose settings to fine-tune the way the comparisons are shown in your document.**

   At the top you see a group of checkboxes under the heading Comparison Settings. Click to put checkmarks next to the changes you want highlighted and marked in the combined document. For example, if you don't place a checkmark next to Moves, text that was moved in the reviewer's document is shown in its new location in the combined document, but you don't see double underscores and double strikethroughs to show the move. It's as if the move has already been accepted.

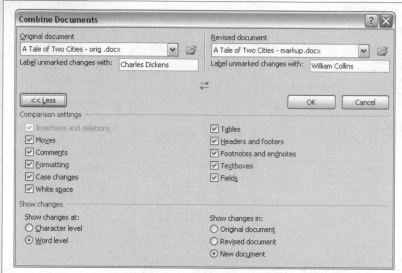

Figure 16-13:
Use the Combine Documents box to merge two versions of a document and to see the differences between the two. The Comparison settings determine which changes are shown in the combined document. Under Show Changes, you can choose to show the changes in the original document, in the revised document, or in a new document.

6. **In the Show Changes group, choose the level of changes you want to view and where you want the combined document to appear.**

   You have two choices to make about the *level* of changes: Word can show changes at the character level or at the word level. It's a little easier to work at the word level. For example, if you change the word "you" to "your," Word highlights the whole word as a change rather than just showing that you inserted an "r."

7. **Under the "Show changes in" heading, choose where you want to see the combined document.**

   In most cases, it's best to choose the last option, "New document"; that way, the combined document is an entirely new document, and you can save it under a new name. This choice leaves your original and the reviewer's documents untouched, so in case of an emergency, you can go back and take a look at them.

8. **Click OK to combine the documents.**

   After a little hemming and hawing, Word shows you something like Figure 16-12, which may be a little intimidating until you decode what's really going on. You see the familiar Reviewing Pane on the left side. In the middle is your Combined Document, sporting underlines and strikeouts to show the changes. The right side of Word's window shows two documents: The original is at the top, and the reviewer's document is on the bottom. All three documents are synchronized, so when you scroll through one document, the other two automatically scroll to the same spot.

9. On the Review tab, in the Compare group, use the Show Source menu (Figure 16-14) to adjust the view so that it works for you.

Viewing the Combined Document and the Original and Revised document at the same time gives you a good picture of how the reviewer changed the document. On the other hand, if you find yourself suffering from vertigo, you can adjust the view using the Show Source menu. If you don't need the Reviewing Pane, you can close that too. Just click the X button in the upper-right corner of the pane.

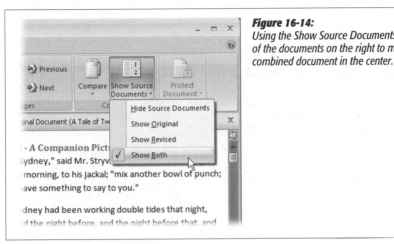

Figure 16-14:
Using the Show Source Documents menu, you can hide one or both of the documents on the right to make it easier to focus on the combined document in the center.

Comparing Two Documents

The procedure for comparing documents is almost identical to combining two documents, and the command is even on the same menu: Review → Compare → Compare. The Compare Documents box is almost identical to the Combine Documents box (Figure 16-13), since you're searching for the same types of changes in your document—moves, comments, insertions, and deletions.

What's different between the Combine and Compare commands are the results. When you combine two documents, the result shown in the center window incorporates the changes in *both* documents. When you compare two documents, the result is a marked up document that shows differences between the two, as shown in Figure 16-15. The result is what's known as a legal *blackline*, detailing all the changes in a clear, standardized way. This type of comparison is handy when two parties are negotiating the details of a contract.

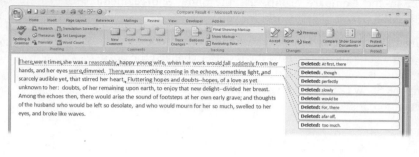

Figure 16-15:
When you compare two documents, Word shows you a marked up copy that points out the differences. The standard markup shows deleted text in balloons and inserted text underlined and in place. A vertical line in the margin makes it easy for you to zero in on changes.

Protecting Your Document from Changes

Sometimes you want to show your document to people, but you don't want them to mess it up with unwanted changes. Perhaps you want them to add comments but not to fiddle with your words. Or, maybe you need them to review and edit a certain section but to leave the rest of the document alone. Using Word's Protect Document options, you're in control (Figure 16-16). You can provide specific permissions to specific reviewers, and you can even password protect the Protect Document settings.

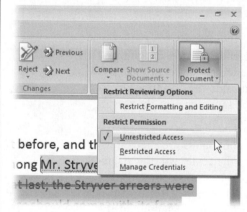

Figure 16-16:
Use the Protect Document menu on the Review tab to limit how other people can change your document. When you choose Restrict Formatting and Editing at the top of the menu, a panel opens on the right side of your document. Use the settings to select the type of edits you want to permit.

The first step to limiting the way others can change your document is to open the Restrict Formatting and Editing pane with the command Review → Protect → Protect Document or the keyboard shortcut Alt+R, PR, F. The pane that appears is divided into three parts, as shown in Figure 16-17.

You use the first two sections to describe how you want to restrict changes to the documents, and then you use the third section to start enforcing protection. (Despite the wording, you don't get a blue hat, a badge, and a nightstick.)

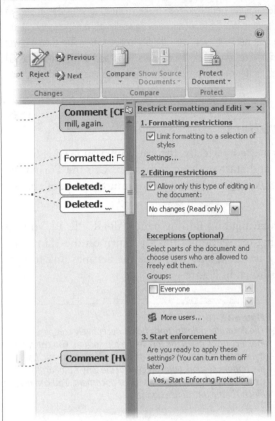

Figure 16-17:
The Restrict Formatting and Editing pane lets you limit the way others can change your document. Use the first two sections, "Formatting restrictions" and "Editing restrictions," to define how you want to protect the document, and then click Yes, Start Enforcing Protection.

Here's a brief description of each section:

- Use **Formatting restrictions** to limit the ways reviewers can make formatting changes to your document. You can also restrict them from choosing new themes and styles.

- Use the **Editing restrictions** to pick and choose from a variety of editing options such as comments and tracked changes. This section also gives you ways to limit reviewers to editing selected portions of the document.

- Use **Start enforcement** to apply the restrictions defined in the other two parts. You can use password protection to keep your reviewers from changing the Protection settings.

The following pages describe your restriction options in detail.

Tip: If you want to give different people different permissions to make changes to your document, you need to designate them as *users*—that is, people Word can identify electronically. It's not as complicated as it sounds: If you're working on a business network, you can identify colleagues using their network address, such as *editorial\chaz* or *chaz@allyear.com*. Click "More users," and add the name to the Add Users box. You can also group individuals under one name, to make it easier to give several people the same type of permission.

Applying Formatting Restrictions

If you've got your document formatted perfectly, the last thing you need is to have one of your reviewers jump in and start messing things up. Use the Formatting Restriction to keep them from making any changes or to limit the kind of changes they can make.

After you open the Restrict Formatting and Editing pane (Alt+R, PR, F), you can apply formatting restrictions using the section at the top. Turn on the "Limit formatting to a selection of styles" checkbox, and then click the Settings link to open the Formatting Restrictions box shown in Figure 16-18.

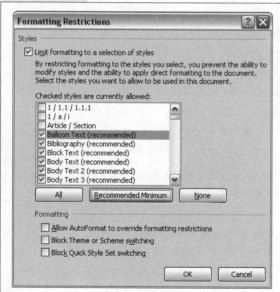

Figure 16-18:
The Formatting Restrictions box is deceptively complex-looking. Just start at the top. In the top section, you can limit the way reviewers can apply styles to your document. Using the bottom section, you can control the way AutoFormat works while reviewers change your document. You can also block Theme and Style changes.

Here are some of the ways you can protect your document:

- **Tracked Changes.** Turn on this setting, and Word tracks any changes that are made by reviewers.

- **Comments.** Permits reviewers to add comments to your document but prevents them from making changes to the text.

- **Filling in forms.** Use this option when you create forms for others to use. You want them to fill in the blanks without changing the boilerplate text. (You can find a whole chapter on creating forms starting on page 335.)

- **No changes (read only).** Prevents reviewers from making any changes. You also use this option when you want to limit editing to specific portions of your document. In other words, the entire document is read only except for specific areas that you designate.

Note: In previous versions of Word you could suggest, with a prompt, that people open your document in read-only mode, but you couldn't enforce it as you can with Word 2007.

Allowing Changes in Parts of a Document

One of the snazzier tricks you can do with Word 2007's document protection is to protect parts of the document but allow people to edit other parts. You can even choose who has access to different parts of the document. Here are the steps to set it up:

1. **Choose Review → Protect → Protect DocumentRestrict Formatting and Editing.**

    The Restrict Formatting and Editing pane opens on the right side of Word's window.

2. **Under Editing Restrictions (number 2), turn on the "Allow only this type of editing in the document" checkbox. Then, from the drop-down menu, choose "No changes (Read only)."**

    After you choose "No changes," some extra boxes appear below the heading Exceptions. You use these boxes, in step 4, to choose groups or the individual who can edit specific parts of your document.

3. **Select a portion of the document where you want to allow editing.**

    First, you choose the portion of your document that you want reviewers to edit. You can drag your mouse to make a selection, for example, or you can use any of the other standard selection techniques described on pages 40–43.

4. **Turn on checkboxes to choose the groups or the individual who can edit the selected text.**

    If you want anyone who gets the document to edit the selected text, click the checkbox next to Everyone in the Groups box. If you want to limit access to some of your reviewers, turn on the checkboxes for just those people in the Individuals box. You can add people to the lists by clicking the "More users" link beneath the boxes, as described in the tip on the previous page.

5. **Repeat steps 3 and 4 to select other portions of your text and give permission to edit to groups and individuals.**

   When you're done, click the "Yes, Start Enforcing Protection" button to turn on protection, and then save your document for distribution.

With the document protected, you distribute it to your reviewers. When the reviewers open the document, they'll be able to make changes only in the regions you've selected. Word provides two buttons on the Restrict Formatting and Editing pane to make it easy to jump back and forth between editable areas (Figure 16-19).

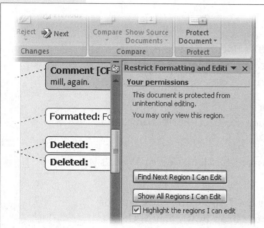

Figure 16-19:
Reviewers working on a restricted document can use these buttons to jump to regions where they're permitted to make changes.

Part Four:
Customizing Word with Macros and Other Tools

4

Customizing Your Workspace

If some aspect of Word's appearance or behavior bugs you, never fear—it's much easier to change than, say, the appearance and behavior of your teenager. In fact, Microsoft is known for providing multiple ways to do the same job, multiple paths to the same dialog box, and multiple ways to view your work. More often than not, you can tweak the aspects of Word that you find annoying.

On the other hand, Word's factory settings work quite well, and you can safely ignore this chapter. Think of this chapter as a laundry list of the settings in the Word Options dialog box, which you can tinker with at your leisure. Scan the headings and the bullet points, and zero in on the features that are important to you. For example, this chapter explains:

- How to put your favorite commands in the Quick Access toolbar in the upper-left corner of most Office programs.

- How to create your own keyboard shortcuts.

- How to change the appearance of menus, tools, and documents.

- How to fine-tune the way Word behaves when you're editing documents.

Customizing the Quick Access Toolbar

The Quick Access toolbar lives in the upper-left corner of all Office programs. Sometimes on the Internet you see it referred to as the QAT, because computer gnomes have a strong affinity for acronyms. New in Office 2007, the Quick Access toolbar is designed to put your most frequently used commands in one spot, no matter which Office program you're using. Best of all, you get to choose which commands you want in the toolbar. Microsoft made a guess at the commands that most people would want and put some choices on the Quick Access toolbar menu to get you started (Figure 17-1).

Figure 17-1:
Click the drop-down button (the tiny down arrow) next to the Quick Access toolbar to open a menu where you can add and remove the icons for common commands to the toolbar. If the command you want isn't on this menu, click More Commands to add it, as described in the steps below.

Adding Commands to the Quick Access Toolbar

Suppose you'd like to add a couple more commands to the Quick Access toolbar. Perhaps you miss the menu in earlier versions of Word that let you quickly switch between open Word documents. Also, say you're a big fan of AutoText, which lets you assign long strings of text to a couple keystrokes (page 24). You can add the AutoText button to the Quick Access toolbar, so you can quickly create and use AutoText entries.

In this tutorial, you see how to add these two commands—Switch Windows and AutoText—to the Quick Access toolbar:

1. **To the right of the Quick Access toolbar, click the tiny arrow button to open the drop-down menu.**

   By checking the commands on this menu, you can add their icons to the Quick Access toolbar. Trouble is, the commands shows that the two commands you want to add aren't even on the menu, so:

2. **Near the bottom of the menu, click More Commands.**

   The Word Options dialog box opens, showing the Customize options (Figure 17-2). The list box on the right shows the commands that are currently shown on the Quick Access toolbar. The box on the left contains commands that you can add to the Quick Access toolbar.

   The "Choose commands from" drop-down menu above the left box reads "Popular Commands." Evidently, the Switch Windows and AutoText commands aren't popular enough to make the cut, because they aren't on the list. Fortunately, you can use the "Choose commands from" menu to display more commands.

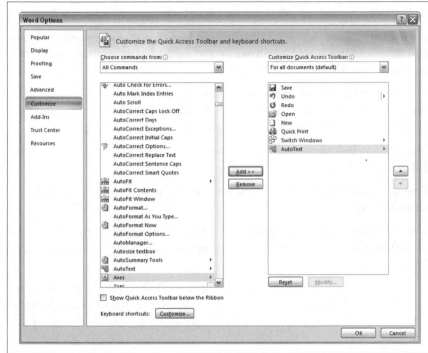

Figure 17-2:
The Customize Pane in the Word Options box lets you add commands to the Quick Access toolbar. Use the "Choose commands from" drop-down menu to show available commands in the box on the left. Double-click a command on the list to add it to the Quick Access toolbar, as shown by the list box on the right.

3. From the "Choose commands from" drop-down menu, choose All Commands.

    The All Commands list is pretty lengthy, giving you an idea of just how many different commands Word has to offer. That's why the "Choose commands from" menu also lets you narrow down your choices by choosing commands from specific ribbon tabs. (The major tabs are listed closer to the top, and the submenu tabs, like those for chart tools and table tools, are listed near the bottom.)

4. Scroll down the All Commands list to select AutoText, and then click the Add button between the two list boxes to add the command to the box with the Quick Access toolbar commands.

    You can use the Add button to add a command to the Quick Access toolbar list, or you can just double-click a command.

Tip: The first entry, <Separator>, isn't a command; it simply places a vertical line in the Quick Access toolbar to help organize the icons. If you have lots of commands in your Quick Access toolbar, you may want to group them between separator bars.

---

5. **Scroll down to select Switch Windows, and then double-click to add the command to the Quick Access toolbar box.**

   Press S to jump down to the commands that begin with S. That makes it a shorter scroll to get to the Switch Windows command. Now that you've filled the list with your desired commands, it's time to arrange them to your liking.

6. **In the Customize Quick Access toolbar list box, select a command, and then use the up and down arrow buttons on the right to arrange them in an order that works best for you.**

   To make it easier to find your new commands, you can add one or two separators described in the previous tip. For example, you may want to group the related Save, New document, and Open document commands together.

7. **Click OK to close the Word Options box and admire your newly configured Quick Access toolbar.**

   When the Word Options box closes, you see your new command on the Quick Access toolbar.

Both the AutoText and Switch Windows commands are more than simple command buttons—they're actually drop-down menus, which can save you a couple of ribbon clicks.

For even greater time savings, you can use keyboard shortcuts to run the commands on the Quick Access toolbar. The commands are numbered from the left to the right, so you can choose them with the Alt key and the number (Figure 17-3).

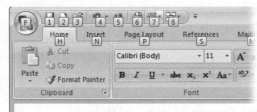

Figure 17-3:
Press the Alt key, and the commands on the Quick Access toolbar sprout little number badges. You can run a command with a keyboard shortcut by pressing Alt with the corresponding number. In this example, Alt+1 runs the Save File command, and Alt+8 runs Switch Windows.

Tip: If you've used earlier versions of Word, you may not like the location of the Quick Access toolbar. So Microsoft lets you move it. Click the Customize Quick Access toolbar button, and then choose "Show Below the Ribbon" (it's near the bottom of the menu). The Quick Access toolbar moves to its own row between the ribbon and your document. In this location, it looks similar to the toolbars in earlier versions of Word.

Creating Keyboard Shortcuts

Savvy Word workers know that taking time away from the keyboard to grasp the mouse wastes precious seconds every time. If efficiency is what you crave, take a cue from the power users and learn the keyboard shortcuts for the commands you use most often (you find them throughout this book). If there isn't a shortcut for one of your favorite commands, you can create one. Or, if you learned word processing on a different program, you may want to change Word's keyboard shortcuts to match the ones that your fingers are used to.

Here's how to customize Word's keyboard commands:

1. **Choose Office button → Word Options. When the Word Options box opens, click the Customize button at left.**

   The Customize window opens. (It's the same window used to organize commands on the Quick Access toolbar, as described in the preceding section, shown back in Figure 17-2.)

2. **At the bottom of the box, click the "Keyboard shortcuts:" Customize button.**

   The Customize Keyboard dialog box opens. As you can see in Figure 17-4, it offers several lists, text boxes, and buttons. At top are two list boxes called Categories and Commands.

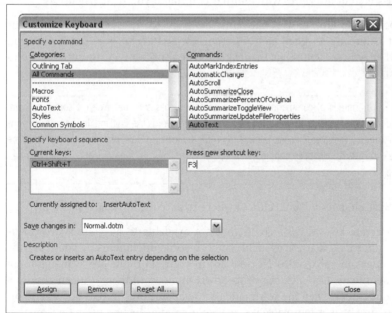

Figure 17-4:
Use the Customize Keyboard box to change the keyboard shortcuts for Word Commands. Choose a category from the box on the left, and then pick a command from the box on the right. Click within the "Press new short cut" box on the right, and then type the keystroke you want to use for your shortcut.

3. **On the left, choose from the Categories options to show commands in the Commands box on the right.**

   When you make a selection in the Categories box, it changes the commands shown in the Commands box. Say you use tables a lot and want to assign a shortcut to the command to insert a table into your document. Choose the Insert Tab in the Categories text box, and the Commands box on the right shows a list of commands related to inserting objects in your document.

4. **In the Commands list, select the command you want to create a shortcut for.**

   When you click, the command gets highlighted.

5. **Below the Commands, in the "Press new shortcut key" box, type the keys for your new shortcut.**

   When you press keys on your keyboard, Word records them in the "Current keys" box on the left. You can use the Alt, Shift, and Ctrl keys in combination with other keys. (Pressing them without another key doesn't record anything.)

Tip: If you make a mistake, hit Backspace to remove it. The Delete key doesn't work, since it's considered one of the keystrokes. So if you press the Delete key, "Del" appears in the text box.

---

6. **Below the "Current keys" box, examine the "Currently assigned to" text box to see if the shortcut interferes with another command you regularly use.**

   It's important to look at the "Currently assigned to" message to learn if your shortcut is already assigned to a different command. So, for example, if you type Ctrl+F, you see a message that explains the shortcut is currently assigned to EditFind.

Note: Word has hundreds of commands and each command has a name. When it comes to commands Word doesn't place spaces between the words so you get words like EditFind. In previous versions of Word this shorthand indicated the Find command on the Edit menu. Now, of course those menus are gone, and the commands have been shuffled around, but Word still uses the original command names. Happy hunting.

---

7. **In the "Save changes in" box, choose where to save the keyboard shortcut.**

   You can create keyboard shortcuts that are available to all your Word documents or shortcuts that are available only to some documents. If you leave the "Save changes in" box set to Normal.dotm, your shortcuts are available to all Word documents. Or, click the drop-down menu, and then you can choose a specific document. Then the commands are available only in that document, or, if the document is a template, it's available to any documents based on that template (see the box on page 136). You may want to limit the shortcut to, say, templates for your work documents if you share a PC with personal activities or other family members.

8. **To save the keyboard shortcut, click the Assign button.**

   Clicking the Assign button saves the keyboard shortcut so you can start using it.

9. **Click the Close button to close the Customize Keyboard box, and then click
   OK to close the Word Options box.**

   If later you decide the keystroke was a mistake, you can come back and change
   it by finding the command (as you did in step 3), and then clicking the Remove
   button at the bottom of the screen.

Tip: If you've really fouled things up, you can click the Reset All button to change all shortcuts back to
their original settings.

Personalizing Word Options

An often-overlooked step in customizing Word is *personalizing* your copy. If you
give Word your name and initials in the Word Options dialog box, the program
"knows" who's typing. Your name is most important when you're collaborating
with your colleagues using Word's reviewing features (Chapter 16). When you
review, edit, and add comments to a document, Word tags your markup with
either your name or your initials.

Word may have added your name and initials when you installed the program. To
check, go to Office button → Word Options. The dialog box opens, showing the
Popular settings (Figure 17-5). At bottom right, you see the text boxes for "User
name" and Initials. If you need to change this information—say you'd rather use a
pseudonym, a nickname, or your company name—type it here.

Changlng Word's Display

Word's ribbon and dialog boxes give you more tools than anyone can ever use.
The key to working efficiently is to arrange your screen so that it shows the tools
you want, where you want them, so don't hesitate to tweak Word's display. Most
of the settings to customize your display are found in the Word Options box,
which you can open with Office button → Word Options or with the keyboard
shortcut Alt+F, I. The other display-related options let you adjust the way Word
shows your document, hidden text, and formatting marks.

The Word Options box shows several buttons on the left side. Each time you click
a button, you see different settings on the right. Three buttons lead to display-
related settings: Popular, Display, and Advanced.

The Popular Display Settings

Open the Word Options box, and then click the Popular button. You see options
that change Word's display under the heading "Top options for working with
Word." See Figure 17-5.

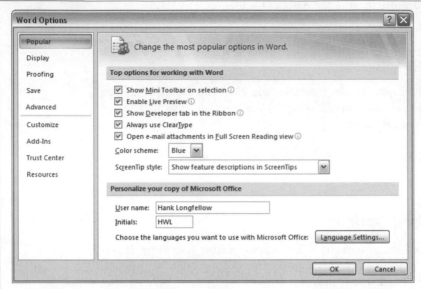

Figure 17-5:
Word stores your name and initials in the Word Options box. It's not some nefarious Microsoft scheme to spy on you. Word uses your name and initials to identify your edits and comments when you collaborate on documents.

- **Show Mini Toolbar on selection.** The Mini Toolbar pops up when you select text in your document, providing common editing and formatting options, as shown in Figure 17-6. When you install Word, this feature is turned on, but if you find the mini toolbar more nuisance than help, you can suppress its pop-up behavior by removing the checkmark from this option.

- **Enable Live Preview.** Live Preview is the feature that immediately changes your document to show you formatting options before you apply them. Live Preview can be too demanding for computers that are slow, underpowered, and graphically challenged. If that's the case, remove the checkmark from this box to turn off Live Preview.

- **Show Developer tab in the Ribbon.** If you're working with macros, forms, templates, or XML, turn on this box to display the Developer tab in the ribbon. The Developer tab provides special tools and buttons that help you create Word documents for others to use.

- **Always use ClearType.** ClearType is a technology developed by Microsoft that's designed to make text on a screen look better. It works for most computers and most monitors, but in some cases, ClearType can make text look worse. For example, if you have a flat panel monitor and you've changed the resolution to something other than the usual recommended (or *native*) resolution, ClearType may not work. In that case, remove the checkmark from this box.

- **Open e-mail attachments in Full Screen Reading view.** Word's Full Screen Reading view is ideal for documents that you want to read but not edit. Use this option to open all email attachments in Full Screen Reading view instead of Print Layout view, where you might inadvertently make changes to the document.

- **Color scheme.** You can change the colors of Word's frame, scroll bars, and other accessories with this drop-down menu. There isn't a way to create your own schemes, so you're limited to choosing from the ones that Microsoft provides. Just choose one whose colors you find soothing and that reduces eyestrain.

- **ScreenTip style.** Screen tips are the messages that pop up when you hold the mouse cursor over a command or a control. You have three choices. Choose "Show feature descriptions in ScreenTips" for a longer, more descriptive message. Choose "Don't show feature descriptions in ScreenTips" for a terse one- or two-word description. Or, choose "Don't show ScreenTips" to eliminate them entirely.

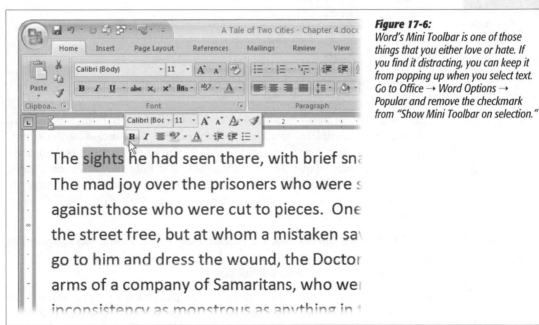

Figure 17-6:
Word's Mini Toolbar is one of those things that you either love or hate. If you find it distracting, you can keep it from popping up when you select text. Go to Office → Word Options → Popular and remove the checkmark from "Show Mini Toolbar on selection."

Changing Display Settings

Open the Word Options box (Alt+F, I), and then, on the left, click the Display button to see and change some of the common display settings (Figure 17-7). The display options are divvied up into two groups: "Page display options" and "Always show these formatting marks."

Page display options

The Page display options change the way Word shows your document in the program window. None of these options affect the way your printed document looks.

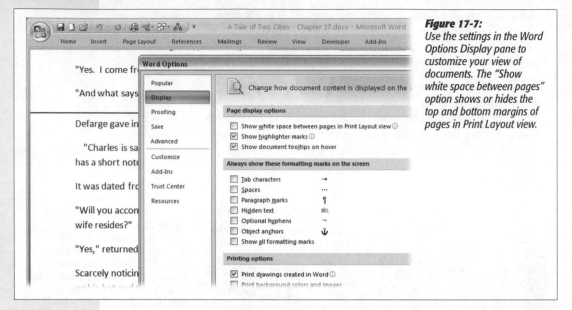

Figure 17-7:
Use the settings in the Word Options Display pane to customize your view of documents. The "Show white space between pages" option shows or hides the top and bottom margins of pages in Print Layout view.

- **Show white space between pages in Print Layout view.** In Print Layout view, Word shows a complete representation of a printed page including the empty, white space at the top and bottom margins. If you uncheck this box, you don't see the extra white space. You can also show and hide the white space while you're working in your document. When you hold the mouse cursor over the area between two pages, the cursor changes to two arrows on pages. Double-click to show or hide the white space.

- **Show highlighter marks.** The highlighter tool on the Home tab lets you call attention to specific parts of text. Word's factory setting is to show highlighted text. If that annoys you, uncheck this box.

- **Show document tooltips on hover.** Document tool tips are things like reviewer's comments and hyperlink addresses that are hidden within your document's text. When you hold your mouse cursor over an item for a couple of seconds, a document tool tip pops up, showing the additional information. Use this option to turn tool tips on or off.

Always show these formatting marks on the screen

Invisible characters lurk within your word documents—tab characters, paragraph marks, and the other formatting marks that are usually hidden in your text. In fact, sometimes when you're wrestling with formatting issues, it helps to bring these guys out of the shadows. You can show and hide most of these marks using the command Home → Paragraph → Show/Hide ¶ or the keyboard shortcut Alt+H, 8. (Figure 17-8 shows how a document looks with all the formatting marks showing.)

If you want a certain mark to *always* show when you create new documents—say you like knowing where the paragraph breaks are—go to Office → Word Options and use the checkboxes under "Always show these formatting marks on the screen" to show and hide:

- Tab characters

- Spaces

- Paragraph marks

- Hidden text

- Optional hyphens

- Object anchors

- Show all formatting marks

Advanced Display Options

Click the Advanced button in the Word Options box to see some of the lesser-used and esoteric settings that let you turn on and off major aspects of the program's appearance. Scroll down to the middle of the box, and you see two groups of settings that affect the look of your documents and the Word window: "Show document content" and "Display."

Show document content

The options under "Show document content" affect the way your document looks when you're working with it. Items with checkmarks in the boxes are visible in your document. Click a checkbox to toggle an option on or off.

- **Show background colors and images in Print Layout view.** Background colors are more for Web pages than printed pages. They can be distracting when you're typing and editing. Turning off this box hides both background colors and background images used as watermarks.

- **Show text wrapped within the document window.** Turn on this box if you want the lines of your text to automatically wrap to fit in the document window. So, if you make your window narrower, Word redistributes the words in the paragraph so that you can see all the words. This setting affects the Draft, Outline, and Web Layout views but doesn't change the Print Layout view. In Print Layout view, if you make Word's window narrower than the lines of text, you hide some of the words.

- **Show picture placeholders.** If you're working on a slow computer with a document that has a lot of pictures, Word can slow down to a crawl. Turn on this box, and all those pictures are replaced with placeholders, as shown in Figure 17-8. Your document scrolls faster, and everything else in Word should be snappier too.

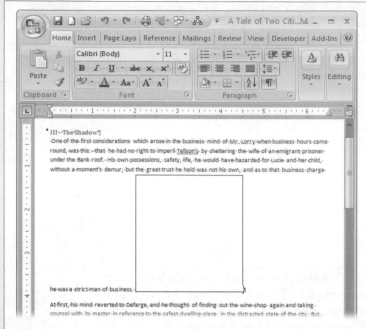

- **Show drawing and text boxes on screen.** Drawings and text boxes show in the Print Layout view unless you turn them off by removing the check from this box.

- **Show text animation.** Animated text is no longer a font option in Word 2007. But Word still shows shimmering letters and marching ant borders in documents created in earlier versions. Mercifully, the powers-that-be in Redmond let you turn off this annoying feature.

- **Show bookmarks.** You use bookmarks to mark locations in your manuscript. Once they're in place, you can jump to them using the Go To command (F5) and refer to the bookmarks by name in macros and Visual Basic for Applications (VBA) programs (page 443). This setting toggles the visibility of bookmarks on the screen. With "Show bookmarks" turned on, they show as gray square brackets surrounding the selected text.

- **Show Smart Tags.** Smart Tags automatically create links to resources on the Internet when you type specific words into your document (see the box on page 155). If you find this quick reference feature annoying, remove the check from this box.

- **Show text boundaries.** Places dotted lines around the text in your document (including text that appears in the headers and footers) that help you line up images and other page elements. (Text boundaries don't appear in printed copies.)

- **Show crop marks.** Crop marks are guides for trimming paper when a document is printed on a piece of paper that's larger than the designated page size (Alt+P, SZ).

- **Show field codes instead of their values.** Field codes usually perform some sort of calculation, and then place the result in the text. For example, a PageNum field code determines the page number, and then places that number in the text. If you want to see the actual field code and not the resulting value, turn on this box. Use the Field shading drop-down menu to highlight fields in your document. The menu provides three options: Never, Always, and "When selected."

- **Use draft font in Draft and Outline views.** The Draft and Outline views don't show your document as it looks on the printed page. You can specify a particular font and size for these two views to make your document more readable on the screen.

- **Font Substitution (button).** When someone gives you a document that uses fonts you don't have on your computer, Word automatically chooses similar fonts to display instead. If you're not happy with Word's choice, use this button to specify substitute fonts.

Display options

To see the advanced display options, go to Office → Word Options → Advanced, and scroll down to about the middle of the window. You see the settings listed below. Click to toggle the checkboxes—a checkmark means an item is visible in Word's display.

- **Show this number of Recent Documents.** When you click the Office button, Word shows the documents you've recently opened and saved. Use this box to set the number of documents listed. The number can be as high as 50, but something in the 10 to 20 range is usually sufficient.

- **Show measurements in units of.** Choose the units you'd like to see in your Word rulers and dialog boxes. You have a choice of inches, centimeters, millimeters, points, and picas.

- **Style area pane width in Draft and Outline views.** A pane listing paragraph styles appears to the left of your text in the Draft and Outline view, as shown in Figure 17-9. Enter a number in this box to set the width of the pane. For example, if you're using inches, enter .5 to devote a half inch to the Style pane. If you don't want to show a Style pane, just set the number to zero.

- **Show pixels for HTML features.** Turn on this box to use pixels as the unit of measure for dialog boxes related to HTML and web pages. For Web page designers, the pixel (short for picture element) is the basic unit of measure. For example, a Web page may be set to 750 pixels wide by 540 pixels tall, a good fit for many computer screens.

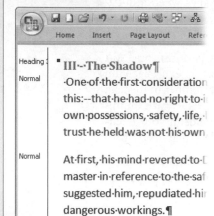

Figure 17-9:
The Style pane shows to the left of your text in Draft and Outline view. But you can decide just how much it shows by adjusting the width. Set the width to zero in Word Options, and it won't show at all. Go to Office button → Word Options → Advanced → Display to find the "Style area pane width" setting.

- **Show all windows in Taskbar.** The Windows taskbar at the bottom of the screen can group Word documents together under one icon, or it can show each Word document as a separate icon. Turn on the checkbox to see separate icons for each document.

Note: Your Windows options also affect how your Word windows appear in the taskbar. To change the Windows settings, click the taskbar, and then choose Properties from the pop-up menu to adjust the taskbar settings.

- **Show shortcut keys in ScreenTips.** You see screen tips when your mouse cursor pauses over a button for a few seconds. This handy setting shows the shortcut keys for the command in the screen tip. It's a good way to learn those shortcuts.

- **Show horizontal scroll bar.** Displays the horizontal scroll bar automatically when you open a new document.

- **Show vertical scroll bar.** Shows the vertical scroll bar when you open a new document.

- **Show vertical ruler in Print Layout view.** Automatically shows the vertical scroll bar in Print Layout view.

- **Optimize character positioning for layout rather than readability.** This option shows character positioning accurately, as it will appear when you print the document. Use this only when it's critical for layout purposes because it can distort the spacing between characters and make the document harder to read onscreen.

Customizing the Save Documents Settings

The Word Options box has several options that affect the way Word saves your documents. For example, suppose you want to always save your document in the older Word file format .doc. Make the change here, and you won't have to change Word's setting every time you save a document. You don't have many options, but some of them are on the computer-geek technical edge of things. To see the Save settings option, go to Office button → Word Options → Save button. You see three groups of settings:

- **Save documents** lets you change the file format and the location in which Word saves your documents.

- **Offline editing options for document management server files** adjusts Share-Point settings if you're working with colleagues on a SharePoint site.

Note: For more details on SharePoint, look to *Essential SharePoint* and *SharePoint Office Pocket Guide*, both by Jeff Webb.

- **Preserve fidelity when sharing this document** gives you a way to make sure your document looks the same on other people's computers as it does on yours. Sounds geekier than it really is.

Here's a brief rundown of the settings for each of the three groups.

Save Document Options

Use the first setting "Save files in this format" to choose the file format you want to use most of the time. You can always override this option when you do a Save As (Office button → Save As). The available file formats include:

- **.docx.** New format for most Word documents.

- **.docm.** New format for Word documents containing macros. (Microsoft is making an effort to increase computer security by reining in Office macros; see page 429.)

- **.dotx,** New format for Word templates.

- **.dotm.** New format for templates containing macros.

- **.doc.** Format for all files created in earlier versions of Word, including Word 6.0, Word 95, and Word 97-2003.

- **.dot.** Format for legacy Word templates.

- **.pdf.** Adobe Reader (also known as Acrobat) files. (Available as an add-in; see the box on page 171.)

- **.xps.** XML Paper specification (Microsoft's answer to PDF). (Available as an add-in.)

- **.mht, .mhtml.** Single file Web page—in other words, all the files that make up a Web page contained in one single file.

- **.htm. .html.** Standard Web page format. This format is like the Web pages you see on the Internet; if the page includes photos or other files, links on the page point to those external files.

- **.rtf.** Rich Text Format, a file format used to exchange files with other word processors and other types of computers like Macs and Linux computers.

- **.txt.** A text file format that does not include extensive formatting.

- **.xml.** eXtensible Markup Language, a standard language for describing many different types of data.

- **.wps.** The old Microsoft Works format.

AutoRecover options

Word can automatically save your document at specific intervals. Just turn on the checkbox, and then type a number of minutes in the "Save AutoRecover information every…minutes" box.

In the "AutoRecover file location" box, type the location where you want to store the temporary AutoRecover files. Word's factory setting (*C:\Documents and Settings\[user name]\Application Data\Microsoft\Word*) should work fine for most computer setups. If you need to select a new location, click the Browse button, and then navigate to a new folder.

Default file location

When you have a new document and click that Save button, how does Word choose a folder to save it in? It uses the folder listed in the "Default file location" box. You can save a lot of time and folder navigation gymnastics by setting this option to match the way you work. Microsoft's factory setting for this is your My Documents folder. That's not a bad choice, but if you have a folder where you keep most of your Word documents, click Browse, and then select that folder. If all your work for the next three months is going to go into a single project folder, you may want to change to that folder for the time being.

Offline Editing Options

If you collaborate with others using a SharePoint network site, these settings may interest you. If you're not a SharePoint collaborator, you can skip this section. SharePoint is Microsoft's network technology developed to help people share the same files and workspace. When you use a shared file, you check it out like you'd check a book out of the library. Others can't make changes to the file you've checked out. When you check it back in, you may add comments to explain how you've changed the file.

Word has to store temporary files while you're working on a document you've checked out. The settings in this group determine where Word saves the file while you're working on it. The factory setting for "Save checked out documents to" is "The server drafts location on this computer." That should work fine for most computer and network setups. If you want to change the location, click "The Web server" button, and then click Browse to designate a new location.

Embedded Font Options

The wonderfully named "Preserve fidelity when sharing this document" option is easier to figure out than it sounds. Here's the scoop: When you create a document and format the text, you're using fonts stored on your computer. Those fonts create the shapes of the letters and, as you know, those shapes vary a lot. For example, just compare the Arial and Algerian fonts (Figure 17-10). If you share the file with someone who doesn't *have* the Algerian font installed, Word just makes a best guess and chooses some other font to display the text. That's not always a good thing: If you're creating an ad or a poster for a concert, the look of the type is critical to the feeling of the piece.

Figure 17-10:
Word gives you lots of fonts to choose from, but when you share a document, how can you be sure other people have the same fonts to view your masterpiece? The solution is to embed the fonts you used into the document file.

To make sure that everyone sees your document with the right fonts, Word lets you *embed*—that is, store—the fonts in the document file. Yes, this makes the file bigger, but it's an invaluable option when you really need it. Go to Office button → Word Options → Save button. The bottom section of this window is where you make choices for embedded fonts. First, use the drop-down menu to choose whether you're changing the setting for a single document or for All New Documents.

Turn on the "Embed fonts in the file" checkbox, and two more options come to life. If you want to reduce the file size, turn on both of them:

• **Embed only the characters used in the document (best for reducing file size).** This option is fine if the person you're sharing the file with is just going to read it and not make changes. (Leave it turned off if the person is going to edit the document.)

- **Do not embed common system fonts.** Some fonts, such as Arial or Times New Roman, are already installed on just about every Windows computer in the world. Turning on this box reduces file size by *not* embedding fonts other people are almost certain to have.

Changing Editing Options

The Word Options box has lots of little checkboxes that control editing options you may never have even considered. For example, you can tell Word which style would prevail when you cut text from one place in your document that's formatted as Heading 2, and then you paste it into a paragraph that's formatted as Normal. If you have preferences about such things, go to Office → button Word Options → Advanced. Two groups of settings deal with the intricacies of editing: "Editing options" and "Cut, copy, and paste."

Editing Options

- **Typing replaces selected text.** The factory setting works this way: If you select text and then start typing, the selected text disappears, leaving only the new characters. If you'd like to keep that selected text, turn off this checkbox.

- **When selecting, automatically select an entire word.** If you're handy with a mouse, you may want Word to select exactly where you click and release. If you always want Word to select entire words even if you snag only part of a word in your selection, leave this box turned on.

- **Allow text to be dragged and dropped.** This favorite editor's tool lets you select text, and then drag it to a new location, saving you lots of cutting and pasting. If you're worried you may accidentally drag text someplace else, go ahead and turn it off.

- **Use CTRL + Click to follow hyperlink.** When you have links to other locations in your document or to the Internet, you can jump to those locations by pressing Ctrl+click to make the move. Turn this option off, and the links in your document work like Web page hyperlinks, where a single click follows a link.

- **Automatically create drawing canvas when inserting AutoShapes.** When you insert a single picture or graphic into a document, you don't need a drawing canvas (page 276). But if you're working with several graphics and you want to carefully arrange their relationship with each other, it's best to use a drawing canvas that holds all the graphic elements. Turning on this setting means Word always creates a drawing canvas when you insert an AutoShape into a document.

- **Use smart paragraph selection.** The paragraph mark at the end of paragraphs "holds" detailed formatting information. In other words, when you select a paragraph with the paragraph mark included, you select all the paragraph's formatting with it. If you select just the paragraph's text without the paragraph mark, you lose all the formatting. If you turn on this option, then Word always includes the paragraph mark when you select an entire paragraph.

- **Use smart cursoring.** *Smart cursoring* is an aid that moves the insertion point to the page you are viewing if you use the arrow keys. For example, if you use scroll bars to move away from the page with the insertion point, and then use one of the arrow keys, the insertion point automatically moves to the page that you're viewing.

- **Use the Insert key to control overtype mode.** In overtype mode, if you insert the cursor in the middle of a paragraph and start typing characters to the right of the insertion point, then the original characters begin to disappear as you type over them. In insert mode, these same characters are just pushed along in front of the insertion point. In previous versions of Word, the Insert key served as a toggle between insert and overtype modes—much to the bafflement of folks who hit Insert by accident and saw their precious words disappear. In Word 2007, the Insert key doesn't act as a toggle between overtype and insert mode unless you turn on this box.

- **Prompt to update style.** Turn on this box if you want Word to give you the option to change the underlying style when you make formatting changes. When you change text that has a style applied to it, Word asks if you want to change the style to match—in other words, if you want Word to change *all* the text that uses the style.

- **Use Normal style for bulleted or numbered lists.** Word usually uses the Paragraph List style for bulleted and numbered lists. Turn on this option if you prefer to use the Normal style.

- **Keep track of formatting.** Consistent formatting is actually a form of communication to your readers, sending messages about the importance of text and grouping similar items by similar appearance. Word can keep track of formatting styles as you create and apply them, which makes it easier to apply the same formatting to other parts of your document using Word's styles.

Tip: To see the styles you create through formatting, you need to make some changes in the Style Pane Options box (Figure 17-11). When you use this option, you can also use the Select Text with Similar Formatting command that shows on the pop-up menu when you right-click selected text.

- **Mark formatting inconsistencies.** This option goes hand-in-hand with the previous item, "Keep track of formatting." Select this option, and Word puts a wavy blue line under text that seems to be inconsistently formatted.

- **Enable click and type.** This option lets you click anywhere on the page and begin typing. Word automatically adds the necessary paragraph marks, indents, and any formatting to place text in the location you clicked. This feature works in Print Layout and Web Layout views. The drop-down menu below this option lets you choose the paragraph style that's applied when you click and type. (Of course, you can always change the paragraph style after you've typed your text.)

Figure 17-11:
Use the Style Pane Options box to adjust the appearance of the Styles Pane and the Style box. To see styles that you create on the fly, set the "Select styles to show" menu to "In current document," and then turn on the three boxes under "Select formatting to show as styles."

Cut, Copy, and Paste Options

As you can guess, the cut, copy, and paste settings control Word's behavior when you use those most common editing commands. That's right—you have control over what Ctrl+V does. To change these settings, go to Office button → Word Options → Advanced button. The second group of settings affects cut, copy, and paste options (Figure 17-12).

The first four settings tell Word how to settle formatting disputes. For example, when you cut text from a document, it already has some formatting. When you paste it into a new spot in a Word document, that location also has font and paragraph formatting. Which prevails—the source formatting or the destination formatting? You may think the whole question makes a mountain out of a molehill, because if you don't like the formatting once you paste the text, it's certainly easy enough to change it. However, computers are finicky machines, and they need rules to decide every little thing. Here's your chance to write the rules. Word divides the issue into four different pasting possibilities:

Pasting within the same document

When you paste text to a new location in the same document, Word leaves the text formatting the way it was to begin with. In Word lingo, that option is Keep Source Formatting. You can change this setting and tell Word to Match Destination Formatting. In that case, most of the text takes on the formatting of the destination. The exceptions are words that are formatted for emphasis with bold or italics, under the assumption that you still want to emphasize these words. The third and final option tells Word to Keep Text Only, which means Word discards everything that isn't text, such as pictures and tables. Pictures and other graphics are left out. The text in tables is converted to paragraphs. The text then takes on the formatting of the destination.

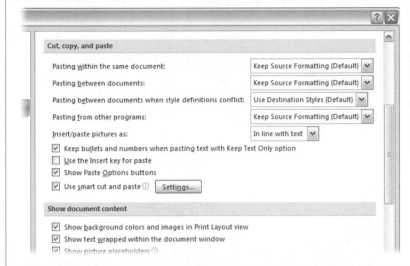

Figure 17-12:
When Word pastes text into a new location, which formatting is used—the source's formatting or the formatting at the destination? Word's standard settings, shown here, work fine for most situations, but you're free to change them to fit your own work style.

Pasting between documents

When you paste text between two different Word documents, you have the same options as within the same document: Keep Source Formatting, Match Destination Formatting, and Keep Text Only. Word needs to resolve an extra detail when you paste between documents that may not have the same style definitions: If you leave this option set to the factory setting (Keep Source Formatting), Word adds style definitions to the destination document if they aren't already there. (The other two options use the formatting of the destination document, so it's not an issue.)

Pasting between documents with style definition conflicts

Ah, but what about two documents that have a Heading 2 style but one is 24-point type and the other is 28-point type? In this case, the factory setting is to Use Destination Style, which makes sense. Most of the time, you probably want the pasted text to conform to the styles in the destination document. However, you can opt to Keep Source Formatting or Keep Text Only instead.

If you choose Match Destination Formatting in this case, Word disregards the *style* definitions in both the original and the destination documents and uses whatever formatting is in effect at the spot where you paste. In most cases, the result is ever-so-slightly different from the default option.

Pasting from other programs

When you paste in text from PowerPoint, Excel, or other programs, you face similar issues, and you get similar options too. The factory setting for this situation is Keep Source Formatting, so your text basically keeps the appearance it had in the original program. You can change this to Match Destination Formatting or Keep Text Only, which behave as described earlier.

Changing Your Security Settings

Microsoft has a bad reputation when it comes to computer security. Granted, one of Word's advantages is that the program is an open book for programmers who want to create add-ins and macros (mini-programs that run within Word). These tools make Word even more useful for the rest of us. Unfortunately, it's also easy for programmer thugs to use the same tools to foul up people's computers, steal information, and generally cause havoc. With Office 2007, Microsoft has taken steps to make your computer more secure. This chapter shows you how to use the features that make the world safer for you and your Word documents.

Since Microsoft takes a multifaceted approach to computer security, so does this chapter. First, you learn how to create your own digital signature to prove your authorship of a document. Even more important, you learn how to check out the digital signatures attached to documents provided by others. Then, a tour of Microsoft's Trust Center explains how keeping a list of Trusted Publishers and Trusted Locations protects you from malicious macros and add-ins. To wrap it all up, you get tips on how to protect your privacy when you share your documents with others.

Tip: You don't have to be a programmer—good or evil—to write macros. You can create macros in Word without writing a single line of code. The next chapter explains how.

Using Digital Signatures

Just like a handwritten signature, a digital signature verifies the source of a document. For example, your signature on a check proves that the check came from you. If someone forges your signature on a check, then that check is void. For contracts and documents that need extra security, you go to a notary. You show proof of your identity, and the notary verifies that you signed the document in the notary's presence. The goal of digital signatures is to provide that kind of security to the documents and programs that you send and receive by email.

Digital signatures give security to both parties—the person who creates and signs a document, and the person who receives it. Of course, digital signatures aren't handwritten—like everything else in the digital world, they're made up of 1s and 0s. However, the cunning, clever software that creates digital signatures ensures that they're unique. As a result, you can use digital signatures to prove that:

- A document came from a particular source or individual.

- A document hasn't been tampered with since it was signed.

- A document was read and agreed upon by the parties that signed it.

You have two ways to sign documents with a digital signature. You can create your own digital ID, which is the digital equivalent of signing a letter or a check without any witnesses. Or, you can purchase a digital ID from a third party that verifies your identity—sort of like signing in front of a notary.

In Word 2007, Microsoft makes it easy for you to sign a document and for someone to verify your signature. The person who receives your document can be confident that it hasn't changed since you applied your signature. That's important for documents like sales contracts—you sure don't want someone changing the agreed upon price.

Creating Your Own Digital Signature

Before you can apply a digital signature to a document, you need to create it. You can create a *self-signed* digital signature—that is, one you make yourself—right in Word.

Tip: If you want to create a third-party signature, you need to contract with a company known as a Certificate Authority. Details on third-party signatures begin on page 419.

Here's how to create your first digital signature:

1. **With your document open in Word, go to Office button → Prepare → Add a Digital Signature, as shown in Figure 18-1.**

   If you don't already have a digital ID, the first time you try to add a digital signature to a document, you see an alert box explaining that Microsoft can't warrant a digital signature's enforceability. Bottom line: The legality of digital signatures hasn't been proven, and may vary from district to district. The box shows two options—"Signature Services from the Office Marketplace" and OK. Click OK to open the "Get a Digital ID" box. From this box, you can either "Get a digital ID from a Microsoft partner" or "Create your own digital ID." (You won't see this box if you've already created a digital signature.)

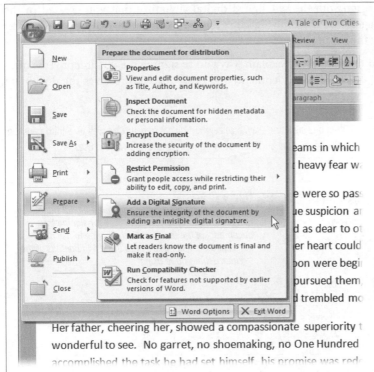

Figure 18-1:
Use the Prepare menu under the Office button to add a digital signature to your document. If you haven't created a digital signature, Word takes you through the steps to create one.

2. Choose "Create your own digital ID." When the Create a Digital ID box opens, type the information you want to appear as part of your digital signature, and then click Create.

   You *must* enter a name, but the rest of the details (email address, organization, and location) are optional. When you click Create, Word stores your identity on your computer.

The ID you've just created will be available the next time you sign a document using the Office button → Prepare → Add a Digital Signature command, as described next.

Signing a Document with Your Digital Signature

After you've created a digital signature, it's simple to apply it to a document. Make sure you're finished editing the document, though. Once the digital signature is in place, you can't make any more changes.

1. With your document open in Word, go to Office button → Prepare → Add a Digital Signature.

   An alert box appears that provides an explanation of digital signatures. It also gives you a chance to go to the Office Marketplace to purchase a third-party signature. (Once you get tired of Microsoft's sales pitch, you can click the "Don't show this message again" checkbox to bypass this alert in the future.)

2. **Click OK to go with the self-signed digital signature that you created in the steps on page 414. When the Sign box appears (Figure 18-2), type your reason for signing the document.**

Now's your opportunity to explain why you're signing the document. This message becomes part of the document, and everyone who receives the document will see it.

Tip: If you have more than one signature—say, a self-signed digital signature as well as a third-party signature—you can click the Change button, and then choose the signature you want to use.

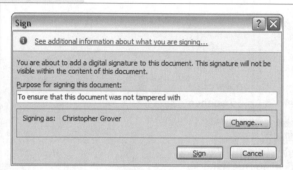

Figure 18-2:
The Sign box appears when you add a digital signature to a document. Type your "Purpose for signing this document" in the text box. Click Change to use a different digital signature or to inspect the details of the signature that you're using.

3. **Click the Sign button to complete the signature. When an alert box pops up saying that you were successful in signing the document, click OK.**

As the alert box also says, the signature will be invalid if the document is changed. And, in fact, Word prevents you from making any changes; most ribbon commands are grayed out, and any attempts to edit text produce an error message. Also, if some nefarious person tries to hack the file in a program other than Word, the Digital Signature system detects the alteration.

After you click OK, Word returns you to your document, but, again, you won't be able to make any edits. The only way to make changes in Word is to remove the signature.

Adding a Microsoft Office Signature Line

Digital signatures like the one described in the previous section are *hidden*. In other words, the signature doesn't show up anywhere on the printed page. In Word, you see a message banner just below the ribbon announcing the presence of signatures. To see them, click the View Signatures button in this banner, or choose Office button → Prepare → View Signatures (Alt+F, EW), to open the Signatures pane. You can apply another type of signature to a document that's a hybrid of a digital and a handwritten signature: the Microsoft Office Signature line (Figure 18-3). It's a good option for contracts or other documents that need a visible signature of one or more people. With a digital signature line, you can send signed contracts back and forth via email—no postage required.

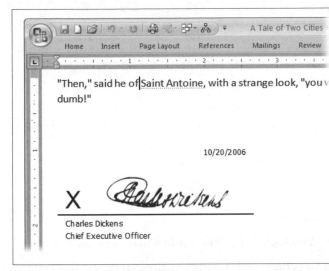

Figure 18-3:
For documents that need to be visibly signed, use the Microsoft Office Signature line. In addition to having all the advantages of a digital signature, the signature line shows up in a printed document.

Suppose you're creating a lease agreement. You write up the contract, add two signature lines, and then sign one of them before emailing it to your business colleague. Here are the steps for this two-party document in detail.

1. **Choose Insert → Text → Signature Line to open the Signature Setup box (Figure 18-4).**

   You may see the alert box offering third-party signature services. If so, click OK to close the alert box and open the Signature Setup box.

2. **In the Signature Setup box, type in the details that are to be included with the signature, and then click OK to close the box.**

   The Signature Setup box provides text boxes where you can enter name, title, email address, and instructions. You see two checkboxes: Turning on the "Allow the signer to add comments in the Sign dialog" box gives people signing the contract a way to communicate when they sign. It's a good idea to turn on the "Show sign date in the signature line" box so that the date the document was signed is recorded along with the signature.

3. **Back in your document, press Tab, and then repeat steps 1 and 2 to insert a second signature line.**

   Specifically, open the Signature Setup box (Insert → Text → Signature Line). Type the details for the second person who will sign the document, and then click OK to close the box.

   At this point, you have a document with two signature lines. No signatures have been attached, so you can still make changes to the document.

Figure 18-4:
Use the Signature Setup box to attach additional information to the signature line. For example, you can include an email address for contact purposes or instructions for other people who are signing the document.

4. **To open the Sign box, double-click the signature line that *you* want to sign.**

   You may see the alert box offering third-party signature services at this point. If so, click OK to close the alert box and open the Signature Setup box. (If you never want to see this sales pitch again, turn on the "Don't show this message again" checkbox.)

5. **In the Sign box, type your signature or choose an image to represent your signature. If the "Allow the signer to add comments in the Sign dialog" option (mentioned in step 2) was turned on, you see a text box labeled "Purpose for signing this document." If you wish, type a message in the box.**

   The Sign box shows a big X where your signature is to appear. You can type your name, and it will appear next to the X in the document. But it's oh so much cooler to have a graphic representation of your signature. If you happen to be using a tablet PC with Windows XP Tablet PC Edition, you can sign on the line with your stylus; otherwise, you need a picture file (such as a JPG or a GIF file) of your signature stored on your computer.

   To use a picture for your signature, click the "Select Image" link next to the box to choose a graphic signature. A standard Windows file box opens to let you select your signature's image file.

Tip: If you've got a graphic tablet on your computer, it's a snap to make a JPG of GIF of your signature. Otherwise, the best way to get a graphic image of your signature is to write it on a piece of paper and use a scanner to bring it onto your computer. You can also try taking a photo of your signature, but it won't be quite as clear as a scanned image.

---

6. **Click OK to close the Sign box and complete the signature.**

   After the box closes, you see the signature on the line next to the X. The document also has a digital signature, and it's locked to prevent any more changes (Figure 18-5).

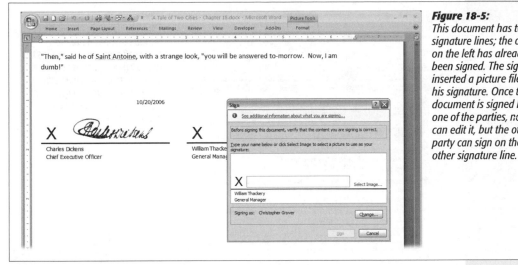

Figure 18-5:
*This document has two
signature lines; the one
on the left has already
been signed. The signer
inserted a picture file of
his signature. Once the
document is signed by
one of the parties, no one
can edit it, but the other
party can sign on the
other signature line.*

Removing a Digital Signature

Once a document has a digital signature, you can't make changes to it. After all, one of the purposes of a digital signature is to prove that a document hasn't been altered since the time it was signed. As a result, sometimes it's necessary to remove a digital signature from a document. Here are the steps:

1. **With the document open, choose Office → Prepare → View Signatures.**

   The Signatures pane opens.

2. **In the Signatures pane, under Valid Signature, click the signature you want to remove. From the drop-down menu that appears, choose Remove Signature.**

   An alert box opens and asks "Are you sure you want to permanently remove this signature?"

3. **Click Yes to remove the signature.**

   You can remove your signature, and often even someone else's signature, from a document. Once all the valid signatures are removed from a document, it can once again be edited.

Getting a Third-Party Digital Signature

Self-signed signatures are great for assuring everyone that a document hasn't been altered after you signed it, but they can't prove that you're actually who you say you are. The *third-party digital signature* is the electronic equivalent of a notarized document. Just as getting a document notarized means extra hassle and expense, third-party digital signatures require more time and effort than the self-signed variety. First, you must subscribe to a service, like the ones provided by one of Microsoft's Partners (Figure 18-6). The annual cost ranges from about $100 to $250, depending on the services you're buying.

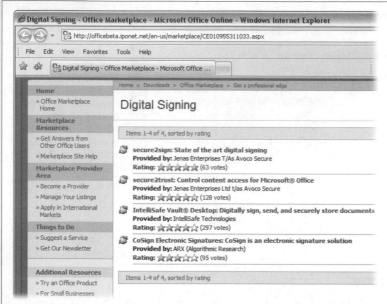

Figure 18-6:
You can purchase a digital signature from one of the Microsoft partners for about $100 to $250 a year. Prices vary depending in part on whether you're purchasing an individual signature or one for several employees in a company.

Once you've purchased a digital signature, you can add it to your documents the same way you added your self-signed signature, as described earlier. The difference is that people who receive your document have the added third-party assurance that you're legit. Third-party signatures are an important factor when you're using a macro or a Word add-in that someone else wrote. In that case, you're the one checking the signature, not the one creating it. The next section explains how to check a digital signature.

Checking a Digital Signature

When you open a Word document that has a digital signature, you see an icon that looks like a medallion in the status bar in the lower-left corner (Figure 18-7). Click this icon to open the Signatures pane (it opens to the right of your document). You can also open the Signatures pane with Office → Prepare → View Signatures or Alt+F, EW. In the Signatures pane, you see any valid signatures that you or anyone else has added to the document. Click a signature in the Signatures pane to open a drop-down menu (Figure 18-8). Choose Signatures Details to open a box that states whether or not the signature is valid and shows the purpose for signing the document. The View button leads to the Certificate box with even more details about the signature (Figure 18-9).

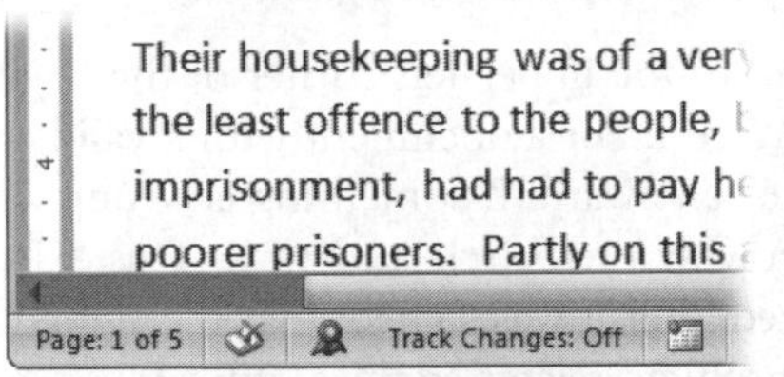

Their housekeeping was of a ver
the least offence to the people, l
imprisonment, had had to pay h
poorer prisoners. Partly on this

Page: 1 of 5   Track Changes: Off

Figure 18-7:
When you open a document that has a digital signature, you notice two things. First of all, you can't make changes to the document. You also see a medallion icon in your status bar (unless you've made changes to Word's factory settings). Click this icon to open the Signatures pane.

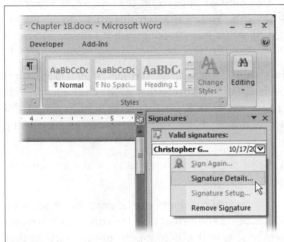

Figure 18-8:
Open the Signatures pane (Alt+F,EW) and you see a list of valid signatures that are attached to the document. Open the drop-down menu attached to a name to view the Signature Details.

Figure 18-9:
When you open a certificate for a digital signature, you see a box with two tabs. The General tab (not shown) lists who issued the certificate and whom it was issued to. Under the Details tab, you see a box showing Fields and Values. Click a field to view the details. For example, click the Issuer field to see the issuer's name and email address.

Here are the things to look for when you're checking a digital signature:

- **The Digital Signature Information icon.** In the upper-left corner of the Digital Signatures box's General tab, you see an icon. For a document with a valid certificate, the icon looks like a certificate or an award. If something is wrong with the certificate, you see a document icon with a red circle and an X. This X icon may mean that the document was altered after it was signed, that the signature has expired, or that there's some other problem related to the certificate.

- **The digital signature is OK.** This message appears on the General tab near the Digital Signature Information icon. You won't see this message if anyone altered the file (by removing a signature or tampering with it somehow) after it was signed.

- **The countersignatures timestamp.** Third-party verified digital signatures receive a timestamp from the certificate authority (that is, the company providing the certificate). The date for the timestamp should be within the "Valid from" date range that's shown in the certificate, which you can view by clicking the View Certificate button.

- **Issue to name.** The name of the person or company that created the document appears here.

- **Issued by name.** The name of the certificate authority, if any, shows up here. Microsoft maintains a list of certificate authorities that are known as Microsoft Root Certificate Program Members, as well as descriptions of the practices they use to authenticate documents. Members include AOL, Certisign, eSign, GeoTrust, and Verisign.

Customizing Trust Center Settings

With its macro-writing language Visual Basic for Applications (also knows as VBA), Microsoft gave programmers the ability to control just about every aspect of Word, along with the PC's file system. In the right hands, this kind of programming power is marvelous. Programmers created all sorts of fancy applications based on Word, Excel, and other Office programs. Companies like Adobe and Symantec wrote programs so that their products could share information and work smoothly with Word. Unfortunately, troublemakers used the same power to create programs that deleted files, scrambled directories, and stole credit card details.

Over the years, Microsoft got boatloads of criticism for the way VBA let evildoers introduce viruses and other malware into unsuspecting computers. So with Office 2007, Microsoft has taken steps to keep macros under control but still let people automate their Word documents.

Protecting Yourself from Malicious Macros

One common security problem is that people often never even know when a macro is running in Word. To introduce a bad program, all the bad guys have to do is email you a Word document. If you open that document, the macro runs, and you're cooked: the malware deletes your files or reads your personal information before you even know it. To some degree, that scenario has changed with the new file formats .docx and .docm. When a file that ends in .docx, you can open it and be confident that it won't run any macros.

Filenames that end with an "m" are a signal that the file includes macros. When you open a document that ends in .docm, Word checks to see whether the document comes from a Trusted Publisher. If it doesn't, Word opens the document, but doesn't run any macros unless you specifically choose to allow it (Figure 18-10). Word templates and other Office programs use a similar file naming system: If a file ends with an "m," as in .dotm, then you know the file contains macros. Whether or not they run is up to you, as described in the rest of this section.

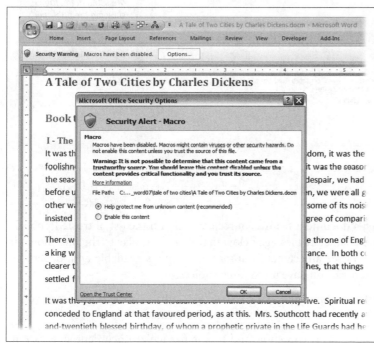

Figure 18-10:
If you know where a document comes from and want macros to run, click Options in the Security Warning box to open the Security Options box, shown here. It provides document information and lets you activate (enable) the macros. If you want to view the settings in your Trust Center, click the link in the lower-left corner.

Choosing Trusted Publishers

With the new file formats and filenames, it's easier to tell when a document contains macros. Still, you want to be able to use templates that have macros and take advantage of all the cool add-on programs out there. You need a way to know whether it's safe to open a file that contains macros. That's why Microsoft created

Office 2007's Trust Center. It lets you run macros and add-ins that come from trusted publishers like Adobe and Microsoft, but warns you before you run macros from questionable sources. Word and the other Office programs use digital signatures (page 413) and a list of Trusted Publishers to make sure documents come from a trusted source.

To see your list of Trusted Publishers, go to Office → Word Options and click the Trust Center button on the left. You see topics like "Protecting your privacy," "Security & more," and Microsoft Office Word Trust Center. Click the Trust Center Settings button at right to see the current settings (Figure 18-11).

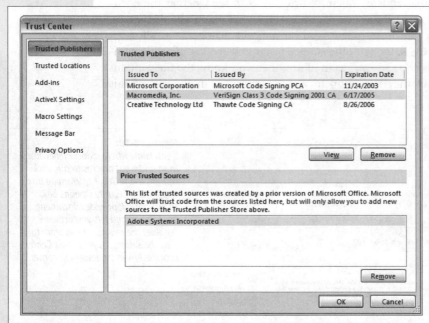

Figure 18-11:
The Trust Center box looks and works like the Word Options box. Click one of the buttons at left to view the settings in the main window. In this view, Trusted Publishers are listed at the top, showing the publisher's name, the Certificate Authority issuing the digital signature, and the certificate's expiration date.

When you open a document from a source that isn't on the list of trusted publishers, Word displays an alert message below the ribbon (similar to the one shown in Figure 18-10). You see any signature information that's available and, depending on the circumstances, you have up to three choices:

- **Help protect me from unknown content.** This option is the safest when you're not sure where a document came from or who created it.

- **Enable this content.** If you know and trust a particular document and want its macros to run, choose this option.

- **Trust all documents from this publisher.** If you know and trust a publisher—your employer or a major software developer, for example—you can add it to your list of trusted publishers. That way, you don't keep getting all these warnings. (This option appears only if the document has a valid digital signature.)

Creating a Trusted Location

Trusted locations are sort of like trusted publishers. You can tell Office programs that files found in a specific folder should be considered safe. When you open a file that is stored in a trusted location, it isn't checked against the list of Trusted Publishers because the assumption is that you've already determined it to be a safe file. Files inside of trusted folders can be opened without being checked by the Trust Center. Typically, a trusted location is a folder on your computer. It could also be a folder on a network, but that's not quite as safe because many other people may get into a network folder. Ideally, your trusted location is a folder inside your My Documents folder.

Here's a step-by-step example showing how to designate a folder named Trusted Stuff as a trusted location. First, create a folder called Trusted Stuff in your my documents folder. For example, go to Start → My Documents to open My Documents in Windows Explorer. Then choose File → New → Folder to create a new folder. Name it Trusted Stuff and then follow these steps:

1. **Go to Office → Word Options → Trust Center.**

    The Trust Center panel shows you information about computer security. On the right side, you see a button named Trust Center Settings.

2. **Click Trust Center Settings to open the Trust Center box. In the list at left, click Trusted Locations.**

    In the Trusted Locations panel, you see a list box with the headings Path, Description, and Date Modified. Word automatically creates a couple of trusted locations, like its template folders and Word's startup folder. You want to add Trusted Stuff to this list.

3. **Near the bottom of the window, click "Add new location" to open the Microsoft Office Trusted Location box (Figure 18-12).**

    The Microsoft Office Trusted Location box shows a warning at top, just to make sure you understand that you're creating a trusted folder. Below the warning you see a text box labeled Path.

4. **Click Browse. When the Browse box opens, navigate to My Documents → Trusted Stuff and then click OK.**

    Leave the "Subfolders of this location are also trusted" checkbox turned off for now. (Security-wise, it's better to give your folders trusted status individually as you create them.)

5. **In the Description text box, type any information that may help you remember what this folder is all about.**

    For example, if the folder contains documents or templates created by the computer gurus at your company, you might type, *These documents and templates were created by the computer geeks at All Through the Year Publishing Company.*

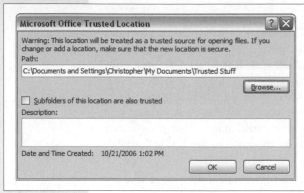

Figure 18-12:
Use the Microsoft Office Trusted Location box to designate a new trusted location. Click the Browse button to add a folder to the Trusted Locations. In this example, the Trusted Stuff folder is selected.

6. **In the Microsoft Office Trusted Location box, click OK.**

When the Trusted Location box closes, you see your Trusted Stuff folder listed at the top of the list (Figure 18-13), with the folder path at left. The Description is in the middle, and the date you added the folder to Trusted Locations is at right.

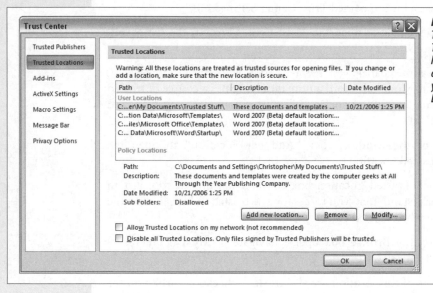

Figure 18-13:
The Trust Center → Trusted Locations panel lists the paths and description for folders you add to the Trusted Location list.

7. **Click OK to close the Trust Center box, and then OK again to close the Word Options box.**

You can repeat these steps to add more folders. When you're through, close the Trust Center and Word Options boxes.

Now that you've designated a folder as a trusted location, use it to store files that you know are safe and that you want to open without Word's Trust Center sending up rockets and warning sirens. For example, suppose some computer expert from inside your company gives you a Word template or file containing macros to make your job easier. Rather than change your Trust Center security options, just put the file in your trusted location. That way, you can open the file easily, and you haven't weakened your security by shutting off Trust Center settings.

Setting Add-in Behaviors

Add-ins are programs that run inside of Word, providing additional features. For example, the Adobe's Acrobat add-in provides special tools for creating PDF files with Word. To change the settings for Word add-ins, go to Office → Word Options → Trust Center and then click the Trust Center Settings button at right to open the Trust Center box. Click Add-ins on the left to see the Add-in options. You see three choices, but depending on your computer setup, they may not all be available (unavailable settings appear grayed out). Here's what the options do:

- **Require Application Add-ins to be signed by a Trusted Publisher.** As long as an add-in comes from one of the publishers on your Trusted Publisher list, it will run just fine. If you turn on this box, add-ins from other sources don't work.

- **Disable notification for unsigned add-ins (code will remain disabled).** If you turn on the first checkbox, then this option becomes active. If you turn on this option as well, not only does Word not run the add-ins, it won't even tell you that the add-ins are there.

- **Disable all Application Add-ins (may impair functionality).** This option is for the super paranoid. Word won't run any add-ins at all, even if they are from a trusted publisher.

Setting ActiveX Control Behaviors

ActiveX controls are powerful widgets that run inside of host programs like Word and Internet Explorer. Examples of ActiveX controls might be a drop-down menu that lets you select from a list of states or a handy toolbar that lets you create an Adobe PDF file from within Word. ActiveX controls can tap into the inner workings of your computer, making them versatile, powerful, and—in the wrong hands—dangerous. For example, a malicious ActiveX control could delete files from your computer or send private information to an Internet address. That's why, in Office 2007, Microsoft lets you limit what ActiveX controls can do on your computer.

You have two ways to protect yourself from dangerous ActiveX controls. First, you can make sure that the control comes from a trusted publisher. Second, with the help of the Trust Center, you can examine the ActiveX program to make sure that it conforms to safe programming practices. Your safest option is to leave the ActiveX security settings as they are when you install Word.

To review and change your settings, open the Word Options box (Alt+F, I) and then click Trust Center → Trust Center Settings. When the Trust Center window opens, click ActiveX Settings to display the options in Figure 18-14.

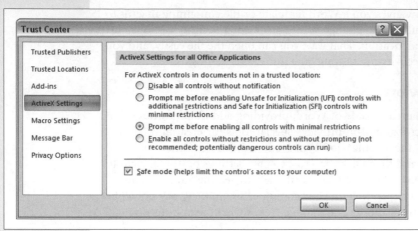

Figure 18-14:
ActiveX controls are widgets like buttons or drop-down menus that can be embedded in Word documents. Use the settings in the Trust Center to rein in the controls, so that they can't run programs without your knowledge and consent.

Here's a description of the different settings:

- **Disable all controls without notification.** This option is safest, since it prevents *any* ActiveX controls from running.

- **Prompt me before enabling Unsafe for Initialization (UFI) controls with additional restrictions and Safe for Initialization (SFI) controls with minimal restrictions.** Just reading this option takes the better part of a day, and understanding it takes about a week. Here's the lowdown: Some controls have additional programs attached to them making them potentially more dangerous. This option behaves differently depending on the type of ActiveX control, putting more restrictions on dangerous-looking controls.

- **Prompt me before enabling all controls with minimal restrictions.** Word uses this option out of the box. The program notifies you before it lets any ActiveX controls work.

- **Enable all controls without restrictions and without prompting (not recommended; potentially dangerous controls can run).** This option is the most dangerous, since it lets any ActiveX control run without letting you know. If you like to walk under ladders and break mirrors on Friday the 13th, give it a try. But the danger with this option is no joke: You can have an ActiveX control running on your computer and not even know if. Even if you're sure that the Word files you open are clean, it's safer to get a prompt as described in the previous option.

Tip: It's good to match your security settings to the way your computer is used. Some computers live safer lives than others. An office computer with only one person using it with company-approved documents is less likely to get into trouble than a computer used by several different people for downloading music, experimenting with shareware, and logging into multiplayer games.

Setting Macro Behaviors

The settings for macros are similar to the settings for ActiveX controls—after all, they're both part of Word's programming environment. While ActiveX controls are widgets that you see in a Word document, macros are programs that run in the background. Macros pop up in all kinds of places, whether you're aware of them or not. For example, you can trigger a macro yourself by choosing from a menu or pressing a keyboard shortcut. Some macros are set up to run automatically when you perform a certain action, like opening a document. An ActiveX control can even trigger a macro as part of its activities.

To review and change the macro settings, go to Office → Word Options → Trust Center and then click the Trust Center Settings button. In the Trust Center dialog box, click the Macro Settings button at left. The Macro Settings panel (Figure 18-15) has radio buttons for the following four settings:

- **Disable all macros without notification.** This super-caution option prevents all macros from running. It doesn't even give you the opportunity to run them if you wanted to.

- **Disable all macros with notification.** If Word detects macros, it pops up a security alert asking whether or not you want to let the macros run. This flexible option is Word's factory setting.

- **Disable all macros except digitally signed macros.** Using this option, macros that have a valid signature from a trusted publisher can run without a warning. Other macros trigger a security alert so you can decide whether or not they run.

- **Enable all macros (not recommended; potentially dangerous code can run).** With this daredevil's option, macros run automatically and Word doesn't even warn you about their presence.

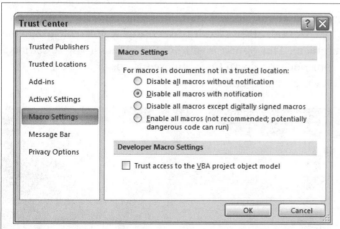

Figure 18-15:
The Trust Center's Macro Settings let you review and make changes to the way macros run in Word. If you're in doubt about the options, just leave the factory setting turned on: "Disable all macros with notification." That way, Word warns you when a document contains macros and you can choose whether or not they run.

Note: At the bottom of the Macro Settings panel, you see a checkbox labeled "Trust access to the VBA project object model." If you value your computer's safety, leave this box turned off. It gives macros access to the inner workings of your computer system.

Showing Warnings

In earlier versions, Word displayed warnings and alerts in message boxes that popped up on your screen. In Office 2007, Word, Excel, and PowerPoint display these warnings in a message bar that appears just below the ribbon. Often, the warning includes an Options button that lets you choose a course of action. For example, suppose you open a file that contains macros. Word shows a warning in the message bar similar to the one in Figure 18-10. The warning explains the situation: Macros have been disabled. If you click the Options button, you see additional information about the situation. In the case of the macro warning, Word tells you that it has disabled macros, most likely because the file doesn't come from one of your Trusted Publishers, or because the digital signature is invalid. You can choose to "Help protect me from unknown content," in which case Word leaves the macros disabled. Or you can choose to "enable this content" if you know the document is safe.

You can choose whether or not Word shows warnings in the message bar. To change the settings go to Office → Word Options → Trust Center, and click Trust Center Settings to open the Trust Center box. On the left side of the Trust Center box, click Message Bar. You see two options:

- **Show the Message Bar in all applications when content has been blocked.** This option is Word's factory setting, and it's a good choice to stick with. The message bar always tells you what's going on and gives you the option to run macros, ActiveX controls, and Add-ins on a case-by-case basis.

- **Never show information about blocked content.** With this option, you never see alerts about macros and other security issues, and you aren't given the opportunity to run them. This option might be appropriate if you're setting a computer up for someone who doesn't need to use macros or add-ins and who might be confused by the security alerts.

GEM IN THE ROUGH

Protecting Your Privacy

Microsoft likes to collect information about how you use your software, how you use their Web site, and when you have problems with their products. The information they collect helps them make business decisions which, in part, help them make better products and, in part, help them make more money.

You'll find an explanation about their policies and how it affects your privacy in Word Options. Go to Office → Word Options → Trust Center and look under Protecting Your Privacy. The links lead to Microsoft Web sites, and it's possible that the explanations and the policies change from time to time.

Removing Personal Information

Word embeds your name in the documents you create, and there's a good chance that it collects other information as you work. To see some of this collected information, choose Office button → Prepare → Properties to open the Document Properties pane above your document. At the very least, you see your name in the Author box. From the Document Properties drop-down menu (in the upper-left corner), choose Advanced Properties to show the full document properties box shown in Figure 18-16.

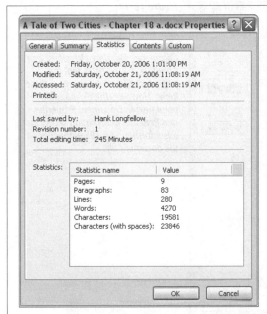

Figure 18-16:
The Document Properties box stores information about you and your document. For example, the Statistics tab keeps track of the number of words and paragraphs. It also keeps track of information you may consider more personal, like total editing time and the number of revisions.

When you turn on Track Changes or enter comments in a document, Word saves even more information in the document file. When you're ready to distribute your document, you may want to remove all personal information. You can run the Document Inspector (a new Word 2007 feature) to get a full report on the details that are included in your document. Choose Office → Prepare → Inspect Document to open the Document Inspector box. You can have Word check for several categories of information:

• Comments, Revisions, Versions, and Annotations

• Document Properties and Personal Information

• Custom XML Data

• Headers, Footers and Watermarks

• Hidden Text

To find personal information, make sure the Document Properties and Personal Information option is selected, and then click the Inspect button in the lower-right corner. After your computer makes a thorough study of your document, it reports back with a box that looks like Figure 18-17. For each type of item the Document Inspector found (comments, document properties, and so on), you see a brief message and a Remove All button. So, for example, to remove the document properties and personal information from your document, click the Remove All button next to that line.

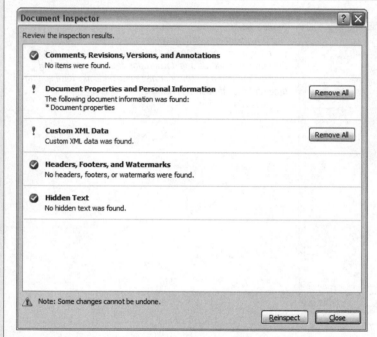

Figure 18-17:
After you run the Document Inspector, you see this box. The circle with the checkmark (as shown next to Comments, Revisions, Versions, and Annotations) indicates that the inspector didn't turn up any of these items. However, the exclamation point next to Document Properties and Personal Information shows that this information is still embedded in the document file.

Introducing Macros and Visual Basic

Macros let you can run several commands with the click of a button or the press of a key. If you find yourself using the same three or four commands over and over again, you can save time by recording those steps as a macro. You can assign the macro to a keyboard shortcut or to a button on the Quick Access toolbar. Then, when you need to run those commands, instead of having to use several keystrokes or ribbon commands, you can do it all with one stroke. And that's just the beginning. If you're interested, you can do much more with macros and the underlying programming language called Visual Basic.

This chapter won't turn you in to a macro-programming wizard, but it will give you a firm grounding in the fundamentals. You learn how to record Word commands and actions as macros by *showing* Word what steps you want the macro to perform. Then, you get to look under the hood and see the Visual Basic programming code that Word writes as it records your actions. This chapter gives you a quick lesson in how to read and interpret Visual Basic code and how to get extra help understanding the language. If you're interested in learning how you can tweak a macro, you can find that here too. If you're game, grab a Jolt cola, turn up the volume on iTunes, and dig in.

Showing the Developer Tab

If you're thinking about creating macros, that automatically makes you a Word developer—a person who creates (or, as programmers like to put it, *develops*) programs, macros, templates, and add-ins. So, the first thing you have to do is make sure you have the Developer tab showing on the ribbon. This tab gives you tools for working with macros and Visual Basic code, content controls, XML settings, and more.

If you don't see the Developer tab on the ribbon, follow these steps to make it visible: Choose Office button → Word Options → Popular. Under "Top options for working with Word," turn on the "Show Developer tab in the Ribbon" checkbox. The Developer tab shows up between View and Add-ins. When you click the tab, you see five groups of commands: Code, Controls, XML, Protect, and Templates. The tools you use most often to create and work with macros are in the two groups on the left—Code and Controls (Figure 19-1).

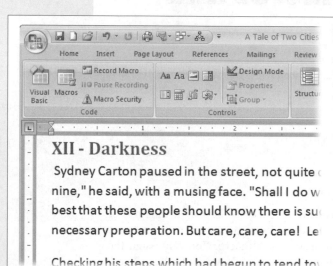

Figure 19-1:
The Developer's tab Code group gives you access to commands to record macros and write Visual Basic code. The Controls group gives you access to Word's content controls as well as the ActiveX controls used in earlier versions of Word (page 427).

Recording Macros

You don't have to be a programmer to create timesaving macros. You'll probably find recording a macro easier than recording a message for your answering machine or a TV show on your Tivo. If you click the Record button, then Word records your keystrokes and mouse clicks, and then, when you're done, you click Stop. The goal for recording a macro is so that you can quickly apply several formatting commands at once. You can combine any number of commands into a single command, making just about any Word command, option, or dialog box faster and easier to use.

Suppose, for example, you work as an editor and frequently select a complete sentence, change its text color, and add a strikethrough effect. Wouldn't it be handy if you could perform all those steps with a single keyboard shortcut? No problem. Turn on the macro recorder, and then do your selecting and formatting. When you're done, click the Stop button on the macro recorder. Simple as that.

Macro Security Warnings

When you open a document that contains macros, Word shows a warning in the Message Bar below the ribbon (see Figure 19-2). If you haven't changed your security settings since you installed Word, the macros are *disabled*—in plain English, they don't work. (See Chapter 18 for the full story on security.)

To *enable* macros so that they can run, click the Options button next to the warning. Word gives you two choices: "Help protect me from unknown content (recommended)" and "Enable this content."

Word's recommendation is the safest route because it prevents macros from running. This security setting is designed to help stop viruses and other malicious code from sneaking onto your computer in the form of macros. On the other hand, if you know that the document is safe—either because you created the macros yourself, or you trust the source—then you can go ahead and choose to "Enable this content."

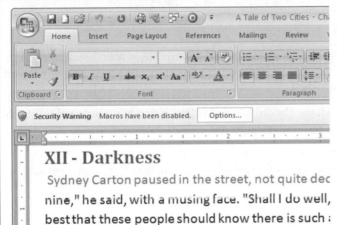

Figure 19-2:
The message bar below the ribbon shows this warning when you open a document that contains macros, even if you're the one who created the macros. To give your document the go-ahead to run macros, click Options, and then, in the Microsoft Office Security Options box that opens, select "Enable this content." As discussed in the previous chapter, you should turn on macros only for documents that you created or that come from someone you trust.

Here's a step-by-step description of the process to create a macro that selects an entire sentence, changes the font color, and applies the strikethrough effect:

1. **Open a document that has at least a couple paragraphs of text, using Office button → Open, and then use Office button → Save As to save it as a Word Macro-Enabled Document (.docm).**

   When you use the Save As command, Word makes a copy of the document, so you can experiment while your original remains untouched. From the "Save as type" drop-down menu, choose "Word Macro-Enabled Document (*.docm)," as shown in Figure 19-3.

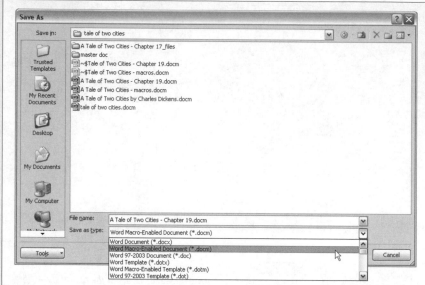

Figure 19-3:
Before you record a macro, you need to save your document with the .docm filename extension. Files that end with .docm can run macros; files that end in .docx can't.

2. **With your document still open, click in the middle of a sentence to place the insertion point. Then, to start recording, click Developer → Code → Record Macro (or press Alt+L, R).**

   Make sure you click the Record Macro button, which has a little red dot in the corner of the icon, and not the larger Macro button.

   The Record Macro box opens, showing a couple text boxes and buttons, most of which you use in the following steps as you name and save your macro (Figure 19-4).

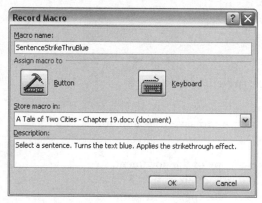

Figure 19-4:
Use the Record Macro box to name your macro and save it in a document or template. You can also assign the macro to either a button or a keyboard shortcut. In the text box at the bottom, you can type a description explaining how the macro works.

Tip: There's also a button in the status bar in the Word window's lower-left corner that you can use to start and stop the macro recorder. It looks like a little Word window with a red dot in the corner. (If this Record Macro button isn't showing, right-click the status bar, and make sure a checkmark appears next to Macro Recording.)

---

3. **In the "Macro name" box, type** *SentenceStrikeThruBlue.*

   Word automatically gives your macro an imaginative name like Macro1 or Macro2, so change it to something that describes what the macro does. You can't include spaces in the macro name, so if the name consists of several words, use uppercase and lowercase letters or use the underscore character to separate words and make the name more readable.

4. **In the "Store macro in" box, choose the name of the document you're using.**

   You can store a macro in a document a template or in *normal.dotm.* When you store the SentenceStrikeThruBlue macro in your document, it is available only in that one document. If you store a macro in a template, then the macro is available in any document based on that template. If you store your macro in *normal.dotm,* it will be available to any document you open in Word. The standard setting that Word uses unless you change it is *normal.dotm.*

5. **In the Description text box at the bottom, type in the purpose of the macro or the actions that it performs.**

   For macros, a good description explains what the macro does. In this case, you can describe three actions: "Selects a sentence. Turns the text blue. Adds a strikethrough."

6. **Click the Keyboard button to open the Customize Keyboard box, where you can assign a keyboard shortcut to the macro.**

   Using the two buttons in the middle of the Record Macro box, you can assign your macro to a button or to a keyboard shortcut. You don't have to do either, but buttons and shortcuts sure make it easier to run your macro. For this example, click the Keyboard button to open the Customize Keyboard box (Figure 19-5).

   As explained in Chapter 17, you can create custom keyboard shortcuts for any of Word's commands, and that includes macros (page 395).

7. **Click in the "Press new shortcut key" text box, and then press Ctrl+Shift+Alt+X.**

   A message appears at left: "Currently assigned to: [unassigned]." That's good; it means your keyboard shortcut won't conflict with any other Word keystrokes. Use the "Save changes in" drop-down menu if you want to save your keyboard shortcut someplace other than *normal.dotm,* the standard setting. For example, you can save the shortcut in your document or in a template if you want it used *only* there.

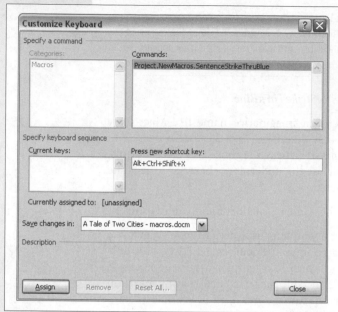

Figure 19-5:
Use the Customize Keyboard box to give your macros a keyboard shortcut. Click in the "Press new shortcut key" text box, and then record your keystrokes. If you make a mistake, use the Backspace key to erase your keystrokes. If your shortcut is already assigned to a command, you'll see the name of the command next to "Currently assigned to:"

8. **Click the Assign button to assign the shortcut to your macro.**

   The keystroke sequence appears in the Current keys box.

9. **Close the Customize Keyboard box.**

   You're done assigning the Ctrl+Alt+Shift+X keyboard shortcut to your macro. Back in your Word document, the cursor sports a new icon showing that you're in Record mode (Figure 19-6). At this point, the macro recording is all set to go. Word records every keystroke and command you choose from the ribbon.

   When you're recording a macro, you can use the mouse to click buttons on the ribbon and to set options in a dialog box, but you can't use it to move the cursor or to select text. You need to use keyboard commands to record those actions.

Note: If you need a refresher on using the keyboard to select text and move around in your document, see Chapter 2 (page 38).

---

10. **To select the entire sentence where the insertion point is flashing, press F8 three times.**

    Each time you press F8, Word selects a bigger chunk of your document. The first F8 starts the selection. The second F8 extends the selection to include a whole word. The third F8 selects an entire sentence—as you can see by the highlight. The macro recorder stores the three F8 keystrokes, which Word knows as the Extend Selection command.

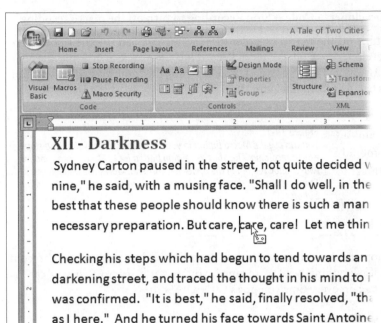

Figure 19-6:
While you're recording a macro, the mouse cursor takes on a new look. Next to the usual arrow, you see what looks like a cassette recording tape. It's your clue that you're in the middle of recording a macro—that is, if you're old enough to remember what a cassette is.

11. **Go to Home → Font. Click the Font Color button, and then choose a blue color from the palette.**

    You can also use Alt+H, FC to open the font color palette; the macro recorder captures the commands either way.

    The text in the selected sentence changes to blue and, at the same time, the macro records the command to set the font color of the selected text to blue.

Tip: If you're using the mouse, click carefully. The macro recorder doesn't pay much attention if you click different tabs looking for a command, but it does record your action any time you click a command button on the ribbon or in a dialog box.

---

12. **With the sentence still selected and highlighted, click Home → Font → Strikethrough.**

    Word applies the strikethrough effect to the selected text and adds the strikethrough command to the recorded actions in the macro.

13. **Click the right arrow key on your keyboard once to deselect the text.**

    To complete the macro, you want to deselect the sentence and remove the highlight from the text. The easiest way to do that using the keyboard is to press the right arrow button.

---

14. Choose Developer → Code → Stop Recording to turn off the macro recoding.

You can turn off the macro recorder three ways. You can use the ribbon command Developer → Code → Stop Recording. Or you can use the keyboard shortcut Alt+L, R. Last and easiest, you can click the Stop Recording button in the status bar, as shown in Figure 19-7.

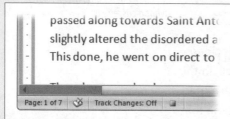

Figure 19-7:
You can use the Macro button in your status bar to both start and stop macro recording. The Start Recording button looks like a Word window with a small red dot in the upper left corner. It works like a toggle, click Start and the Stop button (this tiny square button) is the Stop Recording button.

Once you stop the recording, you're all done. Word has memorized the commands and, if everything went as planned, you've got a macro that you can use over and over again every time you press Ctrl+Alt+Shift+X.

Testing Your Macro

All good programmers test their programs to make sure they work as planned, and you should do the same with your new SentenceStrikeThruBlue macro. To see how your macro works, just click to put your insertion point in a new sentence, and then press the keyboard shortcut you created—Ctrl+Alt+Shift+X. Quick as a wink, you see the plain text change to blue highlighted text. After you run your macro, you should see something similar to Figure 19-8.

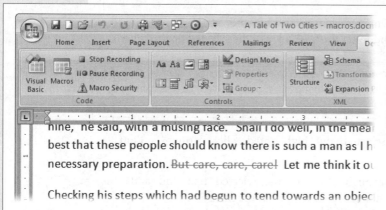

Figure 19-8:
Click in a sentence and run your SentenceStrikeThruBlue macro, and you should end up with a sentence with blue text, with a strikethrough effect. The insertion point should be at the end of the sentence, and the sentence shouldn't be highlighted.

When you create a macro just for your own use, you can test it quickly to see if it behaves the way you planned. If you're creating a macro that's going to be used by others, you need to test it a little more rigorously. You'll find that people often use your macros in ways you didn't expect. Also, it's not unusual for a recorded macro to have some quirks. If you're the only one using the macro, you can learn to work around the quirks, but others using your macro may call your quirks bugs, and complain that your macro doesn't work.

The SentenceStrikeThruBlue macro has a couple of those quirks. For example, it works just fine if you place your insertion point in a sentence that is formatted with plain text. However, if you put the insertion point in text that already has a strikethrough effect, the macro removes the strikethrough line. If you're just using the macro for yourself, you can remember that it works this way and avoid using it with strikethrough text. However, if you're sending it out there into the world for others to use, you may want to change it. On page 445, you see how to fix this particular quirk.

Running Macros

Word gives you three ways to run macros. You can use a keyboard shortcut, as shown in the previous example. Or you can create a button on the Quick Access toolbar (in the upper-left corner of the Word window) that runs your macro. The third option is to run your macro from the Macro box (Developer → Code → Macros). The first two options, keyboard shortcut and button, are the quickest and easiest. The advantage of the Macro box is that it lists all available macros and gives you lots of other options for working with your macros.

Adding a Macro to the Quick Access Toolbar

You can assign your macro to a button when you first create it by clicking on the "Assign macro to" button in the Record Macro box. If you do, you see a new button on the Quick Access toolbar. Then you can run the macro with a click of a button. However, it's still not too late to create a button that runs your SentenceStrikeThruBlue macro. Follow these steps:

1. **Choose Office button → Word Options → Customize to see the settings to customize the Quick Access toolbar (Figure 19-9).**

   The list box on the left shows available commands, and the list box on the right shows commands that are included in the Quick Access toolbar.

2. **In the "Choose commands from" drop-down menu, select Macros.**

   The "Choose commands from" drop-down menu determines which commands appear in the list box on the left. Selecting Macros from the list limits your choices to macros.

3. **Double-click the macro named Project.NewMacros.SentenceStrikeThruBlue to add it to the list of Quick Access toolbar commands on the right.**

   Word macros have somewhat long names separated by dots (.) It's all part of the Visual Basic lingo, and if you choose to spend time working with macros and Visual Basic, it'll become familiar. For now, find the macro with a name

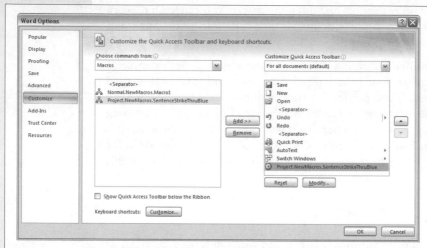

Figure 19-9:
Use the Customize settings in Word Options to assign buttons to the macros you record. In the "Choose commands from" drop-down menu, choose Macros to show the available macros. Double-click a macro name to add it to the list of Quick Access Toolbar commands on the right.

that ends in SentenceStrikeThruBlue. (You may need to drag the right-hand border of the Word Options box to see the full macro names.)

4. **At the bottom of the list box, click the Modify button to change your macro's Quick Access toolbar icon.**

Word gives all macros the same icon, which looks a little like a decision tree or an organizational chart. If you plan to have more than one macro on your Quick Access toolbar, give each one a different icon. When you click Modify, a box opens showing dozens of icons (Figure 19-10).

Figure 19-10:
The Modify Button box shows dozens of icons you can use for your macros. Choose a button that helps identify the actions performed by the macro.

5. **Click to select an icon (the blue bull's-eye is a good choice for this macro), and then click OK to close the Modify Button box. Click OK to close the Word Options box.**

After you close the Word Options box, you see your new macro button at the end of the Quick Access toolbar. When you move your mouse cursor over the blue bull's-eye, a screen tip with the macro's name pops up.

To test the command, just click to place your insertion point in a sentence, and then, on the Quick Access toolbar, click the bull's-eye button.

Running a Macro from the Macros Box

It's quickest to run a macro with a keyboard shortcut or from the Quick Access toolbar. However, at times you may want to run them from the Macros box. For example, since the Macro box lists all available macros in the current document or template (Figure 19-11), it's a convenient way to test or edit all your macros. To open the Macros box, go to Developer → Code → Macros or press Alt+L, PM.

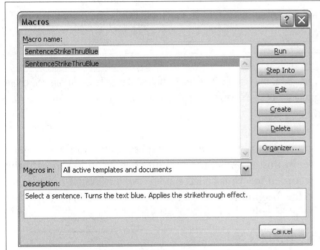

Figure 19-11:
The Macro box (Alt+L, PM) lists the available macros and gives you lots of ways to modify them. Macros are listed in the "Macro name" box. Choose a file or template in the "Macros in" drop-down menu to limit the number of macros showing. The buttons on the right let you run, modify, and create new macros.

To run a macro from the Macros box, just select it in the "Macro name" list, and then click the Run button at top right. The Macro box closes and the macro runs, just as if you'd clicked the button or used the keyboard shortcut.

Tip: You can undo a macro command by pressing Ctrl+X or clicking the Undo button on the Quick Access toolbar. Word steps through the commands, so if there were three commands (as in the SentenceStrikeThruBlue macro), you must press Ctrl+Z three times.

Reading Visual Basic Code

When you record a macro, Word writes the actions and commands. In effect, it's writing a Visual Basic program for you. You can view the program using the Macro box. Simply choose Developer → Code → Macro or go to Alt+L, PM.

In the Macros box, click SentenceStrikeThruBlue, and then click Edit to see the code for the macro you recorded earlier in this chapter. A new window opens with what looks like an entirely new program (Figure 19-12). You're delving into the mysteries of Microsoft Visual Basic.

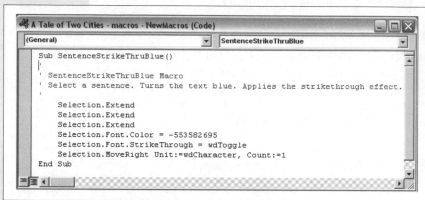

Figure 19-12:
In the Macro box, select the name of your macro, and then click the Edit button at right to launch the Visual Basic editing program. The macro code is in the window at the right. This code is for the SentenceStrikeThruBlue macro.

Note: There's much more to Visual Basic than can be included in this chapter. In fact, you can find entire books on the subject. To learn more about Visual Basic for Applications, check out *VB and VBA in a Nutshell* or *Learning Visual Basic .NET*.

Even if you've never programmed in your life, you can see some familiar English words in Visual Basic code. In this example, the first line begins with *Sub*, and the last line is *End Sub*. Each recorded macro is called a *subroutine* in Visual Basic lingo, and these two lines mark the beginning and end of the SentenceStrikeThruBlue macro.

Here's how to decipher the rest of the code:

- The lines beginning with a ' mark are comments; they don't do anything. They're just used to create blank lines as a way to include informative text and comments. In these comments, you see your macro's name and the description you typed when you created it.

- Moving down, you see three lines with the same words: *Selection.Extend*. You created these lines when you pressed the F8 key, which Word refers to as the Extend Selection command.

- The next line is pretty easy to interpret. *Selection.Font.Color* changes the font color for the selected text. The weird number after the equals sign is Word's term for the color of blue you chose.

- The following line, *Selection.Font.StrikeThrough*, isn't hard to understand either, but the word after the equals sign is a little curious. It reads *wdToggle*. If you're guessing that this command toggles the strikethrough effect on and off, you're right. You deserve an honorary programmer's pocket protector.

- The final line before *End Sub* reads *Selection.MoveRight Unit:=wdCharacter, Count:=1*. Word recorded this code when you used the right arrow key to move the insertion point and deselect the sentence.

When you're done exploring, choose File → "Close and Return to Microsoft Word" to close the Visual Basic window. If you made changes to the code, you see a dialog box asking whether you want to save the changes.

Getting Help for Visual Basic

As described in the previous section, you can read the Visual Basic code for any macro you've recorded. And because Visual Basic uses relatively down-to-earth language, you can interpret many of the lines and figure out what they do. If you're not sure how a particular line of code works or what changes you can make, try using Visual Basic's Help system. It's very detailed and written for programmers, but if you're interested in learning how to tweak your macros after you record them, the help screens have the details you need.

To get help for the details of the Visual Basic code for the SentenceStrikeThruBlue macro, open the now-familiar Macros box (Developer → Code → Macros or Alt+L, PM). Select the macro's name (SentenceStrikeThruBlue), and then click Edit.

The Visual Basic window opens, showing the macro's code in the right box. In the second to last line (*Selection.Font.StrikeThrough = wdToggle*), click anywhere in the word *StrikeThrough*, and then press F1 to open the Visual Basic Help window (Figure 19-13).

You can get more information on any Word command by placing the insertion point in the command and pressing F1. In general, Visual Basic Help is much smarter than Word's Help when it comes to knowing what reference you need. Typically, you see the name of the command or property at the top of the Help box and below a description of the command in programmer's computerese. In addition, you usually find remarks and examples.

In this case, the most helpful text for the StrikeThrough command is the second sentence under Remarks, which explains that StrikeThrough can have three settings: True, False, and wdToggle. True adds the strikethrough effect to selected text, False turns off the strikethrough text, and wdToggle switches the strikethrough effect on and off. The second example shows how to apply strikethrough formatting using the word "True."

Making Simple Changes to Visual Basic Code

Armed with the knowledge provided by Visual Basic Help in the previous section, you know that in Visual Basic the strikethrough effect has three settings: True, False, and wdToggle. When you tested the SentenceStrikeThruBlue macro, you saw that it toggled the strikethrough effect on and off (page 441). It would be better for the macro to always turn it on (or leave it on, if the text is already struck through).

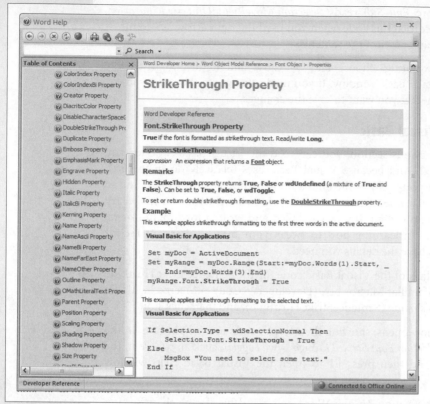

Figure 19-13:
The Help box for Visual Basic is just like Word's Help box. On the left, click a topic, and then you see an explanation in the large window on the right.

In this tutorial, you tweak the code in your macro. (Now's a good time for another sip of that Jolt cola.) Here's how to open your macro in Visual Basic, and then edit the code so that the macro always turns on the strikethrough effect.

1. **In the Macros box (Developer → Code → Macros or Alt+L, PM), click the macro's name (SentenceStrikeThruBlue), and then click Edit.**

   The Visual Basic window opens, with the macro's code displayed in the box on the right (Figure 19-14).

2. **Find the line with the *StrikeThrough* command, *Selection.Font.StrikeThrough = wdToggle*.**

   The way it was recorded, your macro toggles the strikethrough effect on and off. You want to change it so it always turns on the strikethrough effect.

3. **Double-click the word *wdToggle* to select it, and then type the word *True*.**

   Now the line reads, *Selection.Font.StrikeThrough = True*. As you read in the Visual Basic Help window, *True* is one of the options for the *StrikeThrough* command. It sets the strikethrough effect to "on."

4. **In the menu bar, choose File → Close and Return to Microsoft Word.**

The Visual Basic window closes, and you see your document.

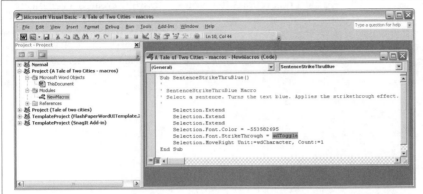

Figure 19-14:
You see a lot going on in the Visual Basic editing window, but there's no need to be overwhelmed. To make simple changes, just focus on your macro's code in the window on the right. This figure shows wdToggle selected and ready to be replaced with the word True.

You can test out your Visual Basic editing to see if it works as planned. Click a sentence, and then run your macro with the Quick Access toolbar button or the keyboard shortcut Ctrl+Alt+Shift+X. The sentence turns blue, and you see the strikethrough effect. Click the sentence again and run the macro again. Instead of removing the strikethrough as it did in the original macro, the text should stay the same—blue with a strikethrough.

More Visual Basic Tweaks

If you thought the previous example was fun, you can try making some more changes to the SentenceStrikeThruBlue macro. For example, you can change the color that's applied to the text by changing the line that begins *Selection.Font.Color =*. Visual Basic can use numbers or special words to identify colors. For humans, the words are easier. Try changing the number after the equals sign to one of these words: *wdColorRed*, *wdColorDarkGreen*, or *wdColorYellow*. The line should look something like this:

```
Selection.Font.Color = wdColorRed
```

In this way, you can change the color the macro changes text to, without re-recording the whole macro.

Poke around and see what else you can change. For example, try changing the number at the end of the line that reads:

```
Selection.MoveRight Unit:=wdCharacter,
Count:=1
```

Try changing the word *Selection.MoveRight* to *Selection.MoveLeft* or *Selection.MoveUp*. All these commands deselect the text that the macro selected at the beginning, but they leave the insertion point in a different place.

Using Digital Signatures

If you get into the practice of creating macros for others to use, you want to create digital certificates that identify you as the author. That way, people can add you to their Trusted Publishers list. First, you must create a digital signature for Visual Basic for Applications Projects. Go to Start → Microsoft Office → Microsoft Office

Tools, and then click Digital Certificate for VBA Projects. You see the Create Digital Certificate box, as shown in Figure 19-15. Type a name for the certificate, and then click OK. An alert box reports that you successfully created a certificate.

Figure 19-15:
Type your name or the company name that you want to show on the digital certificate.

Applying Your Digital Certificate to a Macro

You apply your newly created digital signature to your macro from within Visual Basic. With your macro open in Visual Basic, choose Tools → Digital Signature to open the Digital Signature box. Initially, next to "Certificate name," you see the message "[No certificate]". Click the Choose button to open the Select Certificate box, as shown in Figure 19-16. Choose a certificate from the list, and then click OK. The Select Certificate box closes, and you see your certificate name in the Digital Signature box. Click OK to close the Digital Signature box and return to your macro in Visual Basic.

Figure 19-16:
The Select Certificate box shows the digital certificates that you can apply to your Visual Basic project. Click a certificate, and then click the View Certificate button to see the details.

Creating Your Own Themes and Templates

You don't have to work for a big company to want all your documents to look consistent. Even if you're using Word to dash off letters to the editor, to write a family newsletter, or to harangue local politicians, a few well-coordinated colors, fonts, and maybe even a personal logo can make you seem like you're backed by your own professional design staff. Word is happy to help, thanks to the program's *themes* and *templates*.

Themes control (and help unify) the color scheme and fonts used in your document. With themes, you can easily apply consistent colors, fonts, and effects to entire documents with the click of a button. Word, Excel, and PowerPoint all use the same themes, so if your project involves two or more of these programs, by using the same theme, you can ensure a consistent appearance throughout. Templates help you quickly generate documents that are already loaded up with boilerplate info and design elements. All you have to do is fill in the content. This chapter shows you how to create, modify, and save your own themes and templates.

Note: If you're interested in how to actually *use* themes and templates in your documents, see Chapter 5.

Designing Your Own Themes

Word's built-in themes define three kinds of document elements: colors, fonts, and effects. To create your own theme, you make your own choices from each of these areas.

- **Colors.** Each theme defines a dozen colors for specific document elements such as body text, headings, and accents. These definitions include four text and background colors, six accent colors, and two hyperlink colors.

- **Fonts.** Each theme defines two fonts (also know as typefaces)—one for headings and one for body text.

- **Effects.** Each theme can have one of 20 built-in effects that define graphics features such as shadows, lines, highlighting, and 3-D effects.

The tools you need to create new themes are in the Page Layout → Themes group (Figure 20-1).

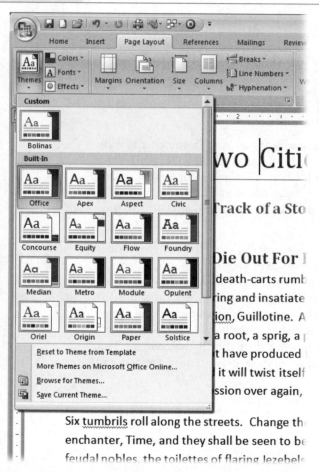

Figure 20-1:
Use the three buttons on the right side of the Themes group to customize a theme by choosing individual fonts, colors, and effects. The Themes menu (open here) shows you the themes you can apply to your document—your Custom created themes as well as the Built-In ones.

Defining Theme Colors

Color is perhaps the most important element in communicating a company's image. Most companies have an identifying color that's prominent in the logo.

When you apply a theme with your company colors to letters, memos, reports, and PowerPoint presentations, everyone knows they came from you. The same goes for colors you identify with your club or group—or yourself as an individual. Right out of the box, Word gives you some serviceable color combinations to use. If these colors aren't quite right for your business, you can create your own theme colors.

You define colors in your theme for three different purposes:

- **Text/Background** colors are the hardworking, everyday colors in your document that are used for the body text. A theme defines light and dark variations, so you have two options—for example, standard black text on a white background and an alternative, like white text on a dark blue background.

- **Accent** colors are the flashier variants used for headers, artwork, table formatting—anywhere you need a splash of color. In your theme, you define six accent colors, but that doesn't mean you have to use all these colors in a document. For most documents, a less is more color policy works best.

- **Hyperlink** colors are used to highlight links in your document and to show links that have been visited.

Here are the steps to create a new color theme:

1. **Choose Page Layout → Themes → Colors (or press Alt+P, TC) to open the drop-down menu.**

   The Theme Colors menu shows all the themes on your computer, with a row of colors beside each name (Figure 20-2).

2. **At the bottom of the Theme Colors menu, choose Create New Theme Colors to open the Create New Theme Colors dialog box (Figure 20-3).**

   At left, you see 12 drop-down menus showing color swatches. At right, you see two examples sporting the theme colors. One example has a dark background, as you may use for a PowerPoint slide; the other example has a lighter background.

   Each theme consists of 12 colors. The four colors shown at the top of the Create New Theme Colors box are text and background colors. Leave the first two colors (Text/Background – Dark 1 and Text/Background – Light 1) set to Automatic, and then you always have black and white available for word processing's white pages and black type.

3. **Using the drop-down menus, replace the Text/Background – Dark 2 and Text/Background – Light 2 colors.**

   When you click the Text/Background – Dark 2 drop-down menu, you see a palette of colors in three groups. At the top, you see the current Theme colors, in the middle you see a group of standard colors and at the bottom you see the colors you recently used.

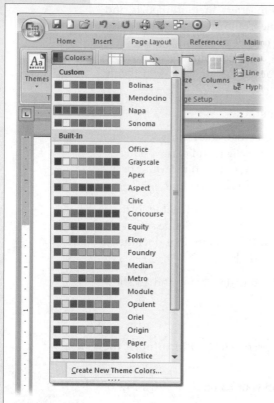

Figure 20-2:
Click one of the color options to change the colors used in your document independently of the fonts and effects. To see all the color themes, you may need to use the scroll bar or drag the menu's bottom border. Custom colors you create appear at the top of the menu while Microsoft's built-in colors are below.

From left to right, each column in the palette lists the same colors that appeared in the Create New Theme Colors box. The colors below the first row are lighter or darker shades of the color in the top row. When you hover the mouse cursor over each swatch, you see the color's name (Accent 5, for example) and a description (Darker 25%), as shown in Figure 20-3.

If you want to make minor adjustments to your theme colors, click one of the lighter or darker Theme Colors shown in the palette. The color you click replaces the Text/Background – Dark 2 theme color. If you're looking for a dramatic change, you want to choose colors that aren't part of the current theme, as described in the next step.

4. **Click the More Colors option at the bottom of the palette to open the Colors box, as shown in Figure 20-4.**

The Colors box gives you a much more varied palette to work from. Click the Standard tab to reveal the Windows color hexagon, which is arranged by hue and by shade. If you need even finer control over color creation, or if you want to specify a color by RGB or HSL number, use the Custom tab. (For details on the RGB and HSL color systems, see the box on page 75.)

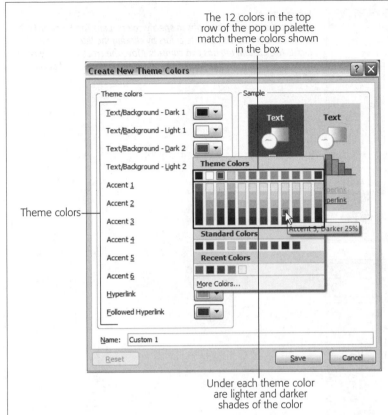

The 12 colors in the top row of the pop up palette match theme colors shown in the box

Theme colors

Under each theme color are lighter and darker shades of the color

Figure 20-3:
The Create New Theme Colors box shows drop-down menus with color swatches. When you click a color, a palette appears. Theme colors are shown at the top. To create select custom colors, click the More Colors button at the bottom.

After you select a color and click OK, the new color shows in the swatch in the drop-down menu. Review your color choices for Text/Background – Dark 2 and Text/Background – Light 2 in the Sample pane. For the sake of your readers' eyesight, make sure there's enough contrast between the text and the background in both examples.

5. **Use the drop-down menus to select colors for the six highlight colors.**

Repeat steps 3 and 4 to select six highlight colors. As you make selections, check the Sample shown on the right. Make sure the highlight colors complement the two background colors while showing distinctly against the background.

6. **Use the last two drop-down menus to choose colors for Hyperlinks and Followed Hyperlinks.**

There are two colors for hyperlinks in documents. Hyperlinks are usually displayed in a different color from other text so people know to click them. After clicking, the link text changes color so readers know they've already followed it. As a general rule, use a brighter color for hyperlinks to make them stand out clearly from (usually black) body text, and a lighter or fainter color for followed hyperlinks for that "used" look.

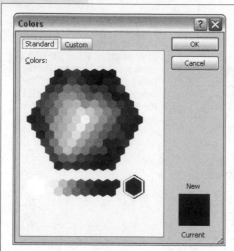

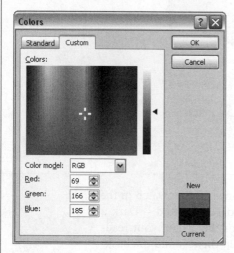

Figure 20-4:
You have a choice of two tabs to specify colors. Left: The Standard tab looks like a prism. You choose colors by clicking the little hexagons. Right: The Custom tab has two controls. Move the crosshairs to select a color, and then move the triangle to adjust the lightness and darkness of the color.

7. **At the bottom of the Create New Theme Colors box, name your new color theme, and then click Save.**

   Always name your themes, or Word will do it for you, and you'll end up with names like Custom 1, Custom 2, and so on. Whatever the name is, your new Color Theme shows up on the Colors menu's Custom group (Figure 20-2).

Defining Theme Fonts

To make changes to the Theme Fonts, click Page Layout → Themes → Fonts, and then click Choose Create New Theme Fonts at the bottom of the menu. The simple Edit Theme Fonts dialog box opens (Figure 20-5). You choose fonts for headings and body text from two drop-down menus. The Sample box on the right side shows how your combinations look together. Use the Name text box to give your new font theme a name.

Tip: Microsoft uses the same name for themes and the colors, fonts, and effect that make a complete theme. You may want to name theme elements consistently as well, so you'll remember which ones go together. For example, if you're creating a theme for your company (All Year), you can create All Year colors, All Year fonts, and an All Year effect.

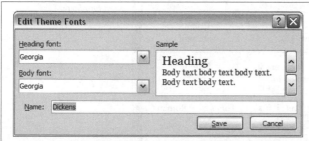

Figure 20-5:
Use the Create New Theme Fonts box to choose two fonts for your theme. Use the drop-down menus to choose a heading font and a font for the body text. The Sample pane provides a preview of your font theme.

UP TO SPEED

Tips for Choosing Fonts

Unless you're a graphic artist, choosing the right fonts can be a little intimidating. You want people to read your documents, so it's important to choose fonts that are easy on the eyes. You have a choice between two major typeface categories (Figure 20-6): serif fonts (like Times and Times New Roman) and sans-serif fonts (like Arial and Helvetica). *Serifs* are the tiny "feet" at the ends of each stroke in a letter or number. *Sans serif* means without serifs, so sans-serif typefaces tend to be simpler, made up of straight lines.

In general, serif types are easier to read, especially when there's a lot of text. The serifs help the reader's eye track along the horizontal line. That's why most magazines and newspapers use serif fonts.

On the other hand, computer screens don't display type as sharply as the printed page, so sans-serif fonts can be more readable on computer screens. You often see sans-serif type on Web pages and on the menus in programs like Word.

Sans-serif fonts tend to be more decorative and stylish. Magazines often use serif type for body text and sans-serif type for eye-catching headlines. Still, matching two fonts can be a tricky business and successful font matching, like beauty, can be in the eye of the beholder. If you're in doubt, you can never go wrong using the same font for both headings and body text. A heading that matches but is larger than the body text always looks good.

New Office 2007 fonts

Reading long documents on the computer screen is a challenge for most people. It's simply not as easy as reading from the printed page. To make matters worse, typefaces that are easy to read on the printed page are sometimes hard to read on a computer screen. In an effort to provide typefaces that are readable both on the computer screen and on the printed page, Microsoft introduced several new fonts in Office 2007. Even if you're familiar with the common typefaces, these names will be new to you. The list below provides a two-second introduction to each font.

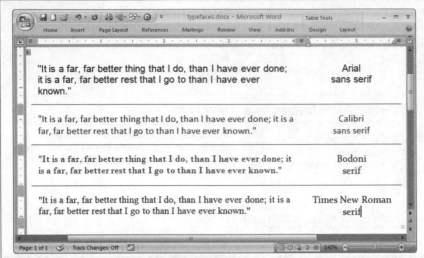

Figure 20-6:
The two fonts (or typefaces) at the top, Arial and Calibri, are sans serif. The two at the bottom, Bodoni and Times New Roman, are serif typefaces.

- **Consolas** is what's known as a monospaced typeface, where each character is exactly the same width whether it's a capital "M" or a lowercase "i." Programmers tend to like monospaced type because each character is distinct, and there are no decorative elements to cause confusion.

- **Calibri** is a modern sans-serif typeface, and you'll be seeing it a lot in the future: Microsoft is positioning it as a replacement for Times New Roman. Calibri is a little more varied in the thickness of its lines than Helvetica or the Helvetica clone Arial, which makes it easier to read in body text than most sans-serif fonts, without the drawback of displaying tiny serifs onscreen.

- **Cambria** is another very readable type, meaning people can quickly discern the letters even at smaller sizes. Cambria is an appropriate typeface for most business uses from letters and memos to Web design.

- **Constantia** is a serif typeface designed for both onscreen viewing and printed documents. Constantia is versatile and looks good in Web pages, letters, email, and printed publications. It's a good choice for PDF or XPS documents that your readers may either print or read onscreen.

- **Corbel** is a sans-serif type with a clean, open look. It's quite readable onscreen even at relatively small sizes, making it good for Web pages or business reports.

- **Candara** is ideal for Web pages. This sans-serif font has an informal, modern, artsy look, similar to Frutiger and Optima.

With the wealth of fonts available in Word, why do you see the same typefaces used over and over? Well, many people are wary about choosing new fonts. And Web designers don't use exotic fonts because they can't be sure their visitors will have the fonts on their systems. Microsoft's new fonts are widely distributed, so you can use them with confidence for good looks and variety.

The chart below lists some of the most overused fonts and possible replacements.

Microsoft font	Similar Mac and Linux fonts	Consider as a replacement	Use for
Arial	Helvetica	Calibri, Corbel, Candara	Web pages, headings, body text
Times New Roman	Times, Georgia	Constantia, Cambria	Printed documents, reports, journals
Courier New	Courier, Andale	Consolas	Computer code, email (monospaced)
Verdana	Frutiger, Optima	Candara, Corbel	Web pages, informal documents

Defining Theme Effects

Effects have less impact in your Word documents than in, say, PowerPoint presentations. The effects in a theme change the line styles, shadow, and fill for tables, charts, and lines. Office's built-in graphics like SmartArt and AutoShapes also take their visual cues from the theme's effects. Unlike colors and fonts, you can't customize any of these effects, you can't create your own, and you can choose only one effect per theme. All you can do is choose one from the available effects. Go to Page Layout → Themes → Effects and click the effect that you want to add to your theme(Figure 20-7).

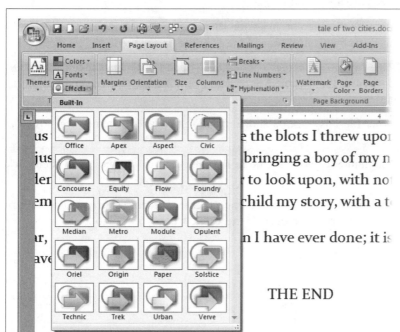

Figure 20-7:
Open the Themes Effects menu with Alt+P, TE, and you see 20 different styles of effects that you can apply to the artwork, charts, and lines in your document.

Modifying and Saving Themes

As mentioned at the beginning of this section, a complete theme is a combination of colors, fonts, and effects. Once you've customized colors and fonts and chosen the effects you want to use, you can name and save the whole bundle. Once you've saved a theme, you can apply it to a document. If you've got a theme that works well for your business, you can distribute it to coworkers.

Here are the complete steps for creating your own theme and then saving it:

1. **Choose Page Layout → Themes → Colors (or Alt+P, TC) to open the Colors menu, and then select colors from the Custom or Built-in color lists.**

   Color themes that you've created appear under the Custom heading. Microsoft's color themes appear under the Built-In heading. If you want to create new custom colors for this project, follow the steps for defining theme colors on page 450.

2. **Go to Page Layout → Themes → Fonts (or Alt+P, TF) to choose heading and body fonts.**

   Consider how your document is going to be distributed, and choose fonts that match the job. You can choose from one of Microsoft's built-in font sets or create your own custom font set. For more details on font choice, see page 454.

3. **Choose Page Layout → Themes → Effects (or Alt+P, TE) to choose the effects you want to use for your document.**

   The menu shows different styles for shapes, lines, shadows, and borders. To select an effects theme, click one of the examples in the menu.

4. **Go to Page Layout → Themes → Themes to open the Themes menu, and then, at the bottom of the menu, click Save Current Theme (it's the last option on the menu).**

   A Windows file box appears showing the folder where themes are saved, as shown in Figure 20-8.

5. **Type a file name for your theme in the "File name" text box, and then click Save.**

   After you type a name and save your theme, the Save Current Theme box closes, and you see your new theme listed when you go to Page Layout → Themes → Themes.

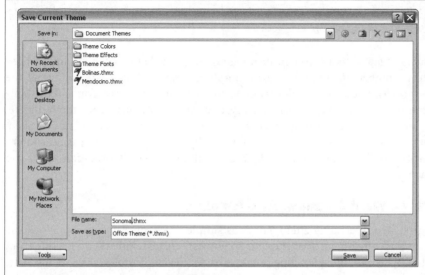

Figure 20-8:
Word automatically saves themes in the Document Themes folder that's inside your Templates folder. As you can see, the colors, fonts, and effects for your themes are each stored in their own folders inside the Document Themes folder.

Designing Document Templates

A template is a special type of document that's used to create new documents. For example, if you write memos as part of your daily work, you can create a memo template customized to your needs. That way, instead of creating a new memo from scratch, you can open a new document that's based on the memo template.

Like all templates, your memo template can include the following elements:

- **Boilerplate text.** Every memo has the same text such as Memo to, From, Date, and Re. You can store text that's used in every memo, so you never have to type it again.

- **Pictures and graphics.** You can include a company logo in the letterhead along with the address, phone number, and other contact details.

- **Styles, themes, and formatting.** Many documents, such as memos, use specific and sometimes complex paragraph styles, margins, indents, and other formatting magic.

- **Headers and footers.** No need to mess with choosing and customizing headers and footers for memos. Save header and footer details in the template, and never worry about them again.

- **AutoText.** The AutoText entries you save in the memo template are available whenever you create a memo.

- **Content controls, macros, and fields.** More complicated templates can include automation elements, like a date picker or a macro.

Note: This section explains how to create and modify templates. The details for using templates to create a new document are on page 136.

In the next few sections, you create a memo template that you can modify and use for any number of purposes. This example is lengthy, but if you follow all the steps, you learn lots of helpful tips and techniques along the way. You add the boilerplate text that should appear in every document generated from the template, plus some content controls (page 340) to save even more typing. You also create a letterhead complete with a graphic logo. Finally, you add a header (using content controls and fields) to automatically provide the pertinent information at the top of each page.

Saving a Word Document As a Template

The first step in creating a template is as simple as saving a document. Word lets you save any document as a template, so you can create templates by starting from scratch or by modifying existing documents. For example, to create a memo template, you can:

- **Start from scratch.** You can open a blank document with Office → New → Blank document, and then add the boilerplate text, paragraph styles, and all the other elements you want stored in your memo template.

- **Use an existing memo document.** If you already have a memo document stored on your computer, you can save some time starting with your existing memo. Remove all the text that's specific to a single memo, but leave the boilerplate text.

- **Modify one of Word's templates.** If you don't have a particular memo style in mind, you may want to use one of the many memo templates that Word provides. You can change the template by adding your own logo, letterhead, and AutoText entries.

Once you've opened the document you want to start from, save it as a template file:

1. **Go to Office → Save As → Word Template or press Alt+F, FT (Figure 20-9).**

   The Save As box opens with the "Save as type" drop-down menu already set to Word Template (*.dotx).

2. **Navigate to the folder where you want to save your template.**

   Since you're creating this template yourself, you probably want to save it in your Trusted Template folders, which is *C:\Document and Settings\[Your name]\Templates*. Templates stored in this folder are easily available when you create a new document using Office button → New or Alt+F, N.

3. **In the File name box, at the bottom, type the name for the template.**

   For example: *Memo – All Through the Year.*

---

4. Click Save to save the template file and close the Save As box.

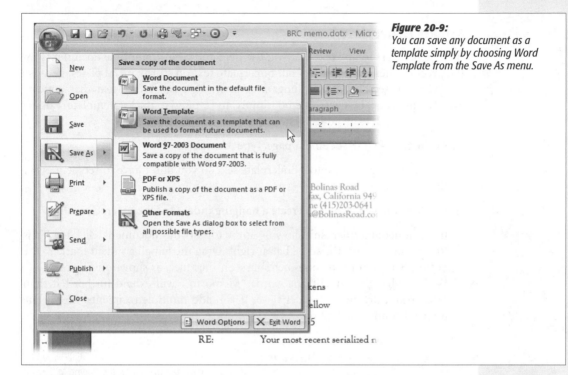

Figure 20-9:
You can save any document as a template simply by choosing Word Template from the Save As menu.

Setting Up the Template Document

The Word settings described in Chapter 3 affect the document as a whole—margins, theme, and so on. Document settings are a big part of template formatting, because you want them to be the same for every document you create from the template. In designing your memo template, you'll get them out of the way first.

1. **Choose Office → New (or use Alt+F, N) to open the New Document box, and then, in the top row of the box, double-click the Blank document icon.**

   A new blank document opens in Word.

2. **Go to Page Layout → Page Setup → Margins, and then choose Normal from the Margins menu.**

   The Normal option sets the top, bottom, left, and right margins to one inch. The Margins menu shows several preset margins. If you don't like any of the options shown, click Custom Margins at the bottom of the menu, and then use the box to set your own margins.

3. **Choose Page Layout → Themes → Themes (or Alt+P, TH) to open the Themes menu, and then select the Equity theme.**

   The Equity theme sets colors for text, background, and highlights. This theme uses the Perpetua font for body text and Franklin Gothic Book for headings.

Last, and perhaps least, the theme selects the Equity effects for your memo template.

Adding Boilerplate Text

Boilerplate refers to any text that you use over and over in multiple documents. In the precomputer days, printers put boilerplate text on sturdy metal plates, because it never changed. In Word, things are easier: You can create text that appears exactly the same in every memo simply by typing it into a template (.dotx) document. (And, as an added benefit, you *can* change it later.)

1. **At the top of your document page, type *Memo to:*.**

   You're making "Memo to:" boilerplate text so you don't have to retype it every time you write a memo.

2. **Use the horizontal ruler to create a hanging indent for the "Memo to:" line.**

   If the horizontal ruler isn't showing at the top of your document, click the View Ruler button above the scroll bar at right. Drag the hanging indent marker (the bottom triangle) to the one-inch mark on the ruler, as shown in Figure 20-10. With the hanging indent, the words "Memo to:" will extend further left than other text, catching the reader's eye. If you add multiple recipients, they'll line up neatly under the first one.

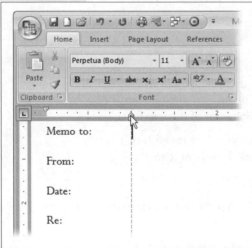

Figure 20-10:
The memo template uses a hanging indent for the "Memo to:" line. The arrow in this figure points to the hanging indent marker on the ruler.

3. **In the right margin next to "Memo to:", double-click to select the entire paragraph. Then use the keyboard shortcut Alt+H, LQ to save the formatting as a paragraph style with the name Hanging.**

   The Create New Style from Formatting box opens.

4. Type *Hanging* in the Name text box.

Word saves new styles in the template, so they're available to any document that uses the template. That way, you can always add more lines under "Memo to:" that align with the same hanging indent ("Subject:" for example).

5. **On new lines, add boilerplate text for the From:, Date:, and Re: lines that make up the top section for each of your memos, as shown in Figure 20-10.**

As you hit Enter to create new lines, Word continues to use the Hanging style for new paragraphs.

Adding Content Controls

The whole point of spending time upfront to create a template is so that you save time later. If most (if not all) of your memo recipients are the same group of coworkers, why spend time typing their names over and over when you can just type them once? You can use a Word content control (page 340) to create a drop-down menu of the names you use most often. You can also use the Date Picker content control to make sure the date gets typed accurately every time.

By adding content controls, you can make the template more useful to others as well as yourself. In this example, you'll see how easy it is to have Word automatically fill in the "From:" line with the name of whoever's using the template. If you make a template like this and distribute it around the office, you may even get a promotion! (Well, you can always hope.) Content controls are also useful if your company wants to create a document database that keeps track of memo subjects, authors, and recipients.

Content controls are like the drop-down menus and text boxes you use when you fill out a form on a Web site. Word makes it easy to create your own, but if you've never used them before, you may want to review Chapter 14 before you follow these steps:

1. **Click the end of the "Memo to:" line, and then press Tab to move the insertion point to the hanging indent position. Then, go to Developer → Controls → Text (or Alt+L, E) to insert a plain Text content control.**

The plain Text content control appears on the "Memo to:" line. (Make sure you don't use the Rich Text control.) This control will hold the names of the memo's recipients.

2. **On the "Memo to:" line, select the text content control, and then choose Developer → Controls → Properties (or press Alt+L, L).**

The Content Control Properties box for this Text control opens.

3. **Change the settings in the Content Control Properties box to match Figure 20-11.**

Type *Memo to* in the Title and Tag text boxes at the top of the Content Control Properties box. Turn on the "Use a style to format contents" checkbox, and then choose Hanging from the Style drop-down menu.

At the bottom of the box, under the Plain Text Properties heading, turn on "Allow carriage returns (multiple paragraphs)." This option lets you enter the names of different recipients on separate lines. Word will store all the recipients' names in the content control. Click OK when you're done.

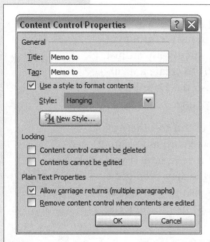

Figure 20-11:
The properties for the "Memo to" content control are set to provide a title and a tag. The Hanging style formats the contents of the control, and the Text content control allows multiple paragraphs.

4. **Go to Developer → Controls → Design Mode (or Alt+L, DM) to switch to Design Mode.**

The tabs around the content controls change, indicating you're in Design Mode. In the next step, you change the prompt text that appears in the "Memo to" content control.

Note: You have to switch to Design Mode before you change the prompt. Otherwise, if you just type new words in the content control, you're not changing the prompt; you're changing the contents of the "Memo to" control.

5. **Select the text in the "Memo to" content control, and then type *Click here to enter recipients.***

This text will appear on the "Memo to" line in your template before you (or anyone using this template) types into it. You're making your template more foolproof by providing prompts that tell people exactly what to do.

6. On the "From:" line, insert a tab, and then use Insert → Text → Quick Parts → Document Property → Author to insert the Author document property.

You can also use the keyboard shortcut Alt+N, QD to open the document properties menu.

Back in your template document, your name appears on the "From:" line. Word gets this information from the Word Options box. If you share this template with others, their names will automatically show up instead.

Tip: If your name doesn't appear, go to Office → Word Options and click the Popular button on the left. Make sure the User Name text box near the bottom of the box is filled in.

---

7. On the "Date:" line of the memo, insert a tab, and then choose Developer → Controls → Date Picker.

The Date Picker control appears in your memo template, displaying the words "Click here to enter a date."

8. On the "Date:" line of the memo, select the date picker, and then choose Developer → Controls → Properties.

The Properties box for the Date Picker control opens.

9. Type *Memo date* in the Title box and in the Tag box. Then, in the "Display the date like this" box, choose the third option that shows a format similar to January 1, 2007.

When you're done, the box should look like Figure 20-12. Click OK.

10. On the "Re:" line of the memo, insert a tab, and then choose Insert → Text → Quick Parts → Document Property → Subject to insert a content control showing the Subject document property.

Like the Author property, the Subject property is one of the standard document properties that you can view using the Office → Prepare → Properties command (or Alt+F, EP).

The text in the Subject content control simply reads "subject." The template will be clearer for newcomers if the content control explains what to do.

11. Select the text in the Subject content control, and then type *Click here to enter a subject*.

The new prompt text shows in the Subject content control.

12. Go to Developer → Controls → Design Mode to turn off Design Mode.

When you're through changing each of the four lines in your memo template, it should look like Figure 20-13.

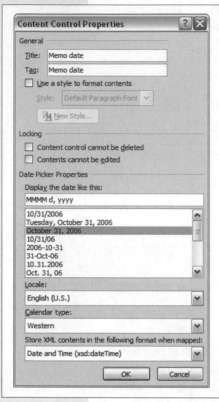

Figure 20-12:
The Properties box for the date picker content control gives you several options for showing dates or both dates and times.

Adding a Header

Headers and footers are a natural for document templates. They let you add elements common to all documents, like a logo, page number, and so on. In the following steps, you also get to try your hand at creating a Building Block using some fancy WordArt.

1. **Double-click at the top of the page.**

   A dotted line appears separating the header from the body of the document. The Header & Footer Tools tab shows on the ribbon.

2. **Choose Header & Footer Tools → Design → Options → Different First Page or press Alt+JH, A.**

   You want your letterhead to show on the first page of your memo, while subsequent pages will show the page numbers and other details.

3. **Go to Insert → Text → Word art to open the WordArt menu, and then choose the WordArt style that looks like an arch (Figure 20-14).**

   The WordArt box opens with a text box showing Your Text Here.

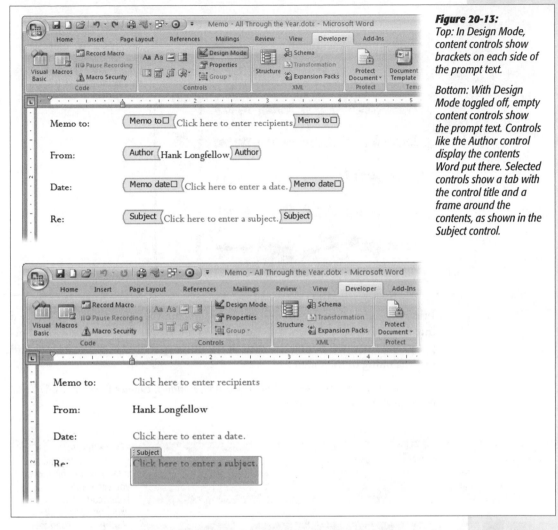

Figure 20-13:
Top: In Design Mode, content controls show brackets on each side of the prompt text.

Bottom: With Design Mode toggled off, empty content controls show the prompt text. Controls like the Author control display the contents Word put there. Selected controls show a tab with the control title and a frame around the contents, as shown in the Subject control.

4. Replace the words in the text box with *All Through the Year* and leave the font set to Arial Black and the size set to 36 points. Then click OK to close the WordArt box.

Your arched text appears in the Header of the memo template.

5. With the WordArt selected, go to Home → Paragraph → Center (or use Ctrl+E) to center the All Through the Year logo horizontally in your memo's header.

If you want to change the color and design of your logo, now's as good a time as any. To do so, double-click the WordArt logo to reveal the WordArt Tools tab.

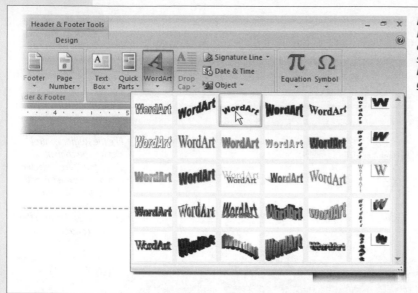

Figure 20-14:
Need to create a letterhead quickly? Give WordArt a spin. It may be a little heavy-handed, but it creates big graphics fast.

6. Press the right arrow key to deselect the logo, and then press Enter to create a line for text under the logo. Type an address for the All Through the Year company, and then press Enter to create some more space between the header and the beginning of the memo.

For example, you can use: *48 Doughty Street, London, England WC1N 2LX.* Your letterhead should look something like Figure 20-15.

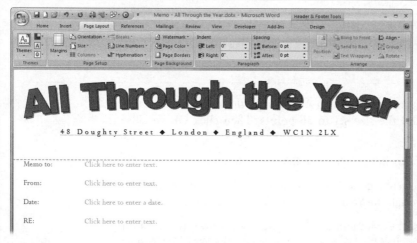

Figure 20-15:
With a WordArt logo and a few typographic tricks, you can create a letterhead. To create this example, use the Alt+N, U shortcut to insert the diamond symbols. Select the diamonds and change their font size (Alt+H,FS) to 7 points. Then select the entire line and change the character spacing (Alt+H, FN) to Expanded by 3 pt.

7. Click back in the body of your document, and press Ctrl+Enter to create a second page. Then double-click the top of the second page to edit the Header for page two and any pages that follow.

You could choose one of the predesigned headers and footers for your memo template; however, this example shows how to create a custom header by inserting content controls and fields.

8. Choose Insert → Text → Quick Parts → Document Property, and then select Subject from the menu to insert a Subject content control in the header.

This way, you can spot the topic of every memo you write at a glace. Mighty handy if you print memos and file them in a folder, or open them onscreen.

9. Press the right arrow key to deselect the Subject content control, and then press Enter to create a new line.

Your insertion point moves to a new line in the page-two header.

10. Type the word *Page*, and then press the space bar. Choose Insert → Text → Quick Parts → Field.

The Field dialog box opens, as shown in Figure 20-16. Time to add some automatic page numbering to your headers.

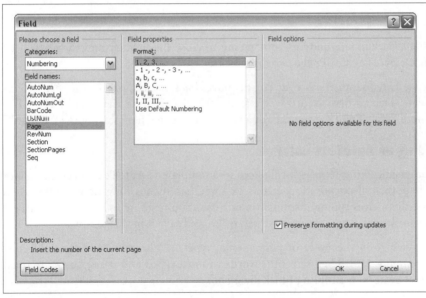

Figure 20-16:
Select a field in the "Field names" list, and then click OK to insert the field in your document. You can use the Categories drop-down menu to limit the fields shown in the list. Different formatting options and field codes appear on the right, depending on what you select in the "Field names" list.

11. From the Categories drop-down menu, choose Numbering. Then in the "Field names" list, double-click Page.

The Field box closes, and the Page field appears in your header. Since you're on the second page of your template document, it displays the number 2.

12. Type the word *of*, and then press the space bar.

    This header is going to show both the page number and the number of pages in the memo.

13. Choose Insert → Text → Quick Parts → Field to open the Field dialog box again. In the Categories drop-down menu, choose Document Information, and then double-click NumPages to insert the number of pages field.

    When you've completed the page-two header, it should look like Figure 20-17.

Figure 20-17:
The header for page two and the following pages in the memo template shows the subject of the memo, the page number, and the number of pages.

14. Click back in the body of your memo to close the header, and then press the Backspace key until page two disappears.

    Page two disappears as your cursor moves back to page one of the memo template. Don't worry. Word won't forget the page-two header details. They'll be there, hard at work, any time you create a multipage memo using the template.

Adding an AutoText Entry

Another juicy little item you can store in a template is AutoText (page 58). Since the hypothetical corporation in this example has such a long name, folks could injure themselves typing it several times a day. You're going to create an AutoText entry to shorten it to a three-letter keystroke, and save it in this template.

1. Anywhere in the body of your memo, type *All Through the Year Publishing Company, LLP*. Then select the words you just typed and press Alt+F3 to open the Create New Building Block dialog box.

   In Word 2007, AutoText entries are part of the new Building Block scheme. In previous versions, they had a separate dialog box.

2. Type the letters *aty* as the name for the Building Block, and then, from the Gallery drop-down menu, choose AutoText. From the "Save in" drop-down menu, choose the name of your memo template: Memo – All Through the Year.

This AutoText entry is available to any memo created using the memo template, but not to other documents. (There's no point in having it clutter up to non-company documents.)

3. In the body of your memo, select the words "All Through the Year Publishing Company, LLP," and then delete them by pressing the Backspace or Delete key.

Now that you've finished creating the AutoText entry, you don't need the words in the body of your memo. Banish them with the Delete key.

Finishing and Saving Your Template

Whew! The heavy lifting is done. Now you just have to put the finishing touches on the document and then save it as a template so you can get started creating new memos from it.

1. At the end of the "Re:" line, click to place your insertion point, and then press Enter to create a new line. Choose Home → Styles → More (or Alt+H, L) to open the Styles menu, and then click the Normal style.

When you press Enter, your insertion point moves to a new line in the memo template. This line marks the starting point for your memo's body text. You don't want to format the body text with a hanging indent, so you change the formatting to the Normal style.

2. Choose Office button → Save (or Office button → As → Word Template if you want to save your template with a new name). When the Save As box opens, type *Memo – All Through the Year* for the file name.

Make sure the "Save as type" box below shows Word Template (*.dotx), the file format for templates that don't include macros. If you included macros in your template, choose Word Macro-Enabled Template (*.dotm) here.

3. Save your template in your Trusted Template folder (*C:\Documents and Settings\[Your Name]\Templates*) or one of its subfolders.

That way, your template will appear when you create a new document using Office → New → My templates.

Test Driving the Memo Template

The steps showed you how to create a template for memos that stored boilerplate text, a paragraph style, content controls, a WordArt graphic, a custom header, fields, and an AutoText entry. Just like you'd test a macro or a program that you designed, you need to test your template to make sure it works as planned. Here are some things to try:

- **Create a document from your template.** Go to Office → New → My templates. You should see your template listed in the New box. If you saved your template in a subfolder, you should be able to find it under one of the tabs. When you open the template, you should see the letterhead slightly grayed-out (Figure 20-18). That's the way headers look when you're not editing them. It will look just fine when you print your document.

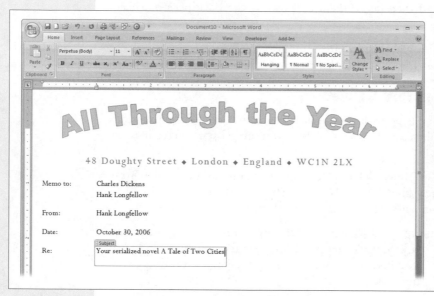

Figure 20-18:
After you create your memo template, take it for a test drive and run it through its paces. Check each of the items that you added to the template: boilerplate text, formatting, content controls, and AutoText entries.

- **Test the** "Memo to:" line. Click the prompt text: "Click here to enter recipients." One click should select the entire prompt. As soon as you type, the prompt should disappear, replaced by your text. Type a name, and then press Return and type another name. They should align neatly one under the other.

- **Check your styles menu.** Open the Styles menu using Home → Styles → More (or Alt+H, L) to make sure your Hanging style is available.

- **Check your content controls.** Your name should appear on the memo's "From:" line. Word uses the name that's stored in Office → Word Options → Popular → User to fill in the Author document property.

- **Test drive the date picker.** Use the Date Picker content control to select a date. The date should appear properly formatted on the Date line.

- **Examine the document properties.** On the "Re:" line, click the Subject prompt and type a subject, like *Your serialized novel A Tale of Two Cities*, for example. Then choose Office → Prepare → Properties to display the Document Properties pane (just below the ribbon).

The memo's subject should appear in the Subject text box. Your name should show up in the Author text box. (You can close the Document Properties pane by clicking the X in the upper-right corner.)

- **Enter text in the body of the memo.** Type some text in the body of the memo, to make sure everything looks okay. If you plan to use headings in your memos, try out the Heading 1, Heading 2, and Heading 3 paragraph styles. Do the same with bulleted lists and numbered lists.

- **Test your AutoText entries.** Type the letters *aty*, and then press F3 to test your AutoText entry. Word should replace the letters "aty" with "All Through the Year Publishing Company, LLP."

- **Examine your memo headers.** With your cursor in the body of your memo, press Ctrl+Enter several times, and then examine the headers on the pages. You should see the memo's subject on one line and then a line that reads something like "Page 2 of 6." (See Figure 20-19.)

Keep in mind that you won't change your template document by making changes to a *document* you created using the template. If any part of your template doesn't work as planned, you need to open the template "Memo – All Through the Year. dotx" (Alt+F, O), make the changes, and then save the file.

Tip: To create a new document from a template, don't open the .dotx file. Instead, use the Office button → New command and select the template in the New Document dialog box.

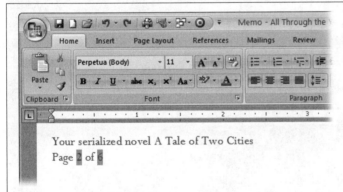

Figure 20-19:
After a subject is typed in on the Re line of the memo, it appears in the page-two header and on any subsequent pages. The line that reads "Page 2 of 6" is a combination of boilerplate text and Word fields.

Using Global Templates

Up to now, this chapter has focused on document templates. The purpose of a document template is to speed up the creation of a specific type of document such as a memo, a letter, or a screenplay. But there's another type of template—a *global template*. The purpose of a global template is to make things like paragraph styles, AutoText entries, and macros available to *lots* of different documents.

Here are other ways that global templates are different from document templates:

- You can use only one document template per document, but you can load several global templates at a time.

- The contents of a document template are available only to documents created with the template. The AutoText, paragraph styles, and formatting options in a global template are available to any Word document, as long as the global template is loaded in Word.

- Boilerplate text and graphics are usually an important part of document templates. The text in the body of a global template is irrelevant; it doesn't show up when a global template is loaded. Instead, global templates are used to take advantage of Word features such as paragraph styles, AutoText entries, and macros.

So, for example, if you want an AutoText entry to be available whenever you're working in Word no matter what type of document you're working on, you need to store it in a global template. Suppose you have a publishing company named All Through the Year Publishing Company, LLP. You create an AutoText entry that assigns that lengthy name to the keystrokes "aty." If you save the AutoText entry in a global template—the Normal template, usually—it'll be available to all your documents (as long as the template is loaded in Word, which you learn about later in this section). See the box below for more detail on the Normal template.

UP TO SPEED

About the Normal Template

The granddaddy of global templates is the *Normal template* (normal.dotm) because it's always loaded and its styles, themes, AutoText entries, and macros are always available. That makes the normal template one very special global template. You may have noticed normal.dotm listed as an option when you saved AutoText entries, building blocks, or macros.

The elements in the Normal template take charge when you create a blank document without any document template attached. The settings in the Normal template tell Word how to format text, set margins, and all the other details Word needs to know.

You can open and change your Normal template just as you'd modify any template. You find it stored in your template folder (*C:\Documents and Settings\[Your Name]\Templates*).

The Normal template is always loaded whenever you have a document open in Word. As explained above, you can have several global templates loaded at one time, so when you load a global template, both the global template *and* the normal template are in effect.

Creating a Global Template

You create and save global templates in the same way that you create document templates. So, to save a file as a global template, you choose Office → Save As → Word Template to open the Save As dialog box. Type the template's name in the File name combo box. Make sure that the "Save as type" box is set to Word

Template (*.dotx) or Word Macro-Enabled Template (*.dotm). Save the file inside your Templates folder (*C:\Documents and Settings\[Your Name]\Templates*) or one of its subfolders.

Loading a Global Template

There's virtually no difference in the file format of a document template and a global template, but there are basic differences in how you treat them. The main difference is the way you load a global template. Here's how to do so:

1. **Go to Office → Word Options to open the Word Options box, and then, on the left, click the Add-Ins button.**

   The Word Options box opens showing Add-ins. The list at the top shows all the add-ins and templates available in Word.

2. **At the bottom of the Word Options box, in the Manage drop-down menu, choose Word Add-ins, and then click Go.**

   The Templates and Add-ins box opens to the Templates tab (Figure 20-20). The text box at the top shows the current document template. The list box at the bottom shows Global templates and add-ins. The checkboxes show which templates and add-ins are currently loaded (that is, the ones Word's currently using). You can load and unload templates and add-ins by clicking the checkboxes. With the two buttons on the right, you add and remove templates and add-ins from the list.

Figure 20-20:
The Templates tab in the Templates and Add-ins box shows the current document template at top. Templates and add-ins available to Word appear in the box on the bottom. Use the checkboxes to load or unload global templates. Use the Add button to add templates and add-ins to the list.

3. **On the right, click the Add button to open the Add Template box.**

The Add Template box shows the contents of your Templates directory so you can choose the one you want to load. The "Files of type" drop-down menu at bottom is set to "All Word Templates (*.dotx; *.dotm; *.dot)," so the files listed in the box are all Word templates.

4. **Double-click a template file to add it to your Global template list.**

When you double-click a template, the Add Template box closes, and the selected template shows in the "Global templates and add-ins" list in the Template and Add-ins box. Initially, the template is checked, meaning that it's currently loaded. If you click to remove the checkmark, the template remains in the list, but it's unloaded, meaning you can't see or use its AutoText entries, macros, and so on.

5. **Click OK to close the Template and Add-ins box.**

The box closes and you see Word and any document that may be open. With the global template loaded, you have access to any styles, AutoText entries, or macros that are stored in the global template.

Part Five: Appendix

5

Appendix: Word Help and Beyond

Word Help and Beyond

Help with Word 2007 is never far away. The first place to look is in the program itself. Word's built-in Help system includes information panels and tutorials stored both on your computer and online. In fact, to support its products, Microsoft has a whole sprawling network of Web sites where you'll find tips, updates, discussion groups, and downloads for templates, themes, and other Word tools.

There's lots of community support out there, too. About 11 years ago, Microsoft developed an MVP program to recognize the folks who freely give their time to help others with Windows, Word, and other Microsoft programs. MVPs aren't Microsoft employees, but they're very good at what they do. On the Internet, you can easily find Word MVPs from around the world—if you know where to look. This Appendix helps you explore all your help options, starting right there on your computer.

Using Word's Built-in Help

When you're working in Word, the most convenient place to look for help is Word's built-in Help system. Press the F1 key, or click the little round button with the question mark in the upper-right corner of most Word windows to open Word Help, as shown in Figure A-1. The Word Help box conveniently opens in its own window, so it's not hard to drag it out of the way when you want to look at your work.

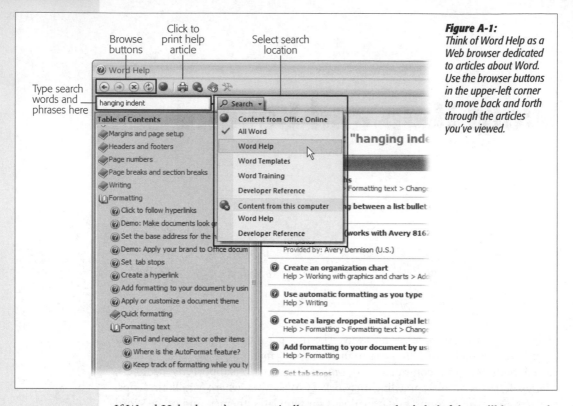

If Word Help doesn't automatically open to a page that's helpful, you'll have to do some searching. You can use two methods for finding the help you need: the Search tool in the upper-left corner or the Table of Contents.

- **Search.** Using the Search text box, type in a word or phrase, like *margins* or *hanging indent*. If you press Enter, or click the Search button, then Word hunts for help. When it's finished, articles that match your search words appear in the right panel. Look through the headings, and then click the one that's most likely to be helpful. If you need to come back and try another topic, click the back button.

  Word can search in several different locations for help. To see a list of the locations, click the triangle to the right of the Search button to open the Search menu. Online resources are listed at the top of the menu, and content that's stored on your computer is listed at the bottom. You can fine-tune the search by directing Word Help to look in a specific location. Use the drop-down menu to the right of the Search text box to choose the locations for the search.

- **Table of Contents.** On the left side of Word Help, the Table of Contents works a lot like a Word outline. You can expand and contract the headings by clicking the little book icons to the left of the words. One click opens a heading and shows the contents. Another click closes the heading, hiding the subheads and articles inside. The icons with question marks are the actual help articles; click them to show the help articles in the pane on the right.

Using Help Articles

For the most part, Word Help works a lot like a Web browser. You can use the buttons in the upper-left corner to browse forward and backward through the articles that you've read. There's even a button to stop and refresh the page, just like on your Web browser. Click an article heading in the Help Window to read the article. Some of the help headings will open your browser and take you to Web pages where you can find resources like templates or view audiovisual demonstrations (Figure A-2).

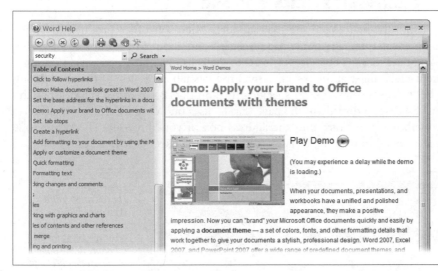

Figure A-2:
Some help articles link to audiovisual demonstrations on the Internet. When you click the Play Demo button, your browser opens to a page on the Microsoft Web site. The demo begins playing as soon as it starts to download to your computer.

If you want to print one of the help articles, click the little printer button at the top of the Word Help window. The Print box opens, and you can choose a printer and make other printing adjustments before you send the article to the printer. For example, on the Margins topic, you may want to print a single page instead of all 10 pages.

The contents shown in Word Help can come from files stored on your computer or from Microsoft's Web site. Use the button in the lower-right corner of Word Help to choose your source (Figure A-3). The help content that resides on your computer is pretty comprehensive. The help content that comes from Microsoft's Web site is kind of a mixed bag that includes all the help articles found on your computer as well as audiovisual demos, templates provided by third parties, clip art, and access to Microsoft's Knowledge Base of technical articles. One advantage of the online help content is that Microsoft continually updates and adds to it.

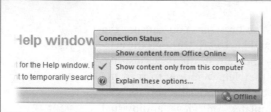

Figure A-3:
A button in the lower-right corner of the Help window shows whether you're online or not. Click the button, and a pop-up menu appears, as shown here.

Using Microsoft's Office Web Site

You'll find the main Web site that supports Microsoft office products at *http://office.microsoft.com*. The home page is slick—and about as helpful as a magazine ad. You need to dig a little deeper to get to the helpful features. To zero in on some more useful articles and links, click the Products tab at the top of the page. Along the left side, you find links to specific office products, including Word. Click the Word link, or go directly to the page that focuses on Word by typing *http://office.microsoft.com/en-us/word* into the address box of your browser. The Word page changes periodically, but it usually looks something like Figure A-4.

Figure A-4:
The Microsoft Word Web page provides links to articles and other resources for the program. At the bottom of the left-hand column under Additional Resources, you find a link to Discussion Groups where you can ask questions and then later come back and read the responses.

Discussion Groups

Discussion groups are one of the great resources of the online world. You can post a question in a discussion group and come back in a couple hours or the next day and other people will be posting answers and debating the fine points of the issue. It's an excellent way to dig deep into a subject and make some online friends in the process. You can also search through the discussion group to see if someone else has asked the same question. Type a word or a phrase in the "Search for" box near the middle of the screen (Figure A-5). After some churning, topics related to your search words appear in the center list. Click a + button to expand the topic, and then click a name to read the contents of the post.

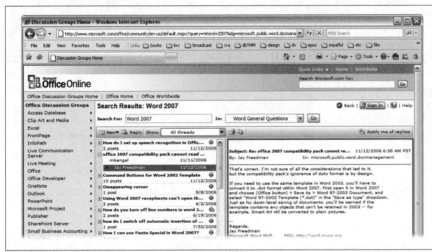

Figure A-5:
The Office discussion groups are a great resource if you have a question about Word. You can use the two columns on the left to zero in on a topic, or you can type a word or a phrase in the "Search for" box near the middle of the screen.

Tip: Before you post your question, it's good online etiquette to check the group to see if a FAQ (frequently asked questions) posting is available. Sometimes experts get annoyed when newbies ask the same question over and over.

The posts in a discussion are listed in chronological order, with the first message at the top. So, start at the top to read the question, and then work your way down the list to read the answers and other responses. Some questions will be answered quickly, with one or two on-target responses. A hot topic can result in a lengthy debate, with a dozen or so responses.

Some of the experts who participate in these discussion groups are Microsoft MVPs. For a description of Microsoft MVPs, see the box on the following page. In general, you'll find the contributions from the Microsoft MVPs both accurate and concise.

What's a Word MVP?

One of the smarter moves Microsoft ever made was to develop a way to recognize the people who voluntarily help others. Each year Microsoft singles out a few individuals who aren't Microsoft employees and dubs them MVPs (Most Valuable Professionals). There are MVPs for all the different Microsoft products, and of course, quite a few are Word MVPs. These folks know how to make Word jump through hoops. You find them offering free advice in computer forums, discussion groups, and newsgroups, and even publishing answers to frequently asked questions on their own Web sites.

Even better, these experts are often experts in other fields in addition to knowing the mysteries of Word. One expert may understand the financial world, while another may be knowledgeable about architecture and construction. Yet another may live in France and be able to answer Word questions particular to that language. This real-world experience along with a love of Word makes MVPs a valuable resource when you have a specific or sticky question.

Third-Party Web Sites

You're certainly not limited to Microsoft-sanctioned resources when it comes to getting help with Word. Many Web sites are devoted to providing advice, services, and add-in software. Some are free, some are pricey, and you'll find everything in between.

If you type *Word help*, or *Word templates*, or *Word Add-in* in your favorite search engine, you'll see dozens of listings like the following:

- **The Word MVP site** (*http://word.mvps.org*). Run by a group of Microsoft MVPs, not Microsoft, this site sets out to tell the whole Word truth and nothing but the truth. As its home page declares: "Word rarely misses an opportunity to perplex." The site divides Word issues into a number of popular topics, and a handy search tool at the top of the home page makes it easy to quickly zero in on what you're looking for (Figure A-6).

- **Woody's Office Portal** (*www.wopr.com*). For years, Woody Leonhard has provided the Word community with expert advice and his WOPR add-in. WOPR stands for Woody's Office Power Pack—a collection of Office-related add-ins. At the time of this writing, WOPR for Office 2007 was not yet on offer, but Woody's probably working on it. (There's been a WOPR for every version since Office 97.) The Web site is a little kitschy, but the information and tools are rock solid. Don't miss Woody's Lounge, an active online forum for Word and other Office programs (Figure A-7). You can read the posts without becoming a member, but to leave a message, you need to sign up. Membership is free, and the sign-up process simply involves agreeing to the rules of the message board. You can sign up for a free email newsletter.

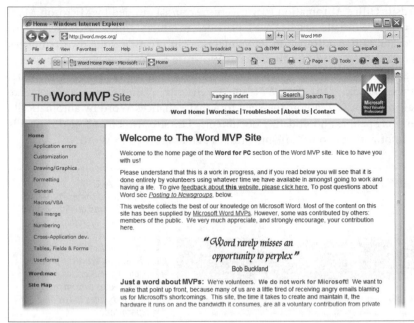

Figure A-6:
The Word MVP site provides a wealth of expert advice. A simple, clean interface makes it easy to browse for a topic, or you can use the search tool at the top of the home page.

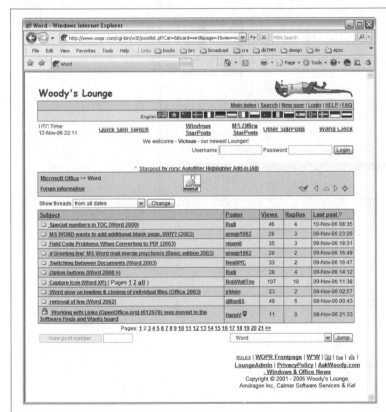

Figure A-7:
Woody's Lounge is an active forum where visitors post questions about Word and other Office products.

• **Wordsite Office Automation** (*www.wordsite.com*). Founded by Microsoft MVP Bill Coan, Wordsite (Figure A-8) provides products and services related to Word and Office automation. Not interested in creating your own templates and macros? You can hire the folks at Wordsite to do it for you. They offer a free analysis of your needs. Wordsite also offers training tailored to individual business needs. On the Wordsite Web site, you find products like DataPrompter 2007, an off-the-shelf tool that enhances Word by automatically prompting people and updating documents. The site also offers free downloads with information about XML and utilities that are related to Word.

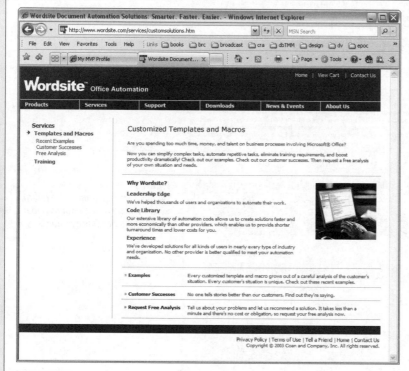

Figure A-8:
If you need some Word expertise and don't have the time to do everything yourself, you can find a company like Wordsite to assist you. Wordsite provides training, sells add-in products, and creates custom macros and templates to customer specifications.

Index

Colophon

Philip Dangler was the production editor for *Word 2007: The Missing Manual*. Rachel Monaghan and Marlowe Shaeffer provided quality control. Michele Filshie wrote the index.

The cover of this book is based on a series design originally created by David Freedman and modified by Mike Kohnke, Karen Montgomery, and Fitch (*www.fitch.com*). Back cover design, dog illustration, and color selection by Fitch.

David Futato designed the interior layout, based on a series design by Phil Simpson. This book was converted by Abby Fox to FrameMaker 5.5.6. The text font is Adobe Minion; the heading font is Adobe Formata Condensed; and the code font is LucasFont's TheSans Mono Condensed. The illustrations that appear in the book were produced by Robert Romano and Jessamyn Read using Macromedia FreeHand MX and Adobe Photoshop CS.

Related Titles from O'Reilly

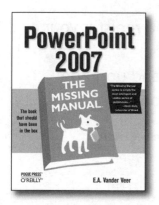

Missing Manuals

Access 2003 for Starters: The Missing Manual

Access 2007 for Starters: The Missing Manual

Access 2007: The Missing Manual

AppleScript: The Missing Manual

AppleWorks 6: The Missing Manual

CSS: The Missing Manual

Creating Web Sites: The Missing Manual

Digital Photography: The Missing Manual

Dreamweaver 8: The Missing Manual

eBay: The Missing Manual

Excel 2003 for Starters: The Missing Manual

Excel 2007 for Starters: The Missing Manual

Excel 2007: The Missing Manual

FileMaker Pro 8: The Missing Manual

Flash 8: The Missing Manual

FrontPage 2003: The Missing Manual

GarageBand 2: The Missing Manual

Google: The Missing Manual, 2nd Edition

Home Networking: The Missing Manual

iMovie HD 6: The Missing Manual

iPhoto 6: The Missing Manual

iPod: The Missing Manual, 5th Edition

Mac OS X: The Missing Manual, Tiger Edition

Office 2004 for Macintosh: The Missing Manual

PCs: The Missing Manual

Photoshop Elements 5: The Missing Manual

PowerPoint 2007 for Starters: The Missing Manual

PowerPoint 2007: The Missing Manual

QuickBooks 2006: The Missing Manual

Quicken 2006 for Starters: The Missing Manual

Switching to the Mac: The Missing Manual, Tiger Edition

The Internet: The Missing Manual

Windows 2000 Pro: The Missing Manual

Windows XP for Starters: The Missing Manual

Windows XP Home Edition: The Missing Manual, 2nd Edition

Windows XP Pro: The Missing Manual, 2nd Edition

Windows Vista: The Missing Manual

Windows Vista for Starters: The Missing Manual

Word 2007 for Starters: The Missing Manual

Other O'Reilly Titles

Excel 2007 Pocket Reference

Writing Excel Macros with VBA, 2nd edition

Excel Hacks

Analyzing Business Data with Excel

Excel Scientific and Engineering Cookbook

O'REILLY®

Our books are available at most retail and online bookstores.

To order direct: 1-800-998-9938 • order@oreilly.com • www.oreilly.com

Online editions of most O'Reilly titles are available by subscription at safari.oreilly.com

The O'Reilly Advantage

Stay Current and Save Money

Better than e-books

Buy *Word 2007: The Missing Manual* and access
the digital edition FREE on Safari for 45 days.

Go to www.oreilly.com/go/safarienabled
and type in coupon code OPKTLZG

Search
thousands of
top tech books

Download
whole chapters

Cut and Paste
code examples

Find
answers fast

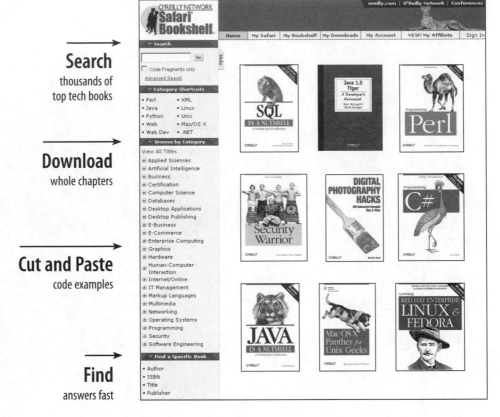

Search Safari! The premier electronic reference
library for programmers and IT professionals.